The University Gets Religion

The University Gets Religion

RELIGIOUS STUDIES IN AMERICAN
HIGHER EDUCATION

D. G. Hart

The Johns Hopkins University Press
Baltimore & London

© 1999 The Johns Hopkins University Press
All rights reserved. Published 1999
Printed in the United States of America on acid-free paper
9 8 7 6 5 4 3 2 1

The Johns Hopkins University Press
2715 North Charles Street
Baltimore, Maryland 21218-4363
www.press.jhu.edu

Library of Congress Cataloging-in-Publication Data
will be found at the end of this book.
A catalog record for this book is available from
the British Library.
ISBN 0-8018-6210-8

George Keller, Consulting Editor

To W. Robert and John R.

Contents

Preface and Acknowledgments

I BEGAN THIS BOOK OVER a decade ago with the submission of a proposal for a postdoctoral fellowship. My intent was to study the effect of academic professionalization on Protestant biblical and theological scholarship in late nineteenth-century America. While historians had given a considerable amount of attention to the emergence of academic disciplines in the natural and social sciences and in the humanities, few had studied the changes wrought by the modern research university within such older fields of learning as theology and the Bible. The fellowship would have provided time to explore the professionalization and specialization of biblical and theological studies.

As it turns out, the effects of academic professionalization on the study of the Bible and theology is still a neglected topic, not simply because my proposal was rejected, but also because, as I was to learn in a different postdoctoral fellowship, the areas of study that constitute the field of religion have never fully been recognized as academic disciplines. Biblical studies is perhaps the one exception to this rule since it was one of the first fields to establish its own professional society in 1880, the Society of Biblical Literature (SBL), and produce its own quarterly, the *Journal of Biblical Literature*. Even so, rare is the college or university that has a separate Department of Bible, a rarity that has forced biblical scholars to find refuge in either ancient Near Eastern studies or Jewish studies programs. Of the other two large fields within religion, church history and theology, the former also boasts its own professional society, the American Society of Church History, and its own journal, *Church History*. But as a field of study, church history has virtually been superseded by religious history, a field that drifts between religious studies and history, depending on the individual college or university, and is fairly marginal to both religion and history programs. Meanwhile, theology has virtually no professional identity, but relies upon various denominational or divinity school publications, while finding its disciplinary niche in various subgroups of religion scholars or ecclesiastical settings. Of course, all fields of study are in a state of flux, but at least most academic disciplines, unlike Bible, church history, or theology, at one time possessed a relatively firm identity and fixed place in American higher learning. The marginality of religion, however, has made professionalization a luxury.

From 1988 to 1989 I was privileged to work under the direction of George M. Marsden at the Divinity School of Duke University on a project exploring the secularization of American higher education. During that year, I began to figure out just how academically peripheral religion has been since the rise of the modern research university and just how recent its emergence as a kind of holding company for the variety of scholars who study different aspects of religious life and thought. As I poked around in the institutional life of academic religion I discovered, somewhat to my surprise, that the American Academy of Religion (AAR), the largest and foremost professional academic society for the study of religion, did not begin until 1964, at roughly the same time that state universities and smaller colleges created religion programs of their own. The academic study of religion did not achieve a formal scholarly recognition until 1979 when the American Council of Learned Societies granted its blessing upon the AAR. I also found out that the AAR was older, but had existed under a different name, the National Association of Biblical Instructors (NABI). That discovery prompted me to wonder about the division of labor between the SBL and NABI. It turned out that the predecessor to the AAR was mainly interested in pedagogical matters related to teaching the Bible in colleges and secondary schools, while the SBL provided a forum for advanced research on the Bible and cognate disciplines. To be sure, the recent professional growth of academic religion is impressive—the AAR rivals the Modern Language Association for membership and resources—but its intellectual pedigree looks considerably less than pure. I began to think that rather than exploring the effect of academic professionalization on theology or biblical studies, simply describing and accounting for the emergence of religious studies as a large but marginal academic field was worthwhile in itself. This book is the result of that decision.

The professionalization of theology or biblical scholarship will have to wait for another time, though the pages that follow cite books and articles that are important for that story, while also providing the context for those developments. Instead, this book focuses on the history of religious studies, a history that has less to do with the procedures and institutions of academic life than with the troubled relationship between American Protestantism and higher education since 1870. Mainstream Protestants, by and large, initiated religious studies, but did so under a distinct disadvantage, namely, that American universities were highly ambivalent about religion. The issue was not so much that American higher education was secular and, thus, hostile to religion. Rather, the issue was that religion did not deliver the goods that research universities promised—the unfettered pursuit of truths that would benefit society. The way Protestants negotiated the obstacles posed by the university determined to a large extent the shape and character of the study and teaching of religion in the United States.

I AM INDEBTED TO many people who helped make this book possible. George Marsden's generosity in providing a year of research and writing at Duke gave me a tremendous opportunity to piece together the hidden history of religious studies while improving my short game. Conversations at Duke with Brad Longfield, Paul Kemeny, Kathy Long, and Diana Hochstedt Butler also proved to be very stimulating and rewarding. I also owe a great debt to George Keller who initially proposed that I develop an earlier article into a longer study and who has been an encouragement throughout the project. Thanks go as well to Sam Logan, Will Barker, and the board of trustees at Westminster Theological Seminary for granting me a sabbatical that provided me with a semester to write. The comments through the years by Mark Noll, David Watt, and Jeff Charles also proved to mean more than any of them probably realize. Ann Hart helped to make the book more readable while also enriching life beyond this study. And Jackie Wehmueller, my editor at Johns Hopkins University Press, deserves much credit for her wisdom, enthusiasm and, above all, for her patience. Finally, to Bob Godfrey and John Muether go hearty thanks for friendship and camaraderie that sometimes make even a vinegary, rigid Calvinist's heart merry.

The University Gets Religion

Why Study Religion?

IT WAS ONE THING FOR Galileo to question the church's teaching about the orbit of the earth or for Charles Darwin to offer an alternative to the Bible in explaining the origins of the human form. But the warfare between science and theology appeared to reach an altogether different level of hostility in 1996 when scholars took on two millennia of reverence for Jesus of Nazareth. Of course, since the mid-nineteenth century, when David Friedrich Strauss questioned the historical Jesus, biblical scholars had been supplying ammunition to the scientific side of the contest between scholarship and dogma. But the 1996 Jesus Seminar struck a nerve with its highly publicized, well-funded, and shrewdly orchestrated findings that Jesus of Nazareth actually said virtually none of the statements attributed to him in the New Testament. During Easter week alone *Time* and *U.S. News and World Report* ran cover stories about the seminar. In addition, *Atlantic Monthly* featured the Jesus Seminar during the Christmas season and the religious periodicals *Christian Century* and *Christianity Today* also weighed in. One theme that appeared in all these reports was the Christ of faith versus the Jesus of reason.[1]

Such coverage no doubt delighted the members of the Jesus Seminar. Just three years earlier they produced their most controversial literary effort, *The Five Gospels,* a book that evaluated the authenticity of Jesus' words in the four gospels along with the apocryphal Gospel of Thomas. Few of those words turned out to be historical but instead were the theological and dogmatic accretions of the church. Yet, the book's dedication was just as provocative as its conclusions.

> This report is dedicated to *Galileo Galilei,* who altered our view of the heavens forever; *Thomas Jefferson,* who took scissors and paste to the gospels; *David Friedrich Strauss,* who pioneered the quest of the historical Jesus.

The editors introduced the book by comparing their efforts to those of Charles Darwin, John T. Scopes, Copernicus, and Johannes Kepler. "The Christ of creed and dogma," they wrote, "can no longer command the assent of those who have seen the heavens through Galileo's telescope."[2]

To be sure, not all members of the American Academy of Religion (AAR), the professional academic society of scholars who study religion, agreed with their colleagues who compiled *The Five Gospels.* But if forced to choose between the authority of theology or that of science, religion scholars would come down squarely with the Jesus Seminar. As one contributor to a forum on the state of religious studies recently put it, the press relished portraying the field as one where the "cultural elite" slay faith "by the scientific sword." Though sensational reports on the academic study of religion often portrayed religion scholars as "menacing God-less atheists," he added, the teaching of religion in modern universities was merely the fruit of the Enlightenment's application of scientific methods to the beliefs, practices, and texts of the faithful.[3]

As useful as the "warfare between science and theology" imagery may be both to selling news weeklies and to the self-understanding of scholars who teach and study religion in American higher education, it has serious limitations. It ignores how religious studies has come to be and why it has taken the peculiar shape that it has. Typically, like press reports about the Jesus Seminar, scholars both inside and outside the field understand the academic study of religion as an outgrowth of the Enlightenment and the triumph of science over dogma. As such, religious studies traces its intellectual origins to such figures as David Hume, Emile Durkheim, Sigmund Freud, and Max Weber, European philosophers and social scientists who freed religion from its ecclesiastical and dogmatic bondage and examined it under the bright light of science and critical reason. Yet, in the context of American learning, the obscure names of O. D. Foster, Robert Lincoln Kelly, Charles Foster Kent, and Clarence Prouty Shedd, mainline Protestant ministers and Bible scholars who in the 1910s and 1920s founded the institutions and formulated the rationale for religious studies, are more important than those of Hume, Durkheim, and company. This book demonstrates why these American Protestants were more important than Enlightenment philosophers or German sociologists to the development of religious studies in the United States. And, perhaps just as important, it suggests why the bulk of religion scholars would prefer that Foster, Kelly, Kent, and Shedd remain in obscurity.

The Science of Religion?

According to the leading practitioners in the field, the contemporary discipline of religious studies has an impressive intellectual pedigree. Here, J. Samuel Preus, who teaches religion at Indiana University, is instructive. The title of his book, *Explaining Religion: Criticism and Theory from Bodin to Freud,* attests to the intellectual roots that many within the field regard as their own. Preus argues that such scholars as Jean Bodin, Herbert of Cherbury, Bernard Fontenelle, Giambattista Vico, David Hume, Auguste Comte, Edward Burnett Tylor, Emile Durkheim, and Sigmund Freud established "a coherent research tradition that produced a new paradigm for studying religion." This paradigm, he explains, treats religion "as an element of culture." Its decisive assumption is that "religion could be understood without the benefit of clergy— that is, without the magisterial guidance of religious authorities," and without any confessional or religious convictions. In other words, the origins of religion should not be assumed to be any different than those of any other aspect of culture. By no means does Preus suggest that this approach to religion is the only one in departments of religious studies. It is the outlook of the university generally and, he writes, "inchoately present but departmentally fragmented in the contemporary university." Nor is he unaware that religious and apologetic motives sometimes informed the academic study of religion. Yet, even if the tradition of scholarship about religion that Preus examines does not dominate the field, he suggests that it is the one most compatible with the scientific and research aims of the contemporary university. Within the environment of the university, Preus argues, religion needs to be addressed "in a cooperative way and from a global perspective."

Theology—the old approach to the study of religion prior to the Enlightenment—is not up to the task in Preus's estimation. Instead, what he advocates, and what the tradition represented in his book provides, is "a scientific-humanistic understanding of religion."[4]

Walter H. Capps, who chaired of the Department of Religious Studies at the University of California–Santa Barbara and held several positions within the profession prior to his death (among them president of the Council on the Study of Religion), follows Preus in ascribing to the field a respectable and serious tradition of academic inquiry. Capps identifies religious studies as a field that "provides training and practice . . . in directing and conducting inquiry regarding the subject of religion." He adds that religious studies uses "prescribed modes and techniques of inquiry to make the subject of religion intelligible." As such, religious studies is "an intellectual discipline," using its own methods of research, pursuing certain "foci of intellectual interest," and producing "'reservoirs' of information and knowledge."[5]

Capps is even more confident in establishing the academic credentials of religious studies when he turns to the history of the field as it developed in the West. In Capps's telling, the story begins with Immanuel Kant, when the "intellectual tradition" characteristically attempted to isolate a religious "first principle," namely, "that without which religion would not be what it truly is." Thus, for Capps, the founding era of religious studies is the Enlightenment. "So prominent were Enlightenment incentives and intellectual sanctions," Capps affirms, "that the tradition of scholarship gives evidence of the utilization of a single methodological paradigm." He concedes that the Enlightenment search for a *sine qua non* in religion had theological roots in Christianity and Judaism. Yet this admission does not undermine religious studies' intellectual vitality and worth. The theological motivation that may have propelled the discipline was a solid ingredient in putting into motion the discipline's "analytical and interpretive processes." It is no wonder, then, that religious studies regularly receives federal grant assistance status from the National Endowment for the Humanities and thus gains even greater academic "respectability."[6]

Professional organizations responsible for maintaining high scholarly standards in the United States provide further examples of religious studies' academic stature. For instance, when in 1970 the American Council of Learned Societies (ACLS) formed the Council for the Study of Religion, an organization that would oversee, sponsor, and coordinate the scholarly study of religion, it relied upon a paper by Claude Welch, then a member of the University of Pennsylvania's religion department. From Welch's perspective, the demands placed upon the religion scholar-teacher were "essentially those that obtain in any other area of scholarly inquiry." Rather than evaluating the professor's competence by standards derived from the religious community, his "knowledge of the field and his critical powers of discrimination, . . . his possession of the appropriate tools of investigation and . . . his integrity in their use" were the best criteria for establishing his academic suitability.[7] Likewise, when the American Library Association devoted to religious studies one of the volumes, *Sources of Information in the Humanities,* in its series of the same name, it followed the conventional understanding of the field. Though the author of this volume, John F. Wilson, professor of religion at Princeton University, admitted that the study of religion in American universities was of a fairly recent vintage and was connected sometimes to the beliefs of specific religious traditions and communities, its academic or "objective" impulse derived from "the Enlightenment interest in religion as a cultural phenomenon." The term *religion* itself, Wilson added, was an intellectual construct of the university that corresponded to "a particular set of social and cultural activities arrived at for purposes of critical analysis."[8]

Perhaps the most poignant expression of religious studies' academic respectability came from the 1985 report of the AAR, in its contribution to the request from the ACLS to Congress for reauthorization of the National Endowment of the Humanities. The authors here contrasted the "quantum leap" that religious studies had taken since the nineteenth century. Religious studies emerged in the period after World War II in need of a "massive reconception." The field could not return to "the halcyon humanistic days of the colonial college or to the cultural isolation of the independent seminary." It had to come to terms with the "new humanistic context," thus explaining the premium that the AAR placed upon "fundamental research and thinking." In other words, the "WASP theology" of the nineteenth-century denominational college would no longer do in the university. It was too sectarian and did not reflect the religious diversity of the American people. So, too, it was not sufficiently scholarly. For this reason the AAR's leadership since the 1960s, especially in sponsoring research and scholarly publications, was crucial to the ACLS's recognition of religion as an academic discipline and its decision to admit the AAR into its membership.[9]

The overwhelming consensus, at least as it emerges from official and professional pronouncements, is that religious studies is a academically rigorous field within the modern research university. The academic study of religion is fundamentally different from church-based inquiry into religion. It is academic, detached, and pluralistic, and makes no judgment concerning the truth claims of the various religions, nor does is it pretend to favor any particular faith. If the study of religion in American universities tends to give more coverage to Christianity and Judaism, this is merely the result of cultural and historical circumstances that have made Christians and Jews the most numerous and influential religious groups in the United States. For this reason, the academic study of religion avoids supernaturalistic explanations of religion that rely upon divine intervention, whether through miracles or special revelation. While theologians and church scholars explain the uniqueness of their own religious traditions by appealing to supernatural activity, the methods of the academy require explanations based upon observable phenomena and empirical methods. In this way, the teaching and study of religion follow the same rules that govern scholars in the humanities and social sciences. A Protestant cleric may be required to affirm and teach the deity of Christ, but in the university seminar Jesus and his teachings are no better or worse than other authors whose sayings or writings became culturally influential. According to the *Encyclopedia of the American Religious Experience,* religion "after a long hiatus [is] once again part of the American academic scene." But "in contrast with the seventeenth, eighteenth, and nineteenth centuries, 'religion' has come to mean not only Christianity and Judaism but a variegated plurality of religious traditions." Meanwhile, the methods used in the academic study of religion "are like those in other academic disciplines, and the aim is not the practice of religion or even indoctrination but rather understanding of religion in its various manifestations past and present."[10]

Dubious Scholarship

Yet, as pure as its intellectual pedigree appears to be, all is not well within religious studies. Recently a number of scholars have accused the field of intellectual vapidity that would make Descartes or Kant blush. For instance, Paul V. Mankowski, in a report on the 1991 annual meeting of the AAR, charged that the papers he heard "were by and large so partisan, so blatantly advocative, that the pretense of a critical method of discourse was seldom even plausible." His accusation did not stem entirely from what he regarded as the AAR's "preoccupation with sexuality."[11] To be sure, Mankowski found some of the presentations to be downright distasteful, if not riddled with jargon, such as the paper, "Sexual Alterities: Otherwise Put," whose abstract read in part: "A feminist-informed, queerly placed interrogation is offered here of the representational matrices within which the stabilizing terms of gender may be opened up and overturned," thus, resulting in "the possibilities of sexual and desiderative alterities."[12]

What was most disconcerting about this particular meeting of the AAR was not so much the overwhelming presence of identity politics but rather the religious orthodoxy that suffused the gathering, an orthodoxy that betrayed the academic pretensions of the organization. "The party line runs like this," Mankowski concluded. "Everything that purports to be 'revelation' . . . is at bottom fiction," the authors of which have constructed such fictions in order to serve their own political purposes. "Fears of sanction and hopes of reward are dangled as carrot-and-stick before the oppressed subject, who is forced into the state of false consciousness called 'faith.'" The goal of religious scholarship becomes one of emancipating the oppressed "faithful" by pointing out the "political motives" behind religious structures supposed to be "divinely ordained." "Finally, members of oppressed populations are urged to invent (or rediscover) fictions of their own in which the notions of authority and obedience have been replaced by that of the lone individual as creator and bestower of value."[13]

Mankowski wrote these words as an outsider within the academic study of religion; he was then a graduate student at Harvard in the field of comparative Semitic philology. But his criticism echoed that of long-time insider Jacob Neusner, who once served as vice-president of the AAR and helped to found the section on Judaism. Neusner trained his eye primarily on the AAR's Judaic scholarship, which seemed to be motivated "not in promoting active scholars and scholarship but in staging the academic equivalent of performance art." Though the topics proposed for the 1993 annual meeting were tamer than the fare that Mankowski sampled—they ranged from "The Holocaust in Historical Context" to "Jewish or Christian Approaches to Textuality, Interpretation, and Suffering"—Neusner believed that the AAR's leadership waffled between Jewishness as an ethnic group and Judaism as a "clearly defined religious tradition." Surely an organization whose business was academic reflection upon religion could come up with a reasonable, though perhaps not convincing to all, basis for including and excluding certain topics for investigation. But instead, the "virus" of the "non-field 'Jewish studies'" dominated. For Neusner the position of the AAR that "everything Jewish is the same as everything else Jewish" showed no "discipline or intellectual rigor." By capitulating to this conception of Jewishness the AAR had actually "excluded the larger part of the scholarly community from [its] study of Judaism."[14]

While Mankowski and Neusner's complaints had the feel of the attacks made by Allan Bloom, Dinesh D'Souza, and Roger Kimball against the Modern Language Association's excesses,[15] advocates for the field have also given less ideological critiques of the academic study of religion. At the 1986 Santa Barbara Colloquy, "Religion Within the Limits of Reason Alone," where distinguished religion scholars met to discuss the purpose and procedures of graduate education in religious studies, Jonathan Z. Smith from the University of Chicago furthered his reputation as provocateur by stating that he doubted "factually, that religious studies constitutes 'a coherent disciplinary matrix in and of itself.'" While such a statement may have been necessary to establish religion departments, the notion "religion" is "not an empirical category," but rather a "second-order abstraction." The field needed to acknowledge, according to Smith, its creation of this academic fiction and, like the creator of Frankenstein, "take responsibility for it."[16] Such outbursts led the convener of the colloquium to warn, though his cautions were not heeded, that the meetings' papers should not be published for fear that they might "trigger a mass exodus of our best graduate students." He went on to sum up the presentations in the following manner: "Religious Studies . . . has no identifiable frame of discourse," it is "our own in-house concoction," it lacks a "cogent legitimation or authority," and it hides behind "western notions of 'rationality'" that no longer cloak "the struggle for power or the distribution of power." In sum, religious studies is "a political compromise, an Ellis Island for the 'considerable company of migrants' who have had to leave their native intellectual homes . . . and who have come to us for refuge."[17]

More recently, the AAR took stock of the discipline and came to equally sobering conclusions. In 1985 the AAR secured funding for a self-study, cosponsored by the ACLS, the Association of American Colleges, the Society for Values in Higher Education, the Association of Theological Schools, and the Society of Biblical Literature. It asked AAR members about the present state and future of the field, the most important issues, and perceptions about the study of religion at members' colleges, universities, or seminaries. According to the report, published in 1991, the "large issues" in religious studies were in flux. For some, diversity and dissonance in the field signified the chaotic nature of the academic study of religion, while for others of a more optimistic mindset, such chaos was the darkness before dawn, "the liminality that inevitably precedes the emergence of new paradigms." The survey also revealed pessimism about the future of religious studies, especially at public universities and small and emerging departments where "hopes had run highest in the past three decades." Though members of the AAR may have differed about the future of their field, the majority of respondents were not confident about their position within American higher education. The report concluded that "the study of religion unquestionably is most tenuous, and has the least security of any of the institutional types in the public sector." "The vast majority of colleagues," it added, "are said to be 'apathetic, indifferent, or hostile toward—and *ignorant* about the study of religion.'"[18] Such conclusions, no doubt, added some tarnish to religious studies' otherwise glittering self-estimate of its intellectual origins.

It got worse. Only three years later, in an issue of the AAR's quarterly journal, the *Journal of the American Academy of Religion,* scholars voiced equally negative estimates. Sam Gill, professor at the University of Colorado–Boulder, reiterated the findings of the AAR's report and of the Santa Barbara Colloquy. The academic study of religion, he wrote, "has failed to advance any sustainable body of theory, any cadre of religion theorists, any substantial body of literature." His conclusion was that "the unsatisfactory defense of the place and role of religion studies in the modern academic environment" has placed religion departments "at a low level of budgetary priority and at risk in many colleges and universities."[19]

Mark C. Taylor, one of the participants at the Santa Barbara Colloquy and religion professor at Williams College, piled on criticisms that paralleled those of Mankowski and Neusner. "Academic discourse in the study of religion," Taylor argued, "is increasingly characterized by intolerance and misunderstanding, which are the symptoms of a politics of identity that claims to defend voices of difference." What had emerged in religious studies, as in other humanistic disciplines, was that "the relativization of the western tradition" had turned into an "absolutism" that Taylor called "fundamentalism of the 'left.'"[20] Most recently Russell T. McCutcheon, who teaches religion at Southwestern Missouri State University, has denied that the notion "religion" exists. He accuses his peers of perpetrating a certain kind of Christian theology under supposedly scientific discourse, and argues that, as such, religious studies is implicated in "the rise and maintenance of the current world capitalist hegemony."[21]

Such assessments of religious studies' intellectual merits deviate considerably from the claims for the field's heady origins in the Enlightenment and the university's liberation from church dogma. This inconsistency, however, is the result of bad or, at least, incomplete history. Though naturalistic accounts of religion have influenced the curricula of many religion departments and inform the investigations of many scholars of religion, a factor of even greater importance to the history of religious studies is one often overlooked, namely, the formal emergence of the field in the period from 1925 to 1965. These four decades witnessed the formation of a body of scholars with a common interest in teaching religion in an academically respectable manner. This was also the time when religion emerged institutionally as an academic department at most of the colleges and universities where it is now taught and studied. And while the history of the teaching and study of religion during these years can appear to be uninteresting—after all, it features the names of those mentioned at the outset, the Fosters, Kents, Kellys, and Shedds of the mainline Protestant world—it is extremely important because it comes closest to accounting for the difficulties confronting the academic study of religion.

The argument of this book, put succinctly, is that to understand the current predicament of the academic teaching and study of religion requires familiarity not simply with the individuals, departments, and organizations that shaped the field but, more important, with arguments used to justify religion as a field of academic inquiry. What these arguments reveal is a strategy for the study of religion in American colleges and universities that a generation of almost exclusively mainline Protestant clergy and academics devised. Their aim, first, was to promote the study of religion under the broad umbrella of the Protestant denominations' campus ministries. Then in the 1960s, when that rationale looked especially tattered, religious studies reinvented itself as an academic field of critical inquiry. But this new academic appearance never hid completely the older ministerial one. As a result, the field suffers from the strain of being pulled in two directions simultaneously, one churchly, the other academic. What is more, as much as religious studies strives to sever ties to communities of faith, it cannot do so without self-immolation. The academic study of religion has not only been dependent historically upon churches, synagogues, and mosques, but it has no object of inquiry without particular religious traditions. As such, religious studies needs communities of faith, and such dependence will always be out of place in the modern university.

The Complicated History behind
Religious Studies

Secularization has been one of the chief concepts used by historians
to describe the changes in American higher education since the rise of
the research university just after the Civil War. Standard accounts of
American higher education and intellectual life generally begin with
the denominational college and its effort to provide authentic Christian
learning. Its classical curriculum provided aspiring ministers with the
necessary skills for studying divinity, its senior year capstone course in
moral philosophy instilled the morality and cosmology of mainstream
Protestantism, and its faculty and administrators consisted primarily of
clergymen. Changes in science spawned by Darwinism as well as transformations in American social and economic life, however, doomed
the antebellum college's endeavors to sustain Christian higher education. Urbanization and industrial growth created a need for college
graduates trained in the social and natural sciences. Furthermore, the
naturalism of Darwin threatened the metaphysical foundation upon
which Christian thought rested. Industrial magnates founded new universities (Johns Hopkins, Cornell, Chicago), and progressively minded
colleges (Harvard and Yale) revised their curricula and conducted other
reforms to respond to intellectual and social challenges. According to
this scenario, the university discarded the naive mental universe of
denominational colleges in order to address new and troubling complexities in nature and society. Philosophers prevailed over theologians,
courses in biology and engineering replaced Greek and Latin, and sociology superseded moral philosophy.[22]

The apparent secularism of the academy would seem to explain the
problems and tensions surrounding the study of religion in American
universities, the late date of the AAR's founding (1964) and its relatively
recently recognition by the ACLS. The "secularization of the academy"
thesis suggests that it took almost a century for a scholarly approach to
religion to emerge which would satisfy academics suspicious of religion. Furthermore, the ethos fueling the creation of the AAR appears
to substantiate this reading. The AAR was founded to promote academically credible and scientifically reliable teaching and study of religion.

Yet the history of religious studies is much more complicated than
the standard accounts of religion and higher education allow. The modern American university was not as hostile to religion as older histories argue, nor was religion marginal to the ethos of the new research

universities which challenged the dominance of denominational colleges. The moral idealism of American Protestantism directly informed the progressive vision of the modern university. Professors and administrators alike were convinced that the pursuit of truth through specialized research would confirm and vindicate the moral teachings of Christianity. Moreover, mainstream Protestant denominations sponsored a series of church and para-church endeavors at universities which drew strong support from students, faculty, and administrators.[23]

The emergence of religious studies in the 1960s as a legitimate academic discipline, therefore, is much more than an instance of religion professors finally reaching a truce in the warfare between science and religion. Rather, it is only one transition in the larger pattern of Protestant involvement in American higher education since the rise of the modern university. Three main periods divide this history. From 1870 to 1925 Protestants embraced the institutions and methods of new learning signaled by research universities. They also adapted beliefs and practices to accommodate the new social arrangements that sustained the revolution in higher education. During this time, because of its associations with academic backwardness, religion was largely an extracurricular activity. The flip side of Protestantism's retreat was the substantial prestige that science enjoyed and the progress that advanced learning promised. This period culminated in the modernist-fundamentalist controversy, a struggle in which liberals and conservatives fought over modern approaches to the study of scripture, new discoveries in the natural sciences, and the church's support for social and political reforms.

The victors in this contest, the modernists, entered the next period, from 1925 to 1965, with the best chance of winning the confidence of the academic establishment. These Protestants, after all, had been arguing that academic work was essential to the establishment of an intelligent, righteous, and just society. But this was also a time when economic upheaval and war demonstrated the limitations of science and progressive social engineering. Rather than supplying enthusiasm for the study of the natural world and human relations, the traditional disciplines of theology, biblical studies, and church history began to be taught in earnest as part of the heritage of western civilization. Consequently, universities not only began to offer courses in religion but also sponsored departments of religious studies. It is no coincidence that the period when religion began to be taught and studied as a normal part of the university curriculum was also the time when the neo-orthodox theology of Reinhold Niebuhr, an outlook that adapted historic Christian teaching about human nature for modern society

and politics, dominated mainstream Protestantism and won considerable favor from American academics. The Judeo-Christian tradition, a
phrase used within increasing regularity, was essential for understanding American culture and western civilization, and for producing civi-
lized graduates.

The final and most recent period in the history of Protestant interaction with American universities began in 1964 with the founding of
the AAR. Larger upheavals in American society surrounding relations
between men and women, blacks and whites, majority and minority
groups, and the United States' posture in international affairs, undermined certainties about the character of America, the legacy of the
West, and the education of undergraduates. With older rationales for
studying religion unraveling, a newer and more academic argument
came to the surface. But the professional commitments of the AAR
could not be harmonized with the older Protestant curriculum in religious studies or the motives of Protestant academics who taught it.
The abstract ideals of science and objectivity did not explain why the
average undergraduate interested in a safe job and comfortable subur-
ban home should study the fiery teachings of the prophet Jeremiah or
the sometimes discomforting views of Martin Luther. Ironically, then,
just at the time when religious studies seemed to be coming into its
own as an academic discipline, American universities were confronting
a series of crises that shook the assumptions and goals of practically all
areas of study, and especially the humanities.

In Search of a Rationale

In many respects the difficulties confronting religious studies reflect
the same obstacles that bedevil other disciplines in the humanities. If
Louis Menand, professor of English at Queen's College, is correct in his
assessment about the place of literary criticism in the university, for
instance, then the academic study of religion's problems may be no
worse than those in other disciplines. In an essay on the merits of academic freedom and the protection it extends to professors from agencies
external to the university, Menand demonstrates that the hierarchy of
doctoral degree-granting programs, peer review prior to publication,
junior appointments, and tenure insures especially well in the natural
and social sciences the "paradigm of professionalism." In this paradigm,
specialists within each field have "wide authority to determine who
the new specialists will be, and in what the work of the specialization

properly consists." But fields such as literary studies, according to Menand, have "the weakest case" for inclusion into the academic structures of the modern university. "The notion that literary criticism is a disinterested, 'scientistic' activity would have seemed absurd to almost any critic before the twentieth century." After all, what is a "true and impartial understanding" of Shakespeare or Chaucer? For this reason Menand concludes that from the beginning of the research university no plausible place existed for literary criticism since "the appreciation and interpretation of works of literature are not obviously scientific."[24]

The same also applies to religious studies where scientific models do not work for the study of theology, Bible, church history, or, for that matter, to the study of the Koran, the Dead Sea Scrolls, or the writings of L. Ron Hubbard. The field of religious studies, like literary criticism whose history in the university is older,[25] has tried to function under the same rules of procedure that have guided the sciences. Those rules worked fairly well when a consensus existed regarding the works that undergraduates should study in order to receive a bachelor of arts degree. But the consensus of a society is often more circumstantial than scientific. And when the agreement broke down about what works of literature or religion were most important for a good undergraduate education, the academic guild's appeal to scientific standards, whether by the Modern Language Association or the AAR, looked defensive if not hollow.

Yet, the difficulties facing religion scholars are not only different but more profound than those confronting other academics in the humanities, difficulties that religious studies' history reveals. As a field of critical inquiry, religion labors under the burden of teaching and studying subjects that come straight from the norms of ecclesiastical sanction or theological normativity. Though members of a small town may have once gathered in semiformal reading clubs, such as an athenaeum, library, or lyceum to discuss works of literature or discoveries in nature, the rules for admission to such discussion did not involve the eternal destiny of the soul.[26] Nor did such study have attached to it the categories of orthodoxy, heresy, communion, or excommunication. Furthermore, the university has virtually supplanted such local forms of literary of scientific interest. But religion continues to thrive outside the academy even while religion scholars use many of the same categories and make many of the same distinctions that members of religious bodies do. To be sure, the study of the Bible and theology in congregations or para-church organizations often advances without the slightest awareness of or deference to the recent findings about the

Gospel according to Mark in the *Journal of Biblical Literature*. Nevertheless, religion professors include or exclude from their writings and lectures subjects that they derive directly from the authoritative interpretations, whether Christian, Jewish, or Muslim, of sacred texts and histories that are required for membership in a specific community of faith. Religious studies, then, cannot escape the perception of being too religious. And whatever challenges the humanities face, the overtly believing or churchly character of religious studies is an encumbrance that the field of religion bears alone in the modern research university.

One way to illustrate this burden is to suppose a curriculum of religious studies that used Arius, Michael Servetus, and Brigham Young— all heretics according to historic Christian teaching—to introduce the categories and methods of religious discourse. The novelty of such an approach becomes apparent once compared to the traditional strategy in religion, one that uses the orthodox expressions mainly of Protestantism, Catholicism, and Judaism to teach the subject. Even though the "canon" of western civilization connotes the notions of orthodoxy and heresy, or mainstream and sectarian, the academic study of Shakespeare, Mozart, and Kant does not use, either implicitly or explicitly, the judgments of cultural authorities deemed by scholars to be dogmatic, sectarian, and superstitious. Because religious studies imports the phenomena of traditional religions into the classroom, it is in the unenviable position of being dependent upon determinations of faith communities for its subject matter, even while rejecting as unscientific the basis upon which those determinations were made.

The tension between religious studies' commitment to scientific standards and its dependence upon the traditions of religious groups is apparent even in the recent survey of AAR members. Results indicated that the overriding "problem or issue" in the field was whether religious studies was different from theological studies. Many respondents believed that the greatest change in the discipline within the last generation of scholarship was a "strong divergence from 'the seminary model.'" For most this change was all to the good since many regarded theological studies as the *bête noire* of religious studies. The friction between religious studies and theological studies reflects the history of a field that throughout its existence borrowed heavily from the curriculum used to train Protestant clergy. Yet, as much as religion professors may want to sever ties to Protestant divinity and churches, in this same survey respondents indicated that the issues of most importance were, in this order, ethics and the Bible.[27] This finding is ironic not only because the ethical teachings of the Bible were a mainstay of religious studies during the era of the Niebuhr brothers, but also because the Bible itself does not exist without the beliefs of churches and synagogues.[28] The parasitic nature of religious studies upon communities of faith could not be more apparent.[29]

Some Qualifications

The history that follows is not of an institutional sort. While it does cover some of the important professional organizations and university programs in the emergence of religious studies, its primary concern is with the rationale that Protestant ministers and faculty employed to justify their work. Nor is this book about the variety of scientific methods used to study religion, whether in religion departments or in other humanistic or social scientific disciplines. The narrative presented is more about the ideas of mainline Protestants who conceived of religion as an academic subject and the academic administrators (many of whom were also Protestant) who accepted that conception. The reason for concentrating on the academic grounds used to establish the field of religion is to understand the ideas behind the institutional history of the many departments and programs in American higher education. Looking at the arguments for including religion in an academic environment apparently dubious of religion's scientific legitimacy, in many cases, makes better sense of the history of specific institutions. In other words, before universities founded religion programs, mainline Protestants had to develop a rational for teaching religion to undergraduates, or for sponsoring graduate programs in religion. The subject of this book, then, is pivotal for any institutional history of a particular department, or for any evaluation of the scholarship that religious studies programs sponsor. This point is all the more apparent in the light of higher education's homogenizing character. With the exception of a few local idiosyncrasies, the histories of individual departments, institutions, or individual scholars will follow generally the contour of the narrative that follows.

The major figures or seminal texts in the field of religion are also peripheral to this study. Other historians have examined, for instance, the fields that comprised religious studies at its beginning—theology, biblical studies, and church history.[30] To the extent that such authoritative texts existed when the field emerged during the middle of the twentieth century, they came directly from the seminary and divinity school faculty of mainline Protestantism. Still, the most persuasive arguments for studying religion in American colleges and universities, the central concern here, rarely came from the prominent theologians, biblical scholars, or church historians whose writings may have been assigned as textbooks. Rarely did the merits of such paradigmatic scholarship prove to university faculty and administrators the wisdom of conferring upon religion the status of academic discipline. Rather, more important to the development of religion as a field of inquiry were the labors and occasional articles of lesser-known figures who worked behind the scenes to advance the study and teaching of religion, who tapped the resources of the mainline denominations, founded national associations of like-minded academics, and articulated a conception of religion's importance for advanced learning. For this reason, much of the evidence for this book comes from relatively obscure journals and little known organizations. Reinhold Niebuhr, H. Richard Niebuhr, and Paul Tillich may been household names that made religion fashionable, but the arguments and efforts of less visible individuals were more important to the success and longevity of religious studies.

The story of religious studies' formation and acceptance divides into three sections. The first covers the era of the research university's origins and how religious scholarship, with its dogmatic and sectarian reputation, had to adjust to the claims made on behalf of science, with its truth-discovering capabilities. After half a century of Protestant scholars trying to show that religious scholarship was not necessarily sectarian, the second section shows how religious studies blossomed in the middle decades of the twentieth century as an academic field even though it was decidedly Protestant. During this time of economic and political uncertainty, the civic faith of mainline Protestants offered an apparently viable religious expression that was inclusive, culturally respectable, and learned. That perception changed dramatically, however, in the decades after 1965, the period covered in the book's last section. At that point what had once been the public theology of mainline Protestantism looked again to be remarkably narrow, intolerant, and sectarian. Within a century, then, religion in the academy had gone through the cycle of being perceived as sectarian, recovering its public acceptability, and turning back to its apparently sectarian roots. The academic study of religion followed this same cycle. Its inclusion and precarious status in the university was and still is bound up with these shifts, both in its advance toward and retreat from scholarly recognition.

PART I

The Age of the University, 1870–1925

ONE

Enlightened Christianity and
the Founding of the University

IF ANYONE WONDERS WHAT side Cornell University took in the debates over religion and science, a casual reading of *The History of the Warfare of Theology with Science in Christendom* (1896) by its president, Andrew Dickson White, should answer most questions. From White's perspective, the history of Christianity was a long series of efforts by the church to restrict scientific inquiry. The sixteenth and seventeenth centuries offered particularly frightening episodes of ecclesiastical interference with science. Copernicus located the sun at the center of the planetary system and received the label of heretic for his genius, escaping persecution only by death. Galileo also endured great opposition from various religious inquisitors. So also in the eighteenth century Laplace's nebular hypothesis generated "an outcry at once against 'atheism,' and war raged fiercely." More recently scientists had challenged theologians about the origins of the human race. White believed that he personally had had to endure the same kind of theological obscurantism when the leaders of several denominational colleges denounced Cornell University as a godless institution. In fact, White wrote his book to answer critics who argued that scientific freedom without ecclesiastical oversight was a sure recipe for infidelity. Even though early Cornell's scientific contributions were hardly advanced,

White was able to start the new university free from religious control and thus establish what would become the pattern for American higher education.[1]

Yet for all of White's hostility to sectarian bigotry or, as he called it, "ecclesiasticism," he maintained that he was no enemy of religion. White opposed dogmatic religion but believed genuine Christianity had nothing to fear from science. The trick was to distinguish between "outworn creeds and noxious dogmas," on the one side, and the "most precious religious and moral foundations of the whole social and political fabric" on the other. White wrote his history of theology and science with this distinction in mind. So, too, he believed that Cornell University, even though free from church oversight, upheld "religion pure and undefiled" while helping to dissolve "this mass of unreason."[2] For this reason, White was unabashed in describing the new institution as a Christian university. "We will labor to make this a Christian institution," he told supporters, but added, "a sectarian institution it may never be."[3] Notwithstanding White's concerns about a hostile public, his policies bore out his profession. Cornell's president instituted daily chapel services and encouraged the work of the Young Men's Christian Association.[4]

Though a skeptical reader of White's rhetoric might regard it as little more than the vestiges of a fast-fading religious outlook, the experience of Felix Adler at Cornell suggests a different perspective. Adler came to the upstate New York university in 1874 to teach Hebrew history and literature. This appointment was consistent with White's intentions to keep Cornell free from religious tests. When Protestants criticized White for hiring a Jew, the president defended Adler as a "graduate of one of our most renowned Christian colleges," implying that some of Christianity had worn off on Adler.[5] When opposition persisted, White finally acceded to the trustees' decision to terminate Adler's appointment. No doubt White thought that he was still above sectarian narrowness and that Cornell remained Christian in a broad and tolerant sense. But Adler saw the inconsistency—if not hypocrisy—of White's action. In a letter, Adler wrote to a friend,

> It seems to me that when [White] used the word Christian he means "moral" in the best sense. But it is precisely this identification of the highest morality with so distinctively a sectarian system as the Christian that is peculiarly grating to the sensibilities of those who are not Christians and do not desire to be classed as such.[6]

As much as American universities have tried to escape the entanglements of religion, they have not been able to dispense with religion or to avoid the restrictions that attend religious beliefs. Though university leaders like White wanted to avoid the bigotry of traditional Protestantism in order to give free reign to science, they were still religious men who believed the new institutions of higher learning in America needed a religious orientation. Theirs, of course, was a religion that veered significantly from historic Christianity, one that they often referred to as "Enlightened Christianity." But this constellation of religious convictions insured that the university movement would be informed by religious motives. In turn these assumptions about Christianity and the nature of higher education in modern society would establish the patterns that shaped the study and teaching of religion in the modern university.

Religion versus Science?

What the 1860 showdown between T. H. Huxley and Samuel Wilberforce was to the warfare between Christianity and Darwinism in England, the 1886 debate between James McCosh and Charles W. Eliot, billed as a "battle between the Titans," was to the debates about religion and higher education in the United States.[7] The specific question before McCosh and Eliot was the place of religious instruction and worship in undergraduate education. Eliot, the president of Harvard, was, of course, one of the great reformers within American universities, advocating the elective system, greater attention to science and modern languages, and specialized research. What was particularly germane to his debate with McCosh were his decisions to make chapel voluntary and religious instruction optional.[8] Sometimes portrayed as an educational neanderthal,[9] McCosh stood for the old ways of the denominational college, with classical languages and literature, and moral philosophy providing the building blocks of the collegiate curriculum, and mandatory daily chapel and required courses in English Bible, ethics, and Christian evidences instilling the basics of Presbyterian orthodoxy in undergraduates at the College of New Jersey (later Princeton University). Eliot and McCosh did not disappoint the audience gathered at New York City's American Art Gallery. Eliot championed the kind of academic freedom for which he was known, especially the idea that higher education should not be bound by Christian dogma. McCosh insisted that an education stripped of its evangelical Protestant moorings was unworthy of the name. Though the tide was turning against McCosh, Eliot's refusal to have his paper published with his rival appeared to give orthodoxy the upper hand.

A year prior to this debate, Eliot and McCosh had also faced off on some of the academic reforms that made Harvard a leader in university circles. Eliot's vision of higher education tapped the deep well of American ideals. The elective system that he favored appealed to American notions about freedom, liberty, and equality. It also had the advantage of opening the seemingly stodgy curriculum of liberal education, with its stress upon Greek and Latin, to the modern subjects of the natural sciences and modern languages. McCosh, however, resisted Eliot's laissez-faire approach. Freedom to choose one's course of study, the Presbyterian insisted, "must be within carefully defined limits." McCosh went on to defend the principle of mental discipline that had governed older models of liberal education. From a set course of study, mandatory class attendance, and required chapel, to the broad and humane learning of a gentleman, McCosh dug in his heels against Eliot's changes. "Education is essentially the training of the mind," McCosh asserted. And the minds of undergraduates, he believed, were not prepared for the freedom Eliot advocated. Just as the administrators and faculty at the College of New Jersey acted *en loco parentis* to insure that students did not patronize saloons or gambling houses, so when it came to classroom instruction students should meet a similar restraint. In a line that undoubtedly endeared McCosh to his largely Presbyterian constituency, he contended that "fathers and mothers should know what is proposed to do with their sons at college."[10]

McCosh's assertion of the parental responsibilities attending the life and education of an academic institution led to the challenge he issued at the end of his first meeting with Eliot. The needs of young men and the duties of colleges made the subject of religion and higher education crucial. So McCosh proposed that he and Eliot meet again in 1886 to debate the future of religion in colleges. In the second meeting McCosh played the conservative, even more so. Eliot, in turn, applied the principle of liberty in education to religion. If colleges could not prescribe a curriculum, how much should they govern the religious life of students? Eliot believed that religion, whether instruction or worship, should be entirely voluntary. Religious liberty on campus did not mean indifference. Eliot conceded that it was virtually impossible to maintain morality without a religious base. But he also believed religious intolerance to be a greater threat to a good education and to the country's prospects than religious voluntarism.[11]

McCosh, however, would have none of Eliot's liberality. Christianity, he believed, had been crucial to the formation of western civilization. The Bible particularly had nurtured everything that educated people valued, namely, Dante, Shakespeare, Milton, and the great expressions of European art—Gothic cathedrals, statues, and paintings. "Withdraw Christianity from our colleges," McCosh threatened, "and we have taken away one of the vital forces which have given life and body to our higher education."[12]

Often overlooked in this debate is how strikingly similar Eliot's and McCosh's views about the aims of higher education were, though they disagreed about particulars. Despite the open disagreement and the conventional depiction of McCosh as the last of a dying breed of educational conservatives,[13] he was, according to J. David Hoeveler Jr., "a liberal and a reformer" within Princeton circles while also being perceived by the larger public as "the eloquent defender" of the older ways.[14] Even in his first debate with Eliot, McCosh displayed an openness to academic reform that got the better of the risk-taking Eliot. If the Harvard president were as committed to enhancing and developing a better awareness of the natural sciences as he claimed, McCosh argued, then the elective system was a poor means for encouraging modern learning. If a student interested in medicine faced a choice between anatomy and physiology on the one hand, and music and lectures on drama on the other, McCosh had no doubt that an undisciplined youth would choose the easier courses. He even wondered what Eliot would say to the student who freely chose courses in baseball and football over the novel subjects of French and modern literature.[15]

McCosh himself, though convinced of the slothfulness of human nature and the need for discipline, was not so tied to older models of education that he excluded the new learning. As a reformer, McCosh saw the value of the natural and social sciences, and of modern languages and literature. He believed these subjects should be included in the curriculum of liberal education. Where he differed from Eliot was in the degree to which standards were necessary for defining a proper education. From McCosh's perspective Eliot offered no standard apart from the fickle choices of undergraduates. In other words, the issue separating Eliot and McCosh was not science versus religion, or the classics versus English literature; it was whether faculty and administrators would set limits on what constituted a good education. For

Eliot liberation provided the optimal setting for the university; for McCosh Christianity yielded the best context.

McCosh also shared with Eliot certain significant convictions about religion. As much as they disagreed theologically—Eliot was a Unitarian—and as much as they held conflicting views about the place of religion in the college or university, both presidents argued about religion in very similar ways. Eliot believed that universities were fundamentally religious in character. "The whole work of the university," he said at Daniel Coit Gilman's inaugural at Johns Hopkins, "is uplifting, refining and spiritualizing."[16] So, too, religion had nothing to fear from the university because the task of both was essentially the same, namely, the construction of a better and freer civilization.[17]

Even though McCosh was adamant about the truthfulness of Christianity and therefore opposed departures from orthodoxy, much like Eliot he defended religion in college education by appealing to Christianity's contribution to the public good. Instruction in Christianity would lead individual students to believe in "high virtues which lift them above the meanness and the selfishness of the world," McCosh said. Religion not only produced upstanding individuals, but also guaranteed the progress of the nation. "All modern history testifies," he wrote, "that the true, the practical method of progress is first to christianize a people, when civilization will follow as fruit grows from the seed." To reverse the order, to put civilization before Christianity was like trying to "civilize those who have as yet no taste for knowledge and refinement."[18]

What stands out about McCosh's views in comparison to those of Eliot is the degree to which this proponent of Scottish Presbyterianism, widely touted as a conservative both religiously and educationally, advocated the inclusion of religion in higher education on grounds determined by his rival, an American Unitarian and social progressive. Rather than arguing for Christianity's intellectual merits or that private religious institutions were within their right to make faith central to their education, McCosh adopted Eliot's criteria of religion's positive influence upon the individual student and the greater social good. Where Eliot saw sectarian Christianity standing in the way of advanced research and restricting religious diversity in the United States, McCosh believed that the best education depended upon orthodox beliefs and that the health of the nation required a daily dose of Christianity. Both Eliot and McCosh, then, argued on the grounds of educational and public utility. In other words, they agreed on how Christianity should be evaluated, that it needed to provide measurable social goods. They disagreed on whether Christianity's influence provided such goods. But their consensus on the best way to judge religion was rooted in a similar conception of the university's purpose and mission.[19]

Protestants and the Enlightenment

The way a Unitarian and an Old School Presbyterian came to evaluate Christianity on utilitarian grounds is a complicated story. But the outline of that narrative involves the means by which American Protestants appropriated the Enlightenment. As Mark A. Noll has argued, the turning point for the relationship between religion and learning in American higher education involved one of McCosh's predecessors at Princeton, John Witherspoon. Almost exactly a century before, and in circumstances similar to McCosh's arrival in the small New Jersey town situated halfway between Philadelphia and New York, Witherspoon came to America from Scotland to preside over the College of New Jersey. Since Presbyterians dominated the institution and because the connections between the American and Scottish theological descendants of Calvin were strong, the trustees' selection of a Scottish Presbyterian minister was not unusual. What was unusual, however, was the curriculum and its philosophical foundations that Witherspoon implemented—a curriculum and philosophy to which McCosh would be greatly indebted.[20]

Witherspoon's predecessor at the College of New Jersey was none other than Jonathan Edwards who, though breaking with certain Puritan practices in promoting revivals, perpetuated traditional Augustinian notions about the way humans know the natural world and the purposes of such knowledge. The basic point of Puritan epistemology and science was to challenge autonomous reason and a self-sufficient universe. Reformed theology placed strict limits upon human reason's capacity to know the world truly because of the Calvinistic understanding of human depravity. What is more, Puritans believed that nature was part of God's revelation, in this case general revelation as opposed the special revelation of scripture. Therefore, an understanding of the physical world would always be partial unless regarded within the context of divine sovereignty in creation and providence, or the outworking of God's decrees. Puritans believed that science gave order to physical objects and human ideas by bringing them into agreement with divine ideals. True science occurred when human knowledge conformed to the mind of God. According to this view of science, especially as articulated by Edwards, human knowledge was ultimately dependent on God who revealed all truth.[21] What Edwards and his Puritan forefathers sought was a theory of knowledge that magnified divine power and glory. All knowledge, including science, came from God and depended upon divine sustenance because the world emanated from the divine mind and communicated God's glory. Accurate understanding of nature was not something achieved through autonomous reason or human powers of observation but depended rather on God's sovereign choice to reveal it.

Until the arrival of Witherspoon in 1768, the College of New Jersey, as an institution established to support the revivals of the First Great Awakening, was firmly under the influence of Augustinian science. But with the Scot's introduction of Common Sense Realism as the foundation for both moral and natural philosophy, the Protestant understanding of science shifted dramatically. Witherspoon departed from the Augustinian distrust of human nature. The College of New Jersey's president denied that human depravity fundamentally impeded the ability of reason to formulate natural virtue, understood the achievements of the scientific study of nature to stem from natural powers of observation rather than the conformity of human intellect to the divine mind, and regarded God in a more remote fashion, as the one who designed the natural world but now stood back from the outworking of creation.[22] Witherspoon's successor at the college, Samuel Stanhope Smith, was the "most capable" systematizer and "leading figure" of the Protestant appropriation of the Enlightenment.[23] Like Witherspoon, Smith believed that human reason was capable of understanding nature and morality truly without recourse to divine revelation, that the advancement of science in both the natural and moral worlds would usher in the millennium, and that the truths of human study would always confirm the truths of revealed religion, namely, Christianity. Though the aim of Witherspoon, Smith, and other adherents of the Protestant Enlightenment was to defend Protestant orthodoxy, by making reason and science autonomous from divine revelation they unwittingly liberated science from first-order considerations regarding the structure of the universe and the nature of human knowledge.[24]

The influence of the Scottish philosophy extended well beyond the College of New Jersey's campus. This method of looking at nature and understanding the relationship between Christianity and science appealed to Protestants of all hues, from Harvard's Unitarians to Kentucky's Disciples of Christ.[25] Part of the Scottish Enlightenment's appeal was clearly apologetic. In America, and even more in France, the

Enlightenment had produced its share of deists and, even worse, skeptics. But by showing that traditional Christian convictions were the reasonable outcome of scientific rationality Protestants appeared to answer Christianity's critics on their own grounds by proving that the best science verified the best religion. At the same time the Scottish philosophy had broad appeal because it appeared to uphold order in a society freed from both monarchy and established religion, the traditional supports for social stability in European culture. Unlike France, where the Enlightenment and anticlericalism went hand in hand, the American Revolution yielded a new political order while also retaining traditional Christian ethics and theology. The Scottish philosophy was to a great degree responsible for this feat, hence its broad appeal.[26]

The legacy of the Protestant Enlightenment had significant consequences for the study of religion. By starting with science as the surest way of arriving at true knowledge of nature and morals and as the certain way to social order and progress, Protestant educators insured that Christian truths would conform to science, a trick that was easier to perform before the specialization of knowledge. Just as important was the effort implicit in the Protestant reception of the Enlightenment to domesticate Christianity for use in public life. The strength of the scientific method was obviously its neutrality or objectivity. Human reason in a scientific mode was free from bias, error, and subjectivity. Scientific truths, then, were democratic and commonly available to all, or at least to all reasonable people. In this sense, science offered a way of knowing that could be easily employed in the public realm. Its methods and results were not dependent on tradition, political authorities, or dogma. Rather, participants in a scientific process gave up prior commitments or presumptions to adhere to the rules of inquiry available through human reason.

In this context, Christianity, or more specifically Protestantism, became synonymous with nonsectarian religion because of its conformity to science and its resonance with public sensibilities. Protestantism coalesced with the Enlightenment in America better than other forms of Christianity not merely because Protestants were more numerous in the United States than Catholics, but also because of what George M. Marsden has called the Whig cultural ideal.[27] In Anglo-American culture, Protestantism stood for the cause of freedom and the progress of human history. The Protestant Reformation, in this view, was a liberation specifically from the tyranny and dogmatism of the papacy, and more generally from the illiteracy and superstition of the Dark Ages. Protestantism encouraged freedom of the individual conscience and a less tradition-bound, if not more scientific, way of interpreting the Bible. Thus Protestantism within Anglo-American culture was closely identified with political liberty from arbitrary power and with freedom of inquiry in the pursuit of truth. Moreover, the survivability of republican forms of government, most American Protestants believed, depended upon the health of Protestantism. If America were to usher in a new order for the ages, it needed moral, responsible, disciplined, and independent individuals, precisely the kind that Protestants thought they produced. In sum, Protestantism and science were essential to the new republic. According to Samuel Stanhope Smith, in an expression that would typify the convictions of many nineteenth-century American educators both before and after the rise of the research university, the truths of Christianity were the "surest basis of public morality," promoting the "tranquility, order, and happiness of society," and the "safety of the republic."[28]

To be sure, most Protestants who embraced the Enlightenment continued to argue for Christianity's truthfulness on the basis of divine revelation. Moreover, the Bible and miracles it reported guaranteed the uniqueness of Christianity and its superiority to other religions. But in the climate of the Enlightenment the defense of Christianity rested less on what appeared to be unreasonable or arbitrary, such as the particularities of Israel's and the early church's teachings and practices, and more on what was reasonable. In the hands of the Protestant Enlightenment, then, Christianity and the study of it moved from the private realm of grace and religious authority (such as the Bible and church office) to the public sphere of nature and the widely accessible criteria of reasonableness. In addition to subjecting Christianity to the demands of public plausibility that scientific methods guaranteed, the Protestant Enlightenment also made religion dependent upon its usefulness for the nation. As long as Protestantism dovetailed with the progress of the American republic, Protestant educators had little difficulty justifying the need for religious instruction in public institutions of learning, whether in common schools or colleges and universities. Not until the twentieth century would the wisdom and legitimacy of that strategy come in for serious question.[29]

The Intellectual Gospel

The assumptions of the Protestant Enlightenment, no matter how superficial it sounds to the modern reader at the end of the twentieth

century, provided the glue that held together the ideology of the research university at the end of the nineteenth century. Even though the
language of the Protestant Enlightenment became less overtly theological in the intervening years, by the time of the debates between McCosh
and Eliot its outlines were still evident. This is why the proponents of
the university movement in the United States could repeatedly speak of
the new institution's dedication to scientific research and graduate study
as fundamentally Christian in orientation. For instance, Daniel Coit
Gilman, the founding president of Johns Hopkins University, a paceset-
ting institution often considered the first secular American university,
said that "American universities should be more than theistic; they may
and should be avowedly Christian . . . in the broad, open and inspiring
sense of the Gospels."[30] So, too, Andrew Dickson White declared in
1872 that Cornell, though free from ecclesiastical control, was a "Christian institution," "governed by a body of Christian Trustees," and "conducted by Christian Professors."[31] Even the least conventionally religious of the university movement, Harvard's Charles Eliot, by the end
of his tenure in 1909 sought an endowment to insure the longevity of
his university's divinity school and voluntary religious services. Eliot's
begrudging acknowledgment of nonsectarian Christianity's importance for higher education was further evidence that, thanks to the
Protestant Enlightenment, science still looked for the blessing of religion.[32] Often regarded by historians of American intellectual life and
higher education as a smokescreen for the strictly academic purposes of
the university, such statements and policies demonstrate the continuing
influence of the Protestant appropriation of science in the age of the
early American republic.[33]

The durability of the Protestant Enlightenment helps to explain
why the changes in higher education after the Civil War were not
nearly as threatening to the churches as the conventional histories of
higher education indicate.[34] Despite the so-called revolution that saw
the research university break with the Christian academy of antebellum Protestant colleges, the evidence of explicit hostility between the
churches and the university—the kind that surfaced in the 1920s with
episodes like the Scopes Trial—is hard to find.[35] In fact, Gilman admitted that "hostility to science by the religious part of the community has
never been noteworthy."[36] The reason for the relatively hospitable
reception of the new universities and their promotion of science has to
be attributed to the widespread influence of the Protestant Enlightenment. To be sure, some Protestant theologians had serious reserva-
tions about some of the novelties of the university, especially whether

reforms of the curriculum would prepare graduates sufficiently in the studies necessary for the training of ministers in seminaries and divinity schools.[37] But Protestant concerns about the university were not the result of hostility to science. American Protestants had drunk so deeply and so long from the well of the Enlightenment that they were loath to consider the possibility of conflict between religion and science. This is not to deny the genuine tension between historic Christianity and the new methods and findings of science. It is only to assert that few Protestants noticed much antagonism, so accustomed were they to showing the religious uses of science.[38]

In fact, the new learning's greatest threat may have been to undergraduate education. To offer more courses in science would require a fundamental overhaul of liberal education. Consequently, the educational reformers who championed the cause of the university did so because of the old-time college's inability to provide an appropriate outlet for scientific teaching and investigation. Prior to the founding of research universities in the postbellum period, to find the serious pursuit of the natural sciences one had to go to scientific schools such as Yale's Sheffield School or Harvard's Lawrence School. These institutions were connected to liberal arts colleges but deemed peripheral to the mission of training learned gentlemen. The university, especially the creation of new ones like Johns Hopkins, Cornell, and the University of Chicago, yielded an unparalleled opportunity to give science sufficient room within American higher education. The question, then, was whether additional study in the natural sciences within the undergraduate program was compatible with a genuine liberal or classical education. For educational conservatives, like Yale's Noah Porter and the College of New Jersey's McCosh, the advanced study of nature meant turning away from the more general questions of the purpose and meaning of human existence and focusing on questions that were utilitarian and materialistic. From this perspective, science did pose a threat to the religious dimension of advanced learning because Christianity had been clearly identified with the higher ranges of human aspiration, as opposed to the more practical matters of how nature and society could become more productive. But, as conservatives noted, science not only threatened religion but all subjects concerned with the invisible aspects of human life, from language to philosophy.[39]

Even so, the advocates of science argued strenuously that it was a rightful partner in the task of liberal education. Gilman, though more conventional than Harvard's Eliot and less conservative than Yale's Porter, was a formidable representative of the university movement's concerns because of his leadership at the ideal research university of the day, the Johns Hopkins University (founded in 1876), and also because he was so moderate in his understanding of science, religion, and the purposes of higher education.[40] Indeed, Gilman's endeavors at Johns Hopkins, much like the Enlightenment in America and its political outworkings, display the conservative as opposed to the revolutionary character of the university movement. Rather than abandoning the educational or religious ideals of the antebellum denominational college, reformers like Gilman appropriated that Protestant heritage and built an institution dedicated to advanced research and the flourishing of natural science.

Gilman's conventional views were especially evident when he defended older conceptions of liberal education and argued that science was thoroughly compatible with them. The purpose of liberal education, he asserted, was the development of virtuous and disciplined character. These traits could only be imparted through the time-honored practice of mental discipline, which for Gilman meant "submission, during adolescence, to the precept, example, criticism and suggestion of those who have themselves been well trained."[41] This recognition that youth required greater structure and less freedom echoed McCosh's criticisms of the elective system. According to Gilman, "young human nature thinking less of preparation for the future than of enjoyment for the present" would likely select "with unerring instinct" a "pleasant" course of instruction. But instead of "reclining upon a bed of roses," undergraduates needed an "orderly" and "required" plan of study.[42] Although studies in classical Greek, Latin literature, and history had supplied this needed order, Gilman believed that science could also instill discipline. "A liberally educated man," according to Gilman, was one who possessed a "vigorous will" and thus was capable of resisting the "downward tendencies of his nature," while sustaining and developing "the upward aspirations of his soul."[43] The study of the natural world contributed to liberal education, then, just as well as studying Greek grammar or reading Thucydides. Scientific methods, namely, "the modes of inquiry, of observation, of comparison, of eliminating error and of ascertaining truth," were disciplines that contributed equally well to the purposes of liberal education.[44]

From this affinity between scientific methods and mental discipline it followed that science was a friend of the higher aspects of human life, especially Christianity. According to advocates of the new university like Gilman, religion had nothing to fear from science properly understood. He believed that the vast increases in human knowledge during his own lifetime had made academics all the more willing to affirm that the "things that are seen are temporal," that the "things that are unseen are eternal," and that "the mysteries of life are just as great as they were in the days of Solomon and Plato." Scientific discoveries revealed a plan that was "incomprehensible" without "belief in one living and true God."[45] By the same token, research universities in no way threatened the religious character of American higher education. If modern science confirmed Christian truth as most Protestant intellectuals by the late 1870s believed, the university's dominant influence could not help but be "highly spiritualizing" and "truly religious."[46] Even the methods of science in Gilman's estimate nurtured piety and virtue. The ongoing task of scientific investigation required seriousness, diligence, and zeal, which made the scientist's vocation sacred. Love of truth engendered a zeal, "an ardor of enthusiasm," not far removed from religious fervor.[47] In fact, there was no better way to secure intellectual and moral integrity "than to encourage those habits, those methods, those pursuits which tend to establish truth."[48] What is more, science increased the scholar's sense of awe and reverence, inculcated wisdom and virtue, and promoted industry. What made science most religious was its moral earnestness. The pursuit of truth was so essential that any dishonesty deserved "a place in the penitentiary of science."[49]

If science instilled the virtues necessary for mental discipline and religious devotion, it also assisted the development of Christian civilization. Like his Protestant ancestors Gilman believed that science had ushered in a new age that would witness the elimination of tradition, superstition, and bigotry while vindicating Christian truth. The university movement, which in Gilman's mind embodied the ideals of scientific inquiry, was, in his words, "a reaching out for a better state of society," "a dim but indelible impression of the value of knowledge," and "a craving for intellectual and moral growth."[50] These were ends entirely consonant with the purposes of higher education in the era of the denominational college. The main difference was the shift from a classical education to one that included new disciplines not just within the natural sciences but also in the humanities and social sciences.[51] But even here, like the antebellum college, the university was responding to the needs of the nation. After the Civil War the modernization of economic and political life meant that the United States needed a different kind of college graduate who was an expert in one of the social or natural sciences. In this way the leaders of the university movement appropriated rationales for higher education that had been in American discourse for at least three-quarters of a century, rationales that included a high estimate of science, the contribution of science to the well-being and progress of the nation, and the important function of colleges in supplying the nation with well-educated leadership. Just as the antebellum Protestant denominational college had benefited from and encouraged the social reforms generated by the Second Great Awakening, so, too, the origins of the research university in the United States lay in a similar Protestant desire for an educated, moral, and religious leadership that would extend the material and spiritual progress exhibited in America's history. As James Dwight Dana, Gilman's mentor at the Sheffield Scientific School, wrote some twenty years before the founding of Johns Hopkins, science guaranteed the progressive discovery of the beneficent laws of a kind God whose design was "becoming a gentle and ready assistant . . . in the material progress of nations, as well as their moral and intellectual advancement."[52]

Though statements like Dana's, which could just as easily have been delivered by Gilman at the turn of the twentieth century, show the lines of continuity between American higher education before and after the Civil War, the argument here denies neither the important changes that occurred within American intellectual life with the coming of the university nor the threat that those changes meant for Christian higher education. The point is that hostilities between Christianity and science, or between academic specialization and liberal education, did not become widely apparent until the twentieth century. According to James McLachlan, "the American university did not emerge *de novo* toward the end of the nineteenth century" but was the result of almost a century of developments in American higher education.[53] Important to that development was the symbiosis of Protestant and Enlightenment norms and assumptions. In the same way that the mixture of evangelical zeal and scientific rigor shaped a whole generation of Victorian scientists, the same blend of faith and intellect guided the architects of the research university.[54]

Enlightened Christianity

If the Protestant appropriation of the Enlightenment shaped the discourse by which university leaders pitched scientific research and academic specialization to the public, it also determined in large measure the kind of religion Protestant educators would support and encourage at American institutions of higher learning. As much as the

younger, nonclerical university presidents affirmed the Christian character of their institutions, they were also quick to add that these Christian universities were not sectarian. Charles Eliot spoke for the whole lot
of American educators when he said at the 1876 inaugural of Johns
Hopkins that "a university can not be built upon a sect, unless, indeed,
it be a sect which includes the whole of the educated portion of the
nation."[55] Andrew Dickson White, as well, believed that his university
was Christian in a nonsectarian sense. Even the conservative Noah
Porter of Yale, to the extent that he had imbibed the Protestant Enlightenment, also swallowed the nonsectarian Christianity that so often
accompanied it. In his spirited defense of the old order in American
higher education, *The American Colleges and the American Public* (1870),
Porter showed remarkable continuity with the Unitarian Eliot by insisting that education was inherently opposed to dogmatism and, accord-
ingly, that the best colleges transcended the parochialism of sect or
creed. In words that epitomized the outlook of Protestant educators
from Baltimore to Cambridge, Porter wrote that the culture of higher
education "is, in its nature, liberalizing," and that genuine Christian
learning would "invariably" recognize "the exclusiveness of any Protestant sect" as "distasteful."[56]

In some ways what university leaders meant by nonsectarian Christianity was only that the religious influence at their campus would not
come from one denomination. In one sense this pose was purely administrative. A repeated concern in the efforts for academic reform was inef-
ficiency of having so many colleges competing for qualified faculty and
scarce resources. Denominational colleges were especially hampered
when it came to financing facilities for scientific research. Better to con-
solidate and coordinate the nation's educational resources, the argument went, at the national level in a few specialized universities than
continue with the inherent mediocrity of so many struggling colleges.[57]

Nonsectarian Christianity, however, also implied a critique of the
denominational college's apparent theological rigor. Even though the
advent of seminaries like Andover in 1808 and Princeton in 1812 had all
but eliminated efforts to teach theology in the undergraduate curriculum, university leaders portrayed the liberal arts college as an institution beholden to the doctrinal convictions of the supporting denomination and, therefore, subject to the bias of dogmatic Christianity. For
them universities had to be free from ecclesiastical control and its
attendant theological restrictions to flourish. Of course, the example
of Noah Porter demonstrated that even Protestant ministers could

embrace the nonsectarian Christianity proffered by the university. But for rhetorical purposes university presidents like White and Gilman appealed for support by threatening Protestant opponents with the stigma of sectarian narrowness and theological intolerance.

Nevertheless, university leaders' conception of Christianity was not simply rhetorical. As sentimental and moralistic as it could sound, Protestant educators were committed to propagating at their institutions an Enlightened Christianity that would yield all of the positive aspects of Christian teaching without the theological baggage. Gilman explained that the essence of this Christianity was capsulized in the Epistle of Saint James, which read, "Pure and undefiled Religion is to visit the fatherless and widows in their affliction and to keep himself unspotted in the world." At other times, Gilman, like many of his peers, would also argue that the "two essentials" of the Christian religion were "the love of God and the love of neighbor."[58] From this perspective, of course, Gilman had a much easier time arguing that the research university was fundamentally a Christian institution. By encouraging science, universities nurtured those habits and disciplines that cultivated individual virtue, and by assisting scientific study that was improving the well-being of society (from medicine to sociology) the university appeared to be doing exactly what Christ required of his followers.

Gilman's former associate at Yale, White, could be more antagonistic to historic Protestantism but ended up taking his stand on Enlightened Christianity. In his autobiography, White, though a proponent of the warfare between science and theology, could hardly conceal his religious convictions. He believed that the world "needed . . . more religion rather than less; more devotion to humanity and less preaching of dogma." Indeed, what repulsed White about denominational colleges and the existing churches was their residual if not explicit creedalism. He complained that the demand that individuals who would "gladly unite with Christians in Christian work, and, in a spirit of loyalty to the Blessed Founder of Christianity" assent to theological formulas "made by no one knows where or by whom, and of which no human being can adjust the meanings to modern knowledge" was, to say the least, "most unfortunate." So like Gilman, White held to Christ's Sermon on the Mount, St. James's pure and undefiled religion of helping orphans and widows, and "some of the wonderful utterances of St. Paul" as the kind of religion that the modern world needed and universities provided. The problem, then, was not with Christianity per se but with the church's control of it. "Religion in its true sense," according to White, "was the bringing of humanity into normal relations with that Power, not ourselves, in the universe, which makes for righteousness." With this understanding of belief and its "absolute, pressing" need, university presidents had little difficulty arguing with a straight face for the religious character of their institutions as well as the fundamental compatibility of Christianity and science.[59]

But this understanding of Christianity was not simply the favorite of academic progressives. It also won the allegiance of educators known for their conventional views about education and religion. Yale's Porter, for instance, wrote that Christian faith "rises above mere worldly tendencies," and "destroys the selfish affections and introduces in their place a love which is warm as well as ennobling." In short, Christian feeling encouraged "whatever in human sensibility is of finer texture" and kept it "fresh and pure."[60] As such, science had nothing to fear from Christianity proper because as "a harmonizing and purifying power" it "liberalizes the mind of each narrow devotee, by lifting his thoughts now and then up to God." For Porter, then, Christianity of the right sort was not sectarian but actually functioned as a check on the sectarian tendency of science to pursue partial or biased approaches to truth. But in the end, Christianity and science both were important for instilling the discipline and nurturing the character that was expected of a liberally educated man. Where Porter differed from Gilman and White was in his reluctance to let science crowd out the study of languages, ancient literature, and moral philosophy.

Princeton's McCosh, though the most conventional of the university presidents in his views, also opposed sectarianism and defended Christianity on broad and ethical grounds. To the charge that prayer and Bible reading at colleges were tantamount to sectarianism, McCosh replied that the prayers and praises offered at most Christian institutions were "of a thoroughly catholic (in the true sense of the term) character" and were said in such a way as not to infringe upon the consciences of non-Christians. In fact, even in Congress, he observed, "religion is publicly honored by devotional exercises without any . . . sectarian peculiarities." And though McCosh still talked about Christ as savior, unlike other Protestant educators who spoke more often of Christ as teacher or the blessed founder, McCosh came down on the side of morality and sentiment rather than creed or divine revelation. Thus, Christianity was crucial to the development of modern civilization because the Bible had inspired all of the great artists and writers. So, too, the survival of morality among the educated classes depended on the sustenance of Christian influences upon the university. Christianity not only inspired great art but also right conduct. Under Christian training, McCosh said, many have been led "to devote themselves to high ends" and have been saved from "the vices into which they might otherwise have fallen." For McCosh the crucial question was none other than the one that Harvard's Eliot had asked, namely, "how to teach morality effectively without religion."[61] This was the great fear that haunted Protestant educators. But Enlightened Christianity furnished the solution; it provided a religious foundation for virtue without the controversies and disputes generated historically by Christian dogma.

Historians of late nineteenth-century American culture have usually observed the close parallels between this enlightened version of Christianity and Victorianism's optimism and innocence. According to Henry F. May, for instance, Victorian culture in the United States was characterized by three beliefs: the universality of moral values, the inevitability of progress, and the importance of traditional literary culture. More recently, Daniel J. Singal has added the radical distinction between civilization and barbarism as another important trait of Victorian culture. Believing as they did in a benevolent God who governed nature by immutable laws and in humankind's ability to derive absolute truth about all aspects of life, Victorians, according to Singal, distinguished between those things that lifted persons above beasts, such as education, refinement, manners, the arts, religion, and the family, and the savage realm of instincts and passions which constantly threatened self-control. In the dichotomies Victorianism appeared to reify, science typically came out on the material, physical, or less noble aspects of human existence along with business, technology, and politics. Because science explored the instinctual or even animalistic aspects of human life, its findings were less capable of fostering the virtues and discipline necessary for civilization.[62]

But the views of late nineteenth-century American educational reformers show that the university could transform the study of the natural world from an endeavor too closely focused on the realm of physical existence into a discipline that actually assisted the cultivation of Victorian ideals. What made this possible at least in part was the cosmopolitan outlook that the Enlightenment encouraged. David A. Hollinger, who has written extensively on cosmopolitanism among twentieth-century intellectuals, defines it as the "desire to transcend the limitations of any and all particularisms in order to achieve a more complete human experience."[63] Though he attributes this desire to America's secular intelligentsia, it also motivated the Protestant educators who built the modern university. Cosmopolitanism, no matter how apparently incompatible with religious affirmations, was at the heart of the Enlightenment project, and one to which mainstream American Protestants were deeply committed.[64] Under the banner of science the Enlightenment promised universal laws of politics and morality as well as a common means for discerning truth. In other words, science promised a universal order for nations and individuals, and a universal method of knowing. The Enlightenment, therefore, provided a way for all people and nations to be free from absolutism, superstition, prejudice, and tyranny, or any system of belief or way of arranging the political order that was partial or parochial, that was not available to all reasonable minds and depended upon special claims of revelation or authority. Reason paved the road to liberty and equality by freeing people from the arbitrary demands of blood, land, or creed. With such heady purposes in mind, it made perfect sense for university reformers to hitch the specialized study of the physical world, even if narrowly focused on the mechanics of nature and sometimes overly pragmatic in orientation, to the Victorian desire to escape the parochial and selfish orientation of the uncivilized.[65]

The appropriation of Darwinism provides an example of just how far Protestant educators could go in transforming science into a civilizing and ennobling area of study. Even though Darwin's conclusion about natural selection apparently yielded a glimpse of nature "red in tooth and claw," and though his lessons about the survival of species suggested a darker side of human nature, by the late 1870s when the university movement had fully come into its own, leaders used evolution to justify not just the prominence of natural science in the university but also the superiority of western civilization.[66] To be sure, this evolutionary rhetoric can be attributed in part to older Protestant and Enlightenment notions about progress. But it also demonstrated the Victorian habit of wanting to rise above, if not also to avoid, the harsher aspects of human existence and look on the bright side of life.[67] In effect, university reformers idealized science, taking the spirit of its methods and its promise of a fairer future, without becoming weighed down by its particulars.

The appropriation of Christianity for the sake of the university followed a similar pattern. Enlightened Christianity was a form of religion that fit well with the liberal and progressive norms of the academy. It was reasonable, moral, and inspiring without being sectarian, dogmatic, or superstitious. That Enlightened Christianity turned out to be Protestant provided no difficulty because, unlike Catholicism, as American Protestants would have it, Protestantism did not depend on the arbitrary whims of the pope or church teaching. Instead, Protestant-ism sustained the ideals of science by liberating Christianity from the bondage of medieval superstition and by making the inductive study of the Bible the chief means for arriving at the truths of Christianity. Here the Protestant ideal of liberty of conscience, especially in the form of the rights of individuals to interpret the Bible for themselves, contrasted sharply with Roman Catholic fears of private interpretation and insis-tence upon the laity's assent to the teachings of the Church's hierar-chy.[68] Just as the university idealized science and its results, so too the Protestant educators who led in the reform of American higher educa-tion idealized Christianity and its effects upon university-trained individ-uals and university-influenced cultures. In effect, university leaders took the ethical and spiritual ideals of Christianity and left behind the partic-ulars of creed, liturgy, and polity. Theirs was a cosmopolitan faith that transcended the parochialism of denominational sectarianism.

Academics and Ecumenism

For this reason the participation of university presidents in the meet-ings and endeavors of the Evangelical Alliance was a natural extension of Enlightened Christianity. Founded originally in London in 1846 but failing to establish an American branch until 1867, the Alliance was intended to bring "individual Christians into closer fellowship and cooperation" on the basis of modest, some would say vague, theologi-cal affirmations.[69] Like the Enlightened Christianity that informed the university, American support for the alliance drew more upon Protes-tant sentiments regarding Christian civilization in America and Whig assumptions about moral progress generated by the Civil War than substantive theological discussion.[70] In addition, many of the threats to America's well-being listed by Protestant educators were also mat-ters that agitated members of the Evangelical Alliance. Especially dangerous were materialism, skepticism, infidelity, and dogmatic reli-gion (e.g., Catholicism), all of which persuaded Protestants to work together on the basis of a religious affirmation that put morality ahead of creedal or liturgical matters.[71] The alliance also manifested the Whig habit of conflating Protestantism, civil liberty, and democracy. Unlike Europe, where various forms of tyranny still existed, America, according to Evangelical Alliance leaders, embodied the best hope for true religion because of the nation's democratic and republican foundations. The United States was, in the words of James McCosh who avidly supported the alliance, "the land of the future" because evangelical principles were thoroughly incorporated in the life and spirit of the country.[72]

At its 1887 meeting, devoted to the theme "National Perils and Opportunities," the leaders of the Alliance asked McCosh to speak. His topic was not higher education as some might have expected. Rather, McCosh spoke on the church's duty regarding "the Capital and Labor Question." For the topic of higher education and how universities contributed to the "Christian Resources of Our Country," the Evangelical Alliance turned to Hopkins's president, Daniel Coit Gilman. Like many of the speeches Gilman gave, this one lacked punch. In a conventional way he responded to the question of whether universities were "helps or hindrances" to religious faith by giving examples of Christian heroes from Wycliffe to Frederick Denison Maurice, and of religious movements from the Reformation to sociology, which had been conceived and nurtured by the university. But these illustrations constituted mainly circumstantial evidence. Gilman went on to argue that the purposes of Christianity and the university were "identical." "The ultimate end of all educational and scientific effort" was the same as "that at which Christianity aims, that which was heralded in Judea nineteen centuries ago, by a multitude of the heavenly host, saying, 'Peace on earth, good-will to men.'"[73]

To be sure, not all members of the Alliance would have agreed with Gilman's understanding of Christianity. Some American Protestants would have defined the Christian religion in more particular terms, emphasizing the incarnation and the uniqueness of the life and death of Christ. But Gilman's presence at the Evangelical Alliance, and his continued activity in Protestant endeavors—in 1901 he stepped down from the presidency of Johns Hopkins in part to become the vice-president of the American Bible Society—speaks volumes about the way the American academy appropriated Christianity and about the legacy of the American Protestant encounter with the Enlightenment. In order to protect Christianity from hostile assault and to insure the positive influence of Christianity upon the republic, Protestant clergy first defended their faith on scientific grounds and in the process stressed those elements of Christianity that provided a united Protestant witness to and influence upon the United States. For this reason, the peroration of Gilman's speech was a poignant, even if undistinguished, appropriation of the older ideals of the Protestant Enlightenment for the future work of American Protestants in the university and, ultimately, in the nation.

With the motto which the Secretary of this Conference introduced upon the title-page of his instructive and impressive volume entitled "Our Country," I will conclude these remarks: "We live in a new and exceptional age; America is another name for opportunity. Our whole history appears like a last effort of the Divine Providence in behalf of the human race."

But I will add to this motto these words of Isaac Taylor: "It is the first characteristic of spiritual Christianity, that it attaches a sovereign importance to TRUTH, as furnishing the only solid support for the motives of self-government, purity and charity."[74]

The Common University

The founding of the modern research university in the United States parallels closely the formation of America's common schools for primary and secondary education. In his book about the rise of public schooling in the United States, *The Myth of the Common School,* Charles Glenn shows how the Enlightenment also informed the ideology of school reforms in the first half of the nineteenth century. Under the guise of universal truths and common ideals, American educators, in this case also Protestant, sought to teach a neutral religion in public schools, thus preserving Christian influence while also avoiding the perils of sectarianism. According to Horace Mann, a Massachusetts Unitarian and leader of the common school movement, public schools had the religious mission of elevating and purifying the race. This mission did not emerge from "the creeds of men" but rather stemmed from the "Religion of Heaven."[75] Even though confessional Christians such as Old School Presbyterians and Roman Catholics thought it impossible to separate Christian morality from Christian doctrine, Mann and his contemporaries purged public schools of sectarian and divisive theology while maintaining the religious character of public education. According to Charles Brooks, another Massachusetts educator, "the technicalities of Christian sects are not taught. By special statute they are prohibited. But those great and eternal principles of moral truth, which all sects allow to be indispensable in the grown-up Christian, are the principles which [the schools] carefully imbed in every youthful heart."[76]

It took longer for this same kind of Enlightened Christianity to make its way into higher education, but the university reform movement of the postbellum era insured its victory within the American academy. Even though denominational colleges were in many cases founded upon the assumptions of the Protestant Enlightenment, their church ties guaranteed at least implicitly ongoing awareness of their creedal, liturgical, and ecclesiological distinctiveness, the very things that university leaders believed to be evidence of sectarianism. As in the case of common school reforms, the religious motives of university leaders stemmed not only from a different conception of Christianity than the one taught by the churches. The religious justification for the modern university also arose from a desire to serve and shape the recently unified nation. This nation-serving character of the university movement meant that all higher education worthy of distinction was public, not in the sense that funding came from the state, but in the sense that it served public or national ends. And just as American Protestants during the War for Independence and initial decades of the republic set aside the particularities of denominational traditions for the sake of building a Christian nation, so public school leaders and later university builders discarded dogma in order to find a common faith that served the public. That this neutral religion resembled liberal Protestantism did not matter because this was the kind of faith needed for the good of the nation.

What is ironic about the modern American university is that despite the pride many of its leaders took in their accomplishments, their understanding of the difficult choices required for maintaining Christian higher education may have been worse than their forebears at the denominational colleges. For instance, William James, writing in 1876 for the *Nation,* complained about the poor quality of philosophical thinking and instruction at the antebellum denominational college. Students, he wrote, "leave college with the generous youthful impulse to reflect . . . dampened and discouraged . . . by the lifeless discussions and flabby formulas that have had to commit to memory."[77] Judging by the vagaries of academic rhetoric displayed by the likes of Gilman, White, Porter, and McCosh, the new atmosphere of the university, even though apparently disciplined by the rigor of science, was just as flabby intellectually as the denominational college. The reason for the university's intellectual girth had a lot to do with the way Protestants had embraced the Enlightenment.[78]

Here Alisdair MacIntyre's assessment of the Scottish version of the Protestant Enlightenment is instructive for recognizing the defects of the modern university's intellectual and religious foundation. According to MacIntyre, liberal Protestants in Scotland made the mistake of judging Christianity not on its own terms but rather by the standards of "enlightened modernity," thus apparently insuring a neutral religion but also making Christianity the same as enlightened modernity and, therefore, failing to allow for real intellectual disagreement in an institution where intellectual give and take is supposed to flourish. The other mistake that Protestant educators made, MacIntyre argues, is one of being blind to the wholeness of a religious tradition. University leaders did not see the place of Christianity's moral teachings "within an overall theological moral scheme, embodying and representing a highly specific conception of human nature." These mistakes have left the university without the ability to justify itself intellectually. By insisting that human rationality, when liberated from external constraints (i.e., religious dogma) would automatically produce "agreement among all rational persons," the "false premises" of university reformers imposed "arbitrary constraints upon liberty of judgment" and overlooked the conditions necessary for a rational defense of their institution.[79]

MacIntyre believes the university has yet to recover from the false premises established by liberal Protestants. The study and teaching of religion are part of the legacy of the university's intellectual assumptions and self-understanding. To be included in the university, religion, in the view of university leaders, would have to serve enlightened and public purposes. This means that the religion studied and taught in American higher education would always be a reduced version of a particular religious tradition, one that avoids the religious practices of the believer or cleric in favor of a sufficiently domesticated and innocuous religious expression. This was the vision of late nineteenth-century academic reformers, men who while still members of the mainstream Protestant denominations had been frustrated by their churches' domination of American learning.

Protestant Divinity in the Shadow of the University

IN 1872 PRINCETON SEMINARY celebrated its sixtieth anniversary as well as the semicentennial of its professor of theology, Charles Hodge. As one of America's oldest seminaries—only Andover being four years older—Princeton benefited from Hodge's remarkable longevity. He taught more students (over two thousand) than any other nineteenth-century American theologian, authored several commentaries and theological textbooks, and edited Princeton's formidable theological journal, the *Biblical Repertory and Princeton Review*. In other words, Hodge had a considerable influence upon his own denomination, the Presbyterian Church in the U.S.A., as well as the wider constellations of institutions, both cultural and educational, of which Princeton Seminary and northern Presbyterians were such a significant part. Upon that occasion Hodge summed up what for many ministers and theological educators was a useful measure of a seminary's mission. "I am not afraid to say," he asserted, "that a new idea never originated in this Seminary." Hodge's confidence was as simple as was Princeton's instruction unoriginal. "The Bible is the word of God. . . . If granted; then it follows that what the Bible says, God says. That ends the matter."[1]

More than a century later it is hard to remember that Hodge was no simpleton, as the greetings and guests at his semicentennial indicated.

In addition to officials from the leading seminaries and divinity schools in the United States and other countries, the current or former presidents of Yale, the College of New Jersey, Bowdoin, Union, Lafayette, Rutgers, the University of Pennsylvania, and the University of the City of New York attended the festivities to honor Hodge. During Princeton's first sixty years it regularly turned out graduates who went on to serve in a variety of capacities in American higher education. In an era well before the fractious debates pitting fundamentalists against modernists, a conservative theological institution like Princeton Seminary was firmly entrenched within the elite institutions of American learning.[2]

Yet, from the perspective of academic reformers such as the presidents of Johns Hopkins, Cornell, and Harvard, Princeton's prominence within the field of biblical and theological studies was precisely the problem with bringing religious studies into the research-oriented and progressive environment of the new university. To be sure, Princeton's control by the northern Presbyterian Church represented the kind of sectarian arrangement that prevented the full-throttle pursuit of truth scientifically defined. But just as troubling was Hodge's commitment to the theological status quo. Even if Princeton was more innovative than Hodge believed, he clearly regarded it a badge of honor not to have generated a new idea. For institutions dedicated to adapting higher education to the realities of post–Civil War America with its expanding economic and political needs, Hodge's tenacious grip upon the past looked more foolish than uninspiring.[3]

But America's seminaries were not without resources that the newly emerging universities could use. Unlike Princeton, Andover presented a more promising understanding of theological studies, one that was compatible with the university presidents' vision for their institutions and for the purposes of American higher education. Or so Daniel Coit Gilman of Johns Hopkins thought. In an 1880 article written for the *Congregationalist,* Gilman praised curricular reforms at the Massachusetts seminary that added a fourth year of study to the standard curriculum and included lectures in modern psychology, scientific methods, and biblical criticism. What the country needed were ministers well equipped to address the difficulties of modern thought. Andover's course was designed to do just that. Its purpose in the study of religion, according to Gilman, paralleled the changes inaugurated by the new research university. Contrary to Hodge, Gilman believed that "the most intelligent people of our day" were not interested in "minor" religious questions from previous "historical epochs." "They care very little for the distinctive tenets of any sect." But there was never a time, he added, "when the foundations of belief were so much the subject of earnest thought and study, or when it was more important to discuss great themes in a manly spirit, rather than petty differences in a narrow way."[4]

The trick, of course, was to find academics who could teach religion in such an enlightened way. With the exception of Andover, most advanced studies in religion took place within seminary and divinity school environments where training clergy was virtually the sole goal. For this reason university reformers who wanted religion of the right kind to have a place in higher education gave a surprising amount of attention to the way Christianity was studied and taught within Protestant theological schools. Only when the seminaries and divinity schools forsook Protestant sectarianism for Enlightened Christianity and began to produce religious scholars capable of participating within the university would the study of religion emerge as a legitimate discipline within American learning. Until then, religion in American universities remained an extracurricular affair.[5]

University Experiments in Protestant Divinity

Harvard University's Charles W. Eliot may have envied the prospects of creating a university unencumbered by what he called "Christian sects," like that of his colleague Daniel Coit Gilman at Johns Hopkins.[6] But like it or not Eliot inherited an institution that not only was founded by Puritans but also came with a divinity school. To be sure, the religious instruction offered in Cambridge was broader than most seminaries because of Harvard Divinity School's Unitarian ties.[7] Still, despite the liberal theological tradition of Unitarianism Eliot wanted Harvard's theological education to be like that of his university, namely, undenominational and scientific.[8] As such he devoted considerable time to questions surrounding the training of ministers.

In an address prepared for the *Princeton Review* in 1883 Eliot elaborated in fairly simple terms the problems with Protestant theological education. The fundamental reality was that the "position and environment" of the minister had changed dramatically within the past one hundred years.[9] Other professions rivaled the ministry, and alternative sources of information such as newspapers, periodicals, and cheap books competed with the sermon. What is more, changes within society required that the minister "have his mind made up, and . . . be ready for action." Pastors and priests had also lost their authority. "The divine right of the minister is dead among Protestants," Eliot wrote, clerical

authority now being derived from "the purity and strength of . . . character" (343). In fact, the problem of the ministry's status was even more
deep-seated. Protestant clergy would not recover their influence with
the American public "until the accepted dogmas of the churches
square with the political convictions of the people." Making matters
worse was the rise and development of the natural sciences. Not only
had new knowledge unsettled received dogma but the spirit of scientific inquiry made the acceptance of any kind of truth prior to critical
scrutiny "an unpardonable sin" (345). The consequence of scientific
advance was that the ministry, unlike any other profession, was under
the constant strain of "intellectual dishonesty" (347). No wonder "young
men of promise" were reluctant to enter the profession.

Eliot's remedy to this state of affairs was better training for ministers
so they could "meet the new demands which modern society makes
upon [them]." Not surprisingly, his reforms for theological education
followed the path of greater academic freedom and more electives in
the curriculum. The basic studies a minister needed were hardly different from a good liberal education and included the biblical languages
and Latin, English literature, psychology, political economy, constitutional history, and natural science. Since ministers preached, homilet-
ics was also essential. Among the traditional theological disciplines
(Old Testament, New Testament, church history, comparative religion,
ethics, systematic theology, and "charitable and reformatory methods"),
Eliot recommended that ministers choose three and master them rather
than becoming acquainted with all (353). Superficial study, he argued,
produced "conceited, presumptuous and rash" students, while the
"master" was "humble, unassuming, and cautious." More important,
ministers needed power rather than information. And the "most important step toward getting mental power" was acquiring "a right method
in work." "The true spirit of research," according to Eliot, was the same
in all fields, "namely, the free, fair, fearless, and faithful spirit of modern
science" (354).

Francis Landey Patton, then a professor of theology at Chicago's
McCormick Theological Seminary, who would eventually replace
James McCosh as president of the College of New Jersey, was not
altogether impressed by Eliot's suggestions for reforming theological
education. He was particularly suspicious of the assumption that the
American public accepted nothing on trust from ministers. "Do
lawyers argue with their clients," Patton asked, or do "physicians hold
consultations with their patients" or do "bankers defer respectfully
to the financial wisdom" of nonbankers? He also challenged Eliot's

charge that religious ideas had to conform to modern notions, especially America's political traditions. "The influence gained by sacrific-
ing the language of Scripture to the vocabulary of American politics
would not be worth perpetuating." In fact, a theology carved out of
the Declaration of Independence was not "the gospel of salvation" and
ministers who preached it had no legitimate claim upon "Christian
sympathy." If the American people had grown "so republican" that
they could not even speak of the kingdom of God, then, Patton
asserted, "they have taken a long step in the direction of discarding
Christianity altogether."[10]

Patton also took issue with Eliot's naive faith in the beneficence
of science by questioning the Harvard president's understanding of the
ministry. The Protestant conception of the minister, Patton thundered,
was that he is a "divinely appointed officer in a divinely founded institution, . . . charged with the duty of declaring a specific and authoritative
message in the name of God."[11] Patton already had a reputation for
such outbursts; recently he had led the charge against the heterodoxy of
David Swing, one of Chicago's more popular preachers, in a heresy trial
that attracted national attention.[12] As old-fashioned and dogmatic as
Patton could sound, he did raise an important objection to the kind of
religious instruction Eliot proposed for ministers. Harvard's president
was tampering with a form of education for which the church, not the
university, was ultimately responsible. "The minister is not merely a
man who is to pursue theological science in a university, but he is a man
to receive support in the service of an ecclesiastical organization." Patton's distinction between the church and the university implied not only
that the purpose of the ministry was different from that of the university—the former being preparation for the world to come, the latter
being instruction for life in this world. It also indicated that the spirit of
the university was antithetical to the character of the church. While the
university was open to truth wherever it might lead, the church "must
either impose its creed upon its ministers or else it will sooner or later
reach a position where it will need no ministers at all."[13] In other words,
though the learning upon which the church and university depended
overlapped, the modern university's mission of liberating religious
truth from dogma and making it serve the public good was fundamentally incompatible with the kind of theological education and ministerial training churches required.

Patton's views did not prevent him from gaining the support of the
College of New Jersey's conservative Presbyterian supporters, but they
were at odds with university reformers' conceptions about the study of

religion. More typical was the outlook of Cornell's Andrew Dickson White. Though he did not have to contend with a nearby or affiliated seminary or divinity school and so did not write about theological education, White clearly showed his sympathies for the newer kind of religious instruction proposed by Eliot. White concluded his survey of the warfare between science and theology with an overview of the scientific study of the Bible. In typically whiggish fashion, the Cornell president showed how progressive biblical criticism was, how it took root in America among "the foremost minds," and how despite bitter opposition from ecclesiastical authorities its scholars "were manfully supported by the more intellectual clergy and laity." Furthermore, the "greater universities" in the United States sided with those scholars who refused to accept the received dogma of Christianity.[14] The reason for taking this position was obvious, from White's perspective. He closed his two-volume history with a flourish on behalf of science that had special application to the Christian religion:

> Thus, at last, out of the old conception of our Bible as a collection of oracles—a mass of entangling utterance, fruitful in wrangling interpretations, which have given to the world long and weary ages of "hatred, malice and all uncharitableness"; of fetichism, subtlety, and pomp; of tyranny, bloodshed, and solemnly constituted imposture; of everything which the Lord Jesus Christ most abhorred—has been gradually developed through the centuries, by the labours, sacrifices, and even the martyrdom of a long succession of men of God, the conception of it as a sacred literature—a growth only possible under that divine light which the various orbs of science have done so much to bring into the mind and heart and soul of man—a revelation, not of the Fall of Man, but of the Ascent of Man—an exposition, not of temporary dogmas and observances, but of the Eternal Law of Righteousness—the one upward path for individuals and for nations.[15]

The university president who had the greatest opportunity to harness the scientific study of Christianity to the progressive mission of the research university was William Rainey Harper, the University of Chicago's founding president and one of America's leading Old Testament scholars. Harper was the new breed of religion scholar that university reformers desired to include on their faculties. Only thirty-six years old when the University of Chicago began, Harper had grown up in the Presbyterian Church and attended a Presbyterian college, Muskingum, near to his home in Ohio. Possessor of precocious language skills (he graduated from college when he was only fourteen years old), in 1875 Harper went to Yale for his Ph.D. to study ancient languages. While teaching at Denison University in Ohio Harper became a Baptist, thus explaining part of his appeal to John D. Rockefeller, who wanted the University of Chicago to be a Baptist institution. From Denison Harper moved to Morgan Park Seminary in Chicago and then in 1886 on to Yale where he became a popular teacher and launched a campaign to make biblical studies a regular part of the college curriculum. But perhaps what made Harper most acceptable to the new leadership of American higher education was his devotion to scientific methods and his ability to study the Bible outside a church context. The fact that Harper was never ordained may help to explain his wider angle of vision in the field of Old Testament studies and his success in introducing the study of religion to the research university. Of all the emerging universities dedicated to the newer ideals in higher education, such as Cornell, Johns Hopkins, Clarke, and Stanford, Chicago was the only one to have what today would resemble a department of religious studies.[16]

Like Gilman and Eliot, Harper's attempt to make the study of religion part of the university was hampered by older restrictions stemming from the training of Protestant ministers. Theological and biblical studies had yet to find an academic justification that was independent of churchly considerations. Even so, Harper developed a new curriculum that moved the study of scripture and related disciplines closer to the university's public and scientific orientation and farther from the parochial and private domain of the churches. He began by recognizing the need for religion to interact with the new learning. Harper faulted the undergraduate education of ministers for concentrating exclusively on the study of antiquity. For religion to be more influential, prospective ministers needed to study both natural sciences and psychology before taking up theological studies. Thus, Harper sided with the curricular changes that incorporated the study of the natural and social sciences, and modern languages, which in turn crowded out the classical curriculum and older assumptions about liberal education.[17]

Within the theological curriculum proper Harper argued for several reforms. In order to make the minister more accessible and to prepare him for real life in the church Harper recommended introductory courses in pastoral training, church administration, and church music.[18] Finally, he advised that seminaries adopt the elective system because the field of study was broad and the choice of a specialty increased learning. These changes meant that the course of study would go from three to four years, with a prescribed course in the basics (Bible, theology, history, and sociology) for the first year, and specialization in the final three years, whether academically or professionally oriented.[19]

Like Eliot, Harper believed that recent developments had made the old ways of studying religion obsolete. What stood out in Harper's mind about "the present state of society," as it also had for Eliot, was the "modern democratic situation." "The atmosphere of the present day," he declared, "is essentially different from the atmosphere of our grandfathers." But the study of theology had not been modified at all. Though Christianity was "democratic through and through," the church had been guilty of antagonizing the democratic spirit. Equally difficult for the study of theology were recent developments in natural science. Finally, economic changes had made old ideas about Christianity ineffective. Just as the church had alienated the lower classes by not being sufficiently democratic, so ministers could not influence the number of wealthy men that was increasing "every decade." In sum, theological education was set up to produce only one thing—a preacher. Such education too frequently cultivated a "narrow and exclusive" outlook. What modern times needed were religious leaders with a "broad and generous spirit."[20]

The breadth and generosity that Harper hoped to nurture in the teaching and study of Christianity was not intended simply for seminary and divinity school faculty. To be sure, religious studies had the longest way to go to acclimate itself to the prevailing ethos of the university. But Harper made breadth and generosity the standard for all academic disciplines in the university. For the University of Chicago president, the university was fundamentally a democratic institution, not merely in the sense that it was "an institution of the people," but also because its ideals were the same as those of democracy. "The university had its birth in the democratic idea," Harper affirmed, "and from the day of its birth this democratic character, except when state or church has interfered, has continued." Thus, the university was a place for study, but study of a particular kind, "an institution privileged by the state for the guidance of the people; an agency recognized by the people for resolving the problems of civilization which present themselves in the development of civilization." The university would train and provide a home for the academic elite by giving them freedom from "interference of any kind, civic or ecclesiastical." But in return the university would apply the insights of this elite to humanity's "great problem." This was a good bargain for both democracy and the university.[21]

Harper's understanding of the democratic nature of the university resembled that of many other university leaders. Indeed, for all of the celebration and encouragement of the research ideal at these new institutions, and the corollary notion that the university permitted scholars to pursue truth wherever it might lead, the logic of academic specialization and the noble pursuit of truth were always restrained by the idea that the university was a servant of the public, a place, as Harper argued, where the great issues of the people could be addressed and even solved, and where modern democracy would find leadership and example.[22] For instance, Harvard's Eliot described the less direct benefits of a university as exerting a unifying social, religious, and political influence. "American universities," he asserted, "are schools of public spirit for the communities in which they are situated."[23] Likewise, even the research-minded Daniel Coit Gilman was no less explicit about the public service rendered by universities. The university, he wrote, "benefits society as well as individual men. It renders service to the community which no demon of statistics can ever estimate."[24] For some reason the leaders of American university were oblivious to the tension between the ideals of serving the public and academic freedom. What happened, for instance, if a scholar's zealous research resulted in truths the people did not want to hear? Equally difficult was the notion that the variety of academic disciplines housed in the university would ever come up with solutions to the problems of civilization, as if economists and biologists would have a similar perspective on the practices of Standard Oil. Of course, hindsight is always better, but the logic of university advocates did not produce intellectual coherence or a means to achieve it beyond the good intentions of honorable men.

This incoherence was especially evident in the way university presidents like Harper and Eliot thought about the teaching and place of religion in higher education. First, the trend of academic specialization could have made it possible for those involved in the study of religion to pursue with greater specificity the methods and subject matter of their research. And this did indeed happen in the theological and biblical disciplines, with the founding of professional organizations such as the Society of Biblical Literature (1880) and the American Society of Church History (1888), blossoming at the same time that other academic disciplines professionalized.[25] Specialization in religious subjects, however, could also encourage greater denominational self-consciousness if not sectarianism. If Presbyterian and Quaker theologians pursued with greater industriousness the topics and distinctive aspects of their respective communions' convictions, then theology would hold even less interest for a generally educated audience, much like advanced studies in the natural sciences became less intelligible to wider publics.[26] Perhaps this was the reason that university presidents chose to regard religion in generalist terms, conceiving of it either as something that assisted democracy and had a vital contribution to make to public life, or, according to Harper, as "something which includes all that is holy and sacred in life . . . whether in relation to home, or country or church."[27] Whatever the explanation, by arguing for the relevance of religion (and the ministry, for that matter) to broader concerns beyond the church proper, university reformers were pulling the study of religion in directions that countered the simultaneous academic push for specialization and professional competence.

Second, intellectual incoherence also followed from the desire for religious studies (and the ministry) to be of greater service to the public. While academic specialization in other disciplines, whether for good or ill, generated the notion of expertise and authority, the arguments made by university reformers on behalf of the study of religion stripped religion scholars of their academic proficiency. When, for instance, Harper wondered how someone trained in science could ever be expected to listen with respect to a minister who, though trained in the Bible and theology, was not similarly trained in science, he did not seem to fathom that his question was just as applicable in the reverse situation; why would someone trained in Old Testament literature listen with respect to a natural scientist who had no background in the advanced scholarship on Judaism or Christianity? In the university reformers' outlook the relationship between religious subjects and other areas of study was a one-way street, with religion being forced to comply with the standards and findings of other subjects, especially the natural and social sciences, having no credible academic standing on its own merits, and garnering no real respect from other academics.

In this way, even though the university was open to the study and teaching of religion, it posed a situation where religion scholars were forced to conform to procedures and criteria of evaluation that did not emerge within the field of religion proper. Instead, the ideals of science and democracy, two notions that made the university a public domain, no matter how individual institutions were funded, thus, were at odds with the norms governing scholars who worked within specific religious traditions. Of course, one could argue that to be a part of an institution like the university religious scholars would have to accept the rules that governed the institution. Consequently, demonstrating the public value of private religion was a natural development. But this understandable outcome does not mitigate the tension between the claims of particular religious traditions being taught in the public setting of the university. How does one handle in public a subject that comes from a particular community of faith? Even though the study and teaching of religion in the university would not emerge formally until the middle decades of the twentieth century, the terms upon which religious studies would be accepted were established in the late nineteenth century as university reformers looked for ways to shape seminaries and divinity schools in the image of the university. And those terms were not friendly to the ways that religious communities, whether Protestant, Catholic, or Jewish, understood and studied their tradition.

Church Experiments in Progressive Divinity

Though presidents such as Eliot and Harper took the lead in establishing the basis upon which religion would be taught and studied in the university, their influence upon the churches is less clear. But at the same time that university administrators were drawing up new plans for the education of ministers—in other words, for the way religion should be taught and studied in modern America—theologians and biblical scholars at some of America's seminaries were also reconfiguring the study of Christianity in ways that would conform more to the standards of the university world than to the categories of the religious tradition out of which they worked. This reconfiguration was probably most obvious at the nation's oldest Protestant seminary, Andover.

When Daniel Coit Gilman gave a favorable press to Andover's new course of study he made a direct connection between the aims of university reformers and those of the men responsible for the New Orthodoxy in New England theology. Gilman's high marks for the Massachusetts's Congregationalist seminary may have been inflated since the Progressive Orthodoxy that came to dominate the school in the last quarter of the nineteenth century still worked within traditional Protestant theological categories that university reformers would have considered too dogmatic.[28] Still, the shift at Andover from the old New England orthodoxy to the new way of articulating Christianity resonated with the optimistic and activistic impulses of the modern university.

Changes within New England were evident as early as midcentury when, through the influence of certain strands of romanticism, ministers such as Hartford's Horace Bushnell began to stress the poetic nature of religious knowledge and the figurative character theological language.[29] But developments within New England theology were sporadic and haphazard until they took institutional form at Andover in the early 1880s. At first the older theology appeared to hold the high ground when the seminary's overseers refused to appoint Newman Smyth, an advocate of Bushnellian theological formulations. But gradually progressive Congregationalists established themselves at Andover and in effect captured the school. Indicative of this coup was the removal in 1884 of the seminary's theological quarterly, *Bibliotheca Sacra,* to Oberlin and the inauguration of a new religious journal in its stead, the *Andover Review,* which functioned as the chief device for spreading the new orthodoxy outside classrooms at Andover.[30]

The Andover progressives' doctrinal innovations were far-ranging and imprecise. The one point that generated the most controversy concerned the notion of future probation, namely, whether an individual could be saved from eternal punishment after death. This doctrine became the litmus test for both conservatives and progressives, with the former opposing and the latter advocating the possibility of conversion in the afterlife. But progressive orthodoxy did not simply advance along a few contested points of Protestant speculative theology. Instead, in the spirit of Bushnell, Andover progressives questioned the rational and systematic pretensions of the New England theology across the board by stressing the experiential and dynamic aspects of religious life and thought. In undermining the traditional dichotomies of Protestant orthodoxy, progressives blurred the older distinctions between God and man, and between the supernatural and nature which had been crucial to the New England system. In place of these categories progressives stressed the incarnation as overcoming the distance between the human and divine, and the immanence of God to show the interrelatedness of the spiritual and the natural worlds.[31]

The blurring of theological distinctions was particularly evident in the Andover progressives' discussion of the Christian life. In the younger Andover faculty's hands the task of the church and that of the individual Christian became one of making the whole world Christian, both institutions and individuals. Rather than regarding the church as a people set apart, and the gospel as a means for bringing those outside into the household of faith, Andover progressives conceived of the church and its mission in global and kingdom-building terms where "the church never denies the courtesy of the Christian name or the hospitality of the Christian hope to those whose lives illustrate Christian virtues."[32] Indeed, to limit definitions of Christianity to the teaching of the atonement and salvation through the meritorious sacrifice of Christ was to make historic Christianity into a kind of "magic." Rather than restricting Christianity to the few, progressive orthodoxy sought to make it an "opportunity for all." As such, Christian influence and character became synonymous with righteousness and virtue. Andover progressives still believed they were preserving the gospel's exclusiveness, but also that they did so by affirming Christianity's universality. "The Christian type," they wrote, was the "only type of man acceptable to God." But now with a few adjustments "every man" had "his right in Christianity."[33]

The inclusive nature of progressive orthodoxy also permitted Christianity to have a greater range of influence, one that extended well beyond the traditional confines of word, sacrament, and missions. Thanks to a broader conception of Christianity, individual believers could participate more fully in all walks of life rather than living in isolation from the world. In a striking passage that reversed older ways of interpreting the early church and its antagonism to the surrounding world, Andover progressives transformed the themes of persecution and martyrdom into the cause of democracy.

> Persecution carried it even to the hearts of persecutors. Sometimes the witness to the faith found expression in protest against prevailing immoralities and cruelties. Christianity declared itself in appreciable and effective ways for the rights of man. The Christian became the champion of humanity. The result of these conflicts . . . was always a deliverance or a reform [and] carried Christianity farther and farther into society.[34]

Consequently, moral influences upon the family, the state, and business became effective means of spreading Christian influence. Andover progressives still affirmed the need for Christian missions and evangelism. But their affirmation of older church practices was always bound up with their broader conception of Christianity, which located its "fundamental predicate" in the gospel's "ethical absoluteness."[35] Daniel Day Williams, who wrote on the Andover progressives at a time when Protestant liberalism was in retreat, summarized well the logic of Andover's new theology. "They had developed a moralistic conception of salvation. To be good is to be saved. . . . Living in right relationships with one's fellows is now conceived as the principal meaning of the Christian life."[36] This conception of Christianity proved to be the seminary world's equivalent of the university's Enlightened Christianity. No wonder that university presidents like Gilman favored the changes at Andover and that the efforts of university presidents like Harper to train ministers for service to society resembled the curricular reforms carried out by Andover's faculty.

Andover's progressive orthodoxy was not the only sign of alignment between theological educators and university reformers. Charles Briggs, an Old Testament scholar at Union Theological Seminary in New York, showed that the kind of theological and curricular changes underway among New England Congregationalists were also influencing their more rigid theological neighbors to the south, the Presbyterians. Though Briggs's views did not speak for all Presbyterians in the northeast, they were the wave of the future. Eventually northern Presbyterians would embrace conceptions of the church's service to society that dovetailed with those of the Andover progressives. Furthermore, Presbyterians would revise patterns of theological education to fit with the newer understanding of the ministry, thus opening greater opportunity for cooperation between church and university in the study and teaching of religion. But even though Briggs blazed a trail for religious studies in the university, he encountered opposition from fellow Presbyterians which not only confirmed university reformers' suspicions about the dogmatism and sectarianism of the churches but also revealed the constraints under which the study and teaching of religion would labor until the 1930s.[37]

In many respects Briggs's contribution to the study of religion was more significant than Andover's. Andover progressives prepared the way for an understanding of Christianity that was compatible with the mission of the university only implicitly by challenging time-honored distinctions within Protestant systematic thought, thus removing objections to Christian dogmatism. Briggs, however, took aim more directly at how religion, particularly the Bible, should be taught in order for it to conform to the scientific standards of the university. Formerly, he wrote in an 1897 article, "the study of the Bible was dominated by dogmatic theology." Seminaries and divinity schools taught students of the Bible, primarily prospective ministers, to interpret the scriptures "by the rule of faith, that is, the traditional dogmatic opinion of his sect." But thanks to the university "the student is taught [now] to study his Bible by scientific principles of interpretation and to correct the rule of faith by the Bible." This kind of study required a multitude of talents, from philology, geography, archaeology, and history to exposition, higher criticism, and theology. But the results of such study were well worth the effort.

A proper investigation of the Bible proved, Briggs argued, that dogmatic theology was "speculative" while biblical theology revealed what was truly "of divine authority." Indeed, modern biblical scholarship was better suited for the university than the seminary because university professors were "free from those denominational and schismatic influences which obstruct the pathway to all scientific study."[38]

Briggs's references to the narrowness and sectarianism of the church did not win him many friends within northern Presbyterian circles but they did constitute a theologically informed rendition of the university reformers' brief on behalf of an academy free from ecclesiastical control. While conservative Presbyterians in New York eventually brought Briggs to trial for appearing to make reason and the Bible equally authoritative and for questioning the biblical fidelity of Presbyterian dogma, Union's Old Testament professor aligned himself clearly on the side of America's new leadership in higher education.[39] In fact, Briggs made use of Andrew Dickson White's imagery of warfare between science and theology, no doubt perceiving himself to be a victim of "ecclesiastical domination," the greatest foe of "all learning." But just as White had argued, so Briggs maintained that the hostility was not between science and Christianity proper, but between science and "dogmatic theology." "Real biblical scholars" had never been troubled by the discoveries of modern science because science did not threaten the Bible. Instead, it exposed "the errors of ecclesiastics."[40] Briggs also endorsed the Enlightened Christianity to which university presidents appealed in order to demonstrate the religious purpose of their institutions. The study of theology and the Bible in the university would eliminate "all material that is merely speculative, all that is merely provisional, all that has sprung from the circumstances of a single denomination" and reveal the "one holy catholic faith of the church."[41] Rightly understood Christianity was not parochial, dogmatic, sectarian, or provincial. Instead it was true and therefore stood above and was able to absorb all partial expressions of the truth, whether religious or not.

For this reason Briggs was confident that Christianity and related disciplines were not only appropriate for but also crucial to the success of the modern university. "The age of irenics has come," he announced, "an age whose supreme conception of God is love, whose highest estimation of Christ is love, whose ideal of Christian perfection is love." And it was love as "the great material principle of theology" that made possible reconciliation between "theology and other departments of learning." With such an inclusive understanding of Christianity Briggs wrote that no reason existed any longer for banishing "religious educa-tion from the public schools, or of ignoring and limiting theologi-cal education in the colleges and universities."[42] His cosmopolitan vision of Christian theology went so far as to claim it alone as the "uni-versal" or "comprehensive science." But this newer version of the queen of the sciences did not lord it over the other disciplines as a monarch who required subservience. Instead, Briggs portrayed the relationship between theology and other areas of learning as that between a mother and her children. "The great departments of learning in the university lead up to theology," he wrote; the university "cannot gain complete-ness without theology."[43]

Briggs's arguments for, as he called it, "the higher study of theol-ogy" were undoubtedly comforting to theological progressives and university reformers. The bargain that the churches and the universi-ties obtained from progressive theology did appear to be a no-lose proposition. The churches gained greater credibility by having minis-ters who were no longer socially useless but could add more public functions to their spiritual responsibilities. Meanwhile the new the-ology made the university more trustworthy to church folk because disciplines once considered marginal to religious life now took on spiri-tual significance; what is more, because the expanded curriculum uni-versities offered in the social and natural sciences and humanities pre-pared ministers to be better leaders in their communities, universities no longer appeared to be inappropriate settings for prospective clergy.

Nevertheless, as good as this bargain looked it still suffered from the problem that plagued all versions of Enlightened Christianity, namely, how to reconcile the universalism of science with the particularism of a specific religious tradition. No matter how Protestant progressives and university reformers tried to make Christianity into a religion acceptable to all citizens, it was still even in the most cosmopolitan ren-dering a form of belief that was exclusive because it required some devotion to Christ. According to Briggs, "to know Jesus Christ and his religion, to hold them before the world in their simple truth and their profound reality" was the "pinnacle of exact and comprehensive schol-arship." Indeed, to show Christ in the "midst of all the religions of his-tory," in "all the speculative systems of philosophy," and in the "blaze of universal knowledge" was to see Christ "invincible and regnant and his religion the universal religion."[44] Though Briggs's Jesus was inclu-sive of all religions and available to all people, he was still superior and so not altogether tolerant of beliefs or traditions that made rival claims about truth and authority. But in the context of an ecclesiastical world

that for the most part placed the authority of ministers in their stew-
ardship of sacred mysteries (i.e., preaching based upon holy writings),
not in their mastery of the new learning, such arguments had to be
made in order to convince the faithful that the university and its education were not a threat to the church. Moreover, in a predominantly
homogenous culture where Protestants of British stock governed elite
educational institutions, claims of Christian hegemony and universalism failed to offend.[45]

Functional Religion and the Utilitarian University

An older generation of historians explained these theological changes
by pointing to the profound challenges that the Bible and traditional
Protestant teaching suffered at the hands of Darwinism, higher criticism, and comparative religion.[46] To the degree that Protestant divines
could not ignore the new learning while continuing to affirm specific
interpretations of the Bible, this explanation has continued to inform
scholarship on late nineteenth-century American intellectual life.[47]
Still, equally important for understanding the way Protestant divinity
began to accommodate the university is to consider the politics of
learning. Progressive theological notions were already available prior
to Darwin's discoveries or the reception of German biblical criticism. In turn, the proponents of theological revision looked to Darwinism and higher criticism for intellectual justification as well as professional legitimation against theological conservatives who held
power within centers of Protestant learning.[48] In some cases, the new
theology even shaped the conclusions derived from the seemingly
inductive study of ancient texts and cultures. Especially important for
understanding this shift in late nineteenth-century American Protestant theology was the legacy of Enlightened Christianity. Protestants
were habitually oriented toward harmonizing Christianity and science
in order to show the truth and therefore the superiority of their convictions and to maintain cultural hegemony in a republic dedicated to
scientific or rational forms of rule. Appropriating the new learning
encouraged by the research university, then, may not have been determined as much by the challenges to scripture posed by scholars as the
need to avoid a form of Protestantism that looked sectarian because it
no longer received assent as true by publicly accessible forms of knowledge. Progressive Protestantism, even though it rested at times more

on optimism and inspiration, was a way of holding together the twin commitments to science as the surest means to truth and to Christianity as the true (or at least truest) religion.[49]

Yet, as formidable as the intellectual challenges of the new science were, an even greater difficulty to the old orthodoxy was new social realities.[50] In a word, the old theology no longer made sense in a world where changes in industrial urban centers posed especially difficult questions about individual responsibility, social determinism, and moral absolutes. Indeed, as crime, violence, and disorder appeared to grow at alarmingly fast rates, the Protestant churches' teachings looked less and less relevant to the average middle-class Northeasterner or interesting to the new cadre of academics. As Bruce Kuklick well argues, in a social context where newly arrived immigrants did not appear to be responsible for their behavior, the older Protestant convictions about individual responsibility and the rewards that came to proper conduct went largely unheeded. Instead, the younger theological progressives ignored the traditional intellectual categories of Protestant divinity and looked for ways to make the Christian religion accessible and relevant to everyday life. Often, the answers produced by the likes of Andover progressives were still tangential to the social question, hence the appeal of philosophy as a "rationale for the new scientific enterprises and for the human connection to them, . . . an enterprise that might be spiritual but was resolutely this-worldly."[51]

Yet, the threat to the intellectual stature of theology came not simply from the epistemic status and practical value of the new science (and disciplines like philosophy that could demonstrate their scientific credentials) but also from the practical concerns to which the research university and new disciplines like sociology responded. While university reformers advocated advanced, specialized research this was no esoteric or detached affair. Like denominational college presidents before them, university leaders were committed to a vision of higher education in service to the nation. The problem, however, was that postbellum American society was increasingly a business culture that required professionals other than simply physicians, lawyers, and clergy. Thus, the new universities were service-oriented and fostered scholarship that applied the advances of science to the new economic realities and to their social and political ramifications. They desired useful knowledge, not science for science's sake. For this reason, the discipline of sociology was probably the field best positioned in the minds of many academics to benefit the wider society and justify the university to the American public.[52]

Protestant seminaries and divinity schools were hard put to respond to the new social disorder and to keep up with the new academic landscape. Not only were the social implications of the old Protestant divinity, as in the case of Andover, too individualistic for the social realities of the industrial economy but traditional Christian theology more generally was otherworldly in orientation. To be sure, the New England Theology had a practical bent because of its preoccupation with the moral accountability of individuals, but the questions surrounding personal morality were still couched in the larger context of ultimate responsibility, that is, whether the individual would go to heaven or hell. This otherworldly orientation made theology flat-footed in the late nineteenth century when the overriding concerns were this-worldly. Unless theological and biblical studies could demonstrate some pertinence for the disorder of the new economy, those with a heavy investment in the new social environment, such as university presidents and university faculty, dismissed religion scholars as backward and, worse, sectarian. In other words, traditional theological education was geared toward a form of religion that was out of step with the aim of the university, and so the study of religion would have to speak the language of the new sciences and their usefulness in order to be included in the new academy.

The training of ministers further handicapped the study of Protestant theology and scriptures. Because the study of religion was designed overwhelmingly for aspiring clergy, religious studies looked even more out of touch with America's greatest needs. No matter how much ministers might be encouraged to become active leaders within their communities on political and economic matters, they still had sermons to prepare and sacraments to administer. In other words, the tasks for which Protestant clergy were uniquely responsible put a further drag upon religious studies from the perspective of the university. If what university presidents pitched to patrons and legislators was an institution providing useful knowledge for society's urgent needs, then academic disciplines to be included in the university would have to show their ability not only to provide such knowledge but also to train professionals who could ply their learning in the newly emergent socioeconomic order.

Where formal instruction in religion did emerge, then, was in the isolated instances of comparative religion, sometimes called the history of religions, and the study of ancient Near Eastern cultures, especially, Semitics, where the study of religion appeared to fit the scientific models championed by the university.[53] At places like the University of

Pennsylvania and Johns Hopkins University scholars such as Morris Jastrow and Paul Haupt the field of investigation concentrated on Hebrew and Semitic culture.[54] But at institutions like the divinity schools at Harvard and Chicago, the study of religion took on comparative dimensions. In both cases, whether studying Hebrew religion or the history of religions, the rationale for such study and teaching rested precisely on the ability of these scholars to study religion scientifically. *Religionswissenschaft*, a brand of religious studies forged in Germany, became the model for similar studies in American universities. This so-called science of religion looked at religion impartially, not for the sake of what ought to be but rather simply in order to describe what is. This outlook fit well with the university's commitment to transcending the sectarian divisions that had hampered denominational colleges.

But even here the dispassionate and objective study of religion bore many of the marks of the religious communions whose beliefs and practices were under investigation. Semitics most often depended on the financial support of believing Jews who wanted a place in the university and upon scholars who although liberal theologically had grown up in the tradition and knew the language and faith first-hand. Likewise the study of comparative religion at university divinity schools bore the influences of liberal Protestant hopes for an understanding of and cooperation among world religions that in the end would vindicate Christianity as the ultimate expression of the essence of religion.[55] In fact, the parallels between the arguments for Protestant ecumenism and the scientific study of world religions are striking. In both cases the ideology of Enlightened Christianity disregarded the particular and parochial expressions of both Protestant denominations and various religious traditions in favor of a universal religious essence that would yield social harmony and international goodwill. The effort to blur the differences among Protestant denominations and among world religions and the endeavor to study religion scientifically or objectively both assumed the existence of a religious essence of which all particular religions were simply a specific manifestation. Most often this religious essence showed an uncanny resemblance to the beliefs of nonsectarian or liberal Protestants. Thus, the kind of scholarship on religion that universities would promote were studies that were scientific, nonsectarian, socially beneficial, and unifying.

But because the churches and the training of ministers still dominated the late nineteenth-century American teaching and study of Christianity, the greatest number of religion scholars, those who taught at Protestant seminaries and divinity schools, were ill-adapted to perform their services within the university context. Consequently, formal religious instruction for undergraduates in the new universities (or even graduate programs) was rare. Instead, religious influences came most often through extracurricular activities or formal religious observances.[56]

This, then, was the dilemma confronting Protestant theologians and biblical scholars. If they persisted in the historic concerns of their fields, namely, the study of theological expressions and sacred literature whose chief concern was the preparation of individual souls for the world to come through the functions of ministers, they would not gain a hearing within or admittance to the research university. At a number of seminaries in the northeast, such as Andover and Union, Protestant theological educators began to take steps in this direction. The Andover progressives and biblical scholars like Charles Briggs recast the curriculum of Protestant divinity in ways they believed demonstrated the practicality of Christianity and that produced ministers capable of speaking to the social issues of the day.[57] The new Protestant theology was well adapted to the needs of the university. Protestant progressives did not adapt their studies simply for the sake of acceptance within the university; their intentions were to carve out a place for Christianity and the churches in an environment that appeared to have passed traditional religion by. Nevertheless, this shift in Protestant divinity, from an otherworldly orientation to one more compatible with social purposes of the university, was necessary if religious studies was ever to emerge as a full-blown field within American universities. By reconceiving the church, reforming the training of ministers, and accommodating the new ways of studying the Bible and theology, Protestant theologians and biblical scholars not only made seminaries and divinity schools more socially responsive but also moved the study of religion in the direction of the university. To be sure, by the end of the nineteenth century these changes had yet to take institutional form since the professional study of Christianity, at least, by the turn of the century was still dominated by the scholars who taught at Protestant seminaries and divinity schools. Still, the changes that occurred in Protestant divinity after the Civil War would be crucial if religious studies was ever to bridge the gap successfully between the training of ministers and the educational purpose of the university.

THREE

The Emergence of a Pattern

THE TONE OF THE second annual meeting of the Religious Education Association (REA), held in 1904 in Philadelphia, suggested that the study of religion in colleges and universities was poised for greater prominence and a surer standing in American higher education. The association had been founded in 1903, with great input and energy from the University of Chicago's William Rainey Harper, as a way to popularize university learning, almost as a kind of extension program, one that Harper saw as essential if the university were to be as democratic as the nation it served. The REA was not simply a means for making the research university more accessible, though. As its name indicated, the association also stemmed from Harper's involvement with the Sunday school movement and similar efforts to extend the blessings of professional biblical study to the wider society. Following the organizational model of the National Education Association, the REA included individuals from a variety of educational, moral, and religious organizations, and sought to be a "timely, and vital step in the development of our Christian civilization."[1]

Prospects looked bright for religious studies, not simply owing to Harper's leadership, but also because the organization was comprised of a variety of academics from reputable institutions. Among its officers were William H. P. Faunce, president of Brown University, E. B. Alderman, president of the University of Virginia, Benjamin Ide Wheeler, president of the University of California–Berkeley, Charles R. Van Hise, president of the University of Wisconsin, and William J. Tucker, president of Dartmouth College.[2] Not only did the cause of religious studies appear to have support from and entrée into influential schools, but the papers presented at the 1904 gathering indicated that the study of religion in higher education had found a justification that was plausible to other academics and consistent with the mission of the university. To be sure, the case still had to be made in many instances by faculty from divinity schools and seminaries. But this rationale for the study of religion showed that the late nineteenth-century reforms of Protestant theological education were beginning to pay dividends.

Professor Benjamin W. Bacon, a biblical scholar at Yale, established the foundation for the proper study of the Bible at American colleges and universities. The best reason for putting biblical literature in the curriculum was that the Bible was capable of "scientific study." Previously, the Bible had been studied as a textbook of science with regard to the natural world and a textbook of theology concerning "orthodox doctrine." But this approach was incompatible with the academy's scientific outlook. Courses bearing on "the Bible in practical and intellectual life" had to be carried on "from the purely objective, scientific, critical, and historical standpoint." Only then would such courses find a rightful home in the university and become "most surely effective" in promoting "genuine religious culture." Bacon insisted that this religious culture would not be explicit or forced. It would flow from the student's private reflections, not from "the moralizing or preaching of some representative" of a sect. In fact, "the sectarian prejudice" had no place in the university. Thus, Bacon's advice to other professors was this: "When you teach Biblical Science, let it be *Science*, not a mask for preaching." Indeed, a scientific exposition of the Bible did not need "the factitious aid of 'Lo! here, Lo! there'" in order to make the student "who has capacity for such things 'behold the Kingdom of God.'"[3]

Bacon's address culminated the moves that theological educators and religious academics had made to show the compatibility of religion with advanced learning. It also pointed the direction for how instructors in religion would increasingly justify their place in the university. In the first three decades of the twentieth century, the study and teaching of religion occurred in a more or less happenstance fashion, with different organizations and individuals taking up the cause. What united these efforts, even though lacking institutional organization, was Bacon's argument that religious studies primarily had to be scientific, coupled with his belief that the study of religion would make students religious. This was scientific means for Christian ends, and made sense as long as the religious aims were not sectarian. By the 1960s, however, these aims would look explicitly sectarian and not very scientific. But the Enlightened Christianity that informed the idealism of the university together with the theological climate of mainline Protestant denominations meant that only a few dissidents recognized the partisanly Protestant cast of the study of religion, even if liberal theologically. Just as the rhetoric of science obscured the Protestant assumptions of the university reformers, so the ideal of biblical science masked the spiritual purposes of religious studies.[4]

Sunday School for Undergraduates

According to Frank Knight Sanders, dean of Yale's divinity school and the first president of the REA, the origins of the association went back some three decades. In 1872 the International Sunday School Association devised the uniform lesson system. This endeavor provided all Protestant denominations with a uniform Bible curriculum for Sunday schools and insured that students in all parts of the English-speaking world would be studying the same text each Sunday. The adoption of one curriculum, an effort to incorporate better methods of studying the Bible, and a recognition of the importance of religious institutions like the Sunday school for what Sanders called, "effective religious service" made the work of the REA necessary.[5] Its purpose was to coordinate the work of religious education in its various components, which included departments of universities and colleges, theological seminaries, elementary and secondary public schools, private schools, teacher training, churches and pastors, Sunday schools, young peoples' societies, the home, libraries, the press, art and music, and the YMCA and YWCA.

As one of the first national organizations concerned with the study of religion in American higher education, the REA's early efforts in colleges and universities were generally typical of the way mainstream Protestants thought about the relations between religion and education. In 1907 the association's Committee of Six issued a report on the "State of Religious and Moral Education in the Universities and

Colleges of the United States."[6] This assessment came primarily from the office of Wallace N. Stearns, one of the committee's six members and professor at the State University of North Dakota. Whatever Stearns's isolation from more reputable East Coast institutions, the committee also included the presidents of Swarthmore (Joseph Swain), Oberlin (Henry Churchill King), Bowdoin (William DeWitt Hyde), and Indiana University (William L. Bryan), as well as a professor from Wellesley (Adelaide L. Locke). The report covered what the colleges and universities were already doing in the area of moral and religious instruction, student regulations and organizations, church endeavors, and future plans.

If Americans feared for a lack of religious instruction in their institutions of higher learning—a naked academic square, as it were—the report gave an apparently encouraging overview of the various courses offered at institutions as diverse as Harvard, Hope College, Johns Hopkins, and Iowa University. Some universities had "flourishing" departments of Semitic languages and literature, Hellenistic Greek, Christian literature and cognate studies. Yet in the graphs charting the spectrum of courses in religion, the heaviest number of Xs lined up in the columns under English Bible, philosophy, and ethics. Theology was the leanest of religious subjects with a smattering of institutions offering instruction in Semitic languages, New Testament Greek, and church history.[7]

When the committee turned to faculty it found that "the teaching staff is not so strong in numbers or specialization" as other departments. The largest number of instructors who took part in teaching religious courses was at Bowdoin (ten), with Princeton running a close second (eight). Beyond that only a half dozen institutions had five or more faculty teaching religion (Boston University, Cornell, Northwestern, Pacific, Tufts, and Wellesley).[8] In almost all cases, except at institutions that had a nearby seminary or divinity school, the lack of a religion department meant that courses had to be offered by a variety of departments.[9] In two-thirds of the institutions reporting, religious instruction received a positive report; "only three institutions reported unsatisfactory results." This may explain why student enrollment in religion courses ran the gamut from as low as 14 percent of eligible students to as high as 41 percent.[10]

What is most striking about the report, however, is not its statistics but what it said about how the academics who participated in the REA conceived of religion in higher education. Numbers and comments about instruction comprised only three pages of the twenty-four-page report. The rest was devoted to chapel, student regulations against tobacco and alcohol, student Christian organizations, and affiliated church colleges at universities (primarily at Canadian schools). The report covered these topics in a matter-of-fact way. For instance, on student regulations the committee wrote that "the ban against intoxicating liquors is emphatic" and that the "use of tobacco is in general limited to the university or college building and grounds." The report also mentioned Harvard's Phillips Brooks House, a parish house connected to the college chapel which extended and united the many "scattered undertakings of religion and philanthropy in the University," and the Christian Union at the University of Chicago, which included the YMCA, YWCA, a settlement project in the stockyards district, Catholic and Episcopalian clubs, and the Student Volunteer Movement, all under the leadership of a faculty member.[11] Where the report did editorialize was in the section on chapel. Here the committee registered concern about the "present state of public opinion" that hampered state universities from providing religious instruction or worship.

The remarks of Richard H. Jesse, president of the University of Missouri, at the 1904 meeting of the REA explain why the association's membership considered chapel and prohibitions against drinking and smoking to be as much a part of religious and moral education as formal classroom instruction. One of the chief purposes of higher education was to develop the character of students or, as Jesse put it, "to lift . . . students to higher life socially and religiously." Previously the college president had assumed this responsibility, "men like Wayland and Hopkins." But in the age of the university the character of students had been relegated to the general goodwill of faculty. Jesse noted that this was not the case for chemistry, English, athletics, or even the supervision of dining halls, where "expert talent" was required. So the question remained whether something as important as religion and morals could subsist on such an "unstable" foundation.[12]

Jesse recognized that institutions such as Chicago, Yale, Princeton, and Harvard made "ample provision" for the religious and moral well-being of their students. But too many colleges and state universities, especially the large ones, neglected religious life. He compared the situation to a hotel that entertained five hundred people daily or a railroad company that transported thousands. In both cases, the larger the organization the better care and comfort provided to guests or passengers. If universities were to offer good service, they would have to give more attention to religion. Though a university was primarily concerned with intellectual matters, the best academic results came "only by those who care for their bodies and order their lives aright." "Faith, hope, humility, truthfulness, justice, and unselfishness," he added, were virtues "without which the fairest bloom of scholarship [was] impossible."[13]

Consequently, Jesse proposed the establishment of a dean of manners and morals who would look after the religious and moral life of students. Such an officer would have to be nonsectarian or "broad enough to stimulate the Jewish Club, the Catholic Club, and the Young Men's Christian Association." But Jesse could hardly cloak his Protestant sympathies. So this dean "might" desire that every Jew become a Christian, or that all Catholics become Protestants, though "as an officer of a university" he had no right to meddle with a student's faith. Even so, the dean of manners and morals could legitimately help Jews aspire to that "righteousness whereunto Abraham attained," thereby living up to the "light" they possessed, which was the equivalent of following Christian teaching. He could also help raise Catholics up "to the heights of holiness" to which previous generations had climbed. Whatever this dean did in his official capacities, Jesse preferred that he not be a preacher since pastors tended to be opinionated and unwilling to follow. The ideal would be an athlete. "Many students will avoid you if you come with a Bible in your hand," he warned. The ideal spiritual leader "must have the Bible in his heart" with a "boxing glove on his hand." His scholarship should be respectable but "his interest should be in men rather than in scholarly things." He could give a few lectures a week. But above all he should have a "deep personal piety" and be "broadly catholic."[14]

Jesse's speech may have made some of the academics present at the REA's meeting cringe, but his remarks were representative of the association's outlook, programs, and understanding of religious scholarship. On the one hand, the biblical scholars, theologians, and administrators at colleges and universities believed in and were committed to the notion that the study of religion had to involve scientific methods. This was not simply rhetoric to gain the favor of skeptical colleagues. Educators like William Rainey Harper thought that the new ways of understanding the Bible were in full accord with the methods used by academics in other disciplines. What is more, the longer legacy of the way Anglo-American Protestants appropriated the Enlightenment and defended the superiority of Christianity pointed the REA's membership precisely in the direction of science being the surest, if not the only, road to truth.[15] Another important part of science's lure was the concomitant need to avoid sectarianism. If church dogma impeded a scientific interpretation of scripture or religious ideals, and almost everyone agreed that it did, then tradition and denominationalism would have to go.

On the other hand, despite wanting to be scientific and nonsectarian, the Protestant academics who were part of the REA turned out to be just as religiously motivated as their peers at traditional seminaries and divinity schools. This form of Protestant exclusiveness, however, assumed the benign and tolerant pose of science. In addition to sponsoring the study of religion in college and university classrooms, the association also nurtured extracurricular student activities that were designed to promote a moral and religious life. Indeed, classroom instruction, even though conducted scientifically, was also supposed to produce in students a Christian character. This explains why the REA's programs were so diversified and so inclusive. These Protestants hoped to cultivate moral and religious instruction that would accompany Americans from cradle to grave. To be sure, the religious sensibility that association members were eager to nurture did not include the fine points of the Church of England's *Thirty-Nine Articles* or Luther's *Small Catechism* and so avoided the dogmatism and narrowness of previous Protestant instruction. Still, the religious motivation was apparent. The worrisome idea that a scientific study of the Bible or Christian ethics might lead some students to reject the Christian religion or to choose a different faith altogether never seemed to occur to Protestant educators.

The Church Follows Its Students

At roughly the same time that the REA was beginning its many programs, mainstream Protestants found another way to sponsor religious learning and activities at American universities and colleges.[16] This effort involved commissioning ministers and pastors to serve at churches either on campus or nearby. In many cases the work of these university pastorates was indistinguishable from that of the REA; indeed, many of these ministers would have been active members in the association. The major difference concerned the auspices under which these pastors worked. Whereas some of the programs of the association involved the staff of colleges or universities, or secretaries from the YMCA, university pastorates received their support directly from denominations. As a result, university pastors were much more self-consciously denominational; Presbyterian university works were geared toward Presbyterian students, for example. Nevertheless, denominational identity did not mean sectarianism, as mainstream Protestants understood that concept. Many of these ministers were oriented toward the same sort of broad and inclusive Christianity that dominated the REA. The two most notable Protestant endeavors came from the Presbyterian Church in the U.S.A. and the Disciples of Christ.[17]

In 1903 northern Presbyterians appointed a special committee to determine the number of Presbyterian students attending secular schools and to explore what could be done "to give them religious culture and safeguard them for our church."[18] Its report to the General Assembly of 1904 not only contained the framework for establishing a program of university pastorates, but also foreshadowed the emergence of religious studies. The most obvious concern for the committee was the number of students attending state universities, that is, institutions which by the nature of constitutional arrangements forbade an explicitly religious orientation on campus. According to a preliminary survey, of the thirty thousand students attending state universities, roughly nineteen hundred were from Presbyterian homes or background. Church officials did not believe this was a sign of dissatisfaction with the existing denominational colleges, but rather reflected the situation in western states where state universities dominated higher education. The committee also believed that the secularism of state universities could be easily exaggerated. The report indicated, for instance, that "very many of the presidents and professors in these institutions are earnest Christian men, some of them even ministers of the Gospel." To denounce state universities as "godless" was, therefore, unjust.[19] The church was not so much alarmed by the direction of American higher education, especially compared to the concerns of educators fifty years later. What did concern Presbyterians, however, was the idea of students attending a college or university that provided no religious reinforcement.

Still, the ideal was to have all Presbyterian students attend a denominational college. The committee had no intention of requiring students to attend such schools. Consequently, the only alternative was to make available to students at state universities the same kind of religious activities and ethos that denominational colleges provided. To this end the report suggested a variety of measures, from providing more Christian academics who would teach and oversee state universities to the formation of denominational student associations that provided wholesome forms of student fellowship. But the one recommendation that the committee itself singled out was the appointment of "special ministers" who would reside at universities, "much after the pattern of army and navy chaplains."[20] This suggestion formed the basis for the beginning of university pastors, ministers who offered spiritual counsel, conducted religious services, and provided Christian instruction. Upon the advice of this committee, the Presbyterian Church in the U.S.A. called ministers to state universities for the specific purpose of establishing religious programs that mirrored what already existed at private eastern universities and colleges, whether denominationally controlled or not. In 1905 the University of Kansas was the first to establish a university pastor, with Illinois (1906), Michigan (1908), Wisconsin (1908), Colorado (1909), Arkansas (1909), and Nebraska (1909) following. The principle duties of these ministers was to give instruction in the Bible "and other allied branches of religious study" and "pastoral supervision" to Presbyterian students.[21]

Despite initial success—at Michigan Presbyterians had a facility worth $40,000 and an endowment of $10,000—church leaders recognized that the strategy of calling university pastors was fraught with difficulties. Joseph W. Cochran, for instance, reported to the Presbyterian Church that some universities were "officially indifferent" to religion and conceded that the work of religious education in the university was in an "experimental state." A 1910 report indicated some dissatisfaction with the extracurricular nature of religious endeavors. No "mature experience" and "expert counsel" in religion were available to students similar to what they encountered in other "intellectual subjects." Consequently, the northern Presbyterian Church created the Department of University Work, an agency that was the first of its kind among American mainline Protestant denominations. This initiative reflected a concerted effort to support university pastors. Church officials still said good things about the YMCA and its activities but also recognized the superiority of explicitly denominational work. According to Richard C. Hughes, who headed up the department, "nothing will take the place of personal face to face dealing with each student by a strong, mature man who knows the meaning and value of life and who has wisdom and experience enough to do this difficult and delicate work." What this endeavor meant for university pastors was better support and a greater recognition of their services. The church paid these ministers better salaries, and provided houses and more equipment for their activities. Financial support from the General Assembly alone rose from roughly $6,000 in 1910 to just over $42,000 by the end of the decade.[22]

The Disciples of Christ rivaled northern Presbyterians in seeking to advance the place of religion in American higher education. Rather than establishing university pastorates, however, the Disciples of Christ created Bible chairs at state universities, again because of the lack of religious activities at publicly funded institutions. Unlike the university pastorate, which added academic responsibilities to a minister's spiritual oversight, Bible chairs were explicitly instructional in orientation. According to Anna R. Atwater, president of the Christian Women's Board of Missions, "religion must be given as full and fair consideration as is given to science, art, law and literature." Because government funds could not be used for teaching religion, such instruction "must come from some organized force of the church."[23]

The Disciples' involvement in creating Bible chairs began in 1893 under the auspices of the Christian Women's Board of Missions at the University of Michigan. Soon thereafter the Disciples enlarged their work to include state universities at Missouri, California, Oregon, Virginia, Georgia, Texas, and Kansas. Initially, the Disciples' investment in Bible chairs involved relatively small and scattered efforts that went primarily for the creation of space at or near university campuses where ministers could work. But over time Bible chairs became the most successful form for offering religious instruction. At the University of Missouri, for instance, where the position eventually blossomed into a Bible college that offered courses for credit, by 1930 five hundred students had enrolled. In the estimate of Clarence Prouty Shedd, who chronicled the early efforts of the churches to establish educational programs within the university, "all of the denominations in their teaching programs in state universities owe much to the Disciples."[24]

Indeed, the Disciples' program was the most self-consciously academic of all Protestant endeavors. W. C. Payne, who directed the Bible chair at the University of Kansas, affirmed that the theory that motivated the Disciples' initiative was to offer the same kind of instruction in religion that students received in science, literature, and art. In fact, religious teaching "should measure up well to university ideals." The other significant assumption that informed the Bible chair movement was the idea that the Bible was a book "for religious education." This meant that the Bible and religion should be studied systematically. Such study included a "growing acquaintance with the facts and truths of the Bible" and a "keener appreciation with personal good." The goal was for students to live "more vital and forceful" lives. While pastoral guidance and social activities were beneficial for university students, "the teaching function" of the Bible chair holder was paramount. Instructors could have no official connection to the university in the sense of receiving salary or other remuneration. But the education offered had to withstand the toughest academic scrutiny.[25]

The creation of university pastorates and Bible chairs seems unlikely almost a century later. Such activity looks much more like the extracurricular campus ministries at universities today. Consequently, the temptation for historians of higher education and American intellectual life is to dismiss these efforts as marginal and peripheral to the mission of universities and colleges, much like faculty today might regard the programs of Campus Crusade for Christ, InterVarsity, or Navigators. Nevertheless, even though university pastorates and Bible chairs did not receive financial and, thus, official support from the institutions in which they functioned, the Protestant ethos that dominated American higher education made most universities a hospitable place for the labors of Protestant ministers.[26] As the Presbyterian report on state universities indicated, many faculty and administrators at American colleges and universities, whether private or public, denominational or state, were church members and desired the spiritual well-being of students. And thanks to Enlightened Christianity, the work of university pastorates and Bible chairs did not appear to be out of sync with the goals of higher learning. To be sure, these denominational programs were peripheral to the curriculum of most institutions and this was the overriding concern of Protestant church leaders. Still, the ideals of the university pastorate and Bible chair movement did conform to those of the university. What the denominations needed, however, was a way for their programs to be integrated into the curriculum.

Assistance came from an unexpected source, the Association of American Colleges (AAC), an organization formed in 1916 to promote the cause of the small liberal arts college. Actually, the AAC was not far removed from the endeavors of university pastorates and Bible chairs in the sense that it emerged from the Council of Church Boards of Education (CCBE), an association of mainstream Protestant officials designed to defend the purpose and mission of the denominational college. The chance to form a bigger coalition of liberal arts colleges, one that included denominational and nondenominational institutions, prompted the executive committee of the CCBE to pour the resources of denominational higher education into the AAC.[27] The AAC thus emerged as part of the response by the largest Protestant denominations to the changes in American higher education during the university era. Though its chief concern was the small college, it championed

the same cause as that of the university pastorate, namely, the importance of religion to a sound education.[28]

The AAC's first president, Robert Lincoln Kelly, set the tone for the
new organization and tapped the broader concerns of American mainline Protestants. A Quaker who grew frustrated with the minimal constraints of his denomination, Kelly grew up in Indiana and did his graduate study at the University of Chicago in education. In 1901 he returned
to his alma mater, Earlham College, to teach philosophy, serve as chaplain, and administer academic programs. In 1903 he became president of
the college and moved Earlham away from Quaker sectarianism toward
a "nonsectarian" denominationalism. This policy eventually led to
opposition from committed Quakers who believed a decline in denominational identity was leading students away from Quakerism. In 1917 he
left Earlham to become executive secretary of the AAC and infused this
organization with nonsectarian denominationalism.[29]

Also a member of the REA, Kelly differed little in outlook from the
spirit of Christian tolerance and ethical idealism that informed the association. Earlham undergrads were known to satirize Kelly's baldness
and verbosity in student publications.[30] Mocking the latter is understandable since Kelly's vision of education was so porous and vague. His
understanding, for instance, of the small college's strength stressed a
unified education, as opposed to the confusion of specialization encouraged by "the analytical tendencies of science and the abuse of the elective system."[31] Not in all cases was the "demand for unity" being met.
Kelly admitted that "relatively few colleges" articulated clearly "the
objective" of their program of study. Nevertheless, he believed that
efforts were afoot through senior seminars and freshman orientation
courses to supply the unity necessary for a truly liberal education.
Indeed, the "liberal college" sat poised after nearly three centuries to discover "the golden threads" that contribute to a "liberal education":

> Whatsoever things are true, in science and philosophy and religion, it
> would think on those things; whatsoever things are good in human
> relationship, in things domestic, ethical, civic, social, without dis-
> criminations as to sex or race or nation or time or place of habitation,
> it would think on these things; whatsoever things are beautiful in
> God's creation and in human character—the joint product of God
> and man—and whatsoever things are beautiful by the rare gift of
> man's artistic touch, it would also think on these things. . . . About
> these golden threads there is now in process of forming, if only we
> have eyes to see, a new golden age which should eclipse all those that
> are glorified by history, because built on firmer foundations.[32]

To be sure, Kelly's words were no more abstract and airy than other administrators' from the era. Still, such a broad understanding of liberal education was unlikely to produce meaningful unity for denominational or liberal colleges.

Kelly also believed that religious education would supply the unifying principle that liberal education lacked. Human history had proved that unity came through three channels, namely, philosophy, religion, and art, which corresponded to the true, the good, and the beautiful. But because an "exponent" of the good also involved the true and the beautiful, "the teacher of religion occupie[d] a most strategic position." Indeed, religion, from Kelly's perspective, provided the greatest resources for remedying the "unique emergency" of American higher education." This point was obvious if only one compared the American educational creed to the teachings of Jesus. "Every American child is educable," "all American children should have an equal educational opportunity," "every American child is free to think, to initiate and to resolve"—such were the presuppositions of American education and these assumptions could easily be "interpreted in the terms of the teachings of Jesus." The teacher of religion could also unify the curriculum by demonstrating the indispensability of religion for the "solution of any life problem." Kelly used the example of science. If students were thinking about the indestructibility of matter they could also be taught about "the indestructibility of life and the Kingdom of heaven which is the symbol of immortality." Such was the ubiquitous character of religion and the avenue by which Protestant administrators like Kelly traveled to make religion part of higher education.[33]

Although the institutions Kelly targeted were different from those at which the Protestant denominations established university pastors and Bible chairs, the rationale for studying religion in both cases was the same. Religion was a socially cohesive, intellectually integrative, and morally reassuring entity that gave the small liberal college its unique character and that gave the state university what it needed to provide a proper education not just for Protestant students but for all Americans. That the religion advocated by administrators like Kelly and university pastors mixed a good bit of spiritual oversight with the study of the Bible and ethics says a good bit about the inability of Protestants, at least, to conceive of religion as strictly an academic subject. For that reason the teaching and study of religion still needed a more thoroughgoing rationale if it were to blossom as a field of inquiry as legitimate as science, math, or literature.

Teaching Religion Scientifically,
Building a Human Community

In the 1920s the study of religion continued to be a decentralized, rag-tag affair within American higher education, with mainline Protestants working through a variety of organizations and venues to establish religious influences upon college and university campuses. Protestant conceptions of religion and higher education also continued to be shaped, on the one hand, by a commitment to first-rate scholarship that studied religion scientifically without the encumbrance of dogma or church authority. On the other hand, it assumed the importance of religious guidance in a way that sentimentalized the faith and undercut claims about academic standards. Nevertheless, the decade of the 1920s brought to a head several developments that were crucial for forging a more viable institutional foundation for the study and teaching of religion.

Charles Foster Kent (1867–1925), the Woolsey Professor of Biblical Literature at Yale, provided important leadership in consolidating mainline Protestant involvement in religious education at American colleges and universities. He also represented the mixture of motives that informed Protestant efforts in the study and teaching of religion in the first half of the twentieth century. A member of the REA and another professional organization for religion teachers in higher and secondary education, the National Association of Biblical Instructors (founded in 1909), Kent was also an accomplished Old Testament scholar, having received his Ph.D. in Semitics from Yale in 1891 and having pursued postdoctoral study in Berlin and Breslau. Thus, he shared the general Protestant concern for morality and uplift that so animated the efforts of Bible chairs and university pastorates while also advocating the scientific study of scripture. Kent sensed no contradiction between the two purposes but actually assumed that good scholarship would give students spiritual and moral direction.[34]

Like his mentor at Yale, William Rainey Harper, Kent was constantly seeking ways to improve the study and teaching of Christianity, especially in American higher education. Part of his concern was the declining biblical literacy of seminarians, and the growing burden for divinity schools like Yale to offer remedial instruction.[35] But like Harper Kent also saw no divergence between the interests of seminaries and American higher education. The kind of religious study that was good for prospective ministers to receive as undergraduates was just as valuable for all college and university students. In fact, Kent believed that colleges and universities had an obligation "to the nation" to provide adequate instruction in the Bible. Thus, he argued for the inclusion of courses in religion on the grounds that students needed to be familiar with biblical history, to have an adequate foundation for "individual thought and belief," and to be prepared for future responsibilities "as parent and citizen." While courses in the Bible yielded these advantages to all undergraduates, Kent also thought that students who desired to go into church ministry or religious education should be acquainted with religious instruction at an earlier stage of study than seminary. Of course, Kent's plan for advancing the study of religion was supposed to avoid the perils of dogmatism and sectarianism since it involved "modern historical and literary methods."[36] He even contrasted the academic approach of modern investigation in religion to the "unscientific," even if "important and excellent," work done by the YMCA. Even so, if the purpose of religious studies so involved the personal religious outlook and moral duties of students, then Kent's understanding of instruction in religion differed little from the aims of YMCA secretaries, university pastors, or Bible chairs.

During the 1920s the Yale professor's vision for the teaching and study of religion took institutional form in two ways. One was the establishment in 1922 of the National Council on Religion in Higher Education (NCRHE). Originally called the National Council of Schools of Religion, the NCRHE was founded to improve the quality of instruction and study of religion in American colleges and universities. Its specific task was to provide support for graduate studies in religion, thereby creating a better pool of candidates for faculty positions. The council ran a host of activities ranging from cheerleading for the cause of religious studies to fellowships for graduate students. In its early years funding came primarily from the Hazen Foundation and John D. Rockefeller Jr. Measuring the success of the council is difficult since the creation of religion programs depended upon the idiosyncrasies of each college or university. But by attracting the support of sizable foundations and by channeling that support in the direction of better training for prospective faculty, the NCRHE did give the teaching and study of religion more academic rigor even though it continued to reflect the moralistic and inspirational ideals of mainstream Protestantism.[37]

The greatest success of Kent and the NCRHE was to lend support to the creation of schools of religion. Two schools founded in the 1920s that offer some insight into the confused and growing presence of religious studies in American higher education were at the Universities of Iowa and Michigan. Of the two, Kent had the most involvement with the University of Michigan.[38]

Efforts to provide religious activities at the University of Michigan, whether inspirational or instructional, went well back into the late nineteenth century, with Episcopalians and Presbyterians providing support for the construction of buildings where students could practice their faith. Protestant denominations followed suit in the first two decades of the twentieth century by appointing university pastors to serve at the Ann Arbor campus. Still, Kent's Harper-like commitment to improving the quality of religious education, especially at the university level, deemed pastor-run efforts inferior. Consequently, he helped to establish the Michigan School of Religion, speaking at the university as early as 1920 on behalf of founding an independent institution for the study of religion. A hospitable reception from faculty and administrators led in 1923 to the school's incorporation. University President Marion Burton said on the school's behalf that religion needed to be included in American education, without "doing violence to the principle of the separation of church and state," because it "contends that there is spiritual reality in the universe." This point of view, he believed, would make higher education "more real" and life in general "more satisfactory."[39]

Kent saw the school primarily in instructional, as opposed to inspirational, terms. Its purpose, as he told potential supporters, was to provide courses to undergraduates in religion, train religious and social workers, and offer graduate instruction for future leaders, whether religious or educational. Still, Kent could not avoid the inspirational purpose of religious study. He wanted courses to be "constructive" so that students would be able "to work out for themselves a practical philosophy of life." He also hoped to provide adequate instruction for students "with real blood in their veins and real religion in their hearts."[40]

In 1925 the school began to offer courses, thirty-six in all. University faculty were already teaching many of the classes (thirty-one) listed in the School of Religion's catalog, and credit for the courses offered by the School of Religion's visiting faculty was not guaranteed, reflecting one of the besetting problems for religious studies in the first three decades of the twentieth century.[41] Administrators grouped these courses under five headings: religion and civilization, religion and thought, religion and conduct, religion and institutions, and religion and feeling. The model for these classes, significantly, turned out to be the instruction offered at high-ranking university divinity schools or older progressive denominational colleges. As one article in the *Michigan Alumnus* informed readers, the School of Religion was to make available at public universities the courses in religion "now offered in such privately supported colleges or universities as Harvard, Yale, Dartmouth and the University of Chicago."[42] The reference to Dartmouth was obscure since it had not necessarily been a pacesetter in providing a program in religion. But the mention of Harvard, Yale, and Chicago linked the NCRHE and its institutions clearly to the Enlightened Christianity of Charles W. Eliot and William Rainey Harper.[43] Lists of visiting faculty made this connection explicit. The Michigan School of Religion brought to Ann Arbor such scholars as Shirley Jackson Case and Edgar J. Goodspeed from the University of Chicago, and Kirsopp Lake from Harvard Divinity School. At one time school officials mentioned the noted modernist preacher, Harry Emerson Fosdick, as a possibility for dean.[44]

By 1927 the School of Religion stopped offering classes and the Michigan experiment for all intents and purposes failed. One reason for the school's demise flowed directly out of the confusing rationales that Protestants used for the sake of religion in the university. Leaders like Kent constantly stressed the intellectual value of studying religion and touted the importance of faculty who investigated religion scientifically. Yet the Michigan school also had a vocational dimension that moved it away from the aims of the academy and closer to the church. School officials would promote the importance of training students for service in religious organizations and social betterment. This gave the Michigan school a bit of the feel of a Bible college, a fundamentalist alternative to college or university that also trained Christian workers for evangelism, missions, and urban ministry.[45] Finally, the School of Religion also included spiritual nurture as part of its mission. According to an early brochure, the school would "cultivate reverence for and faith in religious and spiritual values" and make the teachings of Jesus and the prophets "compelling."[46] To be sure, the academic rationale and credentials of NCRHE leaders separated them from Protestant fundamentalist educators who put religious norms above scholarly standards. Still, the blurring of scientific and spiritual purposes made the NCRHE little different from the REA and an awkward fit at the best American universities.

But the greatest factor in the School of Religion's collapse was financial. School and university administrators employed a variety of fundraising strategies, but few of them looked to the churches who had the biggest stake in the study of religion. As much as the scientific approach to religion attempted to avoid sectarianism, religious studies ultimately depended on religious constituencies for enrollments and, hence, support. Just as great a problem in the case of Michigan was the threat that the School of Religion appeared to pose to the churches. Protestant denominational leaders received the impression that the school's courses, rather than reinforcing the faith of students, may have actually alienated them from their religious upbringing. With lukewarm support from the churches the Michigan School of Religion had no real hope of survival. The small endowment that administrators had raised was designated to support a series of public lectures on religious topics. But this lasted for only three years. In 1937 the school's funds became the property of the university.[47]

The School of Religion at Iowa suffered from similar confusion about educational mission but succeeded precisely where Michigan failed by securing a good relationship with religious communities who were willing to fund the project. The principle brains behind the Iowa school was O. D. Foster, an educator with close ties to Kelly and Kent. Foster, who has been described as a "self-confessed religious liberal who reacted during most of his professional life against orthodoxies and traditionalisms of all sorts," started out as a university pastor for the Congregationalists at the University of Wisconsin.[48] During World War I he worked as a religious director for the YMCA and pioneered in the sort of interfaith cooperation that Gen. John Pershing praised as "one of the greatest builders of morale" in the armed services. After the war Foster served as associate secretary of the CCBE and also as secretary of the board for the NCRHE.[49]

Foster was no less vague in his understanding about the purpose of studying religion. In many respects, the leader of the Iowa school was no different from Kelly and Kent in his thought about the need for and value of the study of religion. "The problem" of religion and higher education, as Foster conceived of it, was that students needed "facilities for the development of their spiritual natures."[50] This problem was most apparent at state universities where legal restrictions prevented instruction in religion. In other words, from the perspective of this Congregationalist minister, the kind of religious teaching and research that was going on at private universities and colleges, especially in the Northeast, was fine. Foster's mission was to bring such nonsectarian and scientific religion to the heartland. The work of university pastors and Bible chairs was admirable, but a different model was necessary, one that "would not dispense with short course voluntary Bible classes but rather render them more valuable by providing better trained leaders as well as by putting before the attention of the groups the availability of high grade instruction in subjects for which he has discovered a relish." A school of religion would do just this. It would provide a place where university pastors could assist new converts, where religious workers could receive adequate professional training, where foreign students could learn that "modern Christian communions" are united in "constructive teaching for world building" and in extending "human brotherhood," where educational evangelism could take place, and where state universities would have a link to colleges and universities that taught theology and the Bible. In sum, an independent school of religion would nurture "respect for religion" and remove the stigma of "Godless university."[51]

What made Foster's plan different from other Protestant leaders, and what contributed to the long-term success of the Iowa school, was his desire for cooperation among Protestant denominations and among Protestants, Catholics, and Jews. In many respects his ideas about cooperation among Protestants fit neatly within the nonsectarian impulses of Enlightened Christianity and tapped the ecumenical spirit of the era.[52] When Foster wrote that "truth knows but one path and has no sectarian proclivities" or that "science plays havoc with strictly denominational interpretations in its insistence upon following the lead of fact," he was playing the same melody that university and Protestant leaders had composed thirty to forty years earlier.[53] Furthermore, Foster's willingness to cultivate Roman Catholics and Jews, while unusual within mainline Protestantism, was simply an extension of an understanding of religion that regarded doctrinal teachings as merely the husk of religion's ethical and inspirational kernel. To say that the differences between Calvinists and Lutherans over the presence of Christ in the Lord's Supper was nothing more than a trifle could lead to a similar perspective on the Roman Catholic Mass and the Jewish Passover.

Still, Foster's efforts at Iowa brought to fruition one of the few institutions to extend the principles of Protestant cooperation to non-Protestants. In 1922 Foster presented a paper at a Conference on Church Workers in Universities. Three such church workers at the University of Iowa, YMCA Secretary Rufus H. Fitzgerald, Herbert L. Searles, who was pastor for Presbyterian students, and Walter Schafer, pastor for

Congregationalist students, were in attendance and called for a committee to study the possibility of implementing a school of religion. After a series of meetings and involvement from administrators and faculty, president Walter A. Jessup went forward with a plan for the Iowa school that had Foster's fingerprints all over it. The school's governing board was to consist of "the religious bodies of the state" in a way that would encourage their "support and control." The constitution called for fifteen trustees, with nine designated for clergy or representatives of religious groups, and the other six slots reserved for university officials. Though the composition of the board was heavily Protestant, it did include one Roman Catholic priest, W. P. Shannahan, and one rabbi, Eugene Mannheimer. This ecumenicity extended to the faculty. In what would later be called "the zoo principle" (meaning a religion department functioning as a collection of different religious species),[54] the Iowa school's faculty at first consisted of one Catholic, one Jew, and one Protestant.[55]

In many respects the Iowa school differed little from Kent's strategy for Michigan. The idea behind both was to improve religious instruction, to move it beyond the ken of ministers and YMCA secretaries, and have it taught by academically trained experts. The effort to improve the teaching and study of religion did not mean a break with the earlier Protestant strategy of following students to campus and provide teaching and spiritual guidance. What it did mean was that for religion to have credibility on campus the people providing the education and counsel needed to have the right credentials. They needed to be academics themselves. But the purposes of the early university pastors and Bible chairs and those of the Schools of Religion were virtually identical. The design of mainline Protestant leaders who established these programs was to promote religion and religious activities. The teaching and study of religion was a means to this end. The assumption behind these efforts was that religion made individuals more virtuous, more responsible, more civic-minded, better adjusted to the difficulties of life. Rarely did they consider that the study of religion could lead to disbelief or that nonreligious people could also be virtuous, civic-minded, and well adjusted.

Even though the funding of the Iowa school deviated from the Kent plan by having churches provide support and control, it underscored just how dependent the study of religion was upon believing communities. Religion as an academic discipline did not emerge from a tradition of scholarly inquiry with established methods and standards the way that some of the social sciences and humanities did. Instead, it stemmed from the endeavors of committed believers for the purpose of nurturing and creating more believers. No matter how scientific Protestant educators tried to be and no matter how nonsectarian they thought their beliefs were, they were still engaged in a form of advocacy. They wanted students not simply to come away from religious instruction and activities with greater understanding of religious ideas, institutions, and traditions, but they also wanted students to be religious. And the study and teaching of religion was a fairly sure bet for making them so.

The other distinctive feature of the Iowa school—the inclusion of Catholics and Jews—was not all that unusual from the perspective of the university's promotion of nonsectarian religion. For someone like O. D. Foster, Protestants were essentially one "in the great field of human betterment," "comrades in the service of mankind, and sons in the worship of God."[56] If other religions could assist the advance of ethical progress, of meeting economic and social needs rather than promoting otherworldly beliefs and practices that were sure to divide, then extending such generosity to Catholics and Jews was not a great stretch. Furthermore, because so many of the subjects that Protestants promoted, especially in the field of biblical studies, overlapped with Jewish and Catholic interests, finding a consensus that students should know about Moses, the prophets, Jesus, and the gospels was not as hard to achieve as providing courses that would satisfy Mormons, Presbyterians, and Buddhists. Such consensus was especially within reach when Christians and Jews went to their respective sacred texts for social teachings that were relevant to modern America. At that point, general humanitarianism was far more decisive for the inclusion of different religious traditions than were creeds or ceremonies.

To be sure, rarely had Protestants been willing to regard Catholicism or other religions as enlightened and as progressive as they. Still, in the hands of Enlightened Christianity all faiths came out virtually the same, much like the way America's melting pot dissolved ethnic differences.[57] As long as Catholics and Jews were willing to support a similar kind of civic religion, strip away from their traditions those things that made them sectarian or divisive or unreasonable, and embrace Protestant cultural norms, they were welcome. In fact, the Catholic and Jewish critics of interreligious cooperation often accused their foes of accommodating American norms to the point of giving up essential beliefs and practices.[58] Thus, the cooperative nature of the schools of religion, even while including non-Protestants, was yet one more example of the outworking of the Enlightened Christianity of America's mainline Protestants.

Sectarianism Defeated, Enlightened
Christianity Victorious

As much as the initial efforts to professionalize the study of religion relied upon the unstable compound of academic, inspirational, and nationalistic purposes, they did help to secure a greater respectability for religion in higher education. What furthered the momentum toward the institutionalization of the teaching and study of religion was the fundamentalist controversy that provided a significant backdrop to the efforts of Foster and Kent. Fundamentalism represented sectarianism in the extreme. In both of its most notable expressions, namely, the contest with liberal Protestants in the mainline denominations (especially northern Presbyterians and Baptists) and the opposition to teaching evolution in tax-supported public schools, Protestant fundamentalism demonstrated precisely what the scientific study and understanding of religion was designed to overcome. Religion, as fundamentalists showed, could be intolerant, bigoted, and anti-intellectual and as such was not socially or personally useful. But religion in the hands of those familiar with scientific standards and academic norms, religion that saw truth whole rather than partially or provincially, was the kind acceptable in the academy and society. Thus, no matter how fundamentalists argued that they were scientific and intellectually responsible, their willingness to exclude liberals from churches and modern biology from schools underscored their sectarianism and made their rout secure. With a foil like fundamentalism, liberal Protestants could appeal all the more to faculty and academic administrators about the value of religion properly understood and make further inroads into university and college programs of study.[59]

A good example of how the context of fundamentalism enhanced the liberal Protestant approach to the study of religion came in the George Dana Boardman Lectures of 1925. These lectures had been endowed in the late nineteenth century at the University of Pennsylvania for the purpose of vindicating the "supreme ethical authority" of Jesus Christ.[60] The lecturer for the year that also witnessed the Scopes Trial and major skirmishes in the Baptist and Presbyterian denominations was none other than Charles Foster Kent. The topic he chose was "The Fundamentals of Christianity." As it turned out, the Boardman Lectures were Kent's last public-speaking engagement. In a sequence that paralleled that of William Jennings Bryan who died a few days after the Scopes Trial, Kent died only a month after giving these lectures.

Kent's views were timely because the foundations of human existence appeared to be tottering, especially in the sphere of religion. On
the one side, many were rejecting all religious teaching from the past
because of the truths of science. On the other side in response, many
were clinging to "an authoritative Church and an infallible Pope" to
shore up these foundations. "Shall we select seven or eight dogmas,
long cherished by certain sections of the church," Kent asked, "and
declare that these alone are the fundamentals on which Christianity
and the religion of today and tomorrow must stand?" And what would
happen if such a selection meant "ignoring a majority of the principles
underlying historic Christianity and the vital truths regarding life
which modern science has laid bare?" Kent's resolution to this conun-
drum was the relatively painless option of acknowledging the teaching
of Christianity, as summarized in Christ's Sermon on the Mount, as
fully compatible with modern scientific learning. In Kent's view, Jesus
was the "most modern of ancient thinkers, the most western of eastern
teachers." He was a "practical scientist who used the scientific method
centuries before it was definitely formulated."[61] In other words, the
faculty, administrators, and students at the University of Pennsylvania
had no difficult choice to make. Jesus was scientific, Christianity was
tolerant and generous, science was fundamentally ethical. No good
reason existed for excluding this kind of religion from the academy. In
fact, the threat of sectarianism and ignorance posed by fundamentalism was all the more reason for exposing students to and training religious leaders in a religious outlook that fit so well with the intellectual
outlook and social mission of the university.

No matter how naive or successful Kent's approach to the study
and teaching of religion, religious studies as an academic discipline still
suffered from a confusion of rationales. Since the founding of the
research university, religious faculty who desired greater room for religion on campus had to prove that their studies were up to the scientific
standards of modern learning, a case that involved breaking sharply
with the apparent sectarianism of the old-time denominational college. Yet, the teaching and study of religion also depended at least for
financial support upon communities of believers. The nonsectarian
study of religion could not flourish without sectarian assistance,
whether by providing financial support or by defining the content of
instruction. In turn, the support of the churches gave the study of religion an inspirational dimension that conflicted with the purely intellectual aspirations of the modern academy. Religion had to be taught,

according to some proponents, so that students would retain their religious identity while away from home. The way Protestant academics resolved this tension between science and catechesis was to demonstrate the social utility of religion. Because nonsectarian religion contributed to the formation of good citizens and social order, the study of it was compatible at least with the larger social aims of the university. Thus, even though such organizations as the REA and the NCRHE helped to solidify the respectability of the teaching and study of religion at American colleges and universities, by 1925 when Kent gave his lectures at the University of Pennsylvania religious studies had yet to gain a sure foothold in American higher education.

PART II

The Age of the Protestant Establishment, 1925–1965

FOUR

Religious Studies and the Humanities

IF ANYONE DOUBTED MAINLINE Protestantism's support for the American nation they did not need to look farther than such late nineteenth-century religious bestsellers as Josiah Strong's *Our Country*. A Congregationalist minister and proponent of a social Darwinian version of the social gospel, Strong argued that Anglo-Saxons in the United States were best equipped to build a superior civilization at home while extending it to inferior races around the world. "Our plea," he wrote, "is not America for America's sake; but America for the world's sake. . . . If I were a Christian African or Arab, I should look into the immediate future of the United States with intense and thrilling interest." Then Strong quoted approvingly a Yale professor who had written that "America Christianized means the *world* Christianized."[1]

Protestants who promoted the teaching and study of religion at America's colleges and universities were no less squeamish in affirming support for the United States and its culture. One member of the National Association of Biblical Instructors, for instance, wrote in 1919 that the origins of America's Declaration of Independence were to be found not in the philosophy of Locke and Rousseau but rather in the Old Testament, which emphasized "the Divine rights of the private citizen or common soldier against the king."[2] These direct links between the Bible and national ideals prompted another professor of religion to conclude that the best way to teach the Bible was to show its relevance for rescuing America from disaster. "The teacher who makes his class a vital center for spreading the great biblical messages of democracy and brotherhood," Laura H. Wild of Wellesley College wrote, "is standing at a strategic point in our national life."[3]

Despite such overt connections between religious instruction and America's well-being, until 1930 or so the major hurdle for those who advocated the study of religion was whether they could demonstrate sufficient scientific and academic sophistication. But with the rise of the undergraduate curricular reforms in the 1920s, spearheaded under the headings of general education and western civilization, the justifications for the study and teaching of religion began to shift. Rather than showing that religion was compatible with scientific advance, academics and clergy who promoted religious studies argued that religion—especially Protestantism or other traditions that embraced Enlightened Christianity—was a crucial piece of western culture. Some even went so far as to argue that any program of cultural studies that ignored religion was simply inadequate. If students needed a better understanding of western civilization and its languages, literature, and traditions, as many American educators began to argue between the first and second world wars, the study and teaching of Christianity was a natural if not essential component. Thus, during the interwar period the arguments favoring the inclusion of religion in American higher education assumed a different form.

The emergence of undergraduate courses in general education and western civilization was a remarkable blessing for the scholars who taught religion. From the initiation of the western civilization curriculum at Columbia University in 1919 to the publication of Harvard University's *General Education for a Free Society* in 1945, the case for studying religion, at least the religions of Protestants, Catholics, and Jews, became much easier to make.[4] None of the reforms to promote greater awareness of western culture mentioned religion explicitly as a full-blown academic discipline. But as religion professors heard with greater frequency their colleagues in the humanities call for more instruction in the West's literature and ideals, they responded by showing that western civilization was precisely their bailiwick. Along the way the teaching and study of religion made perhaps its most significant disciplinary connection within American higher education, a connection that would prove to be decisive for the creation of departments and programs in religious studies.

Taking Stock

In 1930 the Conference of Church Workers in Universities and Colleges of the United States met in Chicago for its triennial gathering of members. This meeting was indicative of the state of religious studies just after the fundamentalist controversy and immediately before religion emerged as an academic discipline with departmental status. In some respects, the status of religion in American higher had not improved considerably since the founding of the Religious Education Association (REA) in 1903. It still depended, as conference speakers showed, upon a broad variety of institutions, such as the chaplain, university pastor, director of religious life, YMCA secretary, and instructor in religion. All of these positions had direct ties to the mainstream Protestant denominations, links that revealed the dependence of religious studies upon the support and mission of the churches, no matter how tolerant those communions could be. So, too, the subject itself, if conference papers were only indications, included such a broad definition that students could find religious meaning almost anywhere in the curriculum, from psychology and the social sciences to the physical sciences. Curiously, the conference did not include a presentation on the humanities or literature. Nevertheless, the paper on "Religion for the Modern Mind" by Charles W. Gilkey, chaplain at the University of Chicago, explained why religion was so pervasive while establishing links with humanistic disciplines. Though science broke "human experience up into specialized fields" and contributed to intellectual "narrowness," religion, like philosophy and art, "sweeps the whole horizon, faces its ultimate questions, seeks its deepest meanings." But religion trumped philosophy and art, in Gilkey's estimation, by calling "men with an insistent imperative back into the valley of everyday living, there to toil and to contend for the fuller realization in human life of the values 'showed in the mount.'"[5] Thus, religion was everywhere and its ubiquity in the curricula of colleges and universities produced difficulties for the church workers who gathered in 1930 at Chicago.

The conveners of the conference acknowledged implicitly the lack of a coherent and well-organized program of religion on America's campuses but the threat of secularism and intellectual fragmentation was even greater. According to Frederick J. Kelly, a lecturer at the University of Chicago, the urgent problem facing the churches was the common perception among students that "the school and the church seem to be opposed to each other." Adding to this was the "apparent conflict between church and state" and the latter's unprecedented control of education. The task of church workers at colleges and universities was to bridge the gap between church and school and "develop a scheme of education in which religious idealism shall play its important part."[6] Courses in religion, then, were just one front in the church's efforts to hold on to students and keep intellectual life from losing touch with spiritual ideals and moral values. Even the proposal by William Clayton Bower, a professor of religious education also from the University of Chicago, for a departmental major in religion, stressed the "integrative character" of religious studies for students.[7] Dissatisfaction with the direction of American higher education made proponents of religious studies, who were overwhelmingly from mainline Protestant denominations, unwilling to invest all of their energy in classroom instruction. Inspiration and nurture were still important parts of the rationale for religious studies.

Yet, despite the lack of a clear rationale, prospects for the teaching and study of religion looked considerably better than they had thirty years earlier. Speakers at the 1930 conference of church workers were just one indication that religion was gaining greater credibility within American higher education. The University of Chicago was disproportionately represented because of the conference's location. But speakers also came from Yale, Princeton, Haverford, Duke, Cornell, the University of Pennsylvania, the University of California–Berkeley, and a number of the big Midwestern state schools. Even though some of these speakers served as campus ministers or chaplains, individuals with legitimate academic appointments in a variety of disciplines also made presentations. Additionally, the conference showed the success of the National Council on Religion and Higher Education's (NCRHE) efforts to establish university schools of religion.[8] Most of the conference's conveners had direct ties to the NCRHE and the Iowa School of Religion accounted for three of the twenty-five papers presented.[9] Another facet of the increasing prospects for religious studies was the financial support of the Edward W. Hazen Foundation, which had underwritten a number of efforts in the 1920s to boost the academic study of religion. Though university pastors and chaplains still dominated the teaching of religion, by 1930 an academic orientation had begun to emerge.

Perhaps the most encouraging sign of religious studies' growing maturity was the proposal for a department of religion and an accompanying major. As Shailer Mathews, dean of the University of Chicago's Divinity School, indicated, if religion were not given the "same recognition" in the curriculum as any other "object of human interest," the tendency would be to treat religion as "a matter of private concern, independent of institutional life."[10] For that reason, William Clayton Bower's outline of a "field of concentration in religion" pointed the way toward greater coherence and stability for a religious presence on campus. To be sure, Protestants had devised programs of study in religion prior to Bower's presentation. But the rising stature of religion at America's colleges and universities meant that his proposal would have a better chance of finding a home.[11] The specifics of Bower's plan were not significantly different from what went before. They started generically with overviews of religion in the first two years of college such as "Introduction to the Practice of Religion" and "Psychology of Religion." In the last two years students would concentrate on the religion of the Bible, with courses on the Old Testament, the New Testament, and the life of Jesus. Such a course of study would acquaint students with the importance of religion in human experience, prepare them for participation in the "religious operations of society," and provide a basis for graduate study in religion.[12]

Bower's hopes for a religion major were not overly optimistic, according to statistics from the 1920s and 1930s on the prevalence of courses in religion. Surveys conducted by the NCRHE and the Council of Church Boards of Education (CCBE) indicated that even though religion was scattered, decentralized, and still very much bound up with the spiritual and inspirational aims of mainline Protestants, the building blocks for programs in religious studies were virtually in place. Private universities and colleges, 71 percent of which were denominational and, therefore, often required religious instruction, clearly provided additional courses and enrolled more students than public institutions. Still, individual tax-supported institutions offered the same number of courses as private colleges and universities even though they failed to attract as many students. At the same time, establishing university pastorates and Bible chairs continued to pay dividends. By 1933, mainline denominations had combined to found 174 Bible chairs, 209 university pastors, and 1,145 churches at tax-supported institutions. To be sure, these ministers had a variety of responsibilities beyond teaching. But thanks to the lobbying of such organizations as the NCRHE university pastors taught a variety of courses for credit, from the generic "Religion and Philosophy," "Religion and Sacred Literature," or "Biblical Literature and Religion," to the more specific "Christianity," "Apologetics," or "Bible and Evangelism." What is more, schools of religion, which were staffed primarily by clergy, began to function as departments of religion. Among the more notable state universities to sponsor these schools were Texas, Missouri, Iowa, Illinois, and Oklahoma.[13]

Surveys also indicate that the study of religion was synonymous with instruction in the Bible or its curricular cousin, ethics. For instance, in its 1923–24 catalogue Colgate offered a total of twenty-six hours in religion, seventeen of which were courses in the Bible or the early church (six of nine courses). Colgate's cross-state rival, Cornell, offered fewer courses in the Bible but made up for this with six of its ten religion courses devoted to ethics (fifteen of twenty-four hours). This pattern was no less true for tax-supported colleges and universities. For instance, a survey conducted for the Institute of Social and Religious Research showed that undergraduate courses in the Old and New Testaments accounted for 27 percent of the courses offered at tax-supported institutions, 34 percent at independent or private colleges and universities, and 37 percent at denominational schools. (The next closest category of course work was religious education, running from 9 percent at private institutions to 20 percent at denominational colleges.)[14]

The same report demonstrated the popularity of Bible courses. It was a chameleon that could fit whatever subject a professor had in mind. Teachers of the Bible might "make their work the occasion for the development of religious personality in our world." Or they might use it to show the importance of the "Christian religion for international relations." Or it could also permit instruction in "the value of knowing the religions of other peoples."[15] Instruction in the Bible revealed a similar adaptability in a survey that the CCBE conducted in the 1930s. At the same time biblical studies could meet curriculum requirements for acquainting students with "great literature," "developing a sense of values," and providing a background for understanding "modern culture." Instruction in the Christian scriptures could also orient students to "life problems" and assist them in "developing a philosophy of life." Or the study of scripture could nurture certain "religious values," such as charity, sympathy, faith, reverence for God, and wholesome "prayer habits." But the "chief objective" of most Bible courses was to build character. Religious instruction "integrates life, develops self-control and unselfishness, guides the will, furnishes the driving power for morals, and gives ideals."[16] Perhaps the pluriformity of motives that Protestants were packing into Bible courses was the reason for Hugh Hartshorne's anxious conclusion that biblical instruction was inferior in quality and explained the choice of those students who turned from religion to the social and physical sciences to understand the "whole of reality."[17]

Improving the quality of biblical instruction was precisely what one group of religious educators had in mind even before the report conducted for the Institute of Social and Religious Research became public. The National Association of Biblical Instructors (NABI) had been founded in 1909 as part of the general mainline Protestant concern about American education at all levels. In many respects its aims were similar to that of the REA, though NABI's niche was more similar to those who taught the Bible at private secondary schools and at colleges and universities. As such, it included a fair number of university pastors and other clergy. Yet NABI would emerge as the forum best suited for discussions and strategies pertaining to the study of religion in higher education because colleges and universities were its chief domain and its members stood the greatest chance of securing academic appointments free from ecclesiastical support or connections. By the 1930s the interests of its membership were sufficiently well defined for the organization to start its own periodical. Prior to this, the journals of the REA and the CCBE would publish the papers and proceedings of greatest interest to NABI's members. But in 1933 NABI launched its own journal, appropriately titled the *Journal of the National Association of Biblical Instructors*. In 1936 the name would change to the *Journal of Bible and Religion*.[18]

From the beginning the purpose of the association had been to improve the quality of biblical instruction throughout American education. Though NABI's membership may have overlapped with the professional academic organization of biblical scholars, the Society of Biblical Literature (SBL, founded in 1880), its interests were pedagogical rather than disciplinary. To be sure, the liberal Protestant cast of NABI meant that members were more likely to favor newer as opposed to traditional or sectarian approaches to scripture and thus stood to benefit from the research and writing conducted by the SBL. But NABI never intended to compete with the SBL; in effect, SBL worked out the theory of biblical criticism in the library and seminar room while NABI applied it in the classroom.

Interestingly enough, Charles Foster Kent, the Old Testament scholar at Yale who championed the founding of schools of religion at state universities, was an active member, officer, and proponent of NABI. At the association's 1919 meeting Kent, as president, outlined NABI's purposes:

1. to cultivate a network of biblical instructors in colleges and secondary schools;
2. to reflect upon the instructional methods;

3. to promote the highest educational standards in biblical education;
4. to standardize a course of biblical instruction from secondary to higher education in private and public schools; and
5. to establish Bible departments in college and preparatory schools.

In the past, Kent lamented, the Bible had been taught for theological and dogmatic purposes. But in the light of scientific methods and the "world situation," educators recognized that the "chief aims and values" of the Bible were "historical, literary, social, education, and in the most practical sense, religious." The Christian scriptures, therefore, had broad public appeal beyond the province of the church and seminary. "Measured by every standard," Kent boasted, "that thrilling chapter in human history which witnessed the rise of Judaism and Christianity and the birth of democracy is the most important in the life of humanity." Consequently, the point of better instruction in the Bible was not simply to provide religious instruction for Christian youth. It was much broader. By providing students "intimate acquaintance with the supreme classics of the human race," they would be trained to function "intelligently and successfully" as individuals, parents "and as citizens in the new world order."[19]

Kent reiterated this rationale in 1924 as president of NABI again, only one year before his death. "The personal and social ethics of the Hebrew prophets and Jesus," he said, "have inspired that which is best in our modern civilization." Still, it was hard for him to keep Protestant piety far from view. Despite the Bible's social and political benefits, ultimately its chief interest was personal. Through the teachings of scripture "hundreds of typical men and women were able to master their baser impulses and to find joy and success as humble servants of the living God."[20]

By 1933, however, NABI's endeavors to promote biblical instruction at the collegiate level appeared to indicate that a more concerted effort was necessary. The first issue of NABI's new publication suggested how this effort could be made. Rather than pursuing the old liberal Protestant strategy of adapting biblical teaching to the categories of modern education, some within the organization believed a more aggressive and confrontational approach was necessary. Thus, a segment of the mainline Protestant proponents of teaching religion in higher education showed signs of the theological shift from liberalism to neo-orthodoxy that was emerging in the 1930s. Religion, especially the study of the Bible, had its own place of importance and did not need to take a backseat to any of the modern academic disciplines.

NABI's assertive tone was evident in the very first article of the new journal, an address by the association's president, Chester Warren Quimby, a professor of Bible at Dickinson College. Quimby faulted the older rationales for studying the Bible because of their timid posture. Religious scholars had bowed and scraped at the door of science, "asking for a certificate of intellectual decency." Though motives may have been honest—"to appear intellectually respectable in the modern world"—too often scholars of religion subjected their studies to "the censorship of ever shifting sciences." "We have forgotten," Quimby insisted, "that religion stands in its own right." The gospel could not be reduced to "every day practical common sense." Rather it was the "power of God unto salvation!" Consequently, biblical instruction needed to recover the conviction that the Bible was "the Word of God." Quimby conceded that this approach was fraught with difficulties. The professor who taught the Bible as the word of God would not find his classes full. Nor would he enjoy "jolly campus popularity." But he could take satisfaction from his own conviction that "the Word of our God shall stand forever!"[21]

Joseph Haroutunian, then a lecturer in biblical history at Wellesley College and author of a fierce neo-orthodox critique of New England theology after Jonathan Edwards,[22] seconded Quimby's jeremiad. Instructors of religion too often treated Jesus "as though here were something which anybody would appreciate and accept." But an honest look at Jesus and the Bible showed a religious outlook that was fundamentally at odds with the modern mind. "The modern religious educator," Haroutunian wrote, "is interested in the building of character, in guiding his pupils to a rich, wholesome, healthy, happy life, in cultivating truthfulness, honesty, generosity, etc. which concern primarily present and practical social situations." But the Bible was foreign to these concerns. Its writers were not interested "in the development of personality." Consequently, modern educators were correct to make the Bible a peripheral matter. "Assuming their perspective we cannot convince them that our enterprise has any value or future" because the Bible was "largely irrelevant to the modern mind." Still, Haroutunian urged biblical instructors to hold their ground, to "present the Bible as the word of God, as the judgment of God concerning the world, as a warning and admonishing voice." He held out no real optimism for changing the temper of the modern academy. But at least teachers of the Bible "shall have done [their] duty." And God would use such teaching "for the transmission of his truth."[23]

Coming as they did before the study of religion had emerged as a recognizable academic discipline, these statements on behalf of the Bible look surprisingly confident, if not partisan. If mainstream Protestants still wanted to increase opportunities for religious instruction, returning to the logic of sectarianism would appear to be unwise. Yet, with the defeat of fundamentalists in the largest denominations and the recognition that liberal Protestant hopes for establishing the kingdom of God through scientific, political, and economic advances were overdone, Protestant educators may have been tempted to take off their gloves and insist on the authority of revealed religion.[24] Whatever the explanation, a more assertive posture on the importance of religious studies came at a time when educators were acknowledging the salience of the humanities more generally and especially the need to acquaint students with questions concerning ultimate meaning and value. Religion professors did not see immediately the ties between neo-orthodoxy's insistence upon the transcendent and eternal character of religion and the humanities' concerns with timeless truths. But as the educational establishment promoted the value of humanistic studies more actively, the study of religion became an attractive ally.

Sunday School No More

The founding of NABI's *Journal of the National Association of Biblical Instructors* (*JNABI*) also marked a growing frustration among some of the associations members with the way mainline Protestants had been approaching religious education generally and biblical instruction specifically since the founding of the REA in 1903. Of course, the older approach, as articulated by the likes of William Rainey Harper, had been designed to break with the piety and simplicity of Sunday school methods. But the newer scientific procedures were seldom stern enough to displace American Protestantism's congenital moralism. Nor were Protestant biblical scholars able to free themselves from the sentimentalism that informed their appropriation of scripture for the rearing of children and the building of a "righteous" nation. Consequently, within some circles the old rationales for biblical instruction came in for serious scrutiny.

Another article in the first issue of *JNABI* came from the man who had in fact questioned the effectiveness of biblical instruction in the report of the Institute of Social and Religious Research, Hugh Hartshorne. In his short essay, he summarized the findings of the report, noting the disturbing tendency of nonbiblical fields, such as the philosophy and psychology of religion, ethics, and comparative religion, to challenge the centrality of the Bible in religious teaching. Hartshorne pointed to Sunday schools as partly responsible for the difficulties confronting the study of religion. "In neither the traditional nor the modern school is the Bible dignified by the manner of its use." In either case, teachers broke scripture "up into unrelated passages of supposedly inspirational value" or they used it as a "glorified proof text for the solution of all human ills." Hartshorne reassured his readers that they were not guilty of these approaches. Neither method was common in the college classroom. But he did believe that in religious instruction faculty had divorced too greatly the biblical material from "the more pressing problems of students." As much as the rhetoric of students' needs sounded like a return to the practices of the Sunday school with its inspirational and moral guidance, Hartshorne was advocating an approach to the study of religion that made the Bible "the focus or integrating center" of a student's education. Thus, Hartshorne concluded with a challenge for college professors "to recognize in some practical way the central place of religion in *contemporary* civilization."[25]

Hartshorne's frustration with older approaches and assertion of the need for a better method of instruction were indicative of the changes afoot in the 1930s among educators responsible for teaching religion. The rationales offered by mainline Protestants came in a variety of forms. But the argument that appeared to improve the fortunes of religion as a full-blown field of study was the idea that religion provided the glue that unified cultural life and so was central to any proper acquaintance with or understanding of western civilization. This rationale played down the churchly and spiritual benefits of religious studies and underscored religion's societal assets. But the public character of these benefits moved beyond stipulations that moral guidance was necessary for good citizenship and reassurances that science was not a threat to belief in God. Here religion was integral to the development of liberal democracy and, ultimately, the progress of human history.

To be sure, vestiges of the older liberal Protestant uplift and moralism survived. For instance, Lloyd V. Moore of the University of Tulsa argued that the task of teaching religion to undergraduates was "to interpret the life of today in spiritual terms." Students needed "to find God" but they needed to do so from their "own value-judgments" and within their "own manner of living."[26] Moore's affirmation of the older liberal Protestant emphasis upon religious experience in daily living appeared to make the Bible marginal even while mitigating tensions between religion and science.[27] Still, the Bible was important if not necessary to the older approach to liberal education. Donald W. Riddle underscored the centrality of the Bible to discovering the "technique of religious life." Even though the Bible represented patterns of living that were "foreign" to the twentieth century, to study the religious experience of the Israelites and first Christians was "extremely valuable" for contemporary religious life.[28]

Perhaps the best expression of the older liberal Protestant rationale for studying religion came from Irwin R. Beiler, who taught English Bible and philosophy of religion at Allegheny College. The religion professor's task was increasingly becoming one of making the Bible's "record of religious experience" more useful for "religious experience itself and its continuous reconstruction" by inculcating within students their own sense of religion's vitality and power. Then, after showing the value and reality of "this heightened sense of the spiritual values in God and in Jesus," faculty should harness it "to the needs of social living."[29] The desire to use the teaching and study of religion for pious ends showed that some habits died hard.

Still, though the new links between religious studies and western civilization and liberal democracy also assumed that students would adhere to religious (i.e., Protestant) traditions, they did present a rationale for religious studies that appeared to be more academically plausible. Walter Clippinger, president of Oberlin College, made a fairly typical, but also persuasive, argument for the connection between the concerns addressed in the study of religion and liberal arts education. A liberal education, he wrote, was one that "liberalizes, that is, frees or emancipates from ignorance, superstition, and prejudice." As such, the liberal arts did not narrow the curriculum to specialized studies or vocational preparation. Instead, their materials came from the "widest possible range." A liberal education "should unify for [the student] all knowledge and enable him to relate himself to it all." Nothing in Clippinger's address referred explicitly to religion or the study of it. But his understanding of liberal culture, a holdover from the Victorian era, was one with which Protestants were most comfortable and appeared to give the greatest room for religious education.[30] "The insistent claim of liberal culture," he wrote, was that "man is a free being in the spiritual realm, unhampered by superstition, fear, ritual or code; whose soul may grow from the consciousness that he is personally related to a boundless universe." And it was the contemplation of this universe that would lead students to "the higher realms of spiritual realities and ultimately to God."[31]

The idea that religion was part of a liberal education or one of the humanities occurred with greater frequency among religion faculty during the 1930s. As such, Protestant educators expressed a view shared by some of America's leading educators. One notable statement of the need to overhaul American higher education in more generalist and holistic directions came from the University of Chicago's president, Robert Maynard Hutchins, in his 1936 book, *The Higher Learning in America*.[32] His plan for a "great books" curriculum that made the important works of the western tradition central to a liberal education was part of the widespread discontent with American universities' overspecialization, scientism, and vocationalism, and, consequently, their fundamentally materialistic assumptions.[33] Not only did Hutchins appear to reinforce the concerns of religion faculty who believed that education should train students to see human experience whole, but his many references to Thomas Aquinas and John Henry Neumann suggested a certain sympathy to religion, even if the Christian figures cited were Roman Catholic. Neither did Hutchins's conclusion that theology could not claim to be the integrating principle of a liberal education phase religion academics. That prominent members of the educational establishment were troubled by American higher education's neglect of the spiritual, philosophical, and ethical realms was sufficient ground for giving greater attention to the teaching and study of religion.

Beatrice Allard Brooks, a religion professor at Western College, was one of the first members of NABI to notice the opening that Hutchins had apparently created for the study of religion. The most frequent criticism of American higher education, she wrote, was its lack of unity. Here Hutchins was just one of many voices in a chorus that ranged from the New Humanists, Norman Foerster and Irving Babbitt, to Alfred North Whitehead. Brooks did not merely use the academic reformers to advocate religious studies. She also believed that too many religion faculties were guilty of neglecting a unifying principle in their teaching. Students in religion courses were in danger of being "lost in a fog of details through which they envisage no guiding light." But the encouragement that she took from the new emphasis on values and ideals as opposed to facts and methods could not be missed. The renewed commitment to making students "see beyond the limited and narrow horizon" and to take a long-range view based on "reflectively rational, morally choosing, and spiritually self transcending" values was exactly what instructors of religion could foster. Indeed, American scholars were "recognizing that an important part of the wisdom of the ages is the religious spirit." Brooks concluded reassuringly that "the study of Religion [was] therefore a legitimate and necessary heritage and possession of the individual."[34]

Charles F. Nesbitt of Blackburn College, a denominational school, was even more encouraged by the opening that Hutchins and like-minded critics of American higher education appeared to be creating for the study of religion. Nesbitt took special delight in Hutchins's definition of a classic piece of literature, namely, a book that "is contemporary in every age." Didn't the Bible, Nesbitt asked, fit precisely this definition? "Is not the Bible the most contemporary book we know, as well as one of our oldest?" No matter that Hutchins had not mentioned the Jewish or Christian scriptures specifically. All the more reason, Nesbitt urged, "why some one should point out the aptness of the situation and the need for a renewed emphasis on the position of the Bible in higher education."[35]

Aside from some naive enthusiasm for demonstrating the Bible's qualifications as a classic, Nesbitt did make a more persuasive point when he discussed Hutchins's definition of a "best book" as one without which it was impossible "to understand any subject in our contemporary world." Again, phrases like this one contained a grandeur that too easily flowed from the lips of Protestants who seemed unaware that others might disagree on intellectually as well as morally respectable grounds. But construed narrowly as the influence of the Bible upon European and North American cultures, Nesbitt's claim on behalf of religion's relevance was one that Protestant advocates of religious studies could employ successfully. The import of religious studies for American cultural and political life looked especially compelling in the years just after the publication and discussion of Hutchins's book, as the United States entered another war. In the context of World War II, the connections between biblical religion and liberal democracy seemed obvious to all but a few skeptics in American higher education. On that basis religious studies moved even closer to a secure position within colleges and universities in the United States.

The concerns of the war were readily apparent in the *Journal of Bible and Religion*.[36] Several editorials between 1942 and 1945 addressed the question of teaching religion in the context of world war.[37] In some cases, the identification between biblical religion and the American cause was explicit. For instance, M. Willard Lampe, who taught at the Iowa School of Religion, rhapsodized about the cooperation between the subject areas of religion, philosophy, and science "for the preservation of the democratic way of life." Yet, he added, religion also had a distinctive mission that was "synthetic in nature." It stood for "unity, solidarity, integration, the integration of the individual, the solidarity of society, the unity of *One World*." These ideals gave religious studies an unprecedented opportunity in the context of political upheaval and international crisis.[38] In other cases, the study of religion did not so readily identify with democracy as it did with freedom against tyranny of any kind, especially religious dogma. So Arthur C. Wickenden touted the liberal Christian tradition, which freed students from sectarianism, "an imposed loyalty that does not commend itself to man's higher reason," while also cultivating a loyalty to the "church and the kingdom of God on earth."[39] Likewise, Charles W. Gilkey warned about those who would turn for "relief and escape" to "what we in this company would call 'queer religions.'" Just as fundamentalism and millennialism surfaced after World War I, so Gilkey feared another attack upon "liberal religion," a form of belief clearly more adept than sectarianism at building a "just and durable peace."[40] Even biblical scholars showed with great diligence the significance of their subject for the contemporary situation. Two separate issues of the *Journal of Bible and Religion* featured articles on the relevance of the Old and New Testaments respectively. Curiously, these articles suggested that the older the writings, the more timely the message. Old Testament scholars were more inclined than their New Testament counterparts to make connections between various stages in Israel's history and that of the United States and the Allies. Perhaps the most egregious example was William R. Irwin's conclusion that Pres. Franklin Roosevelt's "four freedoms" made him a "good expositor of Second Isaiah."[41]

Religion's usefulness for the democratic way of life was also a theme of a series of pamphlets sponsored by the Edward W. Hazen Foundation, probably the largest source of funding for the NCRHE and its network of Protestant educators who promoted the study of religion. Julius Seelye Bixler, president of Colby College and former president of NCRHE, in one of the first pamphlets, *The Resources of Religion and the Aims of Higher Education*, took issue with the antithetical posture of American theologians who followed the lead of Karl Barth. What the times demanded was a "religion of loyalty which in its reasonableness" supplemented the culture. Democracy represented this kind of religion because of its absolute devotion to "justice, equality, and fraternity." It brought the "blessings of heaven" by expressing in human relations the ideas of "reason," "universality," and "justice."[42] Though Bixler was content to leave the connections between democracy and religion rather vague, Ralph H. Gabriel, professor of history at Yale University, was more specific. Gabriel traced the "American democratic faith" to the religion that English Protestants brought to the New World. From Puritanism America derived "its emphasis upon the fundamental moral law and upon the doctrine of the self-disciplined individual." From Quakerism America received the ideals of "individual liberty, the dignity and worth of man and universal brotherhood." Although Gabriel refused to comment on the study of religion in higher education his point was clear. If the United States were to "go steadily on" in its democratic faith, its religious convictions could not be ignored.[43] This was precisely the conclusion of another Hazen pamphlet, *Conversations on Higher Education and Religion.* "Religious faith," these educators concluded, "has nourished a high estimate of men and so added at times a great dynamic to democratic thought and to social and political movements." In fact, the participants wondered if "faith in democracy" could survive unless nourished by "the insight and faith of religion."[44]

Thus, the war gave religion professors a greater opportunity to demonstrate the relevance of the Bible for modern life. But by showing religion's importance to democracy and American institutions it also paved the way for faculty and administrators within American higher education to argue for greater attention to religion within the undergraduate curriculum. A survey of religious instruction during the war indicated how the conflict had allowed faculty to prove the value of their presence on campus. Even though reductions in enrollment overall had forced some professors to teach other subjects, such as sociology or math, the authors of the study concluded that the new situation in most cases permitted religion to be seen "in the context of a total cultural pattern rather than an isolated subject." For instance, at Princeton religion instructors had helped to establish the course, "Man and His Freedom in the Western Tradition," which traced the "great classics from the ancient and modern world," from the Bible to the present. The same was true at Denison, Colby, the University of Colorado, and Haverford. Administrative reasons as well as widespread concern about the crisis of western culture underscored the ties between religion and other humanistic subjects. To be sure, as the survey indicated, the older approach to the study of religion survived, one that regarded it as part of the church's ministry to students. Students facing the question of their own mortality did prompt some faculty to adopt a pastoral pose, such as when one faculty member responded that his aim was to "make the resources of religious faith persuasively present and inescapable."[45] Still, the long-term curricular implications of religious instruction during the war were to make religious studies a partner with the humanities.

During the decade before World War II and at the time of the war itself the teaching and study of religion moved closer to finding an academic niche. Prior to the 1930s instructors in religion had to find ways to connect the specialized work of higher criticism, for instance, with the inspirational demands of campus ministry. But a desire by faculty for serious study of the Bible, questions about the materialistic nature of American higher education, and the crisis of western culture generated by the war—these factors contributed to religious studies' growing stature as an academic discipline worthy of inclusion in American higher education.

Religious Studies and General Education

Educational reforms of the 1940s proved to be propitious for Protestant efforts on behalf of the teaching and study of religion. Two influential reports, Harvard University's *General Education in a Free Society* (1945), and the President's Commission on Higher Education's *Higher Education for American Democracy* (1947), expressed concern about the stress upon research and specialization at the expense of unity and integration. As such these reports showed religion faculty to be in sync with those who advocated general education and humanistic studies as a remedy for American higher education as well as the nation. According to the President's Commission, general education promoted "nonspecialized and nonvocational learning which should be the common experience of all educated men and women." Indeed, general education provided students with the "values, attitudes, knowledge and skills" that would allow them "to live rightly and well in a free society." Lest readers miss the importance of moral considerations for higher education, the report added that students should be acquainted with "ethical values, scientific generalizations, and aesthetic conceptions." The Harvard report also recommended more study of "the intellectual forces that have shaped the Western mind" as a cure for the ills of American education. Consequently, what was necessary for a proper understanding of America's "inherited view of man and society," was an education rooted in "religious education, education in the great books, and education in modern democracy."[46]

Though neither report mentioned religious instruction per se, both fueled interest in the restoration of ethical and spiritual concerns within the college curriculum. In fact, during the 1940s a number of books on the humanities appeared with what Laurence Veysey described as "an entirely new frequency and insistence." What was new and significant about these publications was their defense of the humanities. Traditionally, these subjects had been identified with the preservation of antiquity or the perpetuation of genteel culture. Against the backdrop of academic specialization and prestige of science, the humanities—an odd assortment of disciplines ranging from philology to art—became the province of those studies associated with the eternal values of the past. Whether such study was justified on the restrained grounds of cultural heritage or on the ambitious basis of superior and elevated taste, the humanities were easily distinguished from the natural and social sciences. In a very important sense, then, what made a particular discipline humanistic was its impracticality.

But the humanities found a new rationale during World War II and this had important repercussions for the teaching and study of religion. With the cultural crisis stemming from the war, educators began to stress the humanities' relevance for living an ethically and socially responsible life. Increasingly, faculty and administrators used the terms *spiritual, moral,* and *humanizing* in connection with the humanities, while at the same time putting these subjects at the center of liberal education. No longer associated with timeless truths or mental discipline, a liberal education was ideally suited for a liberal democracy. The American Council of Learned Societies summarized this development when in its report on liberal education it asserted that the humanities would be the "platform upon which democratically and liberally minded citizens throughout the country may now unite and move in greater harmony and efficiency toward our common goal."[47]

This new emphasis upon the humanizing and civilizing qualities of higher education made religious studies an attractive ally in the promotion of curricular reform along the lines of liberal and general education. Many faculty and administrators made repeated and vociferous calls for a common curriculum that included instruction in values and ethics. Most of these recommendations looked to the humanities to supply the requisite instruction, but some also included the study of religion and began to list religion as a humanistic subject.[48] Fifty years earlier American educators had not known where to put the study of religion within the threefold division of academic subjects into natural sciences, social sciences, and humanities. On the one hand, Christian divinity fit naturally with the study of ancient languages and culture. On the other hand, the moralistic and progressive aspects of Protestant liberalism from 1870 to 1930 gave the study of religion loose connections to the disciplines of economics, sociology, political science, and anthropology. Whatever its academic status had been, religious studies moved in the 1940s from a ragtag discipline with little departmental structure and a mixture of academic and devotional aims to a partner in the humanities' effort to revive spiritual and moral values.[49]

Having found a curricular niche for the study of religion among the humanities, Protestant faculty became bolder at the same time that administrators were more generous in allocating funding for religion departments. Between 1945 and 1960, for instance, the number of undergraduate programs in religious studies increased almost 100 percent, moving from twenty to thirty-eight. Enrollment figures indicated that students also appeared to welcome religious studies' higher visibility. During the postwar years, according to one survey, religion courses attracted more undergraduates than any other area of study. This expansion occurred most notably at private nonsectarian institutions. Religious studies also expanded in graduate education as the postwar era witnessed the establishment of sixteen new programs leading to the Ph.D., a 60 percent increase. The growth of graduate programs in religion during the 1950s led to a tripling of Ph.D. degrees awarded in religious studies.[50]

Ironically, however, instruction in religion, despite its affinities with literature, philosophy, history, and general education, could not shake its specifically Protestant orientation. The shape of the curriculum in most of the new departments of religion resembled that of Protestant divinity schools and seminaries. Course offerings followed the pattern of Bible, theology, and church history—the typical course of instruction for ministers. The only subjects undergraduate and graduate programs in religion left to the seminaries was the usual fare in preaching, liturgy, and church administration. The Protestant character of religious studies was self-perpetuating because the oldest and strongest programs for training faculty who would staff the new departments were divinity schools such as Yale, Harvard, Union (New York), and the University of Chicago. With the best candidates for academic positions holding degrees in biblical studies, theology, and church history, it was no wonder that religion departments looked like smaller versions of divinity schools.[51]

The discipline of religious studies had come a long way. It began the twentieth century as a field of study that, according to leaders of the university movement such as William Rainey Harper and Charles W. Eliot, needed to move away from its churchly and, therefore, sectarian identity if it was going to be truly scientific and worthy of the university. But forty-five years later religious studies was guilty of precisely what an older generation of Protestant educators had hoped to avoid, namely, providing courses in the standard subjects of Protestant divinity. The reason for this shift said as much about the study of religion as it did about the universities that were providing it. In the era of the university's founding, the study of religion had to show itself to be sufficiently scientific in order to be academically acceptable. The particulars of Protestant theology had to go. As a result, between 1870 and 1930 religion was largely extracurricular and inspirational. But in an academic environment suspicious of specialization and scientific narrowness, the traditional Protestant theological curriculum was permissible especially when it appeared to assist cultural studies, general education, and western civilization. From 1945 until 1970 religious studies established not only its educational but also its institutional identity as a partner with the humanities. While this strategy allowed the discipline to blossom, the field could not shake its Protestant and ministerial genesis and orientation, thus leaving religious studies vulnerable when the climate of American universities changed.

FIVE

Finding a Place for Theology

ON MARCH 8, 1948, Reinhold Niebuhr, professor of applied Christianity at New York's Union Theological Seminary, became the first theologian to grace the cover of *Time* magazine. Whether they were correct, *Time*'s editors believed that Niebuhr's sober, if not somber, theological views spoke for the mood of American society. The writer, in fact, admitted that Niebuhr's theology of original sin and humankind's need for redemption was not a message for "the tenderminded" but rather a faith for a "Lenten age." Still, the old liberal Protestant theology no longer presented an accurate account of the world and humanity's place in it. "Twentieth-century civilization" had reached its climax and its paradoxes had escalated to "catastrophic" proportions. "Man's marvelous conquest of space has made total war a household experience," the anonymous correspondent explained, "the faster science gains on disease (which ultimately seems to elude it), the more the human race dies at the hands of living men." But against the easy optimism of liberal Protestantism, Niebuhr asserted that "life is inevitably tragic." Thus, almost two centuries after Jonathan Edwards preached about what sinners deserved from an angry God, original sin was back in the news because theology seemed to explain why human history, "even at its highest moments," was not a "success story."[1]

Though Niebuhr's perspective may have resonated with a nation that had lived through two wars and economic collapse, his views were not obviously useful to Protestant faculty and administrators who were responsible for the teaching and study of religion. Clarence Prouty Shedd, a colleague of Niebuhr's brother, H. Richard, at Yale Divinity School, was convinced of the importance of theology for American higher education. "At no time during this present century," Shedd enthused, "have so many outstanding educators been saying that higher education must have religious or theological foundations." For without such foundations higher education would "lose its essential meaning and unity." But while affirming the importance of theology for colleges and universities, Shedd's understanding of higher education did not provide a hospitable environment for Niebuhr's grave estimate of the human condition. The "central touchstone" of an institution's educational program had to be the student's need "now as a citizen in his complex and disturbing college world, his capacity to share in making the college a religious community, his needs as a member of the nation's armed forces facing the ultimates of life, and his future as a potential leader in the work of the world as citizen, as a home builder, and a worker." To be sure, Niebuhr's awareness of human shortcomings and the need for grace might help with some of Shedd's "ultimates of life." But in the end Niebuhr's recognition of the unintended and fallen consequences of even the best and most sincere progressive efforts was lost on Shedd's hopes for "the reunion of a revitalized Christianity and learning." Such a reunion would in Shedd's vision create "better men and a better world."[2]

This tension between the dark side of Christian theology and the justification of it by its social relevance dogged professors given the task of introducing religion to American undergraduates. Though religion faculty never truly resolved this tension in the period between 1945 and 1965, when religion departments came into their own, they were able to find a niche, if only because members of their guild were appearing on the front covers of America's most widely circulated magazines. Frequently, Christianity's teachings would have to be dressed up in the fashion of the perennial questions addressed in literature, philosophy (especially existentialism), and other humanistic disciplines. Or they would have to show political relevance for the threats to liberal democracy posed during the Cold War. But whatever the lure, theology was seldom taught or studied systematically in the classroom, despite the pervasive calls for theological considerations by Protestant faculty and university administrators.[3] Through religious studies, theology had finally come back into American higher education after being exiled by the university reforms of the late nineteenth century. But its return would turn out to be as tenuous as its Christian affirmations.[4]

Antidote to Secularism

In sixty years, Protestant assessments of American academic culture had come a long way. When the university reforms of the late nineteenth century were implemented most clergy and scholars hailed the ideals of scientific inquiry and specialized research as a blessing, sure to result in a vastly improved education, better equipped graduates, and a more prosperous, efficient, and equitable national order. The only dissent from the churches concerned the threat universities posed to denominational colleges. But by the middle decades of the twentieth century the mood of Protestant educators and commentators on higher learning had changed dramatically. No longer did the university appear to be so healthy. If anything, the educational establishment's preoccupation with science appeared to be responsible for the political and economic perils that confronted liberal democracy.

A spate of books and other publications beginning in the late 1930s and running well into the 1960s took issue with what the authors regarded as the secular direction of American universities and higher education's failure to propagate the values necessary for a healthy society. Though few of these authors explicitly offered theology as the medicine for an ailing system of education, their overriding assumption was that a recovery of Christian thought and ideals was crucial to the recovery of the university. Thus, this body of work clearly paved the way for theology, a discipline rejected as dogmatic and sectarian by university reformers, to reenter the classroom and assert its former regal status as the queen of the sciences.[5]

An early example of this line of argument was W. A. Visser't Hooft's *None Other Gods*. The secretary of the World Student Christian Federation, Visser't Hooft was, according to Reinhold Niebuhr, "the most influential leader of Christian young people in the Protestant church," an introduction that was sure to gain the author a wider hearing in the United States than many of the Protestant ecumenical officials working in Geneva would receive. Visser't Hooft's aim in this book was simply to rouse the church community to a better understanding of Christianity and the church's task in the world. Part of that mission was to form a Christian intelligentsia that would present the Christian message to the "secular world" and translate that message into a plan of "concrete action." The need for Christian intellectuals inevitably led to an estimate of the university and its prospects for cultivating such academic leadership. Visser't Hooft did not pull his punches. "It is not easy," he wrote, "to describe the university of our days in other than negative terms." He conceded that it had considerable influence and had extended the benefits of applied sciences to society at large. But if asked to express a clear sense of mission the modern university gave "no clear answer." Here Visser't Hooft agreed with the University of Chicago's Robert M. Hutchins that higher learning "does not know what it is itself."[6]

The reason for the university's loss of direction stemmed from historical circumstances dating back to the Reformation and the Enlightenment. The result of this disintegration of academic purpose was an institution "exclusively devoted to the accumulation of scientific data" without attending to them "in the setting of a common framework." Moreover, the university's demise was taking its toll on students who were tired of being drowned "in a sea of facts," frustrated by professors who failed to give a "sense of vocation and of integration," and were looking elsewhere for "orientation and inspiration."[7]

Yet the church could not abandon the university if it was to fulfill the responsibility of Christianizing the social order. Crucial to this order was an integrated understanding of truth, a comprehensive scheme for assimilating all of the facts at the university's disposal. Visser't Hooft hoped that the failure of various philosophies and ideologies to provide such a framework would force university leaders to "turn back to the faith which founded [the university]." In the meantime, the situation required Christians in the university, both professors and students, to be discerning and distinguish between "the things which are of God and the things which are against God." Christians needed to apply the "central affirmation" of the faith to all the realms of intellectual life. "What the university needs most of all today," Visser't Hooft concluded, "is precisely a body of men who believe in the unity of truth and who therefore force the university back to its real mission of seeking 'Truth' and not merely 'truths.'"[8] A little more theology in the university would clearly supply some of the missing order and unity in academic life.

Visser't Hooft was not the only one to blame the apparent aimlessness of the university on the pursuit of scientific knowledge without a theological or metaphysical frame of reference. In *The University and the Modern World*, Arnold S. Nash, chaplain to the Student Christian

Movement and occasional lecturer in political economy at the University of Toronto, complained as loudly as Visser't Hooft about the purposelessness of modern higher education. And again science, "the established religion for the masses," bore a large share of the blame. The notion that knowledge had to be pursued for its own sake, in Nash's estimation, had prevented scientists from recognizing their "social responsibilities" and had encouraged the university more generally to adopt a spectator's approach to the social order. What liberal democratic societies needed—and Nash was writing during the Second World War—was an intellectual synthesis that would provide unity and meaning to the vast stores of knowledge available in modern learning. To be sure, scientific knowledge, while not providing an "adequate foundation," demanded a place in the university. But the autonomy of the disciplines had to cease. All subjects of study needed to be construed "as a means whereby God the Creator as an ultimate and transcendent end [was] worshiped."[9]

Another book from this period written by an Englishman but which Americans cited frequently to promote religious studies was Sir Walter Moberly's The Crisis in the University. Moberly wrote more about British university life but his concerns echoed those of Visser't Hooft and Nash. Even so, the use of atomic weapons gave Moberly's book a darker side than the others. "The veneer of civilization has proved to be amazingly thin," he wrote on the first page, and added that "the heart of man is deceitful and desperately wicked." The problems confronting the university again stemmed from the triumph of scientific expertise. Science had created an atmosphere of neutrality, bred the fragmentation of knowledge, and neglected moral and spiritual factors. Moberly's assessment of the university left Christian academics with a choice. Either they could regard themselves as a small enclave like the early church in the Roman Empire and thus separate themselves from the majority culture. Or they could, as Moberly advocated, Christianize the university from within as a "creative minority." Such an approach would require the recovery of Christian teaching regarding the "indefeasible value of the individual," "the ubiquity and the humanly ineradicable character of sin," and a Christian hope stemming from "divine providence."[10] Such convictions would, Moberly believed, restore to the university a sense of purpose that integrated knowledge and morals.

Of the American authors who contributed to the literature lamenting the secularization of the university Henry P. Van Dusen's was one of the most forceful. The vitality of his book, God in Education, stemmed not as much from the author's responsibilities as president of Union Theological Seminary where the most popular theologians such as Niebuhr and Tillich taught.[11] Rather, what made Van Dusen's thoughts about religion and education so poignant was the author's own history. He had been ordained a Presbyterian minister in 1924 at the time of the fundamentalist controversy and his ordination was one of the high points of that conflict. At the time of his ordination exams, Van Dusen would not affirm the virgin birth of Christ as an necessary article of Presbyterian theology. Fundamentalists, of course, pointed to Van Dusen as evidence of liberalism in the northern Presbyterian Church. Progressives in New York countered with constitutional arguments drawn up by a young Presbyterian elder, John Foster Dulles, architect of the Eisenhower administration's Cold War policies. After the fundamentalist controversy ended, Van Dusen settled into academic responsibilities at Union, teaching systematic theology, and eventually in 1946 became the seminary's executive officer. To compare Van Dusen's significance in the 1920s to his thoughts about American higher education in the post–World War II era is to see just how much mainstream Protestantism had moved to the right. While conservatives in the 1920s were concerned that progressives like Van Dusen were secularizing the churches, by the late 1940s liberal Protestants showed similar fears. The president of arguably the most liberal mainline Protestant seminary in the United States sounded as alarmed about the declining affirmation of Christian verities as fundamentalists had twenty-five years earlier.[12]

Van Dusen began with quotations from both John Foster Dulles and Douglas MacArthur to demonstrate the widespread diagnosis that western civilization was sick. Dulles insisted that the human effort to control the physical "depends upon the moral." MacArthur agreed that the problem facing the West was "basically theological." The universities were emblematic of western culture's demise because they had relied so heavily on science and empirical methods that they had bracketed out religious and moral considerations. Van Dusen took encouragement from the growing presence of religion departments on American college and university campuses. "The major purpose behind all of these new schemes," he wrote, "is to introduce larger unity, coherence and therefore meaning, into the undergraduate's course of study." But simply adding religion courses was not sufficient to overcome higher education's and the surrounding culture's defective outlook. What the university needed was "a fundamental reorientation of *every* subject in the curriculum and its presentation in every course." "If there be a God at all," Van Dusen advised, "He must be the ultimate and controlling Reality through which all else derives its being; and the truth concerning Him, as man can best apprehend it, must be the keystone of the ever-incomplete arch of human knowledge."[13]

Union's president acknowledged that his approach to education could sound intolerant, if not un-American, a charge that liberals had used against fundamentalists two and a half decades earlier. So Van Dusen closed his book with a discussion of the relationship between church and state in the United States. The "authentic 'American tradition'" was one that affirmed the separation of church and state in such a way that did not prevent educators from acknowledging the "power and goodness of God." Here Van Dusen quoted Dean Weigle on the kind of religion necessary for a good education. "The common religious faith of the American people, as distinguished from the sectarian forms in which it is organized, may rightfully be assumed and find appropriate expression in the life and work of the public schools."[14] For Van Dusen this applied as much to higher education as it did to primary and secondary schooling. Having assured his readers that the Judeo-Christian faith was the bedrock of American education and the way out of the West's cultural decline, Van Dusen believed he had made a persuasive case for the necessity of theology in the university.[15]

Of all the books arguing on behalf of theology's inclusion in the university, only one went beyond general affirmations about morals and spiritual ideals to talk about the task of theology itself within the university. This came from William Adams Brown, long-time professor of theology at the seminary over which Van Dusen presided.[16] The occasion for Brown's reflections on the place of theology in the university was *The Higher Learning in America,* by Robert Maynard Hutchins, who as it turned out wrote the preface for Brown's book. Specifically challenging for Brown was Hutchins's contention that theology offered no principle of unity for university education. As a theologian and a member of Yale's board of trustees, Brown had a strong interest in showing that Hutchins was right in his diagnosis of the problem, namely, that the university lacked intellectual coherence, but wrong in ruling out theology as a viable remedy for higher education's woes.[17]

Brown began by describing the history leading up to theology's marginalization in the university. In the medieval world of scholasticism, for instance, "theology gave the . . . university a unifying principle for conduct" (17). To hear a noted liberal Protestant extolling medieval Roman Catholicism was indeed remarkable. But the need for coherence in the twentieth century was so great that Brown was willing to overlook the authoritarianism of Rome to which he otherwise would have objected. In the United States, however, theology had been reduced to strictly a professional discipline. Brown blamed this in part on the churches for creating their own seminaries and divorcing theological education from liberal education. What the churches needed to overcome this defect was the same kind of union that the American nation had achieved after the Civil War (27–28, 96–117).

Another factor restricting theology was the tradition of the separation of church and state. But this feature of religious and political life in the United States was "so far from being designed by our fathers" that it was "not even anticipated by them." The last thing the founders wanted, according to Brown, was "to establish the newly constituted state upon a purely secular foundation" (24). If "more than half of the citizens belong by their own free choice to the Christian church," why did the United States' system of education ignore "the subject which through all the centuries of its history has held the central place in the life of its citizens" (29)? The greatest detriment to theology came from the consequence of the educational reforms of the late nineteenth century. Here Brown identified Charles W. Eliot's program of electives, which broke down "an educational system controlled by a single consistent philosophy." The other factors driving the demise of a unified philosophy of education were science and academic specialization. "One science after another," Brown lamented, "has broken off from its original connection with philosophy" (37, 38).

Restoring philosophy as the organizing principle of university life would not do, however, according to Brown. Metaphysics did not fare well in a comparison with theology. It could not "create a faith in a meaningful world," nor could it offer a "single system of philosophy" upon which all would agree (48, 49). But theology had exactly what the university needed. By theology Brown meant "the philosophy of the Christian religion," or the sum of efforts that used the "Christian faith to bring unity and consistency into man's thought of the universe" (13). Theology as such yielded knowledge "through the senses" of a real "moral and spiritual order in the universe," and of an "excellent" deity. It also enabled men and women to act upon their ideals so that when they trusted and followed "that which is most excellent [they entered] into communion with the deity" (51–52). Brown conceded that other religions had theology but he insisted on Christian divinity as the appropriate one for American universities. It was religion "which as a matter of fact lies at the heart of our Western culture." It also "furnished democracy with its religious basis." Finally, Christian theology was superior to other theologies because it taught that God created all things, thus supplying meaning to history; dignity to humankind; and a "religious basis" for democracy (112).

When it came to outlining how Christian theology should be taught, Brown displayed the liberal Protestant tendency to avoid specifics. On the one hand, his claims for theology were modest, at least when conceived as a discipline. Brown delineated three senses of theology. The first concerned "the science of revealed religion," where divine revelation communicated truths by means "wholly other than those open to man in other fields of knowledge." While this definition of theology equipped the theologian with a specific sphere of inquiry, thus making theology different from philosophy, literature, sociology, or history, Brown agreed with Hutchins that it was "futile" to look to this kind of theology to provide unity for the university. "Faith in the sense of the acceptance on external authority of unverifiable presuppositions," Brown insisted, "has no place in the program of a great university" (11). Later in his book, Brown even compared Karl Barth's theology to Catholicism and attributed the turn to "a purely authoritarian religion" to "disillusionment" with modern life. Obviously, from Brown's perspective, fundamentalism, or any kind of theology that clung to a religious authority other than science, was unacceptable in the university (92).

Two other kinds of theology, however, offered better prospects for the university. Another definition of theology involved the "scientific study of religion." In this sense, theology would have "a place in the university as one among the many other subjects of research to which . . . professors are giving themselves." As squeamish as Brown may have been about doing theology on the basis of special revelation, he did not hesitate to explain that by religion he meant "the great tradition which meets us in the history of the Christian church" (12). Though some might prefer the teaching and study of other religions, Brown countered that Christianity furnished the "most natural point of departure" for exploring "the permanent issues" and humankind's purpose in the world. Not only was Christianity essential to western culture, it was also through missions "bringing into touch with all the faiths of mankind . . . those living issues with which every philosophy worthy of the name must deal" (63). Thus, in good liberal Protestant fashion, Brown put Christianity at the apex of world religions, the faith that completed the incompleteness of other faiths.[18] But even more significant in the decision to teach and study Christianity was its civic benefit. Christianity "furnished democracy with its religious basis."[19] If "democratic civilization" was to maintain itself, Brown warned, it needed a "philosophy which is born of faith, a philosophy which is in fact, and which is not ashamed to call itself, religious." The founders of the American republic had such a philosophy, he insisted. "And they had it because they were Christians" (77).

Still, to teach and study the Christian tradition was not enough to satisfy Hutchins's requirements. This led Brown to develop a third sense of theology. Here the university needed more than a department where students could study Christianity. To find a unifying principle required a version of theology that transcended specialization and disciplinary fragmentation. Theology of this kind was "the philosophy of the Christian religion." Brown explained that such a philosophy was the sum of attempts to use the Christian faith to "bring unity and consistency into man's thought of the universe." The scholastics of the Middle Ages exemplified such a theology when even though accepting revelation and appealing to faith they still followed the dictates of reason. "They were convinced that the God in whom they believed was the basic reality in the universe and hence the key to the understanding of nature and of man" (13). In fact, European universities had been far more open to theologians than American institutions. Here Brown appealed to Schleiermacher, Kant, Hegel, Locke, and Butler, thus proving that the "American restriction of theology to a purely professional discipline" was an anomaly in the history of higher education (22–24).

In Brown's ideal university the theologian functioned as the academic equivalent of the utility infielder in baseball, the person who stepped in to fill in the holes and keep the overarching purpose of higher learning on track. The theologian's function was to "vindicate man's faith that this is a meaningful world—that the reason and conscience with which God has endowed man make him in a true sense akin to God" and to demonstrate the relevance of religious faith (86–87). Modern developments had made it possible for theology to provide this service because the sharp lines between nature and the supernatural had been erased. This characteristically modernist understanding of theology had implications across the academic disciplines and allowed theologians to speak meaningfully in all spheres of academic inquiry. In the natural sciences, for instance, Brown stated glibly that "metaphysics and theology" were "two sides of one and the same thing" (95). Theology was equally pertinent in the humanities. Historians would give as much attention to the "latest developments in the field of Christian missions or church history" as they would to politics and economics. The department of classics would show that Latin was no dead language but was the medium for most of the world's teaching and worship. Likewise, the social sciences could well benefit from an infusion of theology, with psychologists showing the same kind of sympathy for religious experience as William James had, and with sociologists recognizing the church as a significant social institution (120). In the end it did not matter whether a professor in the humanities, social sciences, or natural sciences was theologically trained for theology to flourish and for the university to find its bearings. Anyone who realized "the central place which religion holds in human life, who [could] recognize it when he sees it" had the vision and the power to "unite men in pursuit of a great and worthy ideal" (123–24).

Arguments such as Brown's were useful for advancing the cause of religion in the university at a time when academic resistance to religious interests was low. His appeal was just one more facet of the growing alliance between mainline Protestant academics and the civilizing and humanizing mission of the humanities. Consequently, Brown, with the assistance of many other theological figures, demonstrated the value of religion to those who were concerned about the growing technological, vocational, and materialistic drift of the university.

But the larger consequence of reasoning like Brown's was less positive. While assuming the place of religious studies as a department within the university, the license Brown gave theologians to intervene in the overall mission of higher education created a dynamic that could boomerang on departments of religion. If religious concerns were relevant across the disciplines, then what precisely did the academics with posts in the religion department study and teach? On the other hand, the assumptions about the superiority of Christianity underlying Brown's case for theology in the university made sense at a time when mainline Protestantism continued to be an important player in America's cultural establishment. But the superiority of Christianity, which was largely assumed, could sound downright exclusive. In the 1930s and 1940s charges of intolerance and dogmatism were easy to foist upon fundamentalists. Mainline Protestants were committed to the same political and cultural ideals as most of their academic colleagues and so could easily escape the stigma of sectarianism. But liberal Protestants like Brown did not prepare for the rainy day when the privileged position of Protestant Christianity could no longer be assumed. Consequently, even though the theological impetus for studying and teaching religion in American higher education was successful in the short run, it put religious studies on an even shakier intellectual foundation.

The Ubiquity of Theology

Walter M. Horton, one of America's theologians who had backed away from liberal Protestantism's rosier assessment of human nature, gave himself the task of assessing American theological developments over the course of the first half of the twentieth century in a book that covered the various theological disciplines. Horton may not have been the most objective but he was certainly well connected within the Protestant mainline, as well as the religious studies establishment. A graduate of Union Seminary (New York) and Columbia University, Horton taught systematic theology at his theological alma mater for three years before becoming the Fairchild Professor of Theology at Oberlin College. He also served in a variety of capacities for the World Council of Churches. Horton believed that after the "realignment" of 1930–35, which witnessed the defeat of fundamentalism and the rise of neo-orthodoxy, American theology had "gathered strength for new constructive endeavors." What is more, a decade and a half of "world chaos, world war, and world leadership" had created a captive audience for "an orderly, constructive credo." Horton sensed that a "period of constructive *system building*" was at hand.[20]

Other students of American theology rendered similar judgments and for good reason.[21] Protestant intellectuals such as Reinhold Niebuhr and Paul Tillich had taken the chief themes of Christian theology and made them accessible to a wider public. Carl Michalson, commenting in another forum on a half-century's development in Protestant theology, declared Niebuhr, even though technically an ethicist, to be "the one American theologian" who most consistently delineated the "historical element" of Christianity for general consumption. Niebuhr, for instance, turned to the Christian doctrine of creation to say that "there is purpose in history no matter how hidden." He also used the doctrine of eschatology to explain why this purpose in history was finally "unrealizable" in this world. Jesus Christ became, in Niebuhr's hands, an indication that "perfection will always be crucified in history." Thus, Niebuhr was able to translate the primary teachings of Christianity to audiences only generically Christian or, even more vaguely, generally American. The Union Seminary professor's writings made Christian theology fit within the broader humanistic categories of western civilization.[22]

Niebuhr's ability to speak to a broader constituency was no less true of Paul Tillich, an Émigré from Nazi Germany who came to the United States in 1933 to teach with Niebuhr at Union Theological Seminary in

New York. An anthology devoted to one of Tillich's favorite subjects, "Religion and Culture," which was assembled in the 1950s, demonstrated his wide appeal. Sponsored in part by a committee that included Albert Schweitzer, Martin Buber, T. S. Eliot, Jacques Maritain, W. H. Auden, and Arnold Toynbee, and with contributions from Karl Jaspers, Karl Barth, Gustave Weigle, Georges Florovsky, Charles Hartshorne, and Gabriel Marcel, this book expressed the gratitude and esteem of a generation that had been "inspired and stimulated" by Tillich's thought. At the root of Tillich's theology were assumptions that resonated with the existential currents running through mid-twentieth-century philosophy and literature. He asserted that God and humankind were related in such a way that human existence was always tinged by the gulf that lay between the infinite and the finite. Though he appealed to metaphysics to articulate these themes, Tillich could also make these abstract concepts accessible through such existentialist topics as alienation, rebellion, anxiety, guilt, judgment, fulfillment, and joy. He also showed the applicability of theological reasoning in his thought about the relationship between religion and culture: "Religion is the substance of culture and culture the form of religion."[23] With concepts as malleable and as evocative as Tillich's, academic theology in mid-twentieth-century America experienced a renaissance that appealed to the "intelligent layman" who had read "Camus, Sartre, Tennessee Williams, Faulkner, Freud, Marx, David Riesman, William Whyte, Jr., and so on."[24]

But while theology of a more general and humanistic orientation appeared to be thriving, theology as an academic discipline was making little headway. Theology's inability to carve out its own scholarly niche was certainly a plausible interpretation of three anthologies published between 1944 and 1952 which were designed to show the relevance of religion for higher education. The first was *The Vitality of the Christian Tradition,* edited by George F. Thomas, professor of religious studies at Princeton University.[25] The second was *Liberal Learning and Religion,* edited by the University of Chicago Divinity School's New Testament scholar Amos N. Wilder.[26] The third was *Religious Perspectives in College Teaching,* edited by Hoxie N. Fairchild, professor of English literature at Hunter College.[27] Each book bore the telltale signs of the institutions and networks that championed the cause of religious studies. For instance, *The Vitality of the Christian Tradition* was dedicated to Charles Foster Kent and the agency he had helped to found, the National Council on Religion in Higher Education (NCRHE). Likewise, all of the contributors to *Liberal Learning and Religion* had been fellows or were officers of the NCRHE, and a grant for the publication of the volume came from the long-time grant maker to religious endeavors in higher education, the Edward W. Hazen Foundation. So, too, *Religious Perspectives in College Teaching* depended upon the generosity of the Hazen Foundation and reflected the Connecticut-based philanthropy's agenda of combating the secularization of American higher education. Each book surveyed the range of disciplines in universities and colleges and argued for the value, propriety, and necessity of teaching academic subjects from a Christian perspective. Yet none of the books included a chapter either by a theologian or on Christian theology.[28]

Of these three books, *The Vitality of the Christian Tradition* was the most explicit in its affirmation of historic Christian teaching. The first half of the book covered the historical development of Christianity out of its Hebraic roots to its ancient, medieval, Reformation, and modern expressions. What emerged from this historical overview was a firm conclusion that Christianity was relevant for the twentieth century, especially with a view to the ideological contest being played out in World War II. For instance, the chapter on the Old Testament by James Muilenberg, professor of Old Testament at the Pacific School of Religion, argued that the concern with history in the Hebrew tradition was closely related to "our own contemporary search for coherence in history, our bafflement in the midst of a staggering historical crisis, and our profound concern for the fate of man."[29] Finding the value of medieval Christianity for twentieth-century Americans was just as difficult as that of discerning ancient Judaism's contemporary relevance. But Lynn D. White, the president of Mills College, was up to the task. Though Americans bore a heavy debt to the Puritans, the lesson learned from the experience of medieval believers was not all that different from the one taught by the spirituality of English-speaking Protestants. "The soul striving for perfection" was a constant struggle throughout all ages and lands, and so was "intimately related to contemporary forms of life."[30] Henry P. Van Dusen's chapter on nineteenth-century Protestantism, however, offered the most directly relevant truths for mid-twentieth-century culture. Though he conceded that Protestant liberalism, one of the great developments of the nineteenth century, was under attack, its "record of expansion, of reinterpretation, of unification, of heroic devotion to the cause of Christ" meant that it held "the seeds of promise for tomorrow."[31] Still, the statement of Christian convictions and their relevance never ventured beyond historical developments into statements of academic or technical theology (such as the Trinity, creation, sin, or grace). The most forthright expression of Christian teaching came in the chapter on ethics where John Moore, professor of ethics and religion at Hamilton College, began with a exposition of Jesus' ethical instructions.[32] At a time of monumental cultural upheaval, the teaching and study of theology in the hands of mainstream Protestants was mustering little more than generic Christian sentiments.

The second half of *The Vitality of the Christian Tradition* ventured into the chief disciplinary divisions in academia with an effort to demonstrate the pertinence of Christianity for American learning. But rather than setting a religious agenda for scholars in the humanities, social sciences, and natural sciences, the best the contributors could do was find the weaknesses in the various subjects and thereby add a mildly Christian perspective to make up for the alleged deficiency. For instance, Amos N. Wilder took encouragement from modernist literary developments. In the poetry of D. H. Lawrence, Wilder found a repudiation of "a society so mechanized and commercialized as to have lost its roots in nature." Yeats was another example of a poet who had recoiled from "scientific rationalism." Though explicit references to Christianity were either lacking or negative, Wilder believed this stemmed from a fundamental misunderstanding of the Christian tradition. Once understood properly, a harmonization of modernist literature and Christianity, in Wilder's estimate, was not only possible but pointed to the conclusion that the "Hebraic-tradition is still a vital force in contemporary culture."[33] Howard B. Jefferson, professor of philosophy at Colgate University, took a similar tack in his essay on the physical sciences. He argued that the "facts of science do not necessitate the rejection of theism or compel the adoption" of materialistic and deterministic world view. Neither, however, did science require the affirmation of theism. In the end, the most important battle was not religion versus science but Christianity versus Fascism and Nazism. In that war, Jefferson hoped, Christianity would find science fighting with it "side by side."[34]

While the other two volumes on Christianity's relevance to American learning made little reference to the struggle between democracy and totalitarianism, their contributors argued for theology's significance in a similar way. They persuaded educators to add a religious perspective to their scholarship and teaching rather than demonstrating the difference that such a perspective made for scholarship. This was a predictable stance for the essays in the humanities. From professors of philosophy to lecturers in English literature, the notion that technical and experimental study could not account for the complexity of human existence had tremendous appeal, and again helped to explain the growing acceptance of religion as an academic discipline. This was precisely the point that Douglas Knight made in his chapter, "The Religious Implications of the Humanities." In a word, the knowledge students received from the humanities or theology was better than that of the physical sciences. "The sense of mystery, almost of miracle involved in the proper study of the humanities," Knight concluded, "results from a recognition of the way in which the known exists with the unknown, suggesting how one may regard that unknown but never usurping the place of the deity by pretending to be the sum of all things." The absolute of the humanities had "humility at its root." Though Knight did not say so, he implied that the physical sciences had pride at theirs. But the humanities' battle was not to send science into exile but to secure more seats at the table.[35]

Nevertheless, the deficiencies of natural science, which educators compounded by making scientific method the criteria for all truth, were not necessarily harmful, as the contributors to these volumes also showed. While humanists and theologians argued for adding another perspective, scientists demonstrated the theological perspective already inherent in their studies. Edward McCrady, professor of biology at the University of the South, insisted that students could not learn biology adequately without reference to religious questions. One such question concerned the compatibility of Christianity and evolution. McCrady believed that the problem was not one of reconciling the biblical account of creation with science but rather that of "accounting for [the Bible's] remarkable adequacy." Here he repeated the standard Protestant arguments from the eighteenth century on design in the natural order. It was impossible to look at the physical world in all of its complexity and conclude that it was not "the product of an intelligent designer." McGrady went further in arguing that evolution not only confirmed the existence of God but also the superiority of the human race, which was part of a process "evolving toward a superorganism of planetary dimensions."[36] In a similar fashion, Talcott Parsons concluded a lengthy chapter, stating that the scientific study of religion by sociologists and psychologists had led to the "overwhelming impression of the fundamental importance of religion in human affairs." The view that reduced religion to the "ignorance and superstition of a prescientific age" was, in Talcott's estimation, "definitely in error."[37] The consensus of these books, then, was that religious convictions mattered. American universities needed to give more attention to subjects where theological concerns normally emerged, such as in the humanities. Also, natural and social scientists also needed to include religion in their studies.

George F. Thomas, who wrote the first chapter for *Religious Perspectives in College Teaching,* summarized best the rationale for including religion and theology in higher education which undergirded each of these books. In Thomas's estimate, western civilization was in a state of moral decay. And this decline reflected a spiritual and cultural crisis of profound significance. Not only had the West witnessed the brutality of two world wars, but the Christian outlook upon which European and American culture had been built was disappearing. Secularization in the forms of scientism and academic specialization had taken an especially hard toll on higher education. Thomas's complaint was not so much that the culture of the academy was hostile to religion as it was that scholars were simply indifferent to ultimate concerns. Under the influence of scientific inquiry and technical mastery American learning had become all too "this-worldly." Graduates of universities and colleges may have had adequate training in a variety of disciplines, but they lacked "religious commitments," "ethical and political convictions," and a "clear purpose or sense of direction." Thus, in order to avoid robbing "our American democracy of its higher meaning" and dehumanizing "the lives of our children and their children," educators needed to renew their religious faith and "make it the basis of [their] teaching." While Thomas conceded the importance of academic freedom and of scholarly expertise in the mission of the university, he still thought it impossible, if not absurd, to teach all subjects without reference to religious and moral presuppositions. His argument was no front for a fundamentalist takeover of the university. "We are arguing," he declared, "for a genuinely 'liberal university' which would not in the name of neutrality evade the ultimate issues but would bring them into the open."[38]

Thomas's point differed little from what mainline Protestant theologians were saying about the importance of religion for correcting the faults of American higher education. But unlike fifty years earlier, when church leaders sensed their marginality to university education and saw little wrong with the new emphasis on research and scientific method, these Protestant educators were now critical of American higher education in ways that would have surprised a prior generation of church leaders. Even more startling was how their sentiments were increasingly winning the day. To be sure, Protestants were not responsible for showing the vulnerability of the university but rather were echoing a humanistic critique of higher education more generally. Still, the change in outlook regarding the university and its ways was as remarkable as the new eagerness to bring theology back into American higher learning.

Evidence of this enthusiasm came in a telling way from none other than Nathan M. Pusey, president of Harvard University. In an address given at the 1953 opening convocation of Harvard Divinity School and later published in *Harper's,* Pusey expressed a general commitment to theological studies, but did so in words that gratified Harvard's divinity faculty.[39] "It is my very sincere hope," Pusey asserted, "that theological studies can here be given a fresh impetus and a new life within this University." Theology's importance stemmed from its answers to life's "deepest hungers and need." The tie between theology and the ministry also did not alarm Pusey. He hoped that by fostering theology Harvard would contribute to the training of "dedicated young men coming into the ministry" who would lead the way in creating a "new and more Christian society."[40]

Aside from Pusey's conspicuous hospitality to theology, his remarks strikingly repudiated the conception of religion and higher education forged by the educational reformers who led the way in creating the research university. Here Pusey took dead aim at his predecessor, Charles W. Eliot. While conceding that Eliot's generation of educators were men of great faith, in the light of twentieth-century history Pusey found their "easy optimism unpalatable." That earlier faith had no place for "metaphysical complexities or magical rites." Pusey even speculated that Eliot would have deemed the doctrine of Christ coming into the world to save sinners to be "so much twaddle." But it had become "frighteningly clear that if you try to ignore metaphysical considerations" they would eventually rise up "in perverted and distorted forms to mock" your efforts. In fact, Eliot "was wrong" to eschew metaphysics "by escaping into a formless empyrean of good will." Christianity was one of the great "vehicles for holding and transmitting truth" from one generation to the next. And what American universities needed was not a religion for the future but a religion of the present. We need, Pusey insisted, to keep "a firm grasp on the spiritual treasure" handed down by the Christian tradition, and "to wrestle more vigorously toward a fresh understanding of 'first things.'"[41] Though this statement concerning the importance of religion may not have deciphered exactly how theology would be integrated into the university, it explicitly vindicated the efforts of Protestant educators.

Theology may not have fully recovered her royal status as queen of the sciences, but at least she had been promoted from campus minister to assistant professor.

Whatever Happened to Theology?

In 1975 the editors of *Christianity and Crisis,* the periodical founded in part by Reinhold Niebuhr to provide an outlet for a theological alternative to liberal Protestant theology, dedicated a whole issue to the question, "Whatever Happened to Theology?" At one of their regular meetings, the editors discovered that when they turned from social, economic, and political matters to theology the conversation moved from a "brisk and animated" pace to deadly silence.[42] The symposium turned into a variation on the theme of why there were no longer public theologians of the stature of Reinhold Niebuhr. One of the contributors, Van A. Harvey, then in the religious studies department at the University of Pennsylvania, traced theology's demise to the position of theologians within the specialization and professionalization of knowledge set in motion and nurtured by the research university. The subject matter of theology was ill-suited to the compartmentalization of knowledge in higher learning, Harvey argued. Some theologians like a Niebuhr or a Tillich of "monumental intellect" could speak intelligibly to the academic community. But when produced "by hundreds of average minds" theology acquired the "ephemeral nature of belles lettres."[43]

Yet, from a different perspective the American theological renaissance of the mid-twentieth century did not depend as much upon the genius of theologians who could engage the various disciplines in an intellectually creative way as it did upon the coincidence of American educators turning away from the constraints of professional academic codes and specialized research to a more general and wholistic notion of learning. And this move from specialization to generalization was bound up with the crisis of world war and Cold War. At a time when the very foundation of liberal democracy appeared to be at stake, technical study appeared to distract from the ideals that united Americans with each other and with other societies that valued political freedom. In this context theology did not so much thrive as participate actively in a lively conversation about the nature of human existence and the purpose of human history, a conversation that involved humanists, social scientists, and, to a lesser extent, natural scientists. This development gave mainline Protestant divinity a hearing it had not enjoyed in the United States since the antebellum era. But it also prevented theologians from think-ing critically about their methods and subject matter. Generalities abounded but specifics lagged behind. With the exception of vague ref-erences to the incarnation or the problem of original sin, sometimes with the polish of existentialist terminology, neo-orthodoxy had no "precise doctrinal formulation."[44] For this reason the theological renais-sance was hollow. It depended upon a shift within American learning, not upon the internal resources of American Protestant theology. The answer to the question "Whatever Happened to Theology?" is that American Protestant theology at midcentury was a mirage.[45]

In the short run the theological renaissance was a blessing for the development of religious studies. The public recognition accorded some theologians helped religion professors attract students and justify their budgetary lines to administrators. Furthermore, theology's con-tribution to the recovery of humanistic study and general education gave religious studies more allies within higher education and provided a solution to the problem of where religion fit within the academic dis-ciplines. In addition, the popularity of theological discourse, no matter how unspecialized, was a boon to other scholars in religious studies. As Sydney E. Ahlstrom argued, neo-orthodox thinkers "rescued" the study of the Bible from "the historian's workshop" and assisted the reclamation of specific periods in church history, especially the Puri-tans and Jonathan Edwards. Even if the midcentury theological renais-sance fizzled more than it flared, it contributed to a general confidence among Protestant scholars which showed up in biblical studies and church history.[46]

In the long run, however, by resting on the laurels of the Niebuhr brothers or Tillich, religious studies became dependent on a shaky intel-lectual foundation. Just as theology failed during this era to carve out its own academic niche, so religious studies did not arrive at an under-standing of the teaching and study of religion that would make sense once the virtues of liberal education and the ideals of western civiliza-tion were not so reputable. At a time when religious studies was coming into its own as an academic discipline, not many religion professors were sufficiently foresighted to see the flaws in George F. Thomas's argument for including religion in American universities. Religion departments may not have been sufficient to correct the secular drift of American higher education but, Thomas argued, they were still a neces-sary first step. But this rationale showed that the study of religion was linked more to the spiritual side of Protestant conceptions of higher education than to sturdier scholarly ideals. In fact, Thomas insisted that teaching subjects from a Christian perspective would not be adequate if a professor did not "establish and maintain a truly personal relationship with his students."[47] So in addition to countering secularism, religion faculty still played the part of campus ministers. That phrase carried a lot of the freight of Protestant efforts in campus ministry. In other words, the study of religion and the development of a religious perspective in academic work continued to be part of the Protestant mission to the United States and the nation's leading institutions.[48] But proponents of religion could not explain why acquaintance with religious subjects or spiritual ways of knowing were necessary for what it meant to be college-educated or university-trained. To be sure, some Protestants believed that without a knowledge of religion higher education was inferior. But the most frequently given reason for studying religion was religious, not academic. Advocates for the study of religion believed that students lacked commitment, inspiration, and courage, not that they were deficient in theological and biblical knowledge.

The irony is that the theological renaissance of the 1940s and 1950s contributed to the weak rationale for religious studies. At a time when the stock of religion in the academy was at an all-time high, religion professors could have spent some of their capital to develop better grounds for teaching and studying religion. But they followed the lead of the theologians, showed how religion permeated all areas of study and all walks of life, and thereby failed to carve out a specialized area of research.

SIX

The Good Book for Tough Times

WHEN HARRY EMERSON FOSDICK WROTE *The Modern Use of the Bible* he had in mind a college-educated audience. The book stemmed from the Lyman Beecher Lectures that Fosdick delivered in 1924 at Yale University. His purpose was to show college graduates that the Bible was still worth reading and even revering. Fosdick believed it possible to honor scripture because it sprang from "the noblest elements in our civilization." Nevertheless, he conceded that modern readers were rightfully "bothered" by many things they found in the Bible. "They have to shift their mental gear too suddenly when they turn from their ordinary intellectual processes to the strange ways of thinking" in the biblical texts. Fosdick's way around this intellectual hurdle was to distinguish between the literal teachings of the biblical authors and the "abiding experiences" that lay underneath the Bible's "childlike and primitive" expressions. After all, what was really so ancient as "Blessed are the pure in heart," "God is love," or "Be ye kind one to another"? The only thing that would make these sentiments old and obsolete was a change so monumental in humankind's spiritual experiences as to make men and women indifferent to "love, friendship, and self-sacrifice," and to "desires for peace, for brotherhood, for a kingdom of righteousness upon the earth."[1] In this way, Fosdick argued, the Bible had as much relevance for the well-educated as it did for the common folk who believed in its outmoded cosmology and miraculous stories.

Fosdick's rationale for a modern person's appropriation of the Bible appealed relatively well to American educators. Once the alliance between humanistic studies and religion was forged in the 1930s and 1940s religion professors could readily make the case that studying the Hebrew-Christian scriptures was little different from reading the classic literary and philosophical works of western civilization. As Fosdick argued, the biblical authors treated the same perennial issues of the human condition and the meaning of life as did all great literature. For this reason, various proposals for liberal education from the post–World War II era had little trouble fitting biblical courses into the humanities curriculum.

To take but one example, in the late 1950s the University of Pennsylvania produced a study of the place of religious instruction in humanistic courses for undergraduates, written by Edwin E. Aubrey. The author said the university had an obligation to teach about religious or spiritual values because they were an "integral" part of human experience, having to do with a "person's primary or ultimate meaning." While avoiding indoctrination the Department of Religious Thought, established in 1949, offered a series of courses that featured the Bible: "the development of religion in the Old and New Testament, and advanced courses on Sources for the Life of Christ, and on the Life and Letters of Paul." Aubrey believed such teaching to be fully compatible with the humanists' commitment not to knowledge but to wisdom, "an awareness of the limits of our established knowledge, with concomitant humility, and a recognition that thought is not possible without sensitivity."[2]

At the same time that biblical instructors were joining hands with other scholars in the humanities, a form of biblical scholarship became more prominent in American Protestant circles which would make the ties between the Bible and English literature a bit more complicated. Biblical scholars of a neo-orthodox persuasion were insisting upon the uniqueness of the Hebrew and Christian scriptures to such a degree that the Bible became a collection of writings entirely different from the great works of literature. What was especially important was the discovery of New Testament theology and eschatology. No longer could scholars regard Jesus simply as the fairest flower of humanity. According to Floyd V. Filson, who urged a recovery of biblical theology in New Testament studies, the center of the biblical message was Jesus

Christ whose "career" could only be interpreted as the fulfillment of "the redemptive work of God." Such Christian particularism not only made biblical instruction sectarian in that its intended audience was the community of faith, but it also set the biblical scholar apart. "It is time," Filson asserted, "to be done with the deceptive myth of neutrality." The study of the Bible required "honesty, integrity, fairness, patience, and a sense of . . . limitations," but to engage in such inquiry "without personal response" was out of the question.[3]

As Filson's comments indicate, the study of the Bible in American higher education was surrounded by numerous intellectual obstacles. Was the Bible simply one of the great works of religious imagination? Should it be studied because of its influence upon western culture? Was it simply indicative of the religious and cultural outlook of ancient Near Eastern civilization? And what should student response be to the Bible? Was the inspiration that the Bible yielded the same as that produced by the study of Homer or Shakespeare? Or was reverence for the Bible different from an appreciation of and love for the poetry of Browning? In the period in which religious studies became an established partner in American universities and colleges these questions were rarely addressed. The study of the Bible proceeded apace by professors fully confident that their instruction matched the broader aims of the humanities, at least, if not the university more generally.[4] Failure to address the weighty matter of why and how the Bible should be studied in a public place like the academy, however, exposed the vulnerability of religious studies.

The Word of God

In April 1944 a new religious journal began publication. Its title, *Theology Today,* was certainly not particularly astounding even if theological journals in the twentieth century were harder to find. In fact, not since the University of Chicago's *American Journal of Theology* changed its name to *Journal of Religion* had an academic quarterly been sponsored by mainline Protestants that was devoted to Christian divinity explicitly. Still, what stood out about the new publication was its frank profession of Protestant convictions. The journal's lead editorial began by outlining the mission that the editors believed "God Himself has laid upon them." This mission included setting forth the central realities of Christian faith and life "in clear and appropriate language." Crucial to this task was a rediscovery of the Bible. "God has spoken," the editors wrote, "the eternal silence has been broken; the meaning of existence has been unveiled; the Truth has been made manifest." To be sure, the recovery of the Bible was a task that could not proceed without biblical criticism or safeguarding the rights of intellectual integrity. "But now more than ever," the lead editorial insisted, "the essential unity of the Book stands out in bold relief, and the progressive revelation within it of God's redemptive purpose, which culminated in the life, death, and resurrection of Jesus Christ . . . has been transfused with new meaning." With an editorial purpose like this, *Theology Today* quickly became one of the chief organs for biblical theology, a concentration within biblical studies that stressed the Bible's status as a revelation from God to humanity rather than regarding it, as liberal Protestants had, as a collection of exceptionally pious and inspiring writings.[5]

Four years later another theological journal appeared with similar religious and academic ambitions. Like *Theology Today, Interpretation: A Journal of Bible and Theology* was committed to "the cause of biblical theology."[6] It was designed to be a middle-brow theological quarterly, not "highly technical" or given to the "vagaries of exposition." *Interpretation* would promote "a positive, constructive expression of biblical and theological studies." And like *Theology Today, Interpretation* sprang from "desperate conditions" and "the failure of man's own devices." A "yearning for light from the Bible" marked the whole trend of western culture.[7] If the church were to respond adequately to the problems of the day its ministers needed to "interpret and proclaim the Word of God." The Bible gave the minister "the only authority he has." "He is to lay the Bible mind, the Bible theology, down upon the problems of his people; he is to allow the Bible heritage to speak through him."[8] Along with *Theology Today, Interpretation* signaled the triumph of neo-orthodoxy and the repudiation, even if muted, of liberal Protestantism's high estimation of science, politics, and culture as the means by which the kingdom of God was realized in human history. No longer intimidated by the findings of modern learning, or frustrated by the apparent irrelevance of sacred texts written several millennia before the development of modern societies, the mainline Protestants who edited and wrote for these journals were convinced that the Bible possessed the only real hope for a war-torn world.

Both of these journals sprang directly from ecclesiastical contexts. *Theology Today* came out of Princeton Theological Seminary and had strong ties to the northern Presbyterian Church. *Interpretation* succeeded the *Union Seminary Review* and drew upon academics and ministers within the southern Presbyterian Church, especially those with links to Union Theological Seminary in Richmond, Virginia.[9] Yet, for all of their ecclesiastical affiliations these journals were also academically respectable, partly because of their mainline Protestant patronage, and also because the teaching and study of religion in American colleges and universities was so heavily oriented toward Protestant divinity and churches. For instance, *Theology Today*'s editorial council included H. Richard Niebuhr. It also included a number of faculty in the humanities from Princeton University, the University of Pennsylvania, and Davidson College.[10] At the same time, the contributors to both journals were primarily faculty at Protestant seminaries, but a sizable minority also taught religion at denominational colleges and private and state universities.[11] Even though some Protestants might dismiss the neo-orthodox theology of Karl Barth as a "purely authoritarian religion,"[12] the preponderance of courses in the Bible within religious studies programs and the training of religion professors at Protestant seminaries and divinity schools meant that undergraduates at public and private institutions would encounter lectures, readings, and faculty who espoused in some way the religious outlook that these journals represented.

At times the emphasis upon the Bible as the word of God by religion faculty could be extreme. For instance, Joseph Haroutunian, who taught at Wellesley before moving to McCormick Theological Seminary and then across town to the divinity school at the University of Chicago, in the third issue of *Interpretation* expressed the confessional character of neo-orthodox biblical theology with apparent disregard for academic etiquette. "The primary and perennial function of the Bible is to bring man into the presence of God," he wrote. "The Bible confronts man with God who is the Almighty Custodian of inviolable truth." Haroutunian rarely paused to answer what such a subject was doing in the classrooms of colleges and universities without ecclesiastical affiliation. But upon closer inspection his confession of faith in the Bible had a humanistic side that made the study of the Bible accessible to students who did not believe in God. Haroutunian explained that the Bible taught that "a decision between right and wrong" was one made in "the presence of God," an explanation that underscored the weightiness of all ethical decisions that confronted believers and nonbelievers alike. "The biblical conception of history," he added, grew directly out of the perception that the chief problem of human existence was moral. The phrase "the law of God in contrast with man's behavior" was Haroutunian's way of raising the stakes of human existence. Still, he moved from the more general statement of the importance of ethics for all people to the explicitly church-bound claim that grounded human morality in a right "doctrine of God" against "human idolatry."[13] Such statements assumed the scholar's audience was exclusively Christian and set up real problems for teaching the Bible to non-Christian students.

G. Ernest Wright, a colleague of Haroutunian at McCormick Theological Seminary, was better at making the aims of biblical theology accessible to a wider audience. The Bible's true significance for Wright was its "proclamation of the word of the nature of God and the meaning of human existence." As such the Bible offered solutions to the most profound problems of life. In fact, Wright believed that the biblical writings spoke to the same questions that had animated the great authors and philosophers of the West. Plato and other Greek philosophers addressed the problem of the good life and how men and woman could attain it. But their answers were flawed because they laid too much hope in human reason and failed to take into account the irrationality of human existence. Consequently, the concerns of biblical literature went to the deeper problem of "human tragedies which have resulted from the misuse of . . . freedom" and how it was possible for men and women to live the good life. The chief aim of biblical study was to bring students to an understanding of the book's solutions to life's problems, and to compare those answers with other religions and philosophies. The study of the Bible for Wright still harbored a certain degree of advocacy; the professor, he believed, should be committed to the truths of the Hebrew and Christian scriptures. But Wright, like other advocates of biblical theology, was able to fit the themes of his teaching into the broader questions addressed in other courses in the humanities.[14]

Floyd V. Filson, who also taught at McCormick Seminary with Wright, tried like his colleague to make the study of biblical theology compatible with the larger aims of higher education. As opposed to the liberal approach in biblical studies, which explored questions of text, grammar, authorship, and literary qualities, and, hence, the uniqueness of each book within the Bible, biblical theology took dead aim at the unity of scripture. "These books," Filson wrote, "rightly deserve special grouping" because they "put us in touch with the basic Christian heritage." From the perspective of biblical theology, the Bible also expressed one basic theme, whether in the Old or New Testament, which stressed "the reality and doings of God." Starting with such an attitude toward the Bible meant that biblical scholarship would highlight the historical Jesus, the centrality of the cross, and the resurrection of Christ. As biased as this approach to the Bible might be, Filson still argued for its value in generic terms. The Bible "reports frankly the wickedness and perversity of man and portrays the corruption of individual character and national life." Such a portrait proved the book to be "a realistic document" that did not hide "man's failure and need." Even so, the sacred writings conveyed a sense of trust and hope, not despair. "Man does not know all; he is often baffled and perplexed." But he could go forward "in hope and walk by faith" because God had acted in human history.[15]

For as explicitly Christian and theological as proponents of biblical theology were, they held their own within the ranks of religion faculty and dominated the pages of the *Journal of Bible and Religion,* the chief outlet for academics who taught religion in colleges and universities.[16] As late as 1957 the president of the National Association of Biblical Instructors, A. Roy Eckardt, department chair at Lehigh University, could speak in his presidential address of religion's "strangeness" in the university curriculum. The oddity of religion stemmed not simply from questions of religious commitment versus disinterested inquiry, or the different ties that bound church communities and the academic guild, though Eckardt acknowledged these concerns. Rather, the strangeness of religious studies stemmed from the subject of its teaching and research, namely, "a word from the God beyond gods." Religion departments, according to Eckardt, served "as critical guardian against the easy habit of idolatrizing particular human insights into the nature of truth." For this reason, a religion based upon divine revelation did not quite fit in the university even though its presence brought welcome benefits. "Religion remains in the world yet not of the world, in the university yet not of the university." In the kingdom of God, Christ would be "the invisible logos of every university." But until the true kingdom of God was established, "the strangeness of religion . . . is inevitable."[17] Though Eckardt's perspective on the teaching and study of religion may not have been shared by all, it did represent the influence of neo-orthodoxy and biblical theology upon a significant wing of religious studies. Indeed, biblical theology provided the overarching purpose for teaching the Bible from the 1940s into the 1960s if only because it supplied order to a field of scholarship that through literary and historical studies could not give unity to the diversity of writings in the Hebrew and Christian scriptures.[18] Biblical theology, in effect, functioned within religious studies as the equivalent of general education within the humanities.

Not all religion professors were comfortable with rhetoric such as Eckardt's. Consequently, charges of sectarianism, anti-intellectualism, dogmatism, and fundamentalism lurked in the background or just below the surface.[19] Proponents of biblical theology in the university classroom answered these criticisms not only by using the more general humanistic themes such as the meaning of existence and the problem of evil. Eckardt himself pointed to religion's transcendence and divine authority as a useful buttress to academic freedom by claiming that such liberty was "grounded in the Truth by which religion too is judged."[20] G. Ernest Wright defended the claims of biblical theology on the grounds that it reflected good scholarship. "The accuracy of this attempt to draw out" the unity of the Bible through "the redemptive purposes of God," he argued, "has been confirmed by both form and literary criticism."[21] Meanwhile, George M. Gibson, a pastor ministering in the University of Chicago's neighborhood, was quick to distinguish neo-orthodoxy and the insights of biblical theology from fundamentalism. The former began with a recognition of the limitations of "naturalistic intellectualism" and moved forward to a recovery of "the classic truths of Christianity and their illumination of the problem of human existence." Along the way biblical theologians "were fully conversant with the contributions of modern science."[22] Floyd V. Filson also attempted to dodge the danger of faith replacing sound scholarship by arguing that "intelligent study is not complete until it brings its work into relation to faith and life." Good scholarship and personal faith, therefore, were not mutually exclusive or even necessarily "hostile to each other." Furthermore, owing to the Bible's treatment of ultimate issues, the teaching of biblical theology "inevitably" combined "intelligent study and responsible personal attitude."[23]

Evidence of just such a synthesis of biblical religion and first-rate scholarship was not hard to find. Though he was an archaeologist and taught at Johns Hopkins University in ancient Near Eastern studies, William Foxwell Albright demonstrated how readily the university world would tolerate claims for the Bible's divine status. His work also exhibits the convergence of neo-orthodoxy, humanistic studies, and fears about the fate of western civilization by which biblical and theological studies secured a foothold for religion as an academic discipline. Albright described himself as a positivist, but his work was not overly technical and actually connected well with the 1940s revival of the humanities. He leavened his lectures with broad overviews of the rise and fall of ancient civilizations, and advocated the superiority of western culture by appealing to the tradition of "classical Christian humanism." Archaeological investigation also allowed Albright to identify with the neo-orthodox convictions of Reinhold Niebuhr and supply evidence for neo-orthodoxy's middle-ground understanding of the Bible's import, a view that avoided the extremes of fundamentalist literalism and liberal Protestant reductionism.[24] His siding with Niebuhr was perhaps nowhere more evident than when Albright would jump from the history of ancient Israel to twentieth-century America. From Albright's perspective, the monotheism of Judaism and Christianity was superior to pagan religions, and the Judeo-Christian tradition was the bedrock of America and the West. "Whatever may have been the individual weaknesses of this or that theologian," Albright asserted, "the theology and ethics of the Judeo-Christian tradition are basic to our modern Western way of life. The Ten Commandments cannot be violated with impunity by any people or by any ideological group," whether fascists to the right or communists to the left.[25]

As Bruce Kuklick notes, the fact that Albright's "sectarian" beliefs were common currency at one of America's premier universities shows that religion was never completely down and out in the academy.[26] But even more significant is what Albright's revealed about the broad appeal of the neo-orthodox conception of the Bible and the privileged position of mainline Protestantism among American educators. If the university could count on the Christian and Hebrew scriptures to combat both secularism at home and totalitarianism abroad, then the Bible was a welcome addition to the university, no matter how sectarian its teachers could sound.

For most members of the religious studies establishment and for many university and college administrators, the arguments of biblical theologians made sufficient sense, if the establishment of religion departments in the two decades after World War II is any indication. No one seriously questioned the legitimacy of biblical theology in the teaching and study of religion. As such, biblical theology served a "useful psychological purpose" by saving individuals from "inner crises, while the world falls to pieces upon them."[27] Proponents of this approach themselves were less reductionistic in accounting for the appeal of biblical studies. Regarding the Bible as the word of God gave professors leverage with students. It took the Bible out of the category of great literature and, in the words of Virginia Corwin of Smith College, restored it to its place as "a great mountain, unique and dominant over our history."[28] Still, however effective biblical theology was in the classroom or in the students' personal lives, it thrived in the field of religious studies chiefly because of the widespread assumption that the Bible was special. As long as proponents of biblical theology did not make the mistake of fundamentalists by condemning liberalism, and as long as they remained in the Protestant mainline's good graces, their approach to the Bible, while perhaps sectarian, was welcome. In the words of Amos N. Wilder, though biblical theology fell properly under the heading "theological study of the Bible," its contribution was worthwhile because it brought to light "the fullest significance of the contents of the Bible."[29]

A Repository of Religious Experience

Although a resurgent interest in Christian themes popularized by the neo-orthodoxy and a more general appeal of existentialism in the humanities provided biblical theology with cover in intellectual circles, its churchly character made necessary more academically rigorous approaches to biblical studies. Consequently, older liberal Protestant methods of biblical scholarship continued to be useful for professors in many religion departments. As Thomas S. Kepler, professor of New Testament at Oberlin College, explained his pedagogical outlook, lower and higher criticism of the Bible still provided constructive results. In the former, biblical scholars were concerned with "the uncorrupted text of the original manuscript," a task that united all students of the Bible from agnostics to fundamentalists. Higher criticism pursued the reasons behind a particular biblical text, its author, date, audience, sources, editors, and cultural and religious significance. The crucial difference between Kepler's approach and that of biblical theology was the degree to which a scholar regarded the Bible as the word of God or special revelation. Kepler preferred to be as objective as possible and taught the Bible "*primarily* in a descriptive fashion." This meant describing first the type of literature into which each particular text in the Bible fell. Closely connected with discovering a writing's genre was attention to the different kinds of religious ideas found in the Hebrew and Christian scriptures. For instance, Old Testament apocalyptic writing reflected the influence of Persian thought, while creation narratives were indebted to Babylonian ideas. Kepler taught the New Testament in a similar way by demonstrating the Greek and Jewish influences upon the various writings, and how those texts also reflected different theological perspectives in the early church. To be sure, the liberal approach included some treatment of the Bible's "suggestions for contemporary living." But the chasm between the world of the Bible, "a civilization which was nomadic, agricultural, of the handicraft stage," and the twentieth century, "a machine age, a period of scientific development," meant that biblical teaching would have to be tested before being applied to everyday life. "Do the ideas of a particular book *work*, do they speak to our lives, are they *pragmatic?*"[30] Such criteria would likely lead to the conclusion that the Bible was not the word of God but only contained it here and there.

One of the ideas found in the Bible that Kepler found "helpful and intelligent for the modern man" was the spirit and teaching of Christ. Liberal Protestants had long regarded Jesus's ethical ideals to be the greatest reason for studying a book that appeared to be so antiquated. In a subsequent article, Kepler noted the problem of modernizing Jesus. Was Jesus anything more than a historical personality "who once lived in Palestine, a good man to be sure, but certainly not one with much insight into twentieth-century problems"? Kepler felt the force of this question but believed that biblical criticism provided a remedy. Historical criticism of the New Testament along with "textual critical methods" revealed the "real Jesus" and the proper way of modernizing his precepts. While for some these techniques reduced Jesus simply to a first-century Palestinian teacher of ethics whom people of the Christian faith venerated, Kepler believed that scholarly methods preserved the uniqueness and relevance of Jesus. The real problem, then, was "not so much the *modernizing* of Jesus" but instead "*learning how to catch up* with His insights in the modern world!"[31]

In the hands of liberal Protestant biblical scholars, Jesus not only emerged as relevant for modern times but also as a figure of therapeutic genius. In the words of Lucetta Mowry, who taught Bible at Wellesley College, the "new and revolutionary ethic" exemplified by Jesus stemmed from his living among people and his use of "personal and direct forms of communication in a practical manner to convey his understanding of the divine will to the individual's dilemma and problem." Mowry contrasted this ethic with John the Baptist's call for repentance. While John threatened his listeners with divine judgment and spoke within the "framework of an intense eschatological crisis," Jesus did not self-righteously abandon sinners "to join the community of saints" but rather made "a positive adjustment of life itself." In effect, John represented the climax of the old order of the Old Testament law with its prohibitions and punishments while Jesus instituted the new order of love.[32] Gone from this understanding of the New Testament was the neo-orthodox sense of crisis, God's intervention into history through saving acts, and a Jesus who suffered on the cross and would one day function as the righteous judge of the human race. For Mowry, as for many liberal Protestants, Jesus continued to command respect and allegiance because of his superior ethical outlook, not because he was connected in some way with a new epoch in salvation history.

While occasionally the differences between liberal and neo-orthodox biblical scholars were only implicit, in other cases they could be direct, though always mild-mannered. For instance, Ralph W. Odom, chaplain and chair of the department of religion at Colorado Women's College, believed that a sufficiently scholarly and critical approach to the sayings and teachings of Jesus led to doubts that "eschatologists are right in their logic that Jesus must have been an apocalyptist because the early church so understood him." Odom's method included the standard techniques of higher criticism—examining the sources, weighing the authenticity, and putting into cultural context the teachings of Jesus recorded in the synoptic gospels. But as much as this kind of study produced "the recognition that Jesus . . . must be understood in the context of his own day," liberal Protestant scholars like Odom could never repudiate the uniqueness and superiority of Jesus. For some of the more radical students of the New Testament, higher criticism not only transformed the Bible from the word of God into the words of men, but reduced Jesus to simply one prophet in a line of Jewish sages who attracted a rather significant following but was surely not God incarnate. For the most part, however, while the liberal approach relied on scientific methods, its case for the uniqueness of Jesus was assumed rather than proved. Odom himself concluded that Jesus emerged from critical study with the stature of a genius whose teaching provided "abiding content" and still had "relevance for our day."[33] This upbeat conclusion was useful with students already sympathetic to Christianity as many undergraduates were. But its sentimental attachment to Jesus, in the face of scholarship that could easily lead to much more damaging conclusions, did not yield a framework for teaching and studying the Bible that could withstand an environment more hostile than that of the postwar religious revival.[34]

Yet, despite Protestant reverence for Jesus, the Life and Teachings of Jesus was not the only course taught by biblical scholars in religion departments. Some institutions offered a full range of biblical instruction, very similar to the curriculum at Protestant seminaries. And when scholars turned to other biblical subjects, the sentimentality so characteristic of liberal Protestant attachments to Jesus was less evident.

A historical approach to the Bible that gave full attention to the human characteristics of the text was more akin to the kind of literary studies undertaken by other scholars in the humanities. For instance, Robert T. Anderson, who taught at Michigan State University, studied the influence of the desert on the religion of the Israelites. The barrenness of the desert made it natural for Israel to conceive of God as a great "Provider" and also explained why water would take on symbolic significance in Jewish rites and ceremonies.[35] Another scholar of Old Testament literature, Lawrence E. Toombs of Drew University, located the origins of Israelite religion partly in the myth patterns of ancient Near Eastern societies. He argued that in the pivotal event of Old Testament history, the Exodus where the Israelites were delivered out of Egyptian bondage, biblical writers borrowed freely from the mythology of surrounding peoples while also mythologizing their own historical experience in leaving Egypt for the wilderness.[36] Rather than emphasizing the divine origins or religious significance of the Bible, as neo-orthodox scholars did, liberal Protestant biblical studies treated the Bible like it was any other collection of ancient writings.

New Testament scholarship followed along the similar lines. In some cases this approach to the Bible could pursue such low-voltage issues as determining the author of a particular book in scripture. Eric C. Titus, professor at the Claremont School of Theology, indicated that students in his classes might be expected to evaluate whether the apostle Paul was the actual author of the thirteenth chapter of 1 Corinthians. Various literary and ideological reasons led him to believe that the chapter was "an interpolation" made by an editor sometime at the end of the first century.[37] Another kind of scholarship, without much chance of causing controversy, was a word study. Alvin A. Ahern, who taught religion at Greenville College, employed such an approach in his teaching on the Epistle to the Hebrews, where he examined the meaning of the Greek word for perfection, and teased out its ethical implications for students.[38] Pinpointing the human as opposed to the divine origins of scripture became threatening to believing students when such topics as the resurrection of Christ came up in the classroom. The way liberal Protestant scholars explained this bit of history associated with Jesus was the fairly conventional nineteenth-century practice of distinguishing literal historical facts from symbols of "spiritual life," as John L. Cheek, religion professor at Albion College, did. He conceded that the older liberal Protestant dualism of miracles versus natural phenomena could not be attributed to the early church and so commended the vigor of early Jewish forms of faith. Still, Cheek was aware that only fundamentalists believed in a real resurrection and would only go so far as trying to incorporate an actual physical appearance of Jesus after his death with the hypothesis that Christ's disciples merely experienced a vision of him.[39]

Nevertheless, as much as liberal Protestants attempted to study the Bible with more academic rigor, treating it more as the product of ancient religions than the canon of divine revelation, they continued to display a reverential attitude toward the Hebrew and Christian scriptures that went beyond, for example, a classicist's love of *The Odyssey*. Generally speaking, liberal Protestant study of the Bible was still supposed to produce both an intellectual awareness of the book's origins and significance and a spiritual regard for the Bible's content. The search for the author of 1 Corinthians 13 was more than an example of historical and literary scholarship. It also was a means to discovering the "inspiring" qualities of Paul's "panegyric on love."[40] Likewise, the Book of Hebrews' teaching on perfection suggested "a metaphysical basis for a teleological Christian ethics of self-realization whose social implications" for students were "far-reaching."[41] Even the practice of form criticism of the Old Testament had a religious effect upon its students. It not only unearthed the oral traditions out of which the Jewish canon emerged, but it also led to a better understanding of the Old Testament as Holy Scripture of both Judaism and Christianity which had "normative significance for faith and life."[42]

Even in those cases where scholars did not feel constrained to add a pious flourish to their critical study of the Bible, the academic study of religion gave preference and therefore assumed the authoritative status of the particular sacred books of Christianity and Judaism, thus treating as less significant the religious writings of Muslims, Hindus, and Buddhists. Liberal Protestant scholarship on the Bible had the advantage of being able to employ the same techniques that other scholars in the humanities used to study ancient texts. This methodological similarity gave biblical studies, which was the core of most religion departments, the aura of an intellectual exercise every bit as academic as the study of Shakespeare, Plato, or Jefferson. What is more, the academic rigor of higher critical approaches to the Bible made it easier to tolerate neo-orthodox scholars within the academy even though the latter were more overtly theological and churchly in their orientation than other biblical scholars. But in the end liberal Protestants were just as biased toward the Christian faith and the church as the neo-orthodox in that they started with the Bible as the point of reference for academic inquiry. The Bible, after all, was the church's book, and its status within the Christian community depended upon notions of divine revelation even if the scholars who taught in religion departments hedged on the matter of the book's sacred origins. The question of why the Bible was unique or why it deserved to be studied more than other Christian or non-Christian writings rarely came up. The Bible's value was simply assumed, an assumption derived more from the allegiance of biblical scholars to the Christian church and its historic influence than from academic standards, per se. As University of Chicago Divinity School professor Robert W. Funk observed in 1976 in his presidential address before the Society of Biblical Literature, "without the benefit of the scriptural ploy" American biblical scholars were hard-pressed "to justify their existence in the secular university."[43] That comment was no less true twenty-five years earlier when religious studies came into its own as a serious academic enterprise.

Why Study the Bible?

Whether they could justify their existence satisfactorily or not, in the years after World War II biblical scholars charged ahead with reasons for studying the Bible which contributed to the general expansion of religion as an academic discipline within higher education in the United States. The overlap between the religious studies curriculum and that of the Protestant divinity school was almost complete and the Bible, a staple of Protestant divinity, was preeminent in the religion department. A description of an introductory course in religion from A. Roy Eckardt reveals the dependence of religious studies on Protestant faith and practice and the centrality of courses in the Bible. "Imagine a diagram of a pyramid consisting of five levels, labeled beginning at the bottom . . . history of religion, Old Testament Judaism, First Century Christianity, Protestant Christian faith."[44] That pyramid contained the basics of a religious studies program and its movement from the bottom, the history of religions, to the apex, Protestantism, said a good deal about what religious studies faculty believed important for a successful curriculum.

Perhaps even more revealing was Eckardt's statement of the purpose of such instruction. Using the pious abstractions that had been available for at least a half century, Eckardt wrote that the goal of religious studies was "to aid in the promotion of intelligent Christian faith and life." That statement had some of the cadence of a William Rainey Harper or a Charles Foster Kent who worked at a time when generic Christian vocabulary had a better chance of fitting with the mood of an academy under the sway of science. But Eckardt also sounded a new note, one that trumpeted the confidence of mainline Protestant leaders who believed the study of religion in general, and the Bible specifically, had a great deal more to offer in a world not quite as sure of its destination as that of Harper's or Kent's generation. "We do our best to teach the Bible in terms of what the Bible teaches," Eckardt wrote. Too often the Bible was taught as "mere genealogy, military history, sociology, and biography." Eckardt agreed that the Bible was biography, but of God rather than of men. As if boasting, he bellowed, "we teach the Bible as a biography of the Lord of history, who holds the destiny of men and nations in the palm of his hand, is working out his sublime purposes in love and in judgment, and who has performed a mighty act for the redemption of men in his only begotten son."[45] Rhetoric like that would not have been heard three decades earlier when Protestants were struggling to have the Bible taught at colleges and universities. Nor would it last beyond another fifteen years or so when the assumed superiority of Protestantism and the presumptuous identification of Protestant divinity with the study of religion finally caught up with the field. But for that brief period of roughly twenty years after World War II Protestants could be far more explicit in expressing religious convictions as scholarly communication. And biblical scholars led the way.

To be sure, not all religion faculty were as arch in pronouncing the purpose of their labors. Some could still fit the teaching of the Bible under the umbrella of the humanities or, at least, try. J. Allen Easley, dean of Wake Forest College's school of religion, stressed that as much as religion scholars properly taught the Bible's religious content, "we cannot afford to overlook its literary character." Easley's efforts in this vein were not entirely successful because he could not resist turning to the parable of the prodigal son into "an interpretation of God and his ways," a story of "universal concern."[46] In her presidential address before the 1952 convention of the National Association of Biblical Instructors, Mary Frances Thelen, professor at Randolph-Macon College, also appealed to the Bible's affinities with the humanities. In the liberal arts curriculum "the core courses in history, literature, philosophy, and the Bible," she said, "seek to emancipate the student from the narrow outlook of the twentieth century and to make him free of the whole history of western culture."[47] Winston L. King, chaplain and professor of philosophy and religion at Grinnell College, appealed to the humanities a little more obliquely, if not more sarcastically, than his colleagues. He was concerned about the problems of teaching biblical eschatology to freshmen who knew virtually nothing about the contents of the Bible and whose outlook was permeated by a "scientistic-naturalistic attitude." Freshmen also suffered from "perennial optimism" and so rarely considered a pessimistic thought about "the nature of man, the progress of science, or the future of the human race." Such were the obstacles of teaching Jewish and early Christian eschatology to undergraduates, obstacles that were equally high for other professors in the humanities. Still, while the humanistic rationale gave biblical instruction a wider appeal, Bible professors could not help relying upon an interest among students for which other humanities faculty longed. King believed that the eschatological perspective of the biblical writers was not altogether different from the undergraduates' instinct that humankind's ultimate hope was in God, not the human race.[48]

During the 1950s, appeals by religion faculty to the Bible as a classic in western literature or to the affinities between religious studies and the humanities were less common once the institutional existence of religion departments was more secure. Virginia Corwin, for example, in her 1951 presidential address before the National Association of Biblical Instructors (NABI), spoke of having to avoid "the Scylla of moralism and piousness" and the "Charybdis of a reductionist approach." This meant that students should come away from the study of the Bible with the idea that its writers "believed themselves to have intercourse with God." Successful instruction in the Bible, she concluded, would show "the eternal God confronting men in their hopes, their decisions, their failures, and their touching triumphs." This was the only way that the "Bible itself can speak to our students."[49] Another officer of the association, O. R. Sellers, dean of McCormick Theological Seminary, appeared to be equally oblivious to the assumptions behind biblical instruction, assumptions that made the Bible unlike any other text studied in the university. "It is incumbent upon us," he told fellow members of NABI, that unless "we believe the Bible in a unique sense to be the Word of God we might as well be following some more lucrative calling."[50] Some academics, less compelled by Sellers's claims for the Bible's uniqueness, might have wondered whether he and other religion professors should have been drawing a paycheck at all if the religious studies establishment could not make a better case for teaching the Bible in the supposedly hostile environment of the university.

Yet, few if any voices were raised against what in twenty years would become a crass example of religious sectarianism. If anything, as William F. Buckley's *God and Man at Yale* indicated, biblical studies was bland, secular, and not sufficiently Christian. In his comments on the most popular religion course at the New Haven institution, Buckley complained that Sidney Lovett's survey of the Old Testament did not "proselytize the Christian faith" or even "*teach* religion at all."

Buckley conceded that Lovett's personal religiosity was indeed "contagious" and that many students, impressed by the professor's "faith and goodness," had taken an interest in religion, even to the point of going on to divinity school. Still, Buckley's point was that courses in the Bible did not make Yale a religious place—no more than teaching a course on *Das Kapital* made the department of economics a hotbed of Marxism.[51] Some could legitimately object to courses that gave professors an outlet for their personal religious devotion. Such teaching was, no doubt, out of character with the religious diversity, at least on paper, of the student body. Just as disconcerting was the idea that teaching a particular religious text primarily from the standpoint of religious experience, rather than from that of historical, cultural, social, or intellectual significance, was an acceptable academic practice at a premier American university. But what made the study of the Bible hardest in the modern university was that such scholarship relied, at least in part, upon norms established by the church rather than the academy. The uniqueness of the Hebrew and Christian scriptures, after all, stemmed from the reverence Jews and Christians showed to them, not because they were philosophically or aesthetically superior.[52] Buckley's indictment of religion at Yale ironically confirmed the point that biblical studies was still beholden to the spiritual and devotional ends of mainstream Protestantism, not the intellectual rigor of critical thought or the university's criteria of what it meant to be learned.

Furthermore, reactions to Buckley's critique from Yale's WASP leadership explain why the study of the Bible could flourish in religion departments without hard questions being asked. McGeorge Bundy, Yale class of 1940 and professor at Harvard, wrote a review of Buckley's book for the *Atlantic* and questioned the younger Yale graduate's character, calling him a "violent, unbalanced, and twisted young man." Bundy also had difficulty understanding Buckley's presumptuousness. How dare an "ardent Roman Catholic" define what was acceptable religious belief for Yale University. Part of the explanation for Bundy's reaction to Buckley's temerity came from the committee appointed to look into the spiritual and political condition of Yale. That body, chaired by Henry Sloane Coffin, a prominent Presbyterian pastor in New York City and president of Union Theological Seminary, found that Yale "is a Puritan and Protestant institution by its heritage." The committee also discovered that religious life at the university was "deeper and richer than it has been in many years."[53] Whether Coffin's committee was simply trying to save face is hard to tell. But the response to Buckley from Yale's administration and prominent alumni indicates how widely accepted the Protestant character of the best and most demanding universities in the United States was. If universities such as Yale needed to defend themselves from the accusation of irreligion and did so by appealing to their Protestant heritage, then the climate in American learning in the decade after World War II was not one that would raise difficult questions about the propriety of biblical studies.[54]

One last consideration that helps to put the study of the Bible in some perspective was the mood of postwar American culture. Unlike an earlier era, when such Protestants as William Rainey Harper or Charles Foster Kent were simply trying to gain recognition for the academic study of the Bible in a setting where science promised more happiness and prosperity than traditional religion seemed to offer, the period after World War II was clearly hospitable to religion. Not only could neo-orthodox theologians make the cover of America's popular weekly magazines or presidents of America's best universities intone about the need for Christianity if western civilization (and their own institution's stake in preserving that culture) were to survive. These were also the years of a religious revival that, in addition to launching the career of Billy Graham, the most recent expression of revivalistic Protestantism, also benefited mainline Protestant churches. As much as this revival, whether mainline or evangelical Protestant, tapped a generic civic faith that World War II and the Cold War nurtured, it did allow professors who taught Bible to undergraduate students, whether at Yale or some state universities, to make claims about the Hebrew and Christian scripture's uniqueness, sacredness, and spiritual significance which if uttered by scholars only a decade and a half later might be deemed at least sectarian if not fundamentalist. So wide was the search for a consensus along biblical grounds that it could lead to such hollow platitudes as president-elect Dwight D. Eisenhower's that the United States' form of government was founded on a "deeply felt religious faith." While Eisenhower admitted that he did not care what that faith was—a remark often lampooned—he added that in America that profound faith was "the Judeo-Christian concept."[55]

But these cultural supports for biblical studies in the long run proved to be a flimsy intellectual foundation upon which to build either the field of biblical scholarship specifically or the discipline of religious studies more generally. As closely tied as the teaching and study of the Bible were to the institutions of mainline Protestant divinity, both the churches and the seminaries, so would the field's fall be precipitous once mainstream Protestantism came under scrutiny in the 1960s. Now biblical scholarship in the university progresses only at the mercy of ancient Near Eastern studies departments or in fear that its Protestant origins will be discovered.[56] But, for a brief period in the twentieth century, biblical studies flourished in ways that Harper and Kent could never have imagined, even functioning as the mouthpiece for American Protestantism's theological renaissance.

SEVEN

Church History for the Nation

IN 1962 HENRY F. MAY, an American intellectual historian at the University of California at Berkeley, delivered a paper at the American Studies Association's annual meeting on the recovery of American religious history. He eventually submitted that essay to the *American Historical Review* (*AHR*), the leading journal of historians in the United States, which published it in 1964. Still, May's assessment of the work being produced on the history of religion in America, as he later recalled, received a "very mixed reaction" from the *AHR*'s readers. In fact, the essay "affronted and upset" some critics who denied May's conclusions about the connection between the religious revival the country was experiencing and the academy's recovery of religious history.[1] Despite these reactions, the essay became a benchmark for evaluating the history of American religion. It may even have been responsible for unleashing the flood of literature on religious history that has poured out of university and trade presses since 1970.[2] May's essay's significance, as most later religious historians would have it, was the secular academy's discovery of religion's importance for understanding American society. In May's own words, "the recovery of American religious history has been the work of thoroughly secular academic historians" for whom religion had been peripheral to "the central American tradition."[3]

While May's positive words appeared to make religious history respectable among historians who generally avoided religion, his assessment also looked back to the important work that church historians had been doing at seminaries, divinity schools, and in religion departments, the scholars he called "believers" (80). May noted especially the work done by the "seminary historians," Sidney Mead, Winthrop S. Hudson, and by pastor-turned-historian Timothy L. Smith. These church historians had added to their "present pastoral duties" an academic concern with American revivalism, tracing its roots and developments to the complexity of American culture (77, 78). The success of church historians was evident in May's very use of the term "religion." Throughout his essay, the religious history that was finding legitimacy among professional historians was that of mainstream Protestantism. The only other religious groups on May's horizon were sectarian Christians, such as Roman Catholics, fundamentalists, and evangelicals. May's paper, then, was not simply a watershed for the kind of scholarship on religion which would emerge in university departments of history, but it was also a recognition of the work that religion scholars had been doing during the middle decades of the twentieth century.

While the growth of religious studies added greater weight to Bible and theology as legitimate subjects in the university, the field of church history also benefited. Historians teaching at Protestant seminaries and university divinity schools rode the wave of interest in the academic study of religion and for a brief moment wove the thread of mainline Protestant history into the fabric of what May called "the central American tradition." Church history, thus, helped to give greater credibility to religious studies. But the price it paid for gaining academic respectability may have been too high.

Second Cousin

The National Association of Biblical Instructors (NABI), the professional academic organization out of which religious studies emerged, was true to its name. It consisted primarily of men and women who taught the Bible in colleges, universities, and seminaries and at the secondary school level. That such an association would join hands with theology was not surprising since the Bible had been used traditionally by Christians and Jews as the basis for the theological enterprise. What is more, in the era of neo-orthodoxy the temptation was always at hand for biblical scholars to venture farther into the territory usually occupied by theologians. Church history was another matter, however. Certainly, the construction of the Christian canon, the sixty-six books that make up the Bible, went well into the fourth century and thus made some study of the church's history necessary for biblical scholarship. But the history beyond the formation of the canon was not directly related to the study of the Bible. At best, a historian of the church could argue that his field of study involved the application of the Bible to the lives, both collectively and individually, of Christians. For this reason, NABI's journal, the *Journal of Bible and Religion* (*JBR*), did not feature many articles on church history.[4] Nevertheless, church history was clearly part of the religious studies curriculum just as it was a piece of Protestant divinity's course of study offered at seminaries and divinity schools. Church historians joined NABI and attended its annual and regional meetings. Naturally, then, religious studies would include church history even if the Bible dominated the field.[5]

Though church history was not as prominent as biblical studies or theology, *JBR* did keep its readers informed of developments in the field of the Christian past. Winthrop S. Hudson, then at Colgate-Rochester Divinity School, for example, wrote regularly on the most recent literature in church history. One of his first efforts showed the effects that neo-orthodoxy was having on religious research. In 1948 he informed readers that the "most conspicuous" feature of historical scholarship was a resurgence of interest in Reformation and Puritan studies. Hudson himself linked this trend directly to the theological renaissance that America's cultural crisis had nurtured. Neo-orthodoxy was part of "a heightened Protestant self-consciousness" that had prompted the descendants of the Protestant Reformation to recover their historical roots. Meanwhile, "the present straits of Anglo-Saxon culture" were behind the interest in Puritanism. Most of the Reformation studies surveyed by Hudson were devoted to Luther and Calvin and were published by denominational presses or in theology and church history journals. Many of those studies concerned the influence of Protestant theology on democracy and liberty. The literature on Puritanism was more diverse and less obviously related to democracy's battle with totalitarianism.[6]

Two years later, Puritanism was still in vogue, according to Hudson's survey of the new literature, even "the most important single current in recent American church history," in the words of Leonard J. Trinterud.[7] The interest in Puritanism had also stimulated a revival of studies in

Augustine. That the Puritans were self-consciously Augustinian was not much of a debating point. By tracing a connection between the history of the Massachusetts Bay Colony and the Mediterranean world of the fifth century Hudson showed that the discipline of church history, unlike the "secular" history of the university that gave precedence to period and region, gave less attention to time and place and more to the continuum of the church. Hudson, in fact, made this approach explicit when commenting on an article by James Hastings Nichols about the methods of church history. The primary responsibility of the church historian, in Nichols's estimate, was to trace the "actualization of the Gospel in human history" and to discern the "signs of the Kingdom," that is, the "subtle indications of the presence of the Risen Christ to his adopted brethren." Here was evidence yet again of neo-orthodoxy's influence. Instead of trying to show how church history could be scientific, as had an earlier generation of church historians, the theological climate made it possible, if not necessary, to display Christian convictions in narrating the church's story.[8]

Almost a decade later, Hudson gave one last report on the field, just on the eve of the academic debates that would shake religious studies free from Protestant divinity. His purpose this time was less to survey the recent literature than to assess how church history had changed since it began as an academic discipline in the late nineteenth century. Hudson commented on the early efforts of church historians to conduct "objective" and "secular" studies, and how they strove to "assimilate" the "field and methodology of general history." Then in the 1930s church history benefited from a "growing awareness" of sociological analysis. But the most significant development of the twentieth century was the theological renaissance of Niebuhr and Tillich. Church history's task was no longer primarily one of emancipating students from the past, but to be, in the words of Sidney E. Mead, "an evangelist by reminding people of their unconscious dependence upon their Christian past." So successful had church historians been in this work that "general historians" were beginning to borrow "interpretive themes from the church historians." What was needed, finally, was a textbook that would present the history of the church in the context of the Protestant theology recently recovered. Hudson's assessment once again reflected Protestant scholars' academic confidence and the way that church history contributed to the larger mission of religious studies.[9]

While mid-twentieth-century developments in church history clearly fit the larger theological trends in religious studies, church historians also showed that they belonged to religious studies by using arguments that closely resembled those of theologians and biblical scholars. For instance, Roland H. Bainton, whose biography of Martin Luther would become a classic within the field of church history during the middle decades of the twentieth century, addressed the relevance of Christianity's historical development.[10] To the question whether church history had "anything more to do with us than varieties of sea shells or butterflies" Bainton responded that the study of the church's past was "useful for edification." "In the story of the church," he explained, "we have many a record of heroism, of sacrifice, of noble endeavor and high living," even of "strengthening faith," which enabled individuals "to surmount with constancy all the trials with which life confronts us." Bainton conceded that not all of the church's history was edifying. The church had burned heretics and witches. It had fostered superstition. And these facts needed to be admitted. But even here, church history could serve the pastoral function of encouraging those who were inclined to leave the church when hearing the news of such grim events. "The church has never lived up to the ideal of Christ," Bainton granted, but "the good has outweighed the ill," and the church, despite all defects, was "worthy of allegiance."[11]

Bainton wrote these words in 1942, a time when religious studies was just beginning to emerge out of the cocoon of campus ministry. But the reasons for studying church history would be similar in the next decade even as more faculty possessed Ph.D. degrees rather than divinity degrees alone. For instance, in 1952, at the same time that Winthrop S. Hudson was informing religious studies faculty about the most recent developments in the field, ones that included the work of Perry Miller, Ralph Gabriel, William Haller, Ralph Barton Perry, and John Higham,[12] Claude Roebuck, chaplain at Williams College, was writing on the American Baptist missionary Adoniram Judson. The first American-born Protestant missionary, Judson, according to Roebuck, was an important figure in the "development of the American church." Yet, the Williams College chaplain, who had completed his Ph.D. in the history and philosophy of religion at Columbia University and Union Theological Seminary (New York), made the point of his article Judson's devotional life. The lesson to be learned from Judson's early years of missionary service was that of "evangelical self-denial." "It is self-denial for the sake of the Kingdom," Roebuck concluded, "not to the end of laying hold of God or of removing the trials of life." Like Bainton before him, Roebuck demonstrated that the purpose of teaching church history was personal. He believed that if students could "enter sympathetically into the life of another," if they could experience "his conflicts and struggle," then they could also "gain insight" into themselves and into "God's ways with men." As such, Judson's life was sacramental, or "as Professor Tillich would say," Roebuck added, "'transparent to the Divine.'"[13]

Church historians not only helped in the arena of personal piety, but also assisted the critiques of secularization from which religious studies benefited and upon which the field advanced after World War II. One notable expression of religion's emerging confidence came from William Warren Sweet, dean of American church historians during the second quarter of the twentieth century and professor at the University of Chicago.[14] Sweet faulted an older style of American history which linked the development of the nation's culture strictly to such materialistic concerns as economics and politics. In the early part of the twentieth century, Sweet complained, a doctoral dissertation on any aspect of American church history would have been unthinkable, so "high-handed" was the superiority with which academics dismissed religion. But by 1946, the time of Sweet's article, the tide had changed. It was "entirely respectable in every major university" to choose a topic in church history for Ph.D. work.[15]

Sweet then summarized his own understanding of the influence of the churches in the settling of the American frontier. The first settlers of the Old Northwest were New Englanders and, according to Sweet, their religion was pivotal in establishing the civilization that would prevail. As he explained, "religion in itself is a cultural influence" that refined manners and taste, created "new and higher interests," changed attitudes, and inspired "new and higher ambitions." In fact, Sweet went so far as to assert that the Baptist "farmer-preacher," the Methodist circuit-rider, the Presbyterian school master, missionaries, officers of the American Tract Society and American Bible Society, and Sunday school teachers "were the advance agents of civilization." The chief influence of these Protestants in taming the frontier was to set the moral standards for society at a time when the moral bar was "pretty generally down." By imposing strict discipline upon local residents, Methodists, Baptists, and Presbyterians maintained public decency. Sweet's own understanding of Christian conduct, what he called "the straight and narrow way," informed his high estimate of the Protestant denominations' work. "The filthy habit of tobacco-chewing found its first organized opposition from the churches," he wrote, "and the debauchery which resulted from the free use of homemade whiskey . . . found in the church an implacable enemy." Sweet concluded from this evidence that the churches' influence was "uplifting" (192, 193).

He went on to recount the role that Protestants played in establishing institutions of higher education and in the distribution of literature. Sweet conceded that the chief motive for founding denominational colleges was to train an educated ministry. But the churches were not simply self-serving. These colleges were also started to "introduce Christianity as a cultural force into western society," or as one college charter put it, "to spread the truths of science and the grace of literature." The churches also advanced civilization by publishing religious journals and denominational periodicals. No less important in contributing to the literacy of the people of the Midwest was the Bible. As if to end all debate about the Bible's positive cultural influence, Sweet pointed to Abraham Lincoln's vast knowledge of the Old and New Testaments. "The moral elevation as well as the perfection of his great state papers," Sweet opined of the sixteenth president, "are due largely to [Lincoln's] familiarity" with the King James Bible (194).

In Sweet's retelling of the Midwest's religious history, the churches did well settling the frontier, but taming the city and the immigrants who flocked to them was another matter. In fact, religion's civilizing task was "relatively simple" compared to postbellum urban developments and "the new immigration." With the Germans, Scandinavians, and Irish came a "large and peculiar conservative religious influence" that Sweet attributed to the migrants' peasant background. He disapproved of the parochial schools established by Lutherans and Roman Catholics. They did not "as a general rule" perform with the same "educational efficiency" as the public schools. But Sweet gave the parochial school credit for keeping "some kind of control, moral and religious, over the homes and the children of the recent immigrant." He even praised the Catholics for "saving Detroit, Cleveland, Chicago, St. Louis, and other large cities" from becoming "worse Sodoms and Gomorrahs than they are today." He was not as positive about the Missouri Synod Lutheran church, which represented a type of German Lutheranism "unlike anything else in Europe or America," and which had "withdrawn so completely within itself." Lutheran and Catholic influences upon the Midwest contrasted sharply with "a distinctive type of religious liberalism" that had emerged among the Anglo-Protestant denominations. It stood for "religious scholarship," and its principal tenet was a "willingness to think." Sweet's own institution, the Divinity School at the University of Chicago, was "chiefly responsible" for this movement (195, 196).

Here was church history leavened by the growing confidence of mainline Protestantism at midcentury and advancing the cause of religious studies in the university. The study of America's religious past no longer needed an apology. This meant that Sweet, along with his colleagues in seminaries and divinity schools, could contribute significantly to the study of American history. As Sweet wrote, any attempt to appraise American culture apart from religion was "a contradiction" in and of itself because culture had to do inherently with "the moral and religious as well as with the intellectual life of a society" (191). Church historians of Sweet's generation still remembered the days of sectarianism and "peculiar" religious conservatism, thus accounting for his effort, in good liberal Protestant fashion, to conduct religious scholarship that transcended parochial and denominational boundaries. Nevertheless, Sweet's confident pose also depended upon neo-orthodoxy's critique of scientific and cultural developments that left religion out. In the era of Niebuhr and Tillich, religion was a desirable cultural good. It was, like the New England Protestants who settled the Midwest, helping to tame and civilize the frontiers of science and secularism. What is more, Sweet's version of church history advanced the larger cause of religious studies by showing that religion could contribute meaningfully to the humanistic efforts of the university. Consequently, even if church history was secondary to biblical and theological studies in departments of religion, it did help to give the field greater legitimacy in the academy.

The Recovery of Church History

One of the reasons why religious studies became more respectable academically and why church history particularly fit so well under the big tent of teaching the Bible and theology was, once again, the influence of neo-orthodoxy during the middle decades of the twentieth century. Henry F. May noticed just such a connection between the mainline Protestant theological renaissance of the 1930s and 1940s and the recovery of religious history that he documented among secular historians. "A new kind of religious history" began to be practiced in the 1930s, according to May, which reflected "the turn toward neo-orthodoxy." Here May compared Reinhold Niebuhr to Jonathan Edwards. Like Edwards, Niebuhr drew upon contemporary European thought to remind Americans that theirs was a society "under judgment." But, like Edwards, Niebuhr also reacted against "the smug society" around him by looking first at American circumstances. "It was not Auschwitz or Hiroshima, but Detroit in the twenties" that prodded Niebuhr away from liberalism's optimism and toward a sober estimate of human nature and American society. Though students of Arthur Schlesinger Sr., Oscar Handlin, and Richard Hofstadter continued to write from a "secular point of view," neo-orthodoxy had a "clear and acknowledged influence" on Arthur Schlesinger Jr. C. Vann Woodward, and George F. Kennan.[16]

If neo-orthodoxy made a mark on mainstream historians in the United States, its impact upon church history was even more discernible. While the academics who taught in history departments found Niebuhr's notion of irony useful in historical explanations, historians who taught the history of the Christian church in religious studies departments and Protestant divinity schools relied upon the changing theological climate to render critical interpretations of the American churches' development.

The kind of American church history practiced in this "golden age" was a break from the approach that had dominated the field during its first fifty years or so.[17] After flirting with "salvation history" in the 1880s, church historians quickly followed the lead of historians in the research university and applied the canons of scientific history to the institution of the church. According to Harvard University's Ephraim Emerton, the methods of church history should be exactly those of the profession at large, namely, the technique of "natural science," or "the observation of facts and inductions from them."[18] This approach required a marked distinction between theology and history. Because the former concerned supernatural and, thus, unobservable phenomena, history, which relied upon the collection of scientific data, was illegitimate if it relied on theological norms. Such an understanding of church history implied a rigid distinction between what was empirical and divinely revealed, a repudiation of explanations that resorted to supernatural intervention or divine providence, and a rejection of faith or religious commitment as necessary for research and writing about the church's past.[19]

A scientific approach to church history contrasted significantly with the outlook of seminary and divinity school historians who worked between 1935 and 1965. Here similar factors to those that had made biblical scholarship more self-consciously theological during the same period were at work in church history. With the defeat of fundamentalists, Protestant academics could be more explicit about their convictions without sounding sectarian. Furthermore, the effort to harness science and industry for Christian ends, as liberal Protestants had tried, looked less laudable in the wake of international war and economic upheaval.

Traditional Christian verities might offer more hope for human suffer-ing than the latest scientific discovery or political initiative. As David W. Lotz argues, the "experience of a profound and prolonged cultural crisis in the West" formed the background for the theological interpretation of the church's history which dominated mainstream Protestantism's self-conscious ascendancy in and through religious studies departments. Meanwhile, the convergence of the humanities, general education, and the study of religion created an atmosphere where Protestant scholars, who were convinced of Christianity's centrality to the development of western culture, could be more explicit in highlighting the positive con-tribution of the church than they had been when trying to show that Christianity was compatible with science.[20] Consequently, the goals of church history manifested four traits in the era of neo-orthodoxy's hey-day: first, it focused on the church as "Holy Community"; second, it was forthrightly ecumenical in purpose; third, its method was "anti-posi-tivist"; and, last, church historians showed little hesitancy to state their religious commitments.[21] Church history became a means to challenge the secular assumptions of scientific history rather than a way to demonstrate academic respectability.

Nevertheless, the seminary-trained or pastor historians that May mentioned as significant for the recovery of American religious his-tory—Timothy L. Smith, Sidney Mead, and Winthrop S. Hudson—per-formed historical scholarship that championed the contribution of Christianity all the while complying with the intellectual standards of the profession. Smith's *Revivalism and Social Reform,* published originally by the Methodist publishing house Abingdon Press, did for revivalistic Protestantism what Sweet had accomplished for the New England Protestants who settled the Midwest. Contrary to historians who inter-preted the revivalism of itinerant Methodist and Baptist evangelists as an inherently rural and privatistic expression of Protestantism, Smith tried to show that its theology dominated mainstream Protestantism (infecting even some Unitarians), that its proponents worked and lived in places like New York and Philadelphia as much as western Kentucky or North Carolina's Appalachian Mountains, and that its adherents were as socially progressive as any twentieth-century liberal Protestant. In fact, what made Smith's interpretation of antebellum Protestantism so stunning was his attempt to give revivalism, as opposed to Protestant liberalism, credit for what later became known as the social gospel.[22] Here he targeted the standard accounts of social Christianity by histori-ans who traced the church's social activism to the aftermath of the Civil War, industrialization, and the growth of cities. Smith argued instead that the holiness theology of revivalists prompted a concern for the poor, the abolition of slavery, and an understanding of America's place in the advancement of the kingdom of God which came earlier than liberal Protestantism and thus provided the actual basis for the social gospel.[23] Whatever the merits of Smith's argument, and even though his book was concerned with Protestants who by the twentieth century were no longer in the mainline denominations, his interpretation fit the general trend of church history in the era of neo-orthodoxy. Smith asserted the primacy of Protestantism in laying the foundation for social causes typically understood as stemming from nonreligious sources.

Like Smith, Winthrop S. Hudson looked to the nineteenth century to find the source of American Protestantism's strength. In *The Great Tradition of the American Churches,* published in 1953, Hudson identified what made American Protestantism unique (when compared to European church life) and accounted for its greatest achievements. The "great tradition," as he called it, was the separation of church and state. It began with the Puritans and flourished in the nineteenth century. This tradition depended upon three convictions that New England's Puritans developed: first, the church must remain independent; second, church membership must be voluntary; and third, the church's power must be limited to spiritual, as opposed to civil, matters.[24] These beliefs, Hudson argued, accounted for the remarkable vigor of American religion, a vitality that attracted the constant attention of foreign observers, from Tocqueville to Bryce.[25] The great achievement of this tradition was the host of reforms and religiously inspired activities, from foreign missions to the YMCA, which American Protestants of the nineteenth century conducted. These endeavors had created an "informed Christian public opinion," one that Hudson believed was necessary in a democracy. By pursuing a voluntary course, rather than relying up the coercive measures of a religious establishment, "religious presuppositions" infiltrated public life, even to the point of stamping the character of the public schools and civic discourse more generally. Such religiously informed opinions "must be a free expression of the mind of the community" and so determine the "basic assumptions" of everyone, from average citizens to elected public officials. The responsibility of the churches in America was to foster the qualities of "initiative, responsibility, relevance, resourcefulness, liberality, missionary zeal, and lay participation" (262). Hudson's book, like Smith's, was a story of the churches' successful pursuit of progressive aims.

But unlike Smith, Hudson wrote with explicit theological and inspirational goals. Whereas Smith tried to rescue the tradition of revivalistic

Protestantism from the obscurity of fundamentalism and thereby restore its place in the dominant narrative of American church history, Hudson wrote with the needs of postwar America in mind. He began the book ominously, in good neo-orthodox fashion, warning that a "day of reckoning" had come for the churches. "All men who can discern the signs of the times"—politicians, scientists and educators—agreed that "the basic problem confronting mankind today is a spiritual problem" (17). Hudson's purpose, then, was not simply an academic one of explaining the history of Christianity in the United States. It was also to find a model for "the task of evangelizing a society that has lost its spiritual rootage" (18). This was the reason for his study of antebellum Protestantism and faith had established the principle of religious voluntarism and had achieved a "reasonably Christian democratic society" (245). Of course, twentieth-century Protestants could not merely restore "the disciplinary habits" of the nineteenth century. The excesses of antebellum Protestantism were far too obvious, especially its "moralistic pettiness, legalism, and at times overweening pretensions to absolute truth" (251). Still, the twentieth-century churches needed "some normative content to their message" like the earlier generations of American Protestants.[26] Thus, just as nineteenth-century Protestants had premised their work on "basic theological convictions," so should the Protestants of Hudson's generation.

Such a conviction showed the author's indebtedness to neo-orthodoxy, and Hudson's acknowledgments made that debt explicit. He cited H. Richard Niebuhr's *The Kingdom of God in America* as one source of inspiration for his narrative, while listing other theologians and historians who had also been influenced by twentieth-century Protestantism's theological renaissance, such as Wilhelm Pauck, H. Shelton Smith, Henry F. May, Hugh Thompson Kerr, and Ernest Trice Thompson. Hudson even went so far as to suggest, as Reinhold Niebuhr had, the value of sectarianism. If churches took theology seriously denominational differences would be the natural result. Such division had the virtue of restoring to the church "an effective Christian witness" against "the prevailing secularism of modern culture."[27] Hudson's message was clear and functioned as historical justification for the neo-orthodox jeremiad. The American churches needed to recover their beliefs in order to rival the advance of secularism.

Another prominent church historian from the post–World War II era was Sidney Mead, who taught at the University of Chicago's Divinity School. His writing was less prophetic and more dispassionate than Hudson's. But it still bore the unmistakable marks of neo-orthodoxy.

One index to his understanding of American Protestant history was the Charles R. Walgreen Foundation Lectures that Mead gave in 1954 at his university, later reprinted in an influential collection of essays, *The Lively Experiment*.[28] Mead made his greatest mark in describing the denominational structure of American Protestantism and, like Hudson, in explaining the effects of voluntarism on religion in the United States more generally. What made American Christianity different, even unique, from all its predecessors was its denominational pattern. Unlike traditional forms of Christianity, which depended on creed, territory and the state, American Protestantism was "purposive." It was basically a voluntary association "of like-hearted and like-minded individuals," who united for the common purpose of "accomplishing tangible and defined objectives."[29] At a time when American religious history was synonymous with denominational history, Mead's attention to the peculiarities of church life in a society dedicated to religious freedom was standard fare for students of Christianity in the United States.[30]

Still, as textbook-like as Mead's tone was, the outline of his lectures revealed the telltale signs of neo-orthodoxy. His title for describing American Protestantism since the Civil War was "From Denominationalism to Americanism," a lecture that like Hudson's book documented the weight gain of a flabby Protestantism that had accommodated its message and work to the fashions of Victorian respectability. "The American denominations," Mead wrote, "have successfully lent themselves to the sanctification of the current existing expressions of the American way of life." This sounded more diagnostic than prophetic but it still had a neo-orthodox flavor. When Mead turned to the first third of the twentieth century, his heading—"From Americanism to Christianity"—had a similar feel. For unclear reasons he stopped his narrative in 1930. But he concluded with a call for ongoing historical scholarship that recognized recent Protestantism's "heightened theological consciousness." These "positive attempts to revitalize the life of the denominations on the basis of theological formulations," Mead believed, should provide the "context" for further study.[31]

Though *The Lively Experiment* lacked the fervency of other efforts in neo-orthodox historiography, Mead was indebted to books such as H. Richard Niebuhr's *The Kingdom of God in America,* which had spearheaded the renaissance of a mainline Protestant historiography as much as it was also responsible for a revitalization of Protestant theological scholarship. As it turned out, Mead's posture was not that different from Niebuhr's. The latter's organization of the history of American Protestantism around the doctrine of the kingdom of God was rarely explicit in telling the American churches what they needed to do. After all, Niebuhr wrote at the early stage of neo-orthodoxy's development, before World War II made theology sound more plausible. The most urgency he could muster was the hope that his book would serve as a "stepping stone" for an "American Augustine" who would write the history of the "eternal city in its relations to modern civilization," or a twentieth-century Edwards who would bring "down to our own time the *History of the Work of Redemption.*"[32] Still, church historians heard Niebuhr's call and for the next three decades, according to Henry F. May, that hope influenced many of the "ablest religious historians."[33] As the work of Smith, Hudson, and Mead suggests, church historians produced scholarship that was theological and churchly in orientation, with the clear intention of using the past to serve the present. In the estimate of Henry Warner Bowden, who has written the best survey of twentieth-century American church historiography, their work was part of a movement that gave church history a clear "theological rationale." Bowden added that this kind of church history "recovered both the self-esteem and the outward respect" the discipline had enjoyed before "science banished transcendence from causal explanation."[34] Church history in the age of neo-orthodoxy, thus, provided ready assistance to the aims and purposes of religious studies. It was theologically driven, self-consciously Protestant, critical of the secularist and scientific drift of both the academy and American culture more generally, and, therefore, profitable for undergraduates in need of hope, moral direction, and inspiration.

An *American* Church History

One of the responses to Henry F. May's influential essay on the recovery of American religious history was the worry that such a topic, implicated as it was in theological considerations, would "stir up the animals." May himself noted that among the ranks of historians who had helped to restore some academic interest in church history could be heard "extreme" statements that repudiated "positivist" history. Here he referred to a wing of Protestant church historians who called for a "separate" history of the "church eternal, invisible, and universal."[35] One of the church historians to whom May was referring was James Hastings Nichols, professor at the Federated Theological Faculty of the University of Chicago. In his presidential address before the American Society of Church History for 1950, Nichols faulted his colleagues for not

holding their own in mainstream Protestantism's theological renaissance and succumbing to the norms established by secular historians.
He argued that the challenge of the church historian was to "trace the
actualization of the Gospel in human history" and describe "the signs of
the Kingdom." The influence of neo-orthodoxy was unmistakable.
Since theologians were writing "an astonishing flood of books" on the
meaning of history, Nichols believed it was high time for historians to
catch up.[36] Church history in the age of the Niebuhrs, thus, coincided
with the larger resurgence of Protestant ecumenism and theology. Seminary and divinity school historians could write the history of their own
denominations or theological traditions with the confidence that they
were contributing to the edification of the faithful and correcting the
faults of secular historians.[37]

Yet May and his colleagues in history did not need to fear the explicitly theological aims of Protestant historiography. For underneath
the laments about secularism and the confident assertions about docu-
menting the history of Protestant denominations in the United States
was a narrative that ordered the church's history around the life and
development of America. Consequently, even though Protestant denominational history flourished at midcentury, it depended heavily
upon national norms and patterns to tell the history of the church.

One way of illustrating the captivity of American church history to
U.S. history is to examine the textbook accounts of American religious
history that seminary and divinity school historians produced during the era of neo-orthodoxy. To be sure, since the scope of investigation was the United States it made sense for historians to let American
developments inform the structure and narrative of the church. Still,
the theological convictions that taught the church's distinctiveness
and centrality to the direction of history were not as apparent in these
works as were the establishmentarian assumptions of mainstream
Protestants who linked the fortunes of their denominations to those
of the United States. Two textbook surveys published at the close of
the era dominated by denominational history, Winthrop S. Hudson's
Religion in America (1965), and Edwin Scott Gaustad's *A Religious History of America* (1966), demonstrate the grip that national life had on
the outlook of church historians.

Gaustad, who taught history at the University of California–River-
side, declared at the outset that his purpose was national, not denominational. "Instead of the rise and progress of ecclesiastical bodies or the
decline and fall of archaic forms," he wrote, the history of the United
States guided the story. His point of view in writing this survey was to

argue for the importance of religion in understanding the life of the nation. Religious history was "significant" and "crucial" to interpreting the American experience and was "as vital and legitimate" as any other approach to national history and, even if controversial, such controversy enriched "democracy and the educative process."[38] Gaustad's narrative included non-Protestant subjects; Judaism and Christianity were the dominant religious traditions and so Jews and Catholics regularly surfaced in his account. But the real subject of Gaustad's history was democracy, the subject of his last chapter. Though religion and democracy could never be identified because of Judaism's and Christianity's higher loyalties, Gaustad feared how long democracy could flourish apart from "moral responsibility and spiritual sensitivity." "Believing in a God of rational order and discernible purpose," he wrote, Americans also believed that the "Spirit of God works in and through the people." Not some representative or faction in government, but the voice of the people best represented "the voice and will of God." Such a narrative prevented Gaustad from erring on the side of churchly sectarianism, but it did run the risk of turning the United States itself into a sect, especially when he ended the book with this rhetorical flourish:

> And so a nation was conceived in liberty and dedicated to the proposition that all men are created equal. And so a people, at worship and at work, go out not knowing where they go. But by faith they go, confident that their destiny is guided by God.[39]

Like Gaustad, Hudson wanted to chronicle "the religious life of the American people," not the histories of individual religious groups. Whether he succeeded in achieving the balance between the unity and particularity of American religious life, Hudson's interests were clearly on the side of unity. The basic outline of America's religious narrative was that of Protestants maintaining hegemony through the assimilative powers of ecclesiastical federation and interfaith dialogue. This began with the establishment of Anglo-American traditions, especially seventeenth-century Puritanism, the flourishing of Protestant denominations during the nineteenth century, and their adjustment and recovery during the twentieth century. To be sure, Hudson covered outsiders, namely, Jews, fundamentalists, Eastern Orthodox, and Roman Catholics. But religious unity, cooperation, and toleration were the chief themes in Hudson's story, thus making mainline Protestants who taught and preached such virtues the major actors. His book gave the impression that the religion to be favored was that which promoted

civic harmony, as opposed to sectarian groups that practiced intolerance. In fact, Hudson ended the book on the upbeat note of Vatican II
and the cessation of "acrimonious exchanges in religious debate" that
this council seemed to promise. He sensed a new mood in the mid-
1960s. "Americans of all faiths, in the presence of diversity," Hudson
wrote, "were learning to live together in a way that was mutually
enriching rather than impoverishing."[40] This comment demonstrated
that the much-heralded recovery of church history would only go so
far, and would not include attention to those unique beliefs and practices of a religious community that made it different from others.

Hudson's use of American norms for evaluating religious history
was also evident in the way he structured his survey. The first part,
"The Formative Years," covered religious developments until the rati-
fication of the U.S. Constitution; the second, "The New Nation," went
until the Civil War; the third, "The Years of Mid-Passage," covered the
decades between the American war and World War I; and the last,
"Modern America," extended the narrative to the present. Hudson
offered no explanation for this arrangement, nor should he have since
it was the conventional outline of any number of American religious
history texts written then and since. But it was a curious outline for
historians who had been bitten by the bug of neo-orthodoxy and a
higher view of the church. Rather than letting the introduction of
new religious teachings or the beginning of innovative liturgical practices determine the narrative, for instance, Hudson let the life, particularly the wars, of the nation-state set the pattern for the story of religion in the United States. Again, this practice was not unusual for
someone writing within the context of a religious establishment that
had defined its mission as one of ministering to the public life of the
American nation. But it was a far cry from the neo-orthodox historiographical approach of "let the church be the church."[41]

In the end the recovery of the church that the theological renaissance
promised left little influence on the narrative that church historians
employed to tell the history of the church in the United States. One way
to establish this point is to compare the surveys produced during
the heyday of Protestant influence to those written when church history appeared to be on the margins of academic history. Here William
Warren Sweet's *The Story of Religion in America* (1930) is useful, a work
regularly located in the period of historiography when historians of religion wrote in a "'scientistic' guise."[42] After all, just a few years subsequent to the first edition of Sweet's book, Lewis Vander Velde would
complain of a enormous chasm between the religious history practiced

by professional historians "whose point of view is detached and objective" and that done by pastors and seminary professors "whose primary interest is religious."[43] If this was the dominant outlook within historical circles, Sweet labored to make his scholarship look credible. To do this he followed the norms of the academy, especially the practice of separating theological concerns from such nonreligious factors as economics, politics, demographics, and migratory patterns. In short, Sweet wrote as an apologist for historians to take the history of Protestantism seriously at a time when the affairs of the churches looked marginal from the academy's perspective.

This set of circumstances makes understandable Sweet's technique of situating the history of religious bodies within the life and development of the United States. In what became the paradigm for the rest of his massive (571 pages) book, Sweet wrote that the "parallels between American political and religious history are both numerous and striking." The relations between the churches and the nation were so strong that the separation of church and state was an erroneous matrix for interpreting American religious history. From an unidentified source Sweet appeared to find justification for the shape of his narrative. "There is after all," Sweet quoted, "a certain unity in American church history, as well as frequent connection between it and the civil history of the nation." This affinity accounted for the outline that followed and ran from the churches forming national organizations at the time of the United States' founding and the churches' division during the sectional crisis to the denominations' support for "the program of the government" during the "great American wars." The story of American religion that Sweet told, then, was one where "the same set of influences produced similar results in church and state" while at the same time both the church and the state had exercised a "constant influence" upon each other.[44] His not-so-subtle point was that if Protestantism was so essential to the history of American society then perhaps the rest of the historical profession should sit up and take notice.[45]

But the circumstances that Sweet's successors faced were markedly different. The so-called religious revival of the 1950s, combined with the theological renaissance associated with neo-orthodoxy, meant that religious historians did not have to be as defensive or apologetic as Sweet had. What is more, many religious historians claimed to be using the insights of the theologians to write a truly churchly or theologically informed history of religion in the United States. But in actual practice the narrative that emerged from the neo-orthodox-inspired church historians differed little from Sweet's. The history of Protestant churches was still part and parcel of the history of the American nation-state just as the success of the churches was measured by criteria derived from public life in the United States. This particular brand of historical writing did not match the theological and churchly rhetoric of the times. Indeed, examples of church history that did not depend upon the outline of U.S. history would come from religious traditions whose identity transcended that of America.[46]

Church history thus emerged, along with religious studies, as a worthy partner in the university. But its victory was pyhrric. For the terms by which church historians had justified their scholarship were no more stable than quicksand. As long as Protestantism (and the religions of Jews and Catholics friendly to Protestants) was synonymous with religion in the United States it was relatively easy to recognize the work of Protestant church historians as credible interpreters of a significant part of American life. Once the links between mainline Protestantism and American culture came undone, however, the interpretations of American religion produced by church historians looked arbitrary if not naive. The irony is that if church historians had taken neo-orthodox theology more seriously, if they had produced history of the church as church, their work probably would not have been mentioned in essays about the recovery of American religious history. But it might have left a record that by their churches' own profession was worth recovering.

How Wide the Recovery?

The religious history that Henry F. May thought had been recovered was indicative of the status of religious studies circa 1965. Taking May at his word, the prospects for the academic study of religion looked bright and the involvement of Protestant academics in that recovery appeared to be successful. In other words, the strategy of teaching and scholarly writing, as opposed to campus ministry and extracurricular religious endeavors, appeared to have gained an adequate foundation for religion in the university. Religious studies was thriving and mainline Protestants deserved the credit. But the religious history that May noticed also showed all of the inconsistencies and troubles that would soon bedevil the broader arena of religious studies. By choosing to write the history of religion in America, instead of church history, the rhetoric of ecclesiastical history to the contrary, mainline Protestants were setting themselves up for a fall. Was the history of the main-stream Protestant denominations (with a few Catholics and Jews thrown in for religious dialogue's sake) really the history of religion in America? Perhaps truth in advertising would have made "church history" the better umbrella. But in a diverse place like the United States "church history" sounded sectarian.

The difficulties of equating America's religious history with the history of American Protestantism were evident in Paul A. Carter's comments on the historiography of Protestantism in the United States, published just a few years after May's essay. Carter noticed the recent phenomenon of "unchurched liberals" who were beginning to write on the history of American Protestantism. Carter put May in this camp. Though these liberals were not as willing to embrace neo-ortho-doxy as the seminary historians, Carter argued, they were prone to another kind of bias. He accused them of harboring "a perspective on the religious history of this country that is in the narrowest sense 'WASP.'" So strong was this bias that in order "to pass muster" and be included in the canon of American religious history a movement had to trace its origins to the "religious pattern of the colonial Eastern seaboard." What about Mormons, Lutherans, Catholics, and funda-mentalists, Carter asked. Ideally, "a post-neo-orthodox, post-'WASP,' and post-eastern seaboard generation of scholars" would revise the his-toriography that seminary historians and "unchurched liberals" had produced during the 1950s and 1960s.[47]

Carter's words would soon prove prophetic. Religious history after the age of neo-orthodoxy yielded a flood of literature that made the narrative of Protestantism look more like the trickle of a creek than the flow of the mainstream.[48] What was true of religious history would also be true of its related discipline, religious studies. The Protestant paradigm for teaching and studying religion in American higher educa-tion would only last for approximately a quarter of a century, until the mid- to late 1960s. At that point the weakness of mainline Protes-tantism's strategy became apparent. It had so identified itself and its studies with the life and soul of the nation that once the public noticed how unrepresentative mainline Protestantism was of the larger society, educators and administrators at colleges and universities would have a hard time arguing that a curriculum designed for the training of Protes-tant ministers should be the pattern for the education of the American public. According to Sydney E. Ahlstrom, who tried to explain the dra-matic reversal of mainstream Protestantism's fortunes, "the sharp crescendo of social strife seemed to demonstrate that the time-honored structures of American church life were 'irrelevant' to the country's actual condition." To many observers, he added, the churches "came to be seen, not as a moral leaven in the land, but as an obstacle to change."[49]

The strategy of teaching Protestantism in America's colleges and universities, therefore, worked as long as people, both inside and outside the academy, equated the well-being of the nation with the health of the most influential churches. And this strategy helps to explain why the history of American religion during the age of the Niebuhrs and Tillich was virtually synonymous with the history of mainline Protestantism in the United States. It was ill-suited, however, to weather the recognition of cultural and religious diversity that would characterize the last third of the twentieth century, a time when the relationship between mainstream Protestantism and the university would return to the pattern that prevailed a century earlier during the so-called war between theology and science. But for one brief interlude the prospects for religious studies looked as bright as the recovery that May heralded as successful.

PART III

The Age of the American Academy of Religion, 1965–Present

EIGHT

Religious Studies and the Failure of the Christian Academy

FOR A TIME PROTESTANT EFFORTS to teach and study religion appeared to pay dividends even larger than constructing departments of religion, establishing a curriculum compatible with other fields in the humanities, and cultivating faculty to offer such instruction. The impetus for religious studies was not simply to set apart one part of the university curriculum where religion could be studied, but also to redirect the overarching purpose of higher education. American educators' preoccupation with science had fostered a secular and materialistic outlook, religious studies advocates said. Attending more to the eternal verities of religion and other humanistic studies would restore a proper perspective on the technical and vocational ends that had distracted the university from its higher purpose.

Signs of Protestant optimism and confidence about their place and function in the university world came in 1952 with the founding of the Faculty Christian Fellowship (FCF). This organization of college and university faculty was dedicated to integrating the Christian religion and the various academic disciplines of the modern research university. Its inspiration came from the spate of mid-twentieth-century literature decrying the secularism of modern higher education.[1] But undoubtedly the growing presence of Protestant faculty teaching religion also contributed to hopes for cultivating Christian scholarship that transcended the theological disciplines. Such academic work would involve believing academics in the natural and social sciences and the humanities. According to Werner Bohnstedt, who reported on the first deliberations of the FCF, Christian scholars had for too long segregated their religious convictions from other areas of their lives, especially their work as scholars. He conceded that "two and two equals four, regardless of faith and philosophy" but the relevance of mathematical truth "may be a different one depending upon whether we are members of the Christian faith, or whether we think of our world as man centered and governed by human reason alone."[2]

The enthusiasm generated by associations like the Faculty Christian Fellowship was short-lived, however. By the mid-1960s the organization had exhausted new ways to talk about Christian perspectives on scholarship and, in the words of one historian, "just faded away."[3] But for the decade or so after the mid-1950s the establishment of a Christian academy appeared to be a realistic possibility. Protestants had rehabilitated religion (that is, theirs) in the world of higher education not only by creating departments of religion but also by urging that believing scholars had much to contribute to teaching and research that for too long had relied exclusively on science. This period culminated almost a half-century of Protestant endeavors to gain a foothold for the mainline churches in an academic environment that had feared ecclesiastical entanglement in American higher education. But the failure of Protestant scholars to show how Christian academics differed from and was superior to work already being produced that made no reference to religious conviction would mean that Protestants would have to restrict the project of integrating faith and learning to religious studies alone. And even here the lure of harmonization in the teaching and study of religion would prove immensely elusive.

The Christian Scholar

One sign of emerging Protestant confidence about the academy was the use of the phrase "Christian intellectual" or "Christian scholar." Here E. Harris Harbison's *The Christian Scholar in the Age of the Reformation* captured the sentiments of many Protestant academics, whether working in the field of religion or not.[4] A professor of early modern European history at Princeton University, Harbison decided to study the scholarly vocation of Erasmus, Luther, and Calvin, which was hardly

exceptional since, as the book's dust jacket put it, his courses on the
Renaissance and Reformation were popular with undergraduates. But
this book was more than an Ivy League historian's treatment of a particular theme in sixteenth-century European history. It stemmed from the
1955 Stone Lectures at Princeton Theological Seminary, where Harbison
was a member of the board of trustees. What is more, Harbison was a
fellow of the National Council on Religion and Higher Education
(NCRHE), one of the older mainline Protestant organizations responsible for promoting religion in American higher education. *The Christian
Scholar in the Age of the Reformation,* then, provided a reading on the
pulse of Protestant aspirations for a Christian academy.

From one perspective the vital signs of Protestant scholarship were
faint if Harbison's overt posture in the book is any indication. True to
his sense of the historian's craft, Harbison treated fairly and learnedly
the relations between faith and reason, theology and philosophy, and
piety and learning in the writings of Renaissance humanists and
Protestant Reformers. A concern for careful scholarship prevented him
from using the lectures as a bully pulpit for a greater Christian presence
in the university world.

Still, in his conclusion Harbison could not refrain from offering a
few reflections about the significance of his study for the American situation. Here his understated manner may have reflected quiet confidence as much as bashfulness. Harbison conceded that if the choice
was between faith and reason the believer would have to choose the
former. But he did not appreciate having to put the choice so starkly
and appealed to the founding documents of Princeton Theological
Seminary, which stated that faith without learning "has usually proved
injurious to the Church." For this reason, scholarship was "a legitimate
calling of high significance among Christians." This was especially true
in the study of the Hebrew and Christian scriptures. But the need for
Christian scholars was also evident in the growing divide between the
university and seminary, a division that did not confront the Protestant
Reformers. Harbison believed this separation was unhealthy for both
institutions, forcing seminaries to be nothing more than professional
schools and universities to cater to the selfish "desire for academic
kudos." He concluded the book with a modest call for scholars in seminaries and universities to "acquire the vision of scholarship as a calling
worthy of a Christian, and of Christianity as a commitment worthy of
a scholar."[5]

Perhaps the restraint Harbison displayed in drawing implications
from his study for post–World War II higher education accounts for

the mild reaction his book received in periodical literature. Reviewers were more than impressed by Harbison's impeccable scholarship and even-handed treatment of Renaissance and Reformation themes.[6] What is more, responses did not miss the implications of the book for cultivating a Christian scholarly community. For instance, John Frederick Olson, who reviewed Harbison's work for the *Journal of Bible and Religion,* opined that "the contemporary Christian scholar will find himself enthused over his calling, and he will wish that these lectures might be read by every anti-intellectual in the land."[7] So, too, the review in the *Christian Scholar* praised Harbison for writing a book that would "place it high on the reading list of all academic people who are concerned with the relationship of Christian faith and academic vocation," though it mentioned in addition that a need still existed for some treatment of Christian scholarship in the "so-called 'secular' disciplines."[8] But Harbison's understated approach prevented his book from being used as a banner to lead the procession of Protestant academics back into the university. In fact, that most reviewers who did note contemporary implications regarded the book as a rebuke to anti-intellectual impulses within the Christian community rather than to skeptics in the university world suggests Protestants felt a measure of comfort and acceptance within the academy. Talk of Christian scholarship circa 1955 was not as oxymoronic as it had sounded a half-century earlier.

Harbison's book was not the only study to make the case for Christian scholarship. A few years later Jaroslav Pelikan, then a historian and theologian at the University of Chicago, began work of the kind that reviewers had desired from Harbison, namely, an updated definition of Christian scholarship that was appropriate for the modern university. In a study that bore significant similarities to Harbison's, Pelikan appealed to Reformation sources to make the case for the Christian intellectual. Only in this instance Pelikan's argument extended beyond the theological and biblical scholarship that absorbed Harbison's attention. The University of Chicago scholar appealed to Francis Bacon's distinction among "three knowledges," namely, "divine philosophy, natural philosophy and human philosophy." In a prior book, Pelikan explored theology, the first of Bacon's divisions. But in his subsequent book he turned to the natural sciences and humanities, which corresponded respectively to natural philosophy and human philosophy. In so doing Pelikan hoped to show continuities between the Reformation and modern thought, thereby making more secure the position of the Christian intellectual in the modern academy.[9]

In the first half of *The Christian Intellectual,* Pelikan discussed the Protestant doctrine of creation in relation to modern science's explanation of nature's origins. At the outset he acknowledged the warfare between science and theology which had pitted the likes of Charles Darwin and Thomas Huxley against Samuel Wilberforce and William Jennings Bryan. "The one fundamental Christian doctrine to which Darwin seemed to pose the most direct challenge was certainly the doctrine of creation."[10] But upon closer ispection, according to Pelikan, the Christian doctrine of creation was far more ambiguous than theological and scientific contestants allowed. What the Lutheran confessions of the sixteenth centuries showed especially was an understanding of creation that put Christ, who was both God and man, creator and creature, at the center. The Protestant doctrine of creation, then, was less concerned with the relation between God and the universe than with that between "God and man" (68).

The result was a conception of creation that was fully mysterious. The Bible presented creation as a mystery, not simply because of "the vast Unknown in the cosmos," but also because of "the quality of the Unknown." Pelikan believed that regarding creation as a mystery would make possible "the reopening of the communication between Christian thought and natural philosophy." The Christian intellectual should speak "as a faithful interpreter" of revealed truth and not go beyond "the charge laid upon [him or her]"; the scientist in turn should "speak with the canons of [his or her] own discipline" (79). With lines of communication open, Christians could move about with greater confidence in the academy.

In the second half of *The Christian Intellectual,* Pelikan turned to the humanities and what, if anything, the Reformation tradition of Luther might have to say. Pelikan began with the Protestant teaching about the destiny and nature of humanity, the Lutheran doctrine of justification, and proceeded to work through the tensions between divine and human justice. But along the way he did not show, as he had with the doctrine of creation and science, how such Protestant convictions related to humanistic scholarship. Pelikan did devote a chapter to the "Theologian as a Humanistic Scholar." But his argument mainly repeated those made two decades earlier by Protestant educators who were alarmed by the scientistic orientation of higher education. For instance, he noted that religion and humanistic scholars shared the recognition that "there is no such thing as an uninterpreted fact and that therefore exegesis free of presuppositions is impossible" (107–8). Pelikan also made a pitch for the value of general education in language again reminiscent of the late 1940s (111–15). For this reason, the overall effect of the book was flat and offered few concrete examples of the ways that the Christian tradition might shape humanistic studies.

Still, Pelikan's reflections suggested that Protestant hopes for a Christian academy were not far-fetched. As the reviewer for the *Christian Century* wrote, "Luther and the Reformers stood honorably 'in the vanguard of intellectuals of their times.'"[11] With a few more books like Pelikan's, the argument seemed to run, twentieth-century Christian scholars could do the same. The Christian intellectual did not need to be a specimen from the past but rather possessed a legitimate calling, with abundant resources upon which to draw. In effect, Pelikan's point was that Christian scholars could and should contribute substantially and without defensiveness to the intellectual community. And together with Harbison, Pelikan demonstrated how much Protestant educators identified with and continued to draw upon the insights of sixteenth-century Christian scholars, thanks in part to the legacy of neo-orthodoxy. The fundamental question was whether Pelikan and Harbison's peers could accomplish in the twentieth century anything that might meaningfully measure up to the Christian scholarship of the sixteenth century.

Faith in Practice or Obscurity?

The *Christian Scholar* was a publication where academics who aspired to the name of the journal could put into practice what Harbison and Pelikan had discussed abstractly. Started in 1953, it continued the former quarterly, *Christian Education,* under the same auspices of the National Council of Churches' Commission on Christian Higher Education. The *Christian Scholar* drew heavily on the constituency that oversaw and supported mainstream Protestantism's denominational colleges. Consequently, its contributions came from faculty at Protestant colleges. But it also functioned as an outlet for Protestant academics who taught at nonreligious private and public institutions and who joined the FCF. The *Christian Scholar*'s editorial board included a broad spectrum of leaders within the Protestant establishment, from Bishop James A. Pike, dean of the Cathedral of St. John the Divine, and Walter E. West, counselor to Protestant students at Columbia University, to William Savage, religion editor at Scribner's, and Douglas Knight, who taught English at Yale University. The *Christian Scholar* became, in effect, the clearinghouse for mainline Protestant academics outside religious studies. But like their religion colleagues, writers for the *Christian Scholar* were committed to the proposition that faith and academics were "complimentary aspects of [their] whole life," with belief and study not being divorced "but in constant tension and dialectic."[12]

Perhaps because intellectual pursuits for Christians involved the constant strain of "tension and dialectic," the *Christian Scholar* featured information on a variety of Protestant networks that provided academics with the sustenance of fellowship and fraternity. Older organizations, such as the Student Christian Movement and the NCRHE, constantly supplied reports on their activities. For instance, in the very first issue of the *Christian Scholar* the secretary of the United Student Christian Council enthusiastically recounted three student conferences held during Christmas vacation of 1952 whose purpose was to promote group study by Christians at college and university, and to provide appropriate literature. Instead of using "bull sessions on religion" as a way to bring students to an understanding of Christianity, the conferences promoted the value and practice of "serious study." The theological justification for "having to study in a nose-to-the-grindstone manner" was Jesus Christ's command to love God with "our 'minds.'"[13] The NCRHE also took advantage of the new publication to promote its ongoing work in "stimulating and assisting American colleges and universities to make more adequate provision for religion," by reminding readers of the deadline for graduate student fellowships, listing criteria for projects, and publicizing recent publications.[14] Such reports not only obviated the longevity of organizations started at the beginning of the twentieth century but also demonstrated that those earlier Protestant efforts, if not responsible for changing the direction of American higher education, had at least cultivated a network of institutions and scholars that were nonetheless a presence within the educational establishment.[15]

The one newcomer to the network of Protestant educational organizations was the FCF, founded in the 1952 with the threefold purpose of nurturing "fellowship and discussion" among Christian academics who viewed teaching as a calling, exploring opportunities for Christian faculty to contribute to the "whole life" of their particular academic community, and prompting greater attention to the relation between Christian belief and modern scholarship. FCF held its first national conference at Berea College, Kentucky, and the theme was the "Responsibility of the Christian Professor in the Academic Community."[16] Though the new journal, the *Christian Scholar*, was designed to publish FCF members' reflections on their vocation and academic disciplines, by holding

its first conference at a small, obscure denominational college, the organizers of the new association showed that their interests may have been
more fraternal than academic. If the primary aim of FCF was to show
the value of Christian scholarship, then holding a conference at Yale, an
institution still friendly to the Protestant establishment, would have
made more sense. But if the objective of bringing Christian academics
together was to respond to the conflicts and uncertainties that the academy presented to believing scholars, then gathering in a more intimate
setting was a wise decision. In fact, the early notices about the FCF
sounded a lot like the rhetoric used in the 1920s and 1930s by the early
leaders of the National Association of Bible Instructors. But now,
instead of advocating the appointment of religion faculty to provide the
spiritual development undergraduates needed, Christian faculty in all
the disciplines were being asked to give religious oversight to teaching
and research. Perhaps because the scholars teaching and studying religion were increasingly seeking to professionalize their own field, the
organizers of the FCF sensed a need for the religious work previously
performed by Bible instructors and chaplains.[17]

The fraternal and explicitly spiritual tone of the FCF was clearly evident at its first national conference, at least as reported to readers of the
Christian Scholar. The highlight of this first gathering was a "sense of
community, the sharing of insights and problems." But even more
important was the presence of God. According to the reporter, what
emerged as the primary realization at the conference was "the Spirit
of God working in the group as a whole." In fact, as one FCF member
put it at the conference's conclusion, "This has been a means of grace."
From such a vantage point the vocation of the Christian scholar
assumed sacramental proportions as faculty examined the "true nature
of the college and university" from a "fuller understanding of a biblical
world-view." The ministerial dimension of Christian faculty was also
evident in the worship service that began the conference. FCF members
shared a sense of dependence upon God and gathering for public acts of
worship was "primary for the Fellowship's corporate life." Only when
the conference turned to theology did matters narrowly academic or
scholarly come into view. Here, the participants divided along the doctrinal lines of classic Augustinianism, neo-orthodoxy, and process theology. But the reverent atmosphere prevented "party lines" from forming.
Only after laying a devotional and theological foundation did the conference turn to the relationship between faith and reason, or theology and
academics. But at this point the program offered a grab bag of topics
from the "nature of objectivity," and the "relation between professorial

and pastoral responsibilities," to the social responsibilities of faculty and the Christian ideal of college education.[18]

So much goodwill and fellowship actually worked against the FCF. Initially, its leaders wanted to avoid an administrative structure even to the point of dispensing with organizational memberships, an indication of just how inspirational FCF leaders believed their meetings could be. But by 1954 plans went ahead for an executive director, an executive committee, and recruiting members.[19] Even so, by 1956 when the FCF staged its second national conference, motivation for the association appeared to be running out of steam. That meeting, for instance, went without mention or comment in the 1956 and 1957 volumes of the *Christian Scholar*. Part of the problem was competition from a myriad of other organizations. Instead, the Don's Advisory Group of the Student Christian Movement, the original inspiration for the FCF, sponsored a conference, as did the World Student Christian Federation, the Commission on Christian Higher Education, the United Student Christian Council, and the National Conference of the Interseminary Movement.[20] Obviously, the FCF faced stiff competition from a broad range of activities sponsored by mainline Protestantism's vast network of educational endeavors. A further example of the multiplicity of Protestant efforts was the First Quadrennial Convocation of Christian Colleges, held in 1954 at Denison University, and sponsored by the Commission on Christian Higher Education of the National Council of Churches. The editors of the *Christian Scholar* devoted a whole supplemental issue to this meeting, from papers that discussed the aims of the Christian college both in the United States and around the world, to appendices that duplicated the liturgies used at the conference along with lists of works played at an organ recital and descriptions of artworks exhibited.[21] The competition of Protestant scholarly endeavors was so confusing that a statement by the director of FCF expressed surprise over the existence of the National Council's Commission on Christian Higher Education. Edward Dirks explained that when he became director of FCF he knew "nothing" of the Commission on Christian Higher Education and was "very conscious" of the FCF's autonomy. But he added that he had come to see the interrelationship between the initiative to cultivate a self-conscious group of Christian faculty and the broader aims of the Protestant denominations in higher education. "Christians in the university and the units which represent them," Dirks explained, "act responsibly only in responsible relation to each other" which involved "a real interaction within a whole."[22] Whether this was an apology for FCF autonomy or a forced response to pressure from the Protestant hierarchy to conform, Dirks's statement of clarification reflected a diminished role for the FCF in Protestant scholarly activities, thus explaining the organization's abrupt demise.[23]

What was true for the FCF was equally so for production of Christian scholarship by Protestant academics. Though the *Christian Scholar* was designed to foster a fruitful synthesis of religious conviction and academic inquiry, the interest of the Protestant establishment in their own educational institutions often hamstrung forays into Christian scholarship. For instance, in its very first issue the quarterly published articles on "The Terrible Responsibility of the Teacher," "The Recognition of Christian Perspective in Liberal Arts Teaching at Beloit College," "Witness on Campus," "The Christian Ministry to the Campus," and "The College and the Church: A Partnership."[24] These titles were indicative of mainstream Protestantism's interest in higher education. The actual doing of Christian scholarship or the transmission of knowledge in the classroom could not be separated from the spiritual and devotional concerns of campus ministry. The impression left by such constant references to the Christian college or the responsibilities of Christian faculty outside the classroom was that Protestant educators were not entirely certain what to do with "pure" scholarship. Teaching and writing that did not result in some pious advice for students or demonstrate the importance of Christianity for the betterment of the human race was not obviously Christian.[25]

When Protestant educators did venture onto the runway of Christian scholarship, they did not soar very high. What became fairly obvious early on in the era of the Protestant scholar was how much academics working in fields other than Bible and theology were riding the coattails of the theological renaissance that such figures as the Niebuhr brothers and Paul Tillich had stimulated. In 1956, for instance, the editors of the *Christian Scholar* dedicated one issue to the "biblical perspective" that provided the framework for Christian scholarship. Not only did the editors want to outline the worldview that guided their efforts, but they also hoped to articulate the message that believing academics would speak to American higher education.[26] To carry out this task, they enlisted the standard names in biblical and theological studies from the National Association of Biblical Scholars.

The idiom Protestants used to speak to the academy was decidedly neo-orthodox. Not only did Ernest Wright and Joseph Haroutunian, two prominent spokesmen for a return to biblical theology, contribute articles to the *Christian Scholar*'s issue on the theological basis of Christian scholarship, but the editors also included an annotated bibliography on trends in biblical theology.[27] The editors also made explicit and positive reference to the efforts of Karl Barth and Rudolf Bultmann to "save the Gospel from 'the acids of modernity.'"[28] With neo-orthodoxy providing the motivation for efforts to integrate Christianity and scholarship, it should have come as little surprise that the editors ran articles on the fundamental doctrines of the Christian religion. In addition to Wright's article on special revelation and Haroutunian's on the church, Walter Harrelson contributed one on creation, Howard Kee on the biblical idea of miracle, and Krister Stendahl on Christology.[29] Still, only one article in the entire issue attempted to link the convictions of Protestant divinity to the work in the academy. Here, Paul S. Minear, professor of New Testament at Andover Newton Theological School, used the biblical types of the first and last Adam to contrast the tension between the Christian scholar's dual desires to be faithful to Christ and to be of service to the world. Though Minear believed these desires were compatible because the peace the world sought could only be found in Christ, the Christian scholar's religious convictions and duties were considerably more important than his academic responsibilities. All of the Christian academic's contributions, Minear wrote, "will flow from his participation in the life of the second Adam." "He will measure his own growth and that of his students by New Testament norms rather than by contemporary German, Dutch or American standards." Gone was the older liberal Protestant strategy of accommodating Christianity to the academy. The neo-orthodox Protestant academy, at least as Minear explained it, hoped to make the scholarly community subservient to Christ.

The possibility of taking the academy captive for Christ was also on display in another issue of the *Christian Scholar*, published later the same year. The theme of this number was how to harmonize the believing academic's religious convictions and scholarly responsibilities. Though the editor introduced the collection of essays with the hypothetical case of a Christian biologist who confessed that he was "torn apart" between Christianity and science,[30] the tone throughout the accompanying articles reflected little of the angst implied by the editor. In fact, this silence also suggested how comfortable Protestants academics felt with their dual identity as Christian scholars. Contributing to such comfort was the oft-repeated assurance that science was no longer as powerful as it had been. Roland Mushat Frye, who taught English at Emory University, invoked this perspective when he wrote of "the widening recognition that 'objectivity' is a weak reed upon which to rest any intellectual structure." The limits of Enlightenment rationality meant that interpretation was integral to rigorous scholarship. And since all forms of knowledge reflected certain interpretive stances, "the Christian landscape of reality" was no less legitimate than other philosophical or ideological perspectives.[31]

Another common refrain for understanding the duties of Christian scholars was to claim—as L. O. Kattsoff, professor of philosophy at the University of North Carolina, did—that the Christian academic could do his work confidently from the perspective of the Protestant doctrine of the priesthood of all believers. Just as shoemakers, engineers, and doctors sought to serve God in their work, so too the task of Christian scholarship was dedicated to "the service of God" and gained significance by revealing "God in his creation."[32] Because the Christian scholar sought to integrate his work within the framework of his belief in God, Protestant faculty had a great stake in the effort to restore unity to the university curriculum. Again, science bore a good deal of the blame for contributing to the fragmentation of knowledge. But with science now seen in more realistic terms, Christian academics could help to recover a sense of perspective and integration that American higher education desperately needed. According to Frye, "Surely we have by now come to the point where mere accumulation of knowledge is no longer our *prime* need, and unless we can somehow place our efforts within a larger context of value and meaning" the amassing of "stockpiles of learning" would be "quite irrelevant." Frye added that even though the humanities facilitated the search for values and meaning, their presence in the curriculum did not guarantee integration.[33] Still, despite this concession, he reinforced the older tie between religion and general education, and drew parallels between religious and humanistic teaching.

One last theme to which Protestant academics rallied was the difference that religious conviction made for personal relationships and interaction on campus. This line of analysis made it sound as if Christian scholars were nicer people, and therefore better colleagues. For instance, Clyde A. Holbrook, department chair of religious studies at Oberlin College, wrote that professors owed each other "a bond of mutual loyalty by virtue of the common task" in which they were engaged. This commitment was not "uniquely Christian," he admitted. But the believing teacher "may more keenly feel the obligation and opportunity for a community of loyalty and openness to each other than others."[34] Meanwhile, Rene de Visme Williamson argued that in the dog-eat-dog world of scholarship Christians would behave noticeably differently because of the example of Christ. Just as Jesus showed love to Pharisees, Samaritans, Sadducees, Romans, Publicans, and Sinners, so Christian faculty would "see in [their colleagues] the elements of greatness they possess." Christian faculty would also, following the example of the early church, form groups for fellowship and mutual support that would attract non-believers to the convictions and ways of believers.[35]

Whether the concerns for Christian scholarship implied confidence about the relationship between faith and knowledge, the failure of Protestant academics to entertain hard questions about the intellectual merits of their beliefs or the success of integrating faith and learning contributed to a form of scholarship that, whether unimaginative or intellectually respectable, remained only vaguely Christian. Protestant discussions about the arts and humanities generally lacked imagination. A 1964 issue of the *Christian Scholar*, for instance, ran several articles on Christianity and literature. At the one end was a basic discussion of the methods governing literary study. Here Joseph H. Summers, chair of the English department at Washington University, contrasted the Christian literary scholar's dual loyalties, one to the truth-telling required by the academy and the other to interpret literature from the perspective of Christianity. Though the first duty of Christian academics "is the discovery and community of truth," they also had a responsibility to "keep alive and potentially available" such religious insights as the affirmation of life, "that heroism is possible," that God is "both Love and Creator," and that no matter how much suffering pervades human existence joy "is a mark of the Christian life."[36] At the other end of the discussion of Christian literature were essays on religious themes in the works of particular writers. Newby Toms, an undergraduate student at Princeton, assessed the soteriology behind T. S. Eliot's *The Cocktail Party,* while Josephine Jacobsen, a freelance writer, explored Christian themes in the fiction of Muriel Spark, Graham Greene, J. W. Powers, and Flannery O'Connor.[37] In between were articles on the differences between philosophy and fiction, and the use of Christ figures in American literature whose authors both assumed a didactic view of art more typical of Victorian literary studies.[38] Overall the level of scholarship was not impressive, while the editors' reliance upon two authors without academic appointments suggested a paucity of contributors from which to draw. (That the *Christian Scholar*'s Protestant editors also included two essays either from or about Catholics also implies that Protestant resources in English literature were weak.)

If the quality of Christian literary efforts suffered, the editors of the *Christian Scholar* provided a more intellectually provocative set of articles on medicine, although even here the task of integrating religion and scholarship ran in familiar paths. For instance, Ronald W. McNeur's (a member of the United Presbyterian Church U.S.A.'s educational leadership) article on the relationship between theology and medicine criticized thoughtfully the influence of Cartesian dualism on the treatment of illness but ended up arguing for a holistic approach to the medical sciences that had the customary ring of the mainline Protestant critique of the fragmentation of modern learning.[39] A similar theme came from the complaint of Otto E. Guttentag, professor of medicine at the University of California–San Francisco, about the mechanistic view of the body that prevailed in western medicine.[40] Another common conviction undergirding Protestant scholarly efforts was that determinism of any kind contradicted what Christianity taught about human responsibility and the sovereignty of God. Reiterating this perspective was the article by psychoanalyst Rollo May on the problems of deterministic methods in his field.[41] Where these themes were not present the authors made little mention of religion or the way it pertained to the topic under scrutiny. For example, Eugene T. Gendlin, a psychiatrist at the University of Wisconsin, wrote an essay on the way individuals understand concepts and psychologist Ludwig B. Lefebre appropriated existentialism for psychotherapy; both addressed recent trends in these fields with no reference to Christian convictions whatsoever.[42] Whatever the merits of these essays, some readers could have easily wondered what difference religion made in producing good scholarship.

The impression created by this series of essays on Christianity and medicine was that the academic caliber of the author was disproportional to his Protestant convictions. In fact, the editor felt compelled to account for so many contributions from non-Protestant traditions, and even from non-Christians. The *Christian Scholar,* he explained, has always sought "to be inclusive of . . . insights from all major Christian traditions" even though the journal's identity was squarely within the heritage of "a central stream of Protestantism." When the editorial board began to assemble a roster of writers for the theme of theology and medicine they recognized that "we who are within the Protestant heritage have not been able to keep up in this important field."[43] This admission was as significant as it was curious. Not only did it raise the issue of the need for a Christian perspective on the field of medicine, and therefore of what was distinctively Christian about the scholarship

Protestants were promoting, but it also did not prompt the editor to explain why some of the contributors had no recognizable religious affiliation or outlook. In other words, if non-Christians could produce research and writing fit for Protestant standards of integrating religion and scholarship, then what was the point of having believers go into the academy or of faulting the university world for excluding religious perspectives? The anomaly of Christian scholarship was all the more glaring when the editor included a piece on medical ethics from Joseph Fletcher, a professor at Episcopal Theological School, who would later gain public attention through his work on situation ethics.[44] His solution to such difficult moral decisions as abortion, contraception, and euthanasia—by applying the Christian teaching that "God is love"—the "only one thing" that was "*intrinsically* good . . . regardless of circumstances"—demonstrated how amorphous and chimerical the Protestant mind had become. If an Episcopal priest was going to say that all ethical decisions were theologically relative, chances were that Protestant attempts to carve out a distinctively Christian academy would be equally vague and equivocal. Consequently, despite the enthusiasm for Christian scholarship, Protestants delivered very little that counted as both good scholarship and serious Christian reflection.

The best that mainline Protestant educators could do was point out the perilous consequences of the professionalization and specialization of knowledge. In fact, this was the wedge that had allowed Protestants a way back into American higher education during the quarter century after World War II. By proposing a religious perspective on modern learning as a way to restore integration and meaning to all of the facts produced by scientific methods, Protestants joined with other educators who believed universities and colleges needed to advocate certain values and ideals, not just provide information, to undergraduates and professors-in-training. Teaching religion was just one phase, even though the most important, of this Protestant initiative. Bringing a Christian worldview to bear on all the areas of human inquiry was another way to demonstrate not just the reasonableness of Christianity but also the need for scholars who could see and impart the larger significance of the subjects they studied and taught.

But the fate of the *Christian Scholar* revealed how fleeting the harmonization of religion and higher education was. By 1967 cheerleaders for a Protestant academy had become hoarse, at least if this journal was any indication. That year marked the resignation of Edward Dirks as editor of the *Christian Scholar*. A professor of Christian methods at Yale Divinity School, Dirks was also well entrenched in the network of mainline Protestant institutions involved in American higher education. Not only did he serve on education committees of the National Council of Churches, but he also held posts at the Edward W. Hazen Foundation, the Society for Religion in Higher Education (supported largely by Hazen), the World Student Christian Federation, and the Danforth Foundation. In addition, Dirks was largely responsible for the creation of the FCF.[45] He typified the outlook and interests of mainline Protestant educators who asserted repeatedly the importance of religious perspectives and moral values for higher education. In the words of J. A. Martin Jr., the Danforth Professor of Religion in Higher Education at Union Theological Seminary (New York), Dirks's contribution had been to lead and facilitate a "more catholic and more responsible" discussion of Christianity in the university "than any that has gone before," a discussion that did not "evade the perennial questions of philosophical and theological foundations."[46]

Yet, part of the reason for the resignation of this "young man" must have been linked to the inability of the Protestant community to carry on that discussion in an intellectually responsible or compelling manner.[47] At the same time that Dirks resigned from his post as editor, the sponsors of the *Christian Scholar* determined to stop its publication and replace it with a new journal, *Soundings*. The change of name was significant. Whereas the *Christian Scholar*'s purpose was to advocate the work of Christians in the university, *Soundings*' aims were far less ambitious. It would be to engage scholars "with issues of value, meaning and purpose." In other words, the Christian position was too sectarian. While the *Christian Scholar* promoted the relevance of Christianity to academic work, *Soundings* made "common human concerns" the unifying element and thus replaced "Christianity as 'the intellectual foundation for all areas of scholarly inquiry.'" The editor of *Soundings* did not regard this as a capitulation to secularism. Rather it was a recognition of the breadth and dignity of humanity. The "Judaic-Christian tradition" narrowly and religion more generally were simply parts of the various fields of learning that "dignifies" man, "illumines his reality, tells a truth about him, challenges him to fuller potential." The commitment of Protestant educators was still to values and meaning, or seeing things whole. In fact, *Soundings* would be a forum almost exclusively for interdisciplinary studies "of genuine interest to a wide audience of scholars in many disciplines."[48] But a generic humanism, rather than Christian teaching, supplied the angle of vision.

Whatever the reason for Dirks's departure, the demise of the *Christian Scholar* and the founding of *Soundings* signaled the failure of the mainline Protestant philosophy of higher education. Despite the repeated claims that theological perspectives made a difference in the academy, the results of Protestant scholarship showed otherwise. The best Protestant educators could do was keep alive an older humanistic understanding of liberal education with a few religious themes thrown in. But as the pages of the *Christian Scholar* indicated, Christianity was hardly essential to that understanding. What is more, Protestant pleas for integration, meaning, and value in American higher education did little to prevent the ongoing specialization and professionalization of higher learning. Ironically, mainline Protestantism's commitment to humane and learned generalism added to the impression that Protestant educators were backward at the same time that their efforts to establish a Christian academy made them look sectarian.

Settling for the Humanities

With prospects for a Christian academy fading into interdisciplinary studies, mainline Protestant educators would have to be content with religious studies as the one place where the importance of religious convictions for scholarly endeavor made a difference. In effect, Protestant participation in the academy required a bargain. In exchange for making Protestant divinity the curriculum in religious studies programs, Protestants would have to learn to live with secularism in other fields. This bargain also required Protestants to relent in their pursuit of integration and general education. Protestant educators naturally could claim to be specialists in Bible, theology, ethics, and religious history, but in other areas religious perspectives would have to take a backseat to the rules of the specific academic discipline.

Around 1965 this bargain did not appear to be too concessive. During the 1960s Princeton University's Council of the Humanities, with generous support from the Ford Foundation, commissioned a survey of humanistic scholarship in American learning. According to the series' general editor, Richard Schlatter, the volumes were designed to give an account of the various humanistic disciplines, "enabling us to see just what that scholarship has contributed to the culture of America and the world."[49] If this series was any indication, the bargain that Protestants had made was paying substantial dividends. Of the thirteen volumes in this series, two were devoted to the field of religion, Clyde A. Holbrook's *Religion: A Humanistic Field* (1963), and *Religion* (1965), a summary of the various fields in religious studies edited by Paul Ramsey.[50] If mainline Protestants had failed to prove to other scholars the benefits that religious convictions yielded in the carrel and classroom, they had at least acquired the authority to determine what constituted the study of religion.

The volume edited by Paul Ramsey, an ethicist at Princeton University, was the most straightforward and hence the most predictable of the two books on religion in the humanities series. It contained essays on the history of religions, New Testament and Old Testament studies, church history, theology, ethics, and philosophy of religion. The book lacked an introduction and functioned like a reference work or guide to religious studies. Ramsey's choices provided a snapshot of Protestant divinity circa the first half of the 1960s. With the exception of the chapter on the study of the Old Testament, written by Harry M. Orlinsky of Hebrew Union College, Ramsey assembled a cadre of scholars well known in Protestant seminary and divinity school circles—Princeton University's Philip H. Ashby for the history of religions, the University of Chicago Divinity School's Robert M. Grant for New Testament, Princeton Theological Seminary's James Hastings Nichols for church history, the University of Pennsylvania's Claude Welch for theology, Yale University's James M. Gustafson for ethics and John E. Smith for philosophy of religion. Except for Orlinsky and Welch, all of the contributors had clear ties to the most important educational institutions of Protestant divinity. If anyone needed proof that mainstream Protestants controlled the field of religious studies, both in its curriculum and leading authorities, this book documented it.

Still, because the Ramsey and Holbrook books were part of a series bearing the imprimatur of Princeton University and the Ford Foundation, they gave the impression that religious studies was more scholarly than Protestant. To be sure, Princeton and Ford were not without their own religious connections, but the structure of peer review implicit in the network of editors and sponsors did not question the series' matter-of-fact description of Protestant hegemony in the teaching and study of religion. Part of this blindness to the parochialism of religious studies could be attributed to the humanistic orientation of the series. The teaching and study of religion had gone forward since the 1940s on the basis of a shared outlook among humanistic scholars and the mainline Protestant community.[51] What is more, the Protestant educators who wrote for and edited publications such as the *Christian Scholar* kept alive the older notion of liberal education as a humanizing, civilizing, and integrating enterprise where values and presuppositions, especially religious ones, were crucial to genuine learning. In other words, no matter how much religious studies was part of the mainline Protestant effort to reform American higher education through the integration of faith and learning, it borrowed enough of the tradition of liberal education to look academically respectable.

But academic respectability also implied good scholarship, which meant following the conventions of the academy. So Holbrook's volume, *Religion: A Humanistic Field,* provided a rationale for the subjects covered in the collection edited by Ramsey. To be sure, the very title of the Holbrook book tapped the older conception of religious studies' humanizing and civilizing capacities. Consequently, for instance, he devoted a whole chapter to the place of religion in the humanities, on the one hand arguing that it was impossible to understand the human experience apart from religion, and on the other mentioning the great benefit of interdisciplinary approaches that included religion scholars along with the humanistic faculty.[52] Holbrook described the existential aspect of teaching and studying religion that assisted the "student in coming to an understanding of himself in the light of a broadened and deepening understanding of religious orientations as found in his own and others' cultures" (82). This side of religious studies picked up not only on the rhetoric of the humanities' cosmopolitan perspective but also on the older rationale of Protestant campus ministry that regarded instruction in religion as a means toward spiritual fulfillment and ethical development.

Nevertheless, Holbrook was well aware that the "religion scholar must accept the ground rules of university education at its best," not seeking any "special privilege" among the humanities (50). Here he had to explain why religion scholars in the United States in some cases were producing inferior scholarship and also why Protestantism was the religion of choice in the religious studies curriculum. On the former difficulty, Holbrook conceded that the common impression was that the "undergraduate professor of religion contributes little to the realm of scholarship" (231). Teaching, too much religious work with students, lack of secretarial support, and inadequate library resources all played a role. Still, upon closer inspection, religion professors had not "been altogether idle" in conducting research and writing scholarly books and articles (234). At this point, Holbrook felt it necessary to introduce his peers in the humanities to the broad range of professional academic organizations in religious studies from the Society of Biblical Literature and the American Society of Church History to the National Association of Biblical Instructors. Whether Holbrook himself knew that NABI's original purpose was pedagogical rather than scholarly is not clear. For all that his readers knew, it could have been as academically oriented as the American Textual Criticism Society. Still, after surveying relevant journals in religion and related topics, Holbrook concluded that religion scholars were publishing at the same rate as other humanistic scholars who wrote on religion. And if books of significance in religion were taken into account, the grade for religious scholarship improved dramatically, so much so that Holbrook could conclude "American scholarship in religion has been vigorously prosecuted." Of course, this was not the place, in a formidable series on the humanities, to air too much dirty laundry. Even so, the fact that faculty outside religion departments and seminaries produced so much of the scholarly literature on religion haunted Holbrook's overall assessment of religious scholarship (250–51).

If religious studies faculty were not up to the level of scholars in other disciplines, even in their own area of study, then why were departments of religion necessary? Holbrook never squarely addressed this question. But he did feel compelled to account for the dominance of Protestantism in the study of religion, both in its curriculum and its faculty (whose graduate training often involved completing Ph.D. degrees at Protestant seminaries and divinity schools).[53] After all, was not Protestantism "a relatively narrow door" by which to introduce students to the subject of religion (156)? In response, Holbrook expressed the kind of presumptuous apology for mainline Protestantism that assumed its superiority on the basis of its tolerance and breadth, a basis that in practice made mainstream Protestantism naively intolerant and sectarian by excluding intolerant faiths. For him the question did not concern the limitations a curriculum put upon the student as much as it did with whether the material offered "a breadth of understanding" for further study of religion. And for Holbrook, Protestantism did just that. It had distinguished itself by "establishing a liberal context more congenial to dealing with other religious traditions than have alternative postures." In other words, mainline Protestants were the only believers whose outlook gave them the manners necessary for life in the university. According to Holbrook, "neither Catholicism nor Judaism has as yet prepared men specifically for teaching and scholarship at the undergraduate level to the degree to which Protestantism has" (157, 159). And since religion was so important for a good education, and mainline Protestants held the vast majority of good Ph.D. degrees in religious studies, hiring them to teach Protestant divinity of the mainline variety was in the best interests of everyone in American higher education. This is why Holbrook could go on to argue that instruction in Protestant conceptions of grace, redemption, and revelation to undergraduates need not be a problem. Protestants embraced an open-ended approach to Christianity that made it possible for theologians "to strike hands" with scholars in other disciplines who confronted "similar problems" and abided by "the accepted rules of intellectual discourse" (166). Enlightened Christianity was alive and well in the American university.

With the imprimatur of the Princeton Council on the Humanities and the Ford Foundation, Holbrook's book appeared as a defense of religious studies by an insider in American higher education.[54] But a few critics of his arguments did surface. One from within the ranks of religious studies was John F. Wilson, a recently appointed assistant professor of religious studies at Princeton University. Wilson accused Holbrook of too easily skirting the entanglement between religious studies and the Protestant establishment.[55] He also criticized him for adhering to a bastardized understanding of the liberal arts, one that had been canonized by Harvard University's *General Education in a Free Society,* but which in Wilson's estimate was a heretical departure from the original curriculum of the *trivium* and *quadrivium.* The historic purpose of the liberal arts was to prepare a man for citizenship, not to "liberalize" or "humanize." But the substance of Wilson's criticism concerned the hegemony of Protestant divinity in the religious studies curriculum and faculty. Instead of replicating "protestant seminary offerings minus the so-called 'practical work,'" Wilson advocated the scientific study of religious phenomena as the one thing holding the academic study of religion together. "The study of religion in the faculties of arts and sciences," he concluded, "should be the study of religious phenomena through the use of as many methods as prove fruitful and appropriate." Philosophical, historical, sociological, and psychological methods would be prominent in such an approach, but would not ignore obvious links to the study of art, literature, archaeology, language, and the history of science.[56]

Wilson's call for religious studies free from ecclesiastical dominance and appropriate to the arts and sciences was one way of trying to resolve the inconsistencies inherent in mainstream Protestant scholarship. Whether in religion or other fields, Protestant scholars claimed to be scientific and therefore open to truth wherever it would lead, but also granted a privileged position to liberal Protestantism.

At the other end of the spectrum was the complaint of Morton White, professor of philosophy at Harvard, who although writing several years before Holbrook's book appeared was no less critical of the approach to religious studies specifically (and to religion in higher education generally) implied by *Religion: A Humanistic Field*. Instead of trying to study religion scientifically, White proposed that religious studies follow the model of philosophy or physics. Being philosophical involved commitment to answering philosophical questions.[57] Being a physicist entailed belief or, at least, the pretended belief in the particular theory taught.[58] On this basis, White speculated that the religious equivalent of teaching philosophy or physics was teaching people to be religious. For him, religion was a "total way of life," something that involved far more than cognitive assent to "bare propositions of theology." Religiosity also included the acceptance of attitudes that were moral, liturgical, and social. The way to teach religion, in White's view, was to appoint faculty who while adhering to different religions shared the same concern of being religious, just as philosophers and physicists respectively held the common concern of being philosophical or scientific. No religious tests should be used to appoint faculty. The only criteria would be religious devotion.[59]

White's argument directly challenged the mainline Protestant strategy for integrating religion and learning, whether through the front door of religious studies or the back door of a religious worldview. The Harvard philosopher did not think it inappropriate to teach students *about* religion since scholars in various fields, such as sociology, anthropology, literature, and philosophy were already doing this.[60] A separate department of religion was unnecessary. Nor did White think it a violation of liberal and scientific standards to instruct students *how* to be religious so long as such instruction occurred in a well-defined space like a divinity school.[61] But White believed the way religion faculty were teaching about religion was two-faced. To avoid the charge of indoctrination religion professors claimed to be teaching only about religion. And to avoid the apparent bias of offering courses only in Protestant divinity they argued that mainline Protestants held the best credentials for faculty status and that mainstream Protestantism was the religion best suited to the ideals of the university. White's critique not only revealed the inconsistencies of Protestant educational efforts but also touched the nerve of religious studies' ministerial and spiritual origins. Not too many years before the publication of White's book the task of teaching about religion was never too far removed from the aim of producing good Protestant church members. In other words, putting religion back into the academy was bound up with the desire of preventing college graduates from becoming irreligious.[62]

Thus, a certain irony accompanied the success of the Protestant academy. Momentum for the integration of faith and learning fizzled quickly once put to the test of producing Christian scholarship. Protestant perspectives on science or art might ward off the increasing secularism of the academy but it rarely resulted in noteworthy scholarship. Meanwhile, the recognition of religion as a legitimate humanistic discipline and worthy partner in American higher education occurred at the same time that the rationale for the teaching and study of religion began to show wear. Teaching and studying religion by the rules of the university was a far more difficult proposition than simply assembling those scholars sufficiently agile to keep one foot in the academy and one in the church. In the end, mainstream Protestant educators had sufficient resources, good connections, and respectable credentials to make religion a going concern in American higher education. But they did not have the intellectual muscle to keep it that way.

NINE

Religious Studies in
Post-Protestant America

IN 1963 THE U.S. SUPREME COURT issued a ruling that threatened the very character of religious studies as it had developed for almost half a century. That decision followed the infamous case of *Abington Township School District v. Schempp.* The justices ruled that the practice of Bible reading and prayer in public schools violated the First Amendment and thus was unconstitutional. Despite arguments to the contrary, they found that the daily reading of the King James Version of the Bible and the recitation of a common prayer was definitely religious in intent. As Justice William O. Douglas wrote, "The religious aims of the educators who adopted and retained such exercises were comprehensive, and in many cases quite devoid of sectarian bias—but the crucial fact is that they were nonetheless religious." The religious nature of devotional Bible reading and prayer, Douglas added, contradicted the commitment of American public schools to "an atmosphere free of parochial, divisive, or separatist influences of any sort." The schools' mission was to "assimilate children" into a heritage that was common to "all American groups and religions."[1] Those who were familiar with the history of religious studies, with its origins in the campus ministry of the nation's largest denominations, its curriculum following that of Protestant seminaries and divinity schools, and its professional academic organization bearing the name, the National Association of Biblical Instructors, could not help but fear that the very identity of teaching and studying religion in American universities and colleges was in the balance. For what the Court's decision concluded about Bible reading and prayer was also true of religious studies; the latter was also sectarian, religious in orientation, and out of step with the public mission of higher education in the United States. In the words of Sydney E. Ahlstrom, the Supreme Court's decision was a "blow" to the Protestant establishment and halted abruptly the religious and theological revival of the 1950s and early 1960s.[2]

But the Supreme Court's ruling also reflected an understanding of the relationship between religion and public education which allowed the faculty in religious studies programs to breath a collective sigh of relief. Justice Tom C. Clark, who wrote the opinion of the Court, believed that a good education was "not complete" without the study of religion, either comparatively, historically, or in "its relationship to the advancement of civilization." This idea certainly comforted those who had argued for the teaching and study of religion on the grounds of its contribution to the understanding of culture. Even more reassuring was Clark's explicit approval of the Bible as a legitimate academic subject. "The Bible is worthy of study for its literary and historic qualities," he wrote. "When presented objectively as part of a secular program of education" the study of religion was "consistent" with the First Amendment.[3] In his concurring opinion, Justice Douglas also stated that the "non-devotional" use of the Bible was constitutional. "The holding of the Court today," he declared, "does not foreclose teaching *about* the Holy Scriptures or about the differences between religious sects in classes in literature or history." In fact, Douglas could not conceive how it would be possible to teach many subjects in the social sciences and humanities "without some mention of religion."[4] This distinction between the teaching *of* or *about* religion was the doorstop by which religious studies could keep the door to the university ajar.

Still, the Supreme Court's ruling had repercussions for religious studies since the field had always mixed devotion and theology into its academic work. Even though the *Schempp* case focused narrowly on public education at the primary and secondary levels, the Court's decision implied that Protestants no longer had the upper hand in articulating and propagating the nation's civil religion. Consequently, if religious studies was to continue as a legitimate discipline in higher education, a new rationale would be necessary, one that relied less on the historic ties between the common purposes of mainstream Protestantism and the

American republic. Proponents of religious studies would still claim to be representative of the religious life of American culture. But they would have to take into account the diversity of American religious life to avoid the fate of prayer and Bible reading.

Interestingly enough, contemporaneous with the Supreme Court's ruling in *Schempp,* the organization primarily responsible for the teaching and study of religion in American higher education, the National Association of Biblical Instructors (NABI), underwent a facelift. In 1964, it changed its name to the American Academy of Religion (AAR), a change that stemmed precisely from the concerns that prompted the Court's decision. A NABI Self-Study Committee provided the grounds for this new designation. Committee members balked at the terms "national," "biblical," and "instructors" in the association's title. "National" suggested only scholars in the United States. "Biblical" was too narrow a category for the diversity of religious scholarship practiced by members. And "Instructors" implied a lack of academic expertise. For these reasons the committee recommended the new name: "American" to suggest the international character of the organization and to recognize members from Canada and Mexico; "Academy" to bolster the association's scholarly orientation; and "Religion" to show that members studied more than the Bible. In sum, the death of NABI was an admission by Protestant educators that religious studies, as it emerged in the era of neo-orthodoxy, had crossed the line between the church and the academy, or between private and public spheres. The AAR, then, was an effort to provide teaching and produce scholarship about religion compatible with the public and academic character of the university. As the report of the Self-Study Committee put it, the AAR would be a forum to cope with the "trilemma of commitments of faith, independence of scholarship, and public professional obligations."[5]

Only fifteen years later the change of name paid handsome dividends. In 1979 the American Council of Learned Societies admitted the AAR into its membership, thus in some way putting American higher learning's seal of approval on the academic discipline of religious studies. The seeds planted by university chaplains and Bible chairs almost seventy-five years earlier had finally produced the fruit of many members who staffed departments at the best universities and could boast that their enterprise warranted the recognition of America's elite scholarly associations. Yet, religious studies' professionalization came at a great price. Not only did this process require the abandonment of the devotional, ethical, and cultural purposes that religious studies founders believed to be essential to their academic work, but the professionalization of the field also left religious studies without an identity. Stripped of the pious and social grounds for studying religion, religious studies could not produce a set of compelling intellectual reasons for its place in the university.

Public Religious Studies

Protestant educators did not need the Supreme Court to remind them of the precarious nature of studying religion in the public environment of the university. Well before the *Schempp* decision advocates for the teaching and study of religion in American higher education were obligated to comment, if only in passing, about how mainstream Protestantism's interest in teaching religion at the university level was not a violation of the separation of church and state. For instance, William Adams Brown's case for theology in the university, back in 1937, recognized that the disestablishment of religion in the United States changed significantly the public status of Christianity. But banishing religion from formal education was not the design of the founders. "They were Christians," he wrote, "and desired to be known as such." That is why they made provision for a national day of thanksgiving, and chaplains in Congress and the branches of the military. The separation of church and state, therefore, did not threaten the Christian character of the United States. For this reason, private institutions, whether religious (the University of Notre Dame) or nonsectarian (Harvard and Yale), could easily offer religious instruction without violating the boundaries that kept religion and public life in balance. The more difficult situation was that of the state university receiving tax support. Public institutions had to observe a "degree of impartiality" unnecessary in other schools. But this did not mean that the state university "must ignore theology altogether." The university was bound to teach about "the living philosophies which claim the allegiance of men." A state school could not commit itself to any particular answer "to the problem of life which the faith of religion raises." It could "at least" acquaint students with the variety of religious answers, "and not the least" the Christian answer. What made instruction in Christian theology all the more compelling for Brown was the connection between "freedom and faith." Here Christianity's resistance to the tyranny of totalitarianism made it especially worthy of study in publicly funded institutions.[6]

What was true for Brown before World War II was also the case for Henry P. Van Dusen writing after the war. The latter aggressively asserted the legitimacy of teaching religion in public institutions, including state universities. The Supreme Court's 1948 *McCollum* decision, which ruled that released time programs in Illinois schools violated the First Amendment, set the president of Union Theological Seminary (New York) off. This "dictum" of the court worked "great mischief" by misreading the intentions of the framers of the Constitution. The so-called separation of church and state was not a "constitutional principle." Nor was the aim of the founders to exclude religious instruction for state universities. Van Dusen pointed to the example of Thomas Jefferson, who made provision for teaching in ethics and "religious opinions" at the University of Virginia. He also quoted Justice Joseph Story, who wrote that the "general, if not the universal sentiment in America was, that christianity ought to receive encouragement from the state." A right understanding of the relations between church and state, Van Dusen concluded, meant that the contemporary practice of teaching religion and conducting chapel at state universities was simply "a perpetuation of the national tradition."[7] Up until the early 1950s, then, Protestants recognized that the principle of separation could restrain the way religion was taught and studied in public universities, but it usually did not. Because the fortunes of America were so entwined with mainstream Protestantism, the disestablishment of religion in the United States rarely extended to the generic piety and morality of Protestants who had the nation's best interests at heart.

By the early 1960s, however, the leadership within the field of religious studies began to feel the pinch of teaching that looked increasingly partisan because of its Protestant makeup. Though they had too much at stake to retreat from the seminary curriculum that dominated the field, they did begin to argue for the value of religious studies in a way more appropriate to the public concerns that increasingly attended discussions about the place of religion in education, higher or otherwise. For instance, in a small monograph published in 1960 on religion programs in state universities, edited by Milton D. McLean and Harry H. Kimber, the issue of the separation of church and state preceded what amounted to a simple description of the courses offered at a number of public institutions. Two methods of looking at the "separation principle" existed, one "strict," the other "broad." According to the strict view, the state was not to "'establish' in any way any such ultimate attitude or belief, religious or anti-religious, rational or revealed, private or institutional, prevalent or esoteric." This meant that courses with a "positive religious orientation" were suspect, though professors could design instruction that was historical or comparative in nature. Still, the editors, McLean who taught at Ohio State and Kimber, a professor at Michigan State, believed the broader reading of the separation principle tolerated courses "with positive religious content." Here, they advocated that such religious instruction be voluntary (i.e., elective courses), ecumenical (i.e., courses in a diversity of religious traditions), and objective (i.e., descriptive as opposed to indoctrination). These restrictions on religious studies at state universities provided the proper "checks and balances" while also guarding against the equally dangerous situation of providing an education that ignored "the religious heritage of the majority of the students."[8]

While religious studies faculty at state universities were particularly sensitive to the issue of the separation of church and state, religion professors at private institutions also paid greater heed to the public character of their schools and the propriety of religious instruction in that setting. In a series of articles published in the early 1960s, professors from the University of Southern California, Duke, and Princeton described the purpose and composition of their religion programs. The series also included a contribution from a faculty member at the public university, Iowa's School of Religion. Whether describing public or private schools, each article demonstrated a concern to present religious instruction in a publicly acceptable way.

Geddes MacGregor, dean of the graduate school of religion at the University of Southern California (originally a Methodist institution), started off the series in a somewhat rueful tone. "It is not difficult," he wrote, "to understand why the academic ideal of a graduate school of religion independent of all sectarian interests and aims has been imperfectly realized." The reason, simply put, was the burden of the church. MacGregor admitted that doing religious scholarship free from bias or prejudice was next to impossible. The student who believed he was coming to the study of religion without any religious commitment was as guilty of self-deception as the political scientist who "disclaimed any tendency to either a conservative or liberal point of view." Still, as much as good scholarship required some conviction to yield the necessary zeal, MacGregor believed that the study of religion had too often been hampered by the interests of theology and the attendant concerns of the church. But the vision of a "truly free" school of religion where "men of all faiths may earnestly study the immensely valuable theological traditions to which they are heir" under the tutelage of the humanistic and scientific work of modern learning was close to realization. "Never before has there been an opportunity like ours," MacGregor boasted, "never before has there been available the scientific equipment we possess."[9] Like Protestant educators almost one hundred years earlier, here were the themes of science and the university working in tandem with a truly enlightened and ecumenical faith against the forces of dogma and sect for the purpose of ushering in a new era in the history of truth.[10]

Paul Ramsey, the Harrington Spear Paine Professor of Religion at Princeton University, was more no-nonsense and less millennial in his report than MacGregor. Ramsey began with an overview of the religion program's history, rationale, and content. In fact, it was the content that forced him to comment on the propriety of Princeton's offering many courses that would be described traditionally as "seminary fields." Ramsey's response was to assert, rather than argue, that such areas as Old Testament, New Testament, history of Christianity, theology, ethics, and philosophy of religion had "their own integrity wherever they may be taught or studied." His appeal went straight to the heart of academic notions of expertise and professional competence. The subject matter in religious studies arose from the "nature of religion as a scholarly discipline." What is more, it was only by a "historical accident" that religious studies had become so closely identified with a "seminary-based curriculum."[11] In effect, Ramsey denied that a problem of bias existed in religious studies. But his assertion of the propriety of the Princeton program was telling. Whether a historical accident or the work of providence, the orientation of religious studies toward the particulars of Protestant divinity at private universities like Princeton was hard to defend on grounds of scholarly objectivity.

Duke's program, as described by Waldo Beach, professor of ethics, like Princeton's, bore the marks of Protestant theological and biblical studies. The three major fields were Old and New Testaments, church history, and systematic theology and ethics. Beach acknowledged that even though Duke was related to the Methodist Episcopal Church, the "tone" of the campus displayed "the same general anarchy of norms and the same polytheism" at any American university. Yet the secular character of Duke helped students preparing to teach at America's institutions of higher learning. It made them aware of the "Christ-culture" problem in an especially poignant way and gave firsthand experience in driving undergraduates to "search for a frame of meaning." Here Beach showed that the older motives for campus ministry still survived even into the 1960s among the religious studies establishment. Yet his remarks also reflected the growing awareness that the hegemony of Protestant theology in religious studies was inappropriate. For Beach, one of the problems with the teaching and study of religion was its decidedly western outlook. Even though scholars taught the Bible, theology, and church history in an "ecumenical spirit," it had become apparent that "non-Christian" religions were a valid part of religious studies. The need for instruction in world religions was "desperate." Westerners needed to be "sufficiently nurtured in non-Western religious thought-forms to be able to get 'inside' other cultures."[12] Beach's comment foreshadowed one of the ways that religious studies would come to terms with church-state issues. By offering instruction in other religions, the field could dodge the charge of giving Protestantism a privileged position.

The last contributor to the series, Robert Michaelsen, an American church historian turned administrator at Iowa's School of Religion, showed how little difference existed between the study of religion at public and private universities. On the one hand, Michaelsen acknowledged the concerns of those who stressed the tensions between communities of faith and the academic enterprise. These tensions would require that theology be barred from the university since it is a form of knowledge "inimical to objectivity." If the university were to include the study of religion it should be "'objective' and 'scientific,'" rather than instruction offered by representatives of particular religious traditions. The study of religion, according to this view, needed to be historical, philosophical, and analytical. But Michaelsen also defended the legitimacy of Iowa's program by arguing for theology as a proper discipline within the university. His school appointed theological scholars of Judaism, Roman Catholicism, and Protestantism, thus recognizing the diversity of religion in American life. Yet, the instruction offered was at once rooted in both the community of faith and in the academic community. Michaelsen's justification for this approach stemmed from the conviction that the only way to do justice to a particular religion is to have a teacher "thoroughly grounded" in the assumptions of that religion. He also appealed to a broad, and fairly abstract, notion of theology as not simply a creed or dogma but rather as the systematization of a religious community's consensus.[13] Thus, though the public funding of a school like Iowa required instruction in a diversity of religions, it did not prevent the study of theology. In other words, religious studies need not be exclusively Protestant, but it was nonetheless the study of divinity. Religion scholars were coming to terms with religious diversity in American life, but they had yet to find a methodology derived strictly from the university.

Perhaps the best index to the religious studies establishment's growing sensitivity to the tension between the public space of the academy and the private beliefs of the churches was an article by Paul Ramsey's junior colleague at Princeton, John F. Wilson, an American religious historian trained at New York's Union Theological Seminary. Wilson saw clearly that indoctrination was the central issue with which religion professors and programs had to contend. Religious studies, he argued, was basically the Protestant seminary curriculum "minus the so-called 'practical work.'" Wilson also perceived that religious studies was basically "the visible tip of the iceberg supported by that massive and hidden pan-protestant establishment." These remarks could be construed as a recognition that religious studies functioned at the level of higher education the same way that prayer and Bible reading did at the primary school level. This made the older and accepted rationale for teaching religion unacceptable in Wilson's eyes. Religious studies was out of sync with the "religiously pluralistic" character of American society. If religious studies were to fit into the public mission of American universities, religion scholars and administrators would have to recognize that their subject was "socially divisive in a way that other subjects simply are *not*." In sum, the study of religion faced many more "pitfalls" than other fields.[14]

For at least four decades, Protestant educators had forgotten how socially divisive the study of religion could be. They had been so intent to show the social utility of religion for the civic purposes of the university that they did not learn the lessons of an earlier generation of academics, those who established the modern university precisely to avoid the sectarian and parochial character of religion. The Supreme Court's decision in *Schempp* awoke religious studies faculty from their neo-orthodox and mainline Protestant slumbers. Yet, as much as the questions about the place of religion in the academy resembled those of the late nineteenth century, the developments of the 1960s were different in one very important respect: the Enlightened Christianity of liberal Protestantism could no longer command the allegiance of the university's constituency. If religious studies was to persist as a worthy academic discipline it would have to sever its ties to what Wilson called "the massive and hidden pan-protestant establishment."

Religious Studies versus Protestant Divinity

Administrators of religion departments and leaders within the NABI could respond to the charge that religious studies had been too Protestant by pointing to the numerous courses offered and articles written about non-Christian religions by the organization's members. The trickle of scholarship on non-Christian religions may not have been steady but it was nonetheless evident even during the heyday of neo-orthodoxy. For instance, in the 1953 issue of the *Journal of Bible and Religion* J. Calvin Keene, who taught religion and philosophy at Howard University, argued for the importance of Ramanuja, an Indian theologian whom Keene regarded as the "Hindu Augustine."[15] As it turned out, Keene's discussion of Hinduism sounded a lot like the classic Christian debate between Pelagians and Augustinians. He thus may not have followed the advice of Floyd H. Ross, a professor of religion at the University of Southern California, who wrote on behalf of a better understanding by Christians of Oriental religions.[16] In fact, both Ross and Keene explained non-Christian religions, not on their own terms, but rather by what they had in common with Christianity. This was also the approach of a third article by sociologist Will Herberg on the similarities and differences between Judaism and Christianity. Herberg's point, namely, that "Judaism and Christianity are at one with each other and poles apart from the non-biblical 'religions of the world,'" underscored the way that religious studies handled religions other than Christianity; unity and continuity with the religion of the Bible made a non-Christian religion worth including in the curriculum.[17] Such an approach was undoubtedly patronizing toward adherents of non-Christian faiths who believed continuity with Christianity was not so easily obtained. Still, their efforts demonstrated that within religious studies some scholars were making an effort to cover non-Christian religions.

Another way that religion scholars handled non-Christian religions was through the field commonly known as the history of religions, or in its German original, *religionsgeschichtlich*. This scholarly method flourished in the early twentieth century during the hegemony of Protestant liberalism. It approached the sacred writings of Judaism and Christianity as those of any other ancient religion, thus trying to avoid taking a side in disputes about the superiority of one particular religion. It also endeavored to approach religion phenomenologically, that is, without reference to theological questions of divine intervention (i.e., miracles) or supernatural revelation (i.e., the inspiration and infallibility of the Bible). The history of religions approach allowed biblical scholars, for instance, to stress continuity between Christianity, Hellenism, Judaism, Gnosticism, and other religions of the Roman Empire. Most often what held these different religions together were the more basic aspects of religion itself, an abstract and hard-to-describe spiritual essence that scholars often defined as an experience of transcendence or the divine.[18]

During the era of neo-orthodoxy, when Protestants were more confident and also more willing to defend the particularism of their beliefs, the history of religions approach only made an occasional appearance. As Noah Eduard Fehl, who taught the history of religions at Seabury-Western Theological School, pointed out in 1959, the gap between biblical studies and the history of religions became especially wide with the "neo-Reformation" emphasis on "dogmatic theology."[19] Consequently, after World War II, when religious studies gained an institutional presence in American colleges and universities, the history of religions functioned as the grab bag for everything non–Judeo-Christian.[20] But even its advocates could not avoid putting the history of religions to Protestant purposes. Fehl, for instance, hoped that the history of religions and biblical scholars would once again find a "common interest," based on the hope for the "imminent realization of the Kingdom of God." In fact, Fehl believed that with the help of the history of religions, biblical scholars would be better equipped to engage in "theological construction" that would communicate the message of Christianity to the "new emerging world culture where there are no privileges of historic traditions."[21] So, too, Harry M. Buck Jr., who taught religion at Wilson College, compared the myths of Christianity to those of Islam and Buddhism in history of religions–like fashion in order to show how Protestants in a post-Protestant era could still hold on to their "matrix of inherited ideas and symbols" as fully "'true,' at least in a psychological sense."[22] Rather than functioning as a less apologetically motivated way to study religion, the history of religions still gave the upper hand to Christianity, thus depending upon the theological agenda that fueled religious studies more generally.[23] In some cases, it did present itself as a less-biased, even scientific, way to study and teach religion. But even here, prior to the 1970s, the stress upon "the personal" or experiential side of religion, as some have argued, betrayed a Protestant understanding of religion.[24]

As much as an increasing attention to non-Christian religions suggested the future of religious studies, the best evidence of Protestant divinity's decline within the field of religion during the 1960s came from the dramatic change in the relationship between religion departments and Protestant seminaries. During the late 1950s the faculty in religion departments and the leadership of NABI showed their Protestant colors in response to reports by the American Association of Theological Schools (AATS) regarding the best course of study for undergraduates preparing for ministry. AATS's "Statement on Pre-Theological Studies," issued in 1956, appeared to catch religion professors off-guard and put them on the defensive. The simple point of this report was to encourage undergraduates not to major in religion. The intent was not to disparage the instruction offered within religious studies. Rather, the seminarians' concern was that a major in religion would prevent the breadth of knowledge and perspective necessary for the ministry. In turn, AATS's Statement recommended English, history, and philosophy as majors more suitable than religion or Bible for preseminary training.[25]

Adding fuel to the fire was the book that appeared a year later, coauthored by H. Richard Niebuhr, Daniel Day Williams, and James M. Gustafson, *The Advancement of Theological Education*. Like the AATS report, this project also examined the general status of theological education and how the training of ministers might be improved. Unlike the AATS report, however, this book carried the weight of three theologians whose work was widely respected in both the seminary and religious studies worlds. Though Niebuhr et al. did not write much about preseminary education, what they did write was sure to catch the eye of religious studies leaders. They refused to take a side in the dispute about whether a religion major was valuable or not. What was "crucial," from the authors' perspective, was that whatever undergraduates studied, it had to lay "a foundation for the dialogue between Christian thought with other human knowledge." Some religion programs did this, they concluded. But their suggestion was that religious studies was by no means the only way to accomplish such preparation.[26] Since religious studies had been premised upon the desirability of such a dialogue between Christian thinking and the other disciplines in a liberal education, the lukewarm response to NABI's efforts must have struck some religious faculty as the damnation usually accompanying faint praise.

Religion faculty responded with defenses of their programs that reaffirmed the humanistic character of the field. J. Allen Easley, who taught at Wake Forest College, appeared hurt that Protestant seminary leaders would ignore religious studies for preseminary students. If English, history, and philosophy acquainted students with people and ideas, what was wrong with religion, "as though Jeremiah and Paul, Augustine and Luther, and the ideas they promulgated were of little importance"? What is more, the academic standards in religion were just as high as those in other humanistic disciplines, and thereby contributed "to the student's ability to think, to understand the world of men and ideas and of human affairs." One additional defense of religion as an appropriate major was the value of students discovering, before they enrolled at seminary, whether they were in the "wrong field."[27] J. Arthur Baird replied to the AATS study with his own survey of undergraduates from his institution, Wooster College, to see how well a religion major had prepared them for seminary. Not surprisingly, the first-hand testimony of Wooster's graduates was favorable, though Baird did admit that religion majors fared no better than history, English, or philosophy majors. Religion did have the advantage of providing familiarity with Greek before entering seminary. Still, Baird believed the distinction between undergraduate religious studies and seminary education was artificial. "Theological education," he wrote, "is a fabric that is woven throughout *both* the undergraduate and the graduate curricula." In sum, seminaries and colleges needed to "join hands in the task of theological education."[28]

Such a joint endeavor was precisely what motivated NABI in 1959 to issue a report of its own entitled "Pre-Seminary Preparation and Study in Religion," written by the Pre-Theological Studies committee.[29] Though the report asserted that it stood for neither the college point of view nor the seminary perspective, the committee clearly argued for the value of religious studies at the undergraduate level. The reasons summarized those that Protestants had used in the 1940s when religion was just emerging as a recognizable field. It contributed to general education by integrating all the learning that took place in a liberal education. Religion was also part of the liberal arts because it contributed to the "cultivation of sensitivity, the sharpening of moral judgment, and the relating of intellectual endeavor to ultimate questions." Finally, religion was a good major for preseminary students because it provided "the fundamental knowledge" upon which theological schools could build. In sum, the committee recommended "that, wherever possible, a major in religion be considered a live option for the future theological student, but only where the program offered is possessed of breadth and comprehensiveness."[30] To be sure, the report did not rate religion programs according to this implicit hierarchy, but it did show the degree to which religion faculty even as late as four years before the Supreme Court rulings about prayer and Bible reading in public schools identified with the concerns of Protestant theological education.

By 1966, however, the ties between religious studies and Protestant theological education had weakened considerably. Ironically, it was the clerics who wanted to be free from the academics. Signs of the growing divorce between Protestant divinity in the university and

Protestant divinity in the seminary were palpably evident after the Lilly Endowment's Study of Pre-Seminary Education, which began in 1961 and finished five years later. This was a joint project of both the AATS and NABI which stemmed from the former's concerns about the pre-seminary education of students at its member institutions and the latter's desire to be the professional academic organization devoted to teaching and research in religion. Though it began amicably enough, with AATS and NABI recognizing a common purpose, it ended on a sour note. The publications generated by the study were decidedly oriented toward the training of ministers and, therefore, slighted religious studies. In the introduction to *The Making of Ministers,* edited by Keith R. Bridston and Dwight W. Culver, the former a theologian at Pacific Lutheran Theological Seminary, the latter a sociologist at St. Olaf College, the churchly purpose of the report was evident even if the book's title did not give it away. The editors wrote that their task, as stipulated by the commission given them from the AATS and NABI, was to explore "the relation of pre-seminary and seminary education in the training of ministers."[31] Religious studies, then, received scrutiny only to the extent that it bore upon the preparation of ministers.

Remarkably enough, the findings of this study concluded that the academic study of religion as practiced by many members of NABI (which became the AAR during the investigation) was inferior. In one chapter of *Pre-Seminary Education,* Bridston and Culver explained why religious studies as an undergraduate major was a poor preparation for seminary and pastoral work. Here they responded explicitly to the complaints of NABI's members concerning the recommendation of AATS against a religion major for undergraduates. First, they observed that religion was still not "intellectually respectable" in American higher education even though it was beginning to emerge as a humanistic field of study.[32] At public institutions, for instance, courses in religion served "pre-seminary purposes" as a means toward creating "a favorable impression on the governing bodies and general constituency" (64). In fact, the authors quoted one administrator who complained that the curriculum of religious studies had been "bootlegged" into the university from the seminary and served "catechetical" rather than "educational" ends (61). Bridston and Culver were even harder on church-related schools where the preseminary orientation of religion departments was more explicit. Religion faculty at denominational colleges, they complained, had the "specific professional task of recruiting, supervising, and teaching future ministers" (69), a task reflected in such course offerings as sermon preparation and ministry in rural churches. Consequently, religious studies fell well short of the standards of the academy. Students invariably came away from religion courses with the impression that the subject was "less than one which can hold its own with other subjects in free intellectual competition" (66).

The reason for steering preseminary students away from religious studies, then, according to Bridston and Culver, was because of the need for ministers who had been trained in the humanities. The recommendation they made to AATS ran as follows: "For the seminary, the purpose of pre-seminary education is to produce educated men—not little ministers" (80). What ministers needed was not college-level courses in Protestant divinity but rather a broad education in the liberal arts. Bridston and Culver explicitly staked the health of the Protestant ministry on the degree to which ministers received a humanistic education. For this reason, they did not back away from the earlier recommendation of AATS to prospective seminary students regarding the value of English, philosophy, and history majors. Aside from its weak academic status, religious studies was undermining the "liberal arts tradition in American higher education" (67). Was the purpose of undergraduate education to prepare students for professional studies or was it to provide a grounding in the humanities and a well-rounded education? Bridston and Culver wanted Protestant seminaries to side with the older tradition of the liberal arts college and the propagation of western civilization. "The task of pre-seminary education is cultivation and its purpose is to produce cultured men," they concluded (84). Explaining AATS's negative assessment of religious studies by appealing to the same cosmopolitan ideals that linked religion with the humanities may have softened the blow. But this explanation also implicitly called into question religious studies' humanistic credentials. Consequently, Pre-Seminary Education ended up adding to the "academic insecurity" of religion faculty noted by the report's authors (77).

If the report by Bridston and Culver was discouraging to religion faculty, the contributions to The Making of Ministers did little to improve the academic reputation of religious studies. The book, true to its title, addressed the education and preparation of Protestant ministers, and so only one section concerned religious studies per se. Readers could have reasonably expected these chapters to vindicate the field, especially since two of the authors, Robert S. Michaelsen, director of the Iowa School of Religion, and Paul Ramsey, had a large stake in the field of religion. Yet, despite the editors' selection of such sympathetic individuals, the writers' assessment was decidedly negative.

Michaelsen's essay was the least controversial. Part of his task was to give an overview of the place of religion in American higher education, a story that began not surprisingly with seventeenth-century Harvard and eighteenth-century Yale, charted the work of nineteenth-century denominational colleges, and finished with Protestant efforts throughout the twentieth century. Michaelsen's judgment of the quantity of Protestant pursuits in American higher education was somewhat hopeful. Though religion still was not receiving the amount of attention given to art or zoology, "the contrast with the situation a generation ago is obvious." But quality was another matter. Religion in the undergraduate curriculum, he wrote, was but a "pale reflection of the seminary curriculum." What is more, the purpose of religious studies still labored under the burden of ministerial motives, namely, "to prepare the students to meet the problems of life." Michaelsen finished on a more consoling note. The shift toward a scientific approach to religion, whether through psychology, cultural studies, or history, boded well for the future.[33] Still, the thrust of his chapter reinforced religious studies' poor academic standing.

Ramsey may have not intended it but was even more devastating than Michaelsen. Like Michaelsen, the Princeton professor argued that the academic standards of religious studies were woefully low. He admitted that the formation of religion departments had sprung from a desire to restore theological studies "to a rightful place" in the world of learning, as opposed to functioning merely as "window dressing" for pious alumni. Still, the strategy that had been pursued by the post–World War II generation of Protestant academics had turned out to be academically thin. Ramsey called the argument that religion was related to all the other fields of study the "'God and . . .' theory of undergraduate education in religion." He conceded that the intent of this approach was to pay theology a high tribute. But at a certain point, if religion related to everything, it was sure to "disappear into everything," or at least could be studied by inquiring into everything else but religion. Ramsey believed it would have been fitting to appoint religion professors as adjunct faculty since in most cases they were "exactly that: they are teacher-chaplains or teacher-ministers in a local church, and not teacher-scholars in their main vocation."[34]

The Princeton University ethicist was just warming up. Ramsey saved his most severe judgment for the mid-twentieth-century Protestant theological revival that had propelled the establishment of religion departments and the appointment of religion faculty. "There is . . . a lack of theological scholars of first rank in the United States," he observed, and the reason he offered was that the neo-orthodox theological revival "has not meant much revival of theological scholarship."[35] To be sure, Ramsey's desire for greater specialization in theology reflected his Protestant interests. Also, when religious studies would finally begin to fortify its scholarly standing, it did so by moving in almost the opposite direction, preferring everything else but Protestant divinity. Still, Ramsey's verdict was a ringing indictment of the way religious studies had been operating for almost half a century; it was academically inferior.

Reactions to the Bridston-Culver report and supplementary volume of essays from members of NABI-turned-AAR were surprisingly mixed. In 1966 the *Journal of Bible and Religion* devoted an entire issue to the report. One set of reactions predictably defended the academic honor of religious studies as then constituted and argued for the autonomy of the field from Protestant seminaries. Another set regarded religious studies and Protestant divinity to have still a large measure of overlap because of common purposes.

Of the nine articles, five were clearly sympathetic to the needs of seminaries and assumed a good deal of overlap between ministerial training and the academic study of religion. For instance, James I. McCord, president of Princeton Theological Seminary, wrote with the needs of "the Protestant Church in America" in mind and how seminaries and religion departments both could help Protestants adjust to the scientific and technological revolution underway in the United States.[36] Other responses conceived of religious studies in colleges and universities as primarily theological in nature and, therefore, valuable both for prospective ministers as well as the laity, a conception that presumed most undergraduates were church members. According to J. Arthur Baird, who sat on the committee overseeing the Bridston-Culver report, the chief purpose of the religion department was to promote "the living dialogue of theology" at the undergraduate level "for future laymen . . . but also for future ministers." About this proposition Baird concluded, "there is really no debate."[37] So too for Jack Boozer, who taught religion to undergraduates at Emory University, the lines between religious studies and seminary could not be so easily drawn. The reason was that the study of Christian theology (as written by Paul Tillich, Rudolf Bultmann, and H. Richard Niebuhr) was "as applicable" to the student preparing for parish ministry as to "any man," whether Christian or not.[38] Such reactions were indicative of a field that had grown up in the cocoon of Protestant divinity and the mainline Protestant denominations' efforts to supply the religious ideals of American higher education.

The other set of reactions, those more defensive, foreshadowed the division between religious studies and Protestant divinity that would characterize the academic study of religion after 1970. These authors may not have been prophetic but used the criticisms of religious studies in the Bridston-Culver report to argue for the superiority of teaching and studying religion outside the confines of seminary or church. Harry B. Adams, associate dean of Yale's Divinity School, believed that the report could push "college religion departments" out of their role either as "a recruiting agency for the church" or as "little seminaries."[39] Clyde A. Holbrook, religion professor at Oberlin College, was not so willing to concede religious studies' "thralldom to the ecclesiastical establishment." The study of religion was not "theological education of the whole church" but instead contributed "to a full liberal arts training." In fact, Holbrook thought seminary faculty could learn a thing or two from religious studies and called for them to join the AAR.[40] Even more confrontational was Edmund Perry, who taught religion at Northwestern University. Contrary to the conclusions implied and stated explicitly in the report, Perry (who advised AAR members to read The Making of Ministers and "forget the Report") countered that religion was "becoming a respected field of academic inquiry" at the same time that religion departments and scholars were being liberated from "the Protestant tyranny." For him the Bridston-Culver report was the straw that broke the back of good relations between religious studies and Protestant divinity. From now on, Perry concluded, the content of religion departments would not be determined by "the service it can render to Protestant seminaries," and would include religions other than the Judeo-Christian tradition.[41]

Despite these mixed reactions the die was cast. As much as some Protestant academics might want to keep religious studies and theological education together, the Bridston-Culver report indicated that if religious studies were to flourish it would have to sever its ties to the Protestant establishment. To be sure, that separation would provoke animosity and take time. Religious studies had been cultivated under the aegis of Protestant theology and with a view toward serving the Protestant churches. Furthermore, most religious studies faculty had received their graduate education at Protestant seminaries and university divinity schools. The ties between religious studies and mainline Protestantism were many, thick, and long. But with the changing perceptions of religion that emerged in the 1960s, mainline Protestants could no longer assume their beliefs were synonymous with the faith of the America people. In response, Protestant clergy put forward their status as professionals as an alternative way for maintaining cultural prestige.[42] For academics engaged in religious studies, recovering their reputation would require improving their scholarly credentials.

Rival Professionalisms

The best way for religion scholars to beat the charge of academic inferiority was to point to their own involvement in graduate studies at the Ph.D. level. Traces of this argument were evident in the lead editorial of the *Journal of Bible and Religion* which introduced the articles on the Bridston-Culver report. The unidentified author noted that undergraduate teaching was "just one element" of the AAR's concerns, making it seem a small one at that. What is more, preseminary education was "not in itself more significant than other challenges faced by the academy." The reason for the increasing insignificance of undergraduate study and preseminary training in religious studies, "as everyone knows," owed to the growing involvement of AAR members in "graduate-school education, as distinct from seminary education."[43] Training Ph.D.'s in religion was a big step for a body of scholars once little removed from the chaplain's office. But the professionalization of religious studies according to the academic ideals of the research university was a surefire way to free the field from the burden of Protestant divinity.

Very quickly the leaders of religious studies made good on the editorial in the *Journal of Bible and Religion*. Only five years after the publication of the Bridston-Culver report, Claude Welch, the chair of the University of Pennsylvania's Department of Religious Thought, wrote *Graduate Education in Religion*.[44] This study, sponsored by the American Council of Learned Societies and funded by the Henry Luce Foundation, originated from a proposal by the old National Council for Religion in Higher Education, recently renamed the Society for Religion in Higher Education. The report received endorsements from the institutional leaders within religious studies—the AAR, the Council on Graduate Studies in Religion, the Society for the Scientific Study of Religion, the Fund for Theological Education, and the Association of American Colleges. On the surface, the Welch report was simply descriptive: with all of the investigation of theological education since World War II, from Niebuhr, Williams, and Gustafson to Bridston and Culver, little attention had been given to graduate education in religious and theological studies. But as it happened *Graduate Education in*

Religion could be plausibly read as religious studies' declaration of independence from Protestant theological education.

If the Bridston-Culver report had made religious studies look academically inferior, the Welch study explained the field's weaknesses. Religion as an academic discipline had labored too much under the burden of the Protestant churches. Teachers in religion, Welch wrote, had been "(sometimes rightly) suspected of covert intentions to proselytize." The teaching of religion had too often been confused with "pastoral care." Religious studies was often viewed, Welch continued, simply as "preludes to theological seminary studies" (13, 14). In one of the best analogies used in the whole report that was as telling as it was humorous, the University of Pennsylvania professor compared the religious studies curriculum to the "Cape Codder's map of the United States."

> Like the distance between Chatham and South Chatham, small differences in the immediate neighborhood seem important and exaggerated; so the curricula carefully distinguish between New Testament and patristics or between Early and Late Reformation; each requires separate faculty appointments and sometimes separate degree programs. Judaism is perhaps like Massachusetts, a little more clearly recognizable and distinguishable. But just as the Cape Codder is alleged to have thought of Minneapolis and Indianapolis as the Twin Cities, somewhere near Spokane and Dallas, so all other religious traditions—nonliterate, classical, Asian, "etc."—are lumped in a single undifferentiated category largely beyond our ken. (20)

But all was not lost. Religious studies had finally developed a new orientation, one that in Welch's estimate was "distinct from theology" (13). Here the author vacillated between description and prescription, with the latter spilling over onto the former as a form of cheerleading. The new version of religious studies was (and had to become more) "cross-cultural" so that proficiency would lead to an informed understanding of more than one religious tradition. For instance, how do sacred texts function in Buddhist and Hindu traditions and is that similar to the way Christians regard the Bible? Religious studies was also using a "plurality of methods" (and should do more of it). Understanding the Hebrew and Christian scriptures with only literary and linguistic tools would not produce as rich and full an understanding as research that also benefited from sociological and anthropological insights. The field had also developed strong ties with "cognate areas" (and should continue to develop more). Here was where the Welch report revealed the biggest discontinuity between the new and the older approaches to religion. Whereas religious studies had typically relied upon the disciplines represented in the theological curriculum, with apologetics or the history of religions having to carry the weight of non-Christian traditions, now religious studies was looking to English, history, philosophy, sociology, and anthropology for reinforcement and collaboration (23–25). By severing its close ties to Protestant divinity, Welch admitted that he was opening the field up to some chaos. The traditional orientation of religious studies did give "depth and breadth within the limits of a major religious tradition" which made specialization at the graduate level possible. But this was simply a reason for making undergraduate departments of religion better, not for going back to the old model of the Protestant theological curriculum (22, 27).

Outsiders to the field of religion may have thought Welch's focus awfully ambitious for an academic discipline whose undergraduate teaching had just received serious criticism. Indeed, graduate education in religion had never been a concern of NABI since originally it was an organization that included secondary school teachers, chaplains, and college faculty. But the shift toward graduate education was a natural development in NABI-turned-AAR circles, not only because religion faculty was increasingly occupied in graduate instruction, but also as a response to the Bridston-Culver report. To counter the claim that clergy needed an education worthy of their professional status, religious studies faculty asserted their own form of professionalism, one rooted in academic rather than ministerial or confessional criteria.

Welch devoted one chapter of *Graduate Education in Religion* to the tension in religious studies between providing training for clergy on the one hand and graduate education in religious scholarship on the other. He appeared to have the Bridston-Culver report in mind. Religious studies should not be in the business of training clergy, Welch concluded, and programs that included the bachelor of divinity degree were by and large academically inferior. To make this case Welch drew on the distinction between professional schools (i.e., law, business, and medicine) and graduate programs whose aim was training teachers for colleges and universities. He also distinguished between seminary degrees that gave graduates entrée into the ranks of leadership within a religious community and academic degrees designed to produce leaders within the academy. Finally, Welch noted the differences between the Th.D., a terminal seminary degree that often carried the baggage of "specialized ministerial skills," and the Ph.D. in religion, which made a larger place for nonwestern religions and did not require seminary training for admission. Welch's point that the best graduate education in religion was one free from Protestant divinity came through emphatically when he wrote, "approximately half of the present Th.D. programs are of dubious academic quality."[45] To be sure, the report took some of the sting out of this finding by arguing that all doctoral programs had to balance between preparing teachers and training scholars. So the problems confronting religious studies did not stem from its ties to Protestant theological education alone (47–51). Nevertheless, the Welch report appeared to be compensating for the earlier verdict by the Protestant seminary establishment. Rather than being academically inferior, religion was now a worthwhile field of graduate study in its own right and therefore a vocation with all the cachet that the research university had to confer.

Yet, as much as the Welch report established a rationale for religious studies independent of Protestant divinity, it left the academic discipline of religion adrift without an anchor. In a very revealing chapter on the university as opposed to seminary context and the cognate fields upon which religious studies could draw, Welch asked the loaded question of whether what took place in a department of religious studies could not be done elsewhere within the university such as in ancient Near Eastern studies, philosophy, sociology, psychology, anthropology, history, and literary studies. His answer was, "Nothing appears in a programs of religious studies that could not appear elsewhere" (55). This conclusion was implicit once the report argued for widening the scope and methodology of religious studies beyond the Protestant theological curriculum (24–25). To establish the academic expertise of the field it only made sense to say that religion was more than Christianity and to point to other scholars in other disciplines who were already doing responsible research on religion from the vantage of one of the university's existing disciplines. But if other faculty were already studying religion, then why bother with a separate department devoted to religion? One answer was the practical argument that "in the university things grow only if they are tended, and that means being given an organizing center, a structure, a budget, some appointive control, and so on." But when it came to an intellectual justification, the Welch report was less than convincing. In fact, his rationalization that religion was "at least as unified a 'discipline' as political science or sociology" was a feeble one for offering Ph.D. degrees in religion (55–56).

To be sure, Welch had a point. All disciplines in the humanities and social sciences face a large amount of overlap and their existence as separate fields are not intellectually self-evident. But to appeal to this weakness in the university is only to raise fundamental questions about modern learning. It does not settle the issue of whether to start a new program in religion. Nor did Welch provide a positive rationale that staked out the scope and methods of religious studies. In effect, his report called for an end to the way religious studies had been done, first as an academic form of campus ministry and then as a way of building upon the intellectual respectability of the midcentury Protestant theological renaissance. Yet, this argument was mainly negative. The Welch report tried to hitch the future of religious studies to the advancement and resources of the university. But without connecting the dots between the study of religion and the purpose of the research university, this strategy was doomed. As much as religious studies had been a covert form of Protestant studies, it lacked a legitimate place in the public intellectual space of the university. But without the coherence that Protestant divinity provided, religious studies was rudderless, a discipline in search of an identity.

Religious studies thus entered the period of its greatest academic accomplishments with a schizophrenic outlook. Though the AAR in 1979 became a member of the ACLS, whenever the scholars in the field turned to reflect on their specific academic responsibilities they mustered only confusion.[46] In some ways, the tension religious studies experienced between its public image and private doubts was not altogether different from that afflicting other academic disciplines. But religious studies' difficulties stemmed directly from the events that rocked the field between 1965 and 1970, developments unique to the teaching and study of religion in the setting of the modern research university. On the one hand, the Bridston-Culver report said that the undergraduate religion major, the traditional heart and soul of religion faculty, was academically inferior, thus, giving a failing grade to the long and arduous struggle of mainline Protestants to restore religion in the university. On the other hand, the Welch report declared that religious studies was good enough to offer Ph.D. degrees in religion. Ever since 1970 religious studies has labored under these divergent readings of its academic worth. It has cobbled together the old Protestant theological curriculum, a course of study designed to serve the churches (that best served the nation), with a variety of scholarly approaches to religion free from theological conviction or the authority of sacred texts. This is why, as an article in *Lingua Franca* recently concluded, religious studies is a "shapeless beast, half social science, half humanistic discipline, lumbering through the academy with no clear methodology or raison d'àtre."[47]

TEN

Religious Studies,
the Would-Be Discipline

IN 1986 THE RELIGION DEPARTMENT at the University of California–
Santa Barbara invited scholars from leading religion programs to assess
the contemporary strength of the field, especially in graduate education. Among the various papers presented, Jonathan Z. Smith's was
arguably the most pointed and disagreeable. A professor of religion at
the University of Chicago, Smith stated brashly that religious studies
did not constitute "a coherent disciplinary matrix in and of itself." He
conceded that the effort to establish "some principle of intellectual
autonomy" for the study of religion made sense in the "politics" of academic funding and university administration. But Smith could find no
polite way to agree with the conference's premise that "a unique idiom
or language of religious studies" existed. The field, he believed, did not
even have a "dialect." At best religious studies possessed "only a mon-
grel, polyglot jargon." Instead of having an identifiable and distinct academic niche, Smith asserted that religious studies was, at its "firmest," a
"would-be discipline." Religion lacked both the methodological consensus and a "corporate consciousness" necessary for an "intact discipline."
Teaching and studying religion, he concluded, was "simply one more
functional way of cutting up the pie in the modern university."[1]

However discouraging Smith's comments may have been to prospective graduate students and recently minted religious studies Ph.D.'s searching for appointments, they aptly summarized the evolution of the field after the publication in 1970 of Claude Welch's *Graduate Education in Religion*. Without the direction and commonalities provided by Protestant divinity, religious studies became an omnibus discipline, governed more by a sense of inferiority than a coherent academic mission. For this reason the most recent period in the history of religious studies has witnessed a proliferation of methodological approaches and the addition of new areas of study whose only organizing principle has been the implicit one of proving that religion was "appropriate to the letters and science mission of a modern, secular . . . university."[2]

One index to the growing diversity of religious studies in the era of the American Academy of Religion (AAR) was the publication in 1970 of *The Study of Religion in Colleges and Universities,* edited by Princeton University professors Paul Ramsey and John F. Wilson.[3] Five years earlier, as Ramsey's volume in the Princeton Council on the Humanities series indicated, the dominant fields in religious studies mirrored the Protestant theological curriculum. That book had included chapters on the history of religions, Old Testament, New Testament and early Christianity, church history, theology, Christian ethics, and the philosophy of religion.[4] By the time the Ramsey–Wilson collection of essays on religious studies was published, however, the editors recognized the need to expand beyond the traditional Protestant boundaries to include Catholic studies, Jewish studies, sociology of religion, comparative religious ethics, religion and literature, and religion and art. A Protestant orientation was still evident, with contributions from professors teaching at the most prominent university divinity schools, and chapters on theology, the Bible, and church history, among others.[5] Still, the Ramsey–Wilson volume demonstrated that Protestant divinity could no longer dominate the field.

What is more, *The Study of Religion in Colleges and Universities* also manifested an awareness of religious studies' awkward position in American higher education which had not been evident in the days when Protestant divinity set the standards. For instance, unlike Jacob Neusner, who in a matter-of-fact manner discussed Jewish studies' contribution to the university,[6] Arthur C. McGill expressed, in a remarkably candid fashion, the tension that confronted Christian theologians in the academy. He acknowledged that the model for modern learning stemmed from seventeenth-century philosophical developments that made truth and knowledge dependent upon rational autonomy or, in his own words, "detached and critical reasoning." Furthermore, since the Enlightenment, religion had become "alien" to the university precisely because faith required an attitude at odds with the epistemological models of science. The "religious attitude," McGill wrote, "involves man's seeing himself in relation to powers that prohibit any trace of autonomy." Theologians, then, could not determine truth by satisfying "the demands of reason." Instead, for them knowledge was "fruitfully responsive to the movements of the gods." Given this situation, McGill had to figure out a way for theology to stay in the university. His solution was to trot out the old neo-orthodox response that the university needed theology because scholars were recognizing the limitations of scientific inquiry. "The tradition of rational autonomy is being questioned today within faculties of arts and sciences," McGill reassured his theological readers. Rational inquiry could only go so far in the pursuit of truth. But including theology in the curriculum of colleges and universities would be the "most effective enterprise for getting the truth-question off the ground again" and would remind all scholars and students that religions were primarily preoccupied "at their very centers with the question of truth and falsity." Theology was necessary for American higher education because, in McGill's estimation "no faculty of arts and sciences can afford to forget [the truth-question] for one moment." Interestingly enough, McGill's awareness of theology's ambiguous position was so great that his brief on behalf of Christian theology never mentioned the Trinity, the deity of Christ, special revelation, or the doctrines of sin and grace. Such silence indicated, perhaps more than he recognized, just how ambiguous theology's place in higher education had become.[7]

If Christian theology had a shaky standing in the academy, the study of the Bible, a book revered as sacred and canonical, looked to be on even thinner scholarly ice. Krister Stendahl, dean of Harvard Divinity School, admitted as much in his chapter on biblical studies, even though his intention was to prove the value of teaching the Bible in the university setting. Efforts to justify the study of the Bible on the same grounds by which other scholars interpreted ancient texts or highly esteemed writings were finally unconvincing, according to Stendahl. Augustine and Luther did not read the writings of the apostle Paul as great literature or part of the West's "great books." "It is precisely as holy writ that the biblical material made its impact on Western culture," Stendahl argued, "not because of its intrinsic literary value but because of its peculiar claim to be the Word of God." The implication he drew from the Bible's divine status was that religion departments had a unique responsibility to treat the biblical writings not simply as great works of literature but to understand them primarily as "religious phenomena." As compelling as this line of reasoning may have been to Stendahl, it could not overcome the principle of autonomous rationality that McGill recognized as crucial to the outlook of modern scholarship. If the outlook of academics was to disregard all claims to truth and authority not based on human reason, then why should the university take the church's word and study the Bible as God's word? A different approach might be to avoid the subject altogether, not unlike the one chosen by the Supreme Court regarding prayer and Bible reading in public schools. Even Stendahl inched in this direction when he distinguished between biblical studies pursued in universities and those pursued under the auspices of seminaries, the former being more critical and public, the latter being more confessional and churchly.[8]

James M. Gustafson's final chapter in the Ramsey–Wilson volume testified further to the strain surrounding religious studies as it tried to stand without the crutches of the Protestant establishment or its divinity. He spoke for most of the Protestant contributors when he wrote that "very few, if any other, fields are as preoccupied with their legitimacy and as introspective . . . as religious studies." Gustafson suggested that the reason for religious studies' inferiority complex stemmed from the uncertainties attending "the religious enterprise in the contemporary world." But religion scholars need not be so preoccupied with their academic status, he believed, as long as they distinguished sufficiently "between scholarly teaching and study, on the one hand, and the vital practice of religion, on the other." With that distinction quickly asserted, Gustafson then led a fairly robust cheer for the academic study of religion. Religion departments had put some distance between themselves and seminaries, developed "a posture of analytical rigor" and "disinterested objectivity," created a body of "significant scholarly work," and carved out a field of graduate studies. In sum, religious studies was overcoming its "Protestant Christian myopia." Scholars recognized that justice needed to be granted "to the wide variety of religious life and thought in human history."[9] Even so, for all the enthusiasm that Gustafson's pep talk yielded, it could not overcome the haunting implication that religious studies was in a defensive posture. Religious scholars may have pointed proudly to their field's strengths precisely because those strengths were at issue. Gustafson was right to call attention to religious studies' declaration of independence from Protestant divinity.

But a negative definition of religious studies—that it is not Protestant theology—did not resolve what constituted the field.

Aside from creating the impression that Protestant divinity was on the run in religion departments, the Ramsey–Wilson volume also underscored religious studies' earlier alliance with the humanities as a way to enjoy legitimacy in the academy. Tom F. Driver, who taught theology and literature at Union Theological Seminary (New York), contributed an essay that assumed the close connection between religion and the humanities. After 1945, when religion scholars looked for ways to make their courses more relevant, he wrote, "for obvious reasons, it has seemed more natural and feasible to initiate this dialogue with the subjects called 'humanities' than with others." One of these reasons concerned the project shared by both literary scholars and theologians, who sought to understand "symbols and myths in a scientific and secular age."[10] A. Richard Turner, who taught art at Middlebury College, reinforced the ties between religion and the humanities in a discussion of the relationship between artistic expression and religion. He recognized the demise of religiously inspired art and admitted that a secular or unbelieving museum-goer might not be able to understand a work of art created for explicitly devotional reasons. But even the aesthetic qualities had religious implications since they "are relevant to the profoundest issues of a man's life" and could "in a certain sense function as models for the composition of an ordered life."[11] Even the comparative study of religion using the history of religions approach ran along distinctly humanistic paths. H. P. Sullivan, professor of religion at Vassar College, argued that the historian of religions used methods that were part science and part art, but ultimately contributed to the study of man. The history of religions deciphered and made intelligible "the mysterious universe [western man] is encountering in his growing confrontation with non-Western cultures," while also contributing to a "greater knowledge of man himself" and in-depth knowledge of human nature.[12] Surprisingly, the authors and editors failed to see the irony of continuing such a strong alliance between religion and the humanities, not only because one of the editors had voiced sharp criticism of such an approach,[13] but also because it perpetuated implicitly mainline Protestantism's dominance in religious studies by using the rationale that Protestant educators had devised in the 1930s and 1940s. Furthermore, religious studies' attachment to the humanities would prove to be especially undesirable once younger university faculty and students questioned the canonical status of western civilization's Great Books. So the question remained whether religious studies could legitimately free itself from its Protestant past. The curriculum might be changing, but the aim of studying religion was still conceived in categories derived from the mainline Protestant experience.[14]

If Protestant divinity could no longer unify the teaching and study of religion, what could? One possibility was the history of religions. As John F. Wilson suggested in the introduction to *The Study of Religion in Colleges and Universities,* the history of religions "might be expected to serve as a distinctive methodology for the developing field of religion" in an analogous way to that played by "neo-orthodox Protestant scholarship during the last several decades." The advantage of history of religions was its promise of systematic and comparative study "of various classes of religious phenomena across diverse traditions and cultures." In other words, religious studies needed to include other religious traditions and could no longer rely on the unified curriculum supplied by Protestant divinity. So instead of achieving unity through subject matter, religion scholars would have to look to method. Here, the history of religions had the additional appeal of science, despite the tendency of its practitioners, like the contributor to the Ramsey–Wilson volume, to construe it as a humanistic science that explored the universal qualities of mankind's religious experience. Wilson observed that this approach sometimes also went by the name "science of religion" or in German, *religionswissenschaft.*[15] If religious studies had been guilty of being too theological, the history of religions offered a way for the field to be more scientific.[16]

If contributions to the *Journal of the American Academy of Religion* (*JAAR*) during the 1970s are any indication, the history of religions failed to give shape to religious studies. Instead, published articles as well as submissions reflected the field's pluralistic and incoherent character. Presidential addresses before the AAR ranged from a mildly liberal Protestant critique of the hidden agenda of humanistic psychology and a standard summary of developments in the field of theology and literature to such innovative studies as "Cargo Cults as Cultural Historical Phenomenon" and "Institutions as Symbols of Death."[17] Articles dealing with explicitly Christian subjects continued to outnumber contributions on other religions. For instance, the combined categories of biblical studies, history of Christianity, and theology accounted for seventy-six articles compared to forty-three for Asian religions and twenty-four for Judaica. Still, essays on Christian topics comprised only 19 percent of the total number of published articles. Moreover, biblical studies (thirty-seven articles) received less attention than religion and the arts (forty-eight). Perhaps even more revealing of changes within religious studies during the 1970s were the subjects of manuscripts submitted to the *JAAR*. While submissions per year in such subjects as Old Testament, New Testament, ethics, and Judaica rarely climbed into double digits, the journal received on average thirty-five manuscripts a year in philosophy of religion and twenty-one on Asian religions.[18]

Despite such diversity one recent study argues that the history of religions has actually dominated the field of religious studies and has done so in a harmful way. Russell T. McCutcheon believes that the approach to religion that underwrites the history of religions, namely, regarding religion as a separate category unto itself, has excluded "sociopolitical analysis from much scholarship on religion."[19] In particular, he traces (and faults) the influence of Mircea Eliade on college textbooks where "the dominant discourse on sui generis religion continues to define the field" and sets the standard for future scholarship.[20] To be sure, McCutcheon gives ample evidence of history of religions in college survey texts. Yet the field of religious studies itself has not proved so submissive. The 1986 Santa Barbara Colloquy on religious studies, as well a special issue of the *JAAR*, gave scant attention to the history of religions.[21] What is more, the existence of a separate scholarly organization, the International Association for the History of Religions (founded in 1950) suggests that the academic discipline of religious studies is much bigger than this one approach and thus hardly dominated by it.[22] In sum, the history of religions may have a corner on the freshman college-textbook market as a relatively coherent way to teach all the religions of the world in one semester, but it has not been able to unify the field, let alone set the agenda for graduate studies.[23]

Social-scientific approaches in religious studies have been even less successful in shaping the field, despite the growing prominence of sociology of religion and the apparent need for a scientific, as opposed to theological, methodology. Again, if articles published in the *JAAR* are any indication, scholars working specifically in the field of religious studies were loathe to use the methods of anthropology, sociology, and psychology. As in the case of history of religions, part of the problem for social scientists studying religion concerned a desire for professional uniformity in a field that had always avoided methodological rigor. Religious studies was and is bigger than any particular method of studying religion. Consequently, even though social scientists in Europe, and to a lesser extent in America, had developed a body of theoretical literature as well as field studies that extended back to the nineteenth century and included the work of Edward Burnett Tylor, James Frazer, Emile Durkheim, Max Weber, and William James, for instance, they did not find an academic home in American departments of religion.[24] In fact, the social scientific teaching and study of religion has most often been conducted in anthropology, sociology, and psychology departments. Social scientists interested in religion have also developed a separate scholarly organization, the Society for the Scientific Study of Religion (SSSR), that is more congenial to their procedures. Indicative of the differences between social scientists and religion scholars was the decision by SSSR in 1969 to pull out of the omnibus professional organization, the Council for the Study of Religion, in which the AAR and the SBL were prominent.[25] Perhaps the assessment of Paul M. Harrison, writing on the sociology of religion in the Ramsey–Wilson volume, was pivotal for understanding the inherent antagonism between social scientific and humanistic approaches to the study of religion. He concluded that sociologists could only make a contribution to religious studies if they were willing to recognize their "limitations" as well as their "powers."[26] Over the last three decades social scientists have not been so humble and neither have the majority of scholars in the AAR recognized the value of the social sciences.[27]

The recent history of religious studies, therefore, reflects a loss of coherence in the wake of Protestant divinity's demise. A recent report on the religion major, produced for the Association of American Colleges by an AAR task force, admitted as much, all the while arguing that such instability in the field constituted its strength and vitality. At the outset the report, *The Religion Major,* conceded that religious studies prior to the 1960s had been "unabashedly sectarian." The task force also observed that the 1970s had witnessed a "time of pedagogical experimentation, curricular innovation of many kinds, revisionist scholarship, some confusion and a great deal of intellectual ferment." Yet, despite such humble beginnings, the academic study of religion had "matured into a discipline in its own right." This cheery conclusion followed sentences that granted that religious studies used methods shared by other disciplines and, later, that no one definition of religion prevailed in the field; the category, "religion," was merely a "heuristic" device.[28]

Similarly, the Santa Barbara Colloquy's statement on graduate studies in religion reached similarly inconclusive results, even though resisting mightily the temptation to ask whether the field could legitimately go on in such disarray. Graduate students, according to this report, needed to be trained in "highly specialized subject areas" such as Apache puberty rites, classical Sanskrit texts, and sixteenth-century Spanish mysticism. At the same time, scholars with a Ph.D. in religion needed to have some general method or theory that would allow them to make sense of all faiths. The requirement that religion scholars be both master of one religious expression and jack of all traditions meant that in the melting pot of the academic study of religion all faiths came out tasting blandly like the "human need for symbols of transcendence."[29]

But such a resolution, as others have argued, is very little different from older liberal Protestant efforts to salvage the inspiring ideals from the sordid particulars of the various world religions.[30] It differs little, in fact, from the Enlightened Christianity that shaped the way university reformers at the end of the nineteenth century understood religion. Simply put, this outlook regards as sectarian any commitment to a particular religious tradition, and instead promotes religious ecumenism or cosmopolitanism on the presumption that all religions have a common point of reference. Thus, the claim that religion is essentially a "multicultural study" mimics the rhetoric of diversity that dominates academic discourse without providing tools for critical reflection on the nature of such diversity.[31] It not only reflects the triumph of Enlightenment categories in efforts to study religion, but also bears the marks of mainline Protestantism, except that Protestants now recognize that the truths of their religion, once thought to have universal significance, are simply one patch on the colorful quilt of world religions.[32] As one religion professor recently wrote while reflecting on the problems besetting the field, the openness to diversity that has characterized the academic study of religion over the past thirty years, once thought to be a strength, "now seems to be a weakness." If the study of religion is nothing more than the agglomeration of methods used in other disciplines to study religion, and if particular religious traditions are better understood in departments or areas other than religion, "then little would seem to be lost by abolishing programs in religion and teaching the subject in other departments."[33]

Without the older centripetal forces of providing spiritual guidance and adding humanistic depth, religious studies lacks a center. It is now little more than a collection of those academics who have inherited the older Protestant structures and rationales for religion, conceded that the old way was too exclusive, and added to the mix non-Christian religions. More important, the scholars whose primary professional academic identity is in religion departments and the AAR have yet to articulate an understanding of undergraduate and graduate education that makes religion a natural fit in higher education. Postmodern posturing to the contrary, the modern university is still committed to the Enlightenment ideal of the rational, autonomous individual following human powers of observation and reasoning wherever they lead, irrespective of tradition, revelation, or existing structures of power. The environment of the modern university has never been hospitable to religion since religions depend on divine revelation, tradition, and priestly authority. The current problems surrounding religious studies only prove the point.

The irony is that religious studies' incoherence has become obvious at precisely the same time the field has undergone professionalization. In a certain sense, recent developments within the academic study of religion merely reflect the outworking of academic specialization in the United States that began in the late nineteenth century with the founding of research universities.[34] The new approach to the teaching and study of religion signaled by the AAR followed the same kind of developments that attended other humanistic disciplines and social sciences in the last third of the nineteenth century.[35] Just as history, literature, and psychology, for instance, did not start from scratch but emerged instead from an already existing cultivated elite with its own professional outlook, religious studies came out of a set of professional organizations and networks dominated by the mainline Protestant clergy and theological educators. The organization from which the AAR emerged, the National Association of Biblical Instructors (NABI), was not intended to be a professional scholarly society. Instead, its early aims were pedagogical and it ceded academic expertise to such professional associations as the SBL and the American Society of Church History. The cultivated generalism of the Protestant ministry dominated NABI's orientation and its ambitions dovetailed remarkably well with the emphasis on general education and the humanities that flourished in American higher education between the beginning of World War I and the launching of Sputnik.[36] Yet, as religion scholars became rooted in the university during the 1960s, as their ties to mainstream Protestantism looked more suspicious, and as the educational mission that had sustained a humanistic education during the 1940s and 1950s came under attack, the academic field of religion shifted its orientation from the church to the academy. Advanced research free from sectarian prejudice, rather than the social role of religion, became the norm. The demands of the academy required scholarship and teaching to be scientific and specialized. In turn, a younger generation of religion scholars rejected as amateurish and too churchly the older style of teaching and studying religion. Rather than contributing to the propagation of western civilization and American political ideals, religion now had to prove itself as a specialized field replete with its own methods of research, models of learning, centers of graduate education, professional associations, and scholarly publications.[37]

Yet, religious studies does not fit the typical pattern of academic professionalization in two important respects. One difference is that while professors in the social sciences and humanities broke away from amateur fields of scholarship in order to hone their own academic expertise, religion has functioned as a clearinghouse for a multitude of scholarly approaches to religion whose only source of unity is the vague concept of "religion." Professors in religion departments often have more in common academically with scholars in other departments than in their own. Another important difference is that for the humanities and social sciences academic professionalization yielded a sense of intellectual purpose and scholarly pride. Late nineteenth-century American professional historians and sociologists, however naive their academic pretensions might have been, believed that their standing in the world of advanced learning was secure not simply because their work was superior to that of amateurs but also because their scholarship conformed to the scientific ideals of the new university. In contrast, the professionalization of religious studies has been accompanied by constant fears of inferiority and being viewed as academic misfits. In the words of the conveners of the Santa Barbara Colloquy on religious studies, the field has suffered from a "notable reluctance . . . to play a leadership role in setting the intellectual agenda in the university's task of self-appraisal. If anything, Religious Studies has tended to go out of its way to assure the academy that it fully accepts and affirms the academy's 'standards.'"[38] Ironically, then, liberation from the bondage of the church and its theology has not resulted in intellectual coherence or professional confidence. Religious studies is afflicted with the psychological disease of "cut[ting] a poor figure" in the university.[39]

The sense of academic inferiority within religious studies is undoubtedly part of the larger uncertainty that afflicts the humanities and social sciences more generally owing to questions surrounding methodology, the authority of a canon of texts, and boundaries between disciplines. Still, religious studies labors under an even greater burden, which the intellectual ferment within contemporary American higher education only compounds—its past. It came into American colleges and universities through the efforts of Protestants who first wanted to keep sons and daughters of the church from leaving the faith, and then found in the teaching and study of religion an antidote to the sickness of scientific materialism and secularism, and a buttress to the walls of western culture and liberal democracy. Without those spiritual and cultural functions, the professional study of religion has had to adjust to an academic environment that was originally established to be free of church control and religious dogma. Reckoning with this environment has imposed upon religious studies a unique set of impediments from which the field may only be free when its practitioners wrestle with the peculiar consequences of the way that religion has been studied and taught in American colleges and universities.

Whither Religion in the University?

AT THE BEGINNING OF THE 1993–94 academic year the members of the University of Pennsylvania's Department of Religious Studies received a communication from the dean that spoke volumes about the disarray within the academic study of religion in American universities. The letter informed faculty about recommendations to close the religion department. To be fair, the administration did not single out religion. The need for administrative restructuring also meant closing the American civilization program as well as regional science. But the soul-searching among religion faculty prompted by the decision of the University of Pennsylvania underscored the burden of religious studies. Ever since Claude Welch issued his report on graduate education in religion the field limped along without coherence or consensus.[1] Perhaps Welch's departure from the University of Pennsylvania for the Graduate Theological Union in 1971 foreshadowed, even in a small way, the administration's decision to shut down the religion department.[2]

The reflections by one member of Penn's religion department, E. Ann Matter, a scholar of medieval Christianity, suggest that for all of Welch's talk about the value of religious studies as an academic discipline his report may have been more exaggerated than accurate. Matter blamed the difficulties of her department on the same phenomenon that the legal scholar Stephen J. Carter saw in American culture more generally. In her account of the history of religious studies at Penn, the teaching and study of religion had always mixed belief with academics since the days when the university provided space for the revivals of George Whitefield. But more recently Penn had "erased the religious side of its history, leaving only the pious memory of the rather 'unreligious' Benjamin Franklin to guide us." Just as Carter argued in his book, *The Culture of Disbelief,* that religion was a source of embarrassment to American intellectuals, so Matter believed for similar reasons that "many academics think that the study of religion deserves to be starved out, demoted, or disposed of somehow."[3]

So Matter and her colleagues started a campaign to save their positions and educate the administration about the worth of religious studies. Valuable support came from faculty in such other fields as philosophy, English, classicism, and Asian and Middle Eastern studies. Representatives from student religious organizations, such as the Christian Association, the Hillel Foundation, and the Newman Center, also told the administration how important a "central and 'objective' locus" for religion in the university was for believing students. The religion department also brought in Carter for a public lecture "at a huge price" and made sure the dean was in attendance.[4] Carter's point that religion needed to be taught in public schools was welcome news to religion faculty seeking to hold on to their departmental status. If primary and secondary schools were introducing a "more sensitive understanding of the role of religion in American history and culture," how much sense did it make for a university to gut its department of religion?[5] Finally, by the end of the year such persuasive tactics, along with the findings of a task force appointed by the dean to study the department's strengths and weaknesses, saved the religion program. On June 10, 1994, the board of trustees approved a plan to strengthen rather than close down the university's Department of Religious Studies.

Despite the successful conclusion to this struggle, the University of Pennsylvania's decision to retain the religion department remains highly debatable. Matter herself offered few reasons for the academic study of religion that were free from the sort of argument that Protestant academics used after World War II to show the importance of religion to American culture. What is more, the arguments for closing the department may have owed more to declining enrollments and mediocre scholarship by Penn's religion faculty than to the alleged secularist motivations of the administration. Even more troubling was Matter's appeal to Carter and his arguments for the importance of religion in America. His chapter on religion and education, first of all, had nothing to do with higher education. Second, his sympathies for prayer and teaching values in the classroom (while conceding the constitutional difficulties of doing so in public schools) were hardly the sort of pedagogy upon which the members of the American Academy of Religion (AAR) have come to pride themselves.[6] Even more surprising was the inability of religion scholars to see where their appeal to Carter might lead. According to his line of reasoning, if university-level religious studies does not teach religious values—if it abandons instruction in divinity, whether Protestant or not—it may be as responsible for cultivating a culture of disbelief as timid public school superintendents or activist Supreme Court justices were.

The Academic Culture of Disbelief

Carter's book was the first of several to point out an alarming inconsistency in American public life.[7] The First Amendment guarantees religious freedom for all Americans, thus preventing the government from taking sides in religious or ideological disputes. Americans are, within reason, free to believe whatever they want and to worship in any way they desire. At the same time, because government may not make any particular belief or set of opinions normative for citizenship or holding office in the United States, religion does not appear to matter to the ordering of public life. If the president of the United States may be a Quaker, Buddhist, or atheist, then clearly his religious convictions before the law are irrelevant to his running for and holding office. As Carter put it, the United States is "one of the most religious nations on earth . . . but we are also perhaps the most zealous in guarding our public institutions against explicit religious influences." The result is religious schizophrenia. It is fine to be religious in private but "there is something askew when those private beliefs become the basis for public action." Carter argued that in the sphere of education this schizophrenia produces unwholesome consequences. On the issue of prayer in school, he wrote that public schools may not use the "apparatus of government" to coerce religious belief, but this is not the same as prohibiting prayer in school. Carter also saw a large inconsistency in the disputes over teaching values in public schools. If students cannot be taught that abstinence is a good thing, then how can teachers "convince children that bigotry and avarice, for example, are wrong"? Carter added that schools have gone overboard when it comes to teaching about religion,

as if mentioning religious beliefs and practices in the classroom constitutes endorsing those beliefs and practices. "The movement to teach
about religions in the public schools," he asserted, "is not, as some
might imagine, a smokescreen for infiltration of the education system
by the religious right."[8] Here, Carter appeared to invoke the very same
distinction on which religious studies faculty have relied since the
Supreme Court's rulings on prayer and Bible reading in public schools.
It is one thing to *teach* religion, but it is altogether different and acceptable to teach *about* religion. No wonder the religion faculty at Penn saw
Carter as an ally.

It did not take long for others to apply Carter's observations about
public schooling to higher education in the United States. Perhaps the
most eloquent of these was George M. Marsden's *The Soul of the American University,* a book published only one year after Carter's. The sub-
title of Marsden's book, *From Protestant Establishment to Established
Nonbelief,* summarizes well his narrative. His story of religion in
American higher education demonstrated how the university, which
once thrived upon the religious zeal of liberal Protestants in establishing research and academic specialization as ideals, came to make religion marginal to its educational and social mission. "While American
universities today allow individuals free exercise of religion in parts of
their lives that do not touch the heart of the university," Marsden
argued, "they tend to exclude or discriminate against relating explicit
religious perspectives to intellectual life." Thus, Marsden saw the
same anomaly in American colleges and universities that Carter
observed in American public schools. Yet, Marsden went one step farther and noted that the university's commitment to pluralism is
incredibly inconsistent if such diversity excludes religion. He also
appealed to postmodern critiques of the Enlightenment, which in
Marsden's estimation looked hollow if they harbored the same hostility to faith that eighteenth-century philosophies made fashionable.
Marsden was careful to avoid repeating the mistakes of the past. The
university should not be open to anything that would not "pass
muster academically." "Procedural rationality" should still be the
norm for academic life. Still, "there is no reason why it should be a
rule that *no* religious viewpoint shall receive serious consideration."[9]

Warren A. Nord, the director of the humanities program at the University of North Carolina, made a similar argument in another widely
circulated book about religion and education. He began with the same
paradox noted by Carter and Marsden. If Americans are so religious,
"why does our educational system ignore religion?" Nord conceded

that religion is a very divisive subject, but also stated that it is too important both historically and in the present to be excluded from primary, secondary, and higher education. He was especially critical of the liberal pattern of saying the schools should maintain a posture of neutrality toward religion. This posture merely disguises hostility. By not taking sides educators have deemed religion insignificant and marginal to the academic enterprise. Nord's conclusion followed thoughtful assessment of the variety of issues that bear upon religious education, from constitutional matters to the history of academic freedom. Because of the "massive importance of religion," because public institutions must be open to "the full range of ideas in our marketplace of ideas," because the Constitution requires neutrality "between religion and nonreligion," and because "the truth has become elusive even for intellectuals," religion "must be taken seriously in public schools and universities." Specifically, the curriculum must equip students to understand "religion from the 'inside'" and allow religious ideas to contend with secular outlooks.[10]

Marsden and Nord have not been the only academics to write about religion and higher education. In a review essay of several books, including Marsden's and Nord's, Alan Wolfe, who teaches sociology at Boston University, suspected that "the next major issue facing American higher education may well be the revival of religious faith."[11] Wolfe's suspicions were apparently confirmed when the editors of *Academe,* the magazine published by the American Association of University Professors, devoted an entire issue to religion and higher education. Of the five articles, three referred explicitly to the anomaly of the university's exclusion of religion. As William Scott Green put it, "Religion is one of America's basic symbols of freedom from government control. It is a curious irony that religion should be made peripheral in higher education in the name of the very freedom it represents."[12] The other two pieces, one by Martin E. Marty on the adventure of teaching religion, the other by Isaac Kramnick and R. Laurence Moore on the value of the university's secularism, helped to round out the discussion. But the issue gave the clear impression that religion is a subject that academics have ignored too superficially and that deserves more thoughtful coverage in the university.

Curiously absent from complaints about higher education's neglect of religion is any sustained discussion of religious studies. Marsden, for instance, argued for including religious perspectives in academic work across the board and appealed to the widespread assault upon Enlightenment notions of objective truth which had excluded religion in the first place. Though references to special revelation may be illegitimate, he still asserted that no adequate reason existed for excluding religious viewpoints "from serious consideration."[13] Here, as Marsden made clear in a subsequent book, he had in mind scholars in a variety of disciplines bringing religious perspectives to bear upon their own teaching and scholarship.[14] He also advocated greater institutional pluralism. Accrediting agencies should be more tolerant of religious colleges and universities rather than forcing them to maintain the same kind of policies and procedures required of public colleges and universities.[15] Nord was even more detailed in prescribing a solution to the inequitable treatment religion receives in higher education. He recommended that colleges and universities require a three-course sequence that starts with world religions, a course that includes the beliefs and practices of "the great world religions," then a course on religion and modernity that covers such themes as secularization, pluralism, religious disestablishment, and concludes with a course in moral philosophy that applies both religious and secular points of view to contemporary political and social debates.[16] The irony, of course, is that religion departments already do what Marsden and Nord think should be done. To be sure, their course offerings are not required, nor do they come packaged the way Nord might desire. Still, administrators at most colleges and universities could have come away from Marsden's and Nord's books thinking that the religious studies program at their school already accomplished what these authors thought was missing.

Why, then, does the recent discussion of religion in higher education overlook religious studies? Again, Marsden and Nord are instructive. Marsden concluded that religious studies in the 1960s all too readily capitulated to the naturalistic assumptions of the university, especially under the pressure to professionalize the field and to get rid of the image of religion as a "second-class discipline." "Thus religious studies," he wrote, "would have a methodology more like the social sciences. The new trend was to study religion 'phenomenologically,' so that the object of study was the abstraction 'religion.'"[17] Nord, likewise, treated religious studies as part of the problem rather than the solution. He cited the AAR's self-study, which described religious studies as "scholarly neutral and non-advocative study of multiple religious traditions."[18] From Nord's perspective, the neutrality and non-normative character of religion departments was contributing to the university's neglect of religion. "The value of religious studies in a liberal education," he declared, "hinges on its ability to throw light on spiritual matters." In the end, religious studies cannot avoid normative religious claims. For this reason he argued that theology should be included in universities and colleges because "there should be room for *normative* reflection on religion, whether that takes the form of arguments for or against particular religious claims."[19] In other words, religious studies reflects the very same intolerance of religious points of view or normative religious judgments that characterizes the university's culture of disbelief. The not-so-subtle implication is that the academic study of religion is a failure when it comes to making the university a more hospitable place for religion.

Marsden and Nord were not alone in their assessment. While the general discussions of religion and American higher education rarely mention the discipline of religious studies, a number of other books have appeared since the publication of *The Culture of Disbelief* which substantiate the failure of religion departments to make the university more tolerant of religious beliefs and practices. In his book on twentieth-century Protestant academic theology, W. Clark Gilpin concluded rather optimistically that Protestant theologians have correctly understood their task to be one as a "public intellectual" and persistently orient their work, with that of other academic disciplines in the university, "toward the public good."[20] While Gilpin sees this as a positive outcome, the history of religious studies suggests that the field's public orientation, though understandable, was precisely responsible for creating the impression that the study of Protestantism, with a dose of world religions mixed in, constituted the study of religion. Additionally, by making religion a public matter—that is, by trying to shift it from a churchly to an exclusively academic orientation—religious studies failed to carve out an academic field while also watering down its religious character. Applying theology to public life may help theologians achieve a sense of relevance, but it moves theology outside its own scholarly conventions to those of political and social scientists.

Conrad Cherry's work on the history of university divinity schools was less sanguine than Gilpin's. Cherry saw that the Protestant understanding of religious scholarship and ministerial training fueling these institutions never lived up to the goal of shaping American culture and intellectual life, even though the tradition they represent still affords possibilities for the future. Cherry's claim that this tradition of "divinity education led to unbiased scholarship, the integrity of the life of the mind, and the scholarly exploration of the unusual," however, would have to be seriously revised.[21] Not only has religious studies throughout much of its history manifested a bias toward the beliefs and practices of mainline Protestant churches, whether inculcating Protestant views or reacting against all things Protestant, but the field has also failed to produce first-rate scholarship. From Holbrook's assessment of religious studies in the 1960s down to recent laments about the field's desultory nature, the academic study of religion has limped along behind other academic disciplines.[22] Of course, some would explain religious studies' poor performance as what happens when scholars try to mix faith and academics. Even so, if the strength of religious studies has not been academic, neither has it been religious since none of the religious detractors of the university look to the academic study of religion as a positive example of religious activity in the academy.

Douglas Sloan's recent study of Protestant theology and twentieth-century higher education only confirms the inadequacies of religious studies. Though neo-orthodox theologians offered some insightful critiques of scientism, naturalism, and secularism, the very perspectives that mainline Protestants believed were unwholesomely dominating academic life, the net effect of their arguments was a failure to make any significant dent on American higher education or the epistemological foundations of the modern research university. Sloan concluded that the Protestant effort to provide an alternative to scientific naturalism and thereby unite faith and knowledge was unsuccessful because it "fell back on and accepted uncritically, often enthusiastically, the dominant university conceptions of knowledge."[23]

Most recently, Russell T. McCutcheon, who eschewed any notion of religious studies' responsibility for the moral fiber of the university, nevertheless argued that the effort of studying religion *sui generis,* an approach that dominates survey textbooks and freshmen courses in the field, was the construction of scholars at once beholden to liberal Protestant theological traditions and to "the current world capitalist hegemony."[24] Though McCutcheon's self-congratulatory identification with the world's oppressed peoples trivialized a genuine concern about the university's dependence on big business and big government, his book offered a scathing indictment of religious studies' decrepit academic foundation.[25]

The Mixed Motives of Religious Studies

The history of religious studies, then, demonstrates at least the difficulty if not the impossibility of giving religion greater prominence within the university. Here is a specific instance of religion receiving special recognition in circles of higher learning. Yet, religious studies is not sufficiently religious for the university's believing critics because it is too scholarly. Neither is the field sufficiently scholarly to meet the academy's standards because of the legacy of its religious motivation. In which case, by failing to satisfy both believers and scholars, religious studies proves that religion is at best an awkward fit in the university. The failure of older Protestant efforts to give religion greater prominence in American higher education is a lesson that recent critics of the university's secularist bias fail to learn. In fact, the history of religious studies reveals that after World War II religion found its way back into U.S. colleges and universities for almost exactly the same reasons that religion's recent advocates use. Yet, those who argue for greater attention to religion in the academy offer no provisions for avoiding the mistakes that have afflicted religious studies.

As this book shows, the teaching and study of religion emerged from the efforts of mainstream Protestant ministers and educators who wanted to retain a religious influence in American higher education. In the first phase of those efforts, from roughly 1900 to 1935, Protestants worked mainly through such extracurricular agencies as the Student Volunteer Movement, the YMCA, and campus chaplains. They also saw that courses in religion, especially the Bible, would be crucial to gaining academic credibility. Consequently, the churches founded Bible chairs at the same time that individuals independent of the churches Protestant set up agencies and schools of religion that would teach students what they needed to know about the Bible and Christianity. This instruction was designed to ensure religious literacy and to provide spiritual guidance to the sons and daughters of the church.

In the second phase of religious studies, from 1935 to 1965, a variety of circumstances made Protestant efforts more successful. America's involvement in international politics, both in World War II and the Cold War, underscored the need for understanding and preserving western culture at the nation's colleges and universities. No longer did scientific and technological developments hold the promise they had during the first fifty years of the research university's dominance of American higher education. Instead, through a renewed interest in liberal or general education, the humanities recovered a certain measure of importance in the academy and the culture more generally. Religious studies fit well with the mood propelling the humanities' resurgence. Not only was Christianity important to European history, and likewise Protestantism to the development of the United States, but many educators regarded religion as an important ingredient in the

West's stand for liberal democracy against the tyranny of fascism on the right and communism on the left. The recognition of religion's importance gave Protestants significant leverage in establishing programs and departments that taught the Bible, theology, and church history, all with the understanding that such instruction contributed to the well-being of students and American society, and fit with the university's mission of preserving western civilization.

In the most recent period, after 1965, religion faculty and administrators discovered that the older spiritual and cultural reasons for teaching and studying religion were inadequate in a climate where America's religious and political ideals were, to put it mildly, contested. Contrary to Carter's reassurance that the study of religion is not a "smokescreen" for the politics of the religious right, the social and political debates of the 1960s exposed the teaching and study of religion as part of the cultural and political interests of mainline, as opposed to fundamentalist, Protestants. Once the close fit between Protestantism and liberal democracy became debatable, religious studies had to find another rationale, one more academic and less dependent on the mainline Protestant churches or the political and economic order that they supported. Religion professors were no longer able to count on the cache of western civilization, affinities to the humanities, or the prestige of the Protestant establishment. Yet the search for an academic justification for religious studies has yet to produce one that gives the field coherence, carves out religion as a distinct method of inquiry that is different from the way other academic disciplines teach and study religion, or even defines the concept of religion in a way that is useful for scholarly purposes. The only academic convention that has gained the consent of most religion faculty is the one that regards religious studies as the opposite of Protestant divinity.[26]

Yet, ironically, the anti-Protestant animus in religious studies once again proves the point that the teaching and study of religion in the United States has been dependent, if not parasitic, on Protestant churches and seminaries.[27] Mainstream Protestantism has either determined which subjects comprise the field of religion or, more recently, has been the object against which the discipline defines itself. In either case, the hegemony of Protestant divinity in the academic study of religion has left the field without a center. The older spiritual and cultural arguments for religion, though given a recent facelift, are still out of place in the public, naturalistic, and pluralistic ethos of the university. The transformation of the NABI into the AAR proves as much. The current disarray within the field is the result of both religious studies'

Protestant heritage and the much more difficult question of deciding what constitutes the scholarly study of religion, a question that the mid-twentieth-century Protestant proponents of religion conveniently brushed aside.

The history of religious studies, then, is instructive for anyone who believes that including religion in higher education will remedy the defects of the modern university. First, it shows that religion's cultured admirers made similar arguments fifty years ago, that religious studies was the upshot of those arguments, and how the recent version of those arguments will likely turn out if the failure of religious studies is ignored. Second, it reveals what usually happens to religion in the academy. Protestant academics have typically appealed to moral, spiritual, and cultural considerations for including religion in education. This is true of both mid- and late twentieth-century arguments. But what recent critics of the secular university fail to consider is that those older rationales for studying religion could not withstand the reorientation of American culture in the 1960s when mainstream Protestantism lost its privileged status in American education.[28] What once had been a field of teaching and study that acquainted students with their cultural heritage and the spiritual dimension of human existence found itself needing reasons that were as intellectually persuasive as those for other academic disciplines. This shift from religious and cultural warrants to academic grounds was inevitable once the cultural consensus that had provided coherence for American higher education no longer existed. At that point, religious studies, along with the humanities more generally, had to derive their authority from academic norms and procedures rather than a shared understanding of American culture and western civilization. No matter how contested by postmodernists, the methods and practices of critical reason supply the only coherence to the modern university short of liberationist and egalitarian ideologies. How else do the diverse disciplines of Spanish literature, biochemistry, and urban studies share a common vision of intellectual life?[29]

If the current state of religious studies is what happens when the university, in response to religious advocates, attempts to take religion seriously, then, contrary to recent arguments about religion and higher education, the university's trivialization of religion may be entirely reasonable and even praiseworthy. Although the first generation of university reformers, the Andrew Dickson Whites, Daniel Coit Gilmans, and Charles W. Eliots of American higher education, believed the research university was fundamentally compatible with Christian convictions of the right sort, they excluded theology because they wanted the natural sciences to be the standard of truth and believed that theology would obstruct an open-ended search for truth. The university would be a place free from dogma or revealed religion, devoted to the pursuit of scientifically verifiable truth. For them, teaching religion would have meant a return to the pious and sectarian designs of denominational colleges.

When religion some seventy years later returned to American universities as an academic discipline, it did so with the help of political and cultural circumstances, not by refuting the epistemological impulse that had propelled the modern research university. In the words of Kramnick and Moore, the only way for religion to re-enter the university is through the kind of "sail trimming" performed by liberal Protestantism, a task that involved the bargain of treating faith as an object of inquiry as long as religion faculty conceded that its truth claims were "subject to endless revision." "You cannot think your way to the Judeo-Christian God," they conclude, "without the lift provided by Biblical revelation."[30] The only problem with this construction of the tension between religion and higher education is that Kramnick and Moore, like Carter and Marsden, basically ignore the existence of religion departments and the arguments that led to their founding. If the university was as secular as they think, then how did the Judeo-Christian God receive such a sizable share of funding when religion departments were founded? Also, to suggest that the liberal Protestants who taught in religious studies were immune from appealing to special revelation is to forget those early days of religious studies when Bible faculty, many of whom were under the spell of neo-orthodoxy, argued explicitly that the text they taught was the very Word of God. After two world wars, economic depression, and constant fears of atomic weapons, many observers thought the university might very well use a little "lift" from divine sources.

The good intentions and vast resources of mainline Protestants in religious studies, however, could not alter the dilemma, described well by Alan Wolfe, that inevitably confronts religion in the modern academy. "Give religion priority of place," he writes, "and a certain alienation from success in an increasingly secular and meritocratic culture followed; adjust to America's mobility and economic dynamism, and the old-time religion would have to go."[31] Wolfe wrote this primarily with the history of Christian colleges and universities in mind.[32] But the same is no less true of religious studies where the religious and ministerial aims of Protestants were never far from view. And once those aims became illegitimate in the 1960s, religious studies secularized just like many Protestant colleges had a century earlier. To professionalize the field meant that the old-time religion, even of a neo-orthodox sort, would have to be left behind. Furthermore, if religion scholars did not professionalize, they would have been consigning themselves to the periphery of the university. Yet, by shifting from religious to academic norms, religious studies had to confront the reality that scholars in other fields already taught and studied religion in ways at least as, if not more, scholarly than the religious studies curriculum. Could it be that the university does not need a religion department for the academic study of religion? This question has haunted the field since 1970 when the efforts to professionalize religious studies became more earnest. In a throwaway line that could have caused the closing of religion programs throughout American higher education, Claude Welch admitted in his report on graduate religious studies that "nothing appears in a program of religious studies that could not appear elsewhere."[33]

The Blessings of Excluding Religion

But, some might argue, if religion receives only the attention already given by disciplines where religious history, texts, and ideas naturally emerge, such as in history, sociology, philosophy, and ancient Near Eastern studies, to name a few, the academy gives the wrong impression that religion is unimportant and therefore not a valuable part of America's heritage and vitality. This argument, however, assumes rather than proves religion's importance. For instance, without trying to trivialize the subject, is religion any more important than sex or food for the survival of the human race? Or, to put it another way, have food and sex been any less important to the construction of the American nation? Then why not give sex and food separate departments of study that teach the variety of beliefs and practices about procreation and eating? Some aspects of human existence may still be important even if not accorded departmental status in the modern university.[34]

Arguments for religion's importance also need to establish the criteria by which to measure such significance. Though surveys, polls, and statistics indicate a high degree of religious adherence in the United States, what is not clear is whether religious beliefs or convictions order the behavior and lives of the American population more than the policies of government or the commodities of big business. Since most Americans work outside the home and need to make personal decisions on the basis of economic and political considerations over which they have little control, religion may be even more marginal in American society than its advocates imagine it is in the university. In other words, the point that Talal Asad makes for science may be equally true for the nation-state and multinational corporations. "Religion is indeed now optional in a way that science is not," he asserts. "Scientific practices, techniques, knowledges, permeate and create the very fibers of social life in ways that religion no longer does."[35] If Asad is correct, then the university's exclusion of religion may be quite reasonable.

Yet, critics of the academic secularism counter that such bias contradicts the university's commitment to academic freedom. In the name of tolerating most points of view, some argue, religion should be included in academic life, especially since "there is scarcely any danger . . . of a dominant religious belief leading to the imposition of general restrictions on free inquiry."[36] But, as Louis Menand argues, academic freedom is not the same thing as freedom of expression. The former does not give license (though it has) to any point of view, no matter how reasonable or noble its pedigree. Instead, academic freedom is designed to protect the university from external restraints, especially those of politics and religion, and thereby establish its own professional standards. In Menand's construction of academic freedom, such liberation from external restraint lies at the heart of the research university. In place of such restrictions, the regulations that govern academic life and keep it free are the hierarchical order of doctorates, peer review prior to the publication of dissertation research, and junior and senior faculty appointments, with tenure standing at the pinnacle.

Ideally, then, academic freedom is inherently exclusive of nonacademic outlooks, whether the platform of the Democratic Party or the creed of the Presbyterian Church. Menand writes, by "being free to regulate itself, the profession is free to reject what does not intellectually suit it and essentially to compel, by withholding professional rewards . . . , the work that does."[37] The exclusion of religion, then, is fully compatible with academic freedom since the modern university has been premised upon the notion that religious tenets based on special revelation may play no explicit part in the task of research and teaching.[38] Of course, the establishment of religion departments has been a notable exception to this commitment. In fact, religious studies may be an early example of the therapeutic assumptions and identity politics that led in the 1960s and 1970s to the creation of women's, black, Native American, and gay/lesbian studies programs.[39] Just as marginal groups have argued for inclusion in universities and colleges on the grounds that black, women's, and Native American points of view and histories had been unfairly excluded, so religious studies programs emerged from mainline Protestant complaints that the university had ignored religious perspectives. By forming religion departments, university administrators capitulated to the pressures of mainline Protestants in the same way that they later succumbed to African-Americans, women, and gays, for example. Of course, this analogy is debatable. But if true, it underscores all the more the tenuous position of religion in the academy.

Closely related to the appeal to academic freedom is the one that argues for religion by resorting to the logic of multiculturalism. If the university includes such ideologies as Marxism, feminism, Afrocentrism, and Queer studies, it surely has few legitimate reasons for excluding religious points of view. And if it does, it risks breaking all rules of fairness. For instance, Nord wrote that education should be multicultural "in the sense that it should give voice to various subcultures—religious subcultures included—which currently have little say in the world of intellectual and educational elites."[40] This argument rightly notes an inconsistency within the contemporary academic world but does not prove that religion is compatible with the university's academic procedures. Instead of asking colleges and universities to give more attention to religion, critics of the university might well plead with the educational establishment to adhere to its scholarly standards more consistently by excluding religion and other special-interest-group areas of study, rather than making an exception (which happened when religious studies became an academic discipline). Here, Wolfe's point about the debates over speech codes and sensitivity training is instructive. "The university," he concluded, "ought not to be in the business of healing the afflicted or comforting the aggrieved."[41]

But by striving to reintroduce faith into the university, proponents of religion end up politicizing it, thereby furthering the intellectual flabbiness of American higher education. This is why Menand writes that "universities can decide the things people ought to know, and they can decide how those things should be taught. But universities cannot arbitrate disputes about democracy and social justice, or govern the manner in which people relate socially to one another, or police attitudes." Menand could just as plausibly have added religion to his list. The university may well be asked to make religion more important to its mission and show its significance to modern society, but, in Menand's words, "it is not designed to arbitrate among antagonistic interest groups, or to discover ways of correcting inequities and attitudes that persist in society as a whole."[42]

In the end, the university's disregard of religion may not only be a good thing for higher education but also for religion itself. H. L. Mencken once criticized liberal Protestants for trying to "get rid of all the logical difficulties of religion and yet preserve a generally pious cast of mind." The problem with this effort, he explained, even though pursued with the best of intentions, was that what was left after such "imprudent scavenging" was "a row of hollow platitudes as empty [of] psychological force and effect as so many nursery rhymes." Religion, Mencken believed, was something "far more deep-down-diving and mud-upbringing."[43]

What Mencken detected in liberal Protestantism has been equally true of religious studies, a not altogether startling conclusion since mainstream Protestants have dominated religion as an academic discipline. In fact, what has been common in the study of religion has been the marked absence of anything that might reasonably be described as religious polemic. Instead of teaching the real conflicts and disagreements that exist among religious traditions, a practice that obtains in other academic disciplines, religious studies has invariably promoted interreligious dialogue. According to Paul J. Griffiths, who teaches at the University of Chicago, religious studies studiously avoids "the polemical dimensions of intellectual life." As such the academic study of religion fosters "a repudiation" of "the struggle for truth."[44] From a different perspective, R. Laurence Moore has argued that discussions of religious diversity among religion scholars have generally assumed that "unfriendly feeling is somehow abnormal in a religiously plural society." But for religion to be taken seriously, as recent critics of the university desire, institutions of American higher education must allow for differences to be "aggressively asserted because they are meant to matter."[45] The way to fix this may mean that religious studies should, as Gerald Graff has argued for literary studies, teach the conflicts.[46] But unlike literature, such conflicts would require the university to tolerate doctrines that are explicitly dogmatic and sectarian, and that appeal to sacred texts whose authority rests upon standards that modern scholarship is incapable of adjudicating. In which case, the modern university, which was created to be a site free from ecclesiastical and dogmatic conflict, would become the home of the very things its founders wanted to exclude.

Which is just another way of saying that religion does not do well in the hands of academics, whether they are sympathetic to it or not. Because the university is incapable of evaluating dogmatic claims and supernaturally inspired texts, the religion it tolerates tends to be the thin variety that Mencken described. To exclude those religions that assert their own exclusive claims to truth, then, is to do them a favor. Academic inquiry, if the history of religious studies is any indication, waters religion down to the point where faith makes no actual difference.

Ironically, then, by excluding religion as a field of academic study, the university may be paying religion great respect.[47] That was certainly the intent of the first generation of university administrators and faculty who did not include religion in the original curriculum. Still, whatever the aims of the university's founders, the history of religious studies gives good grounds for the argument that religion does better without the blessing of the university. According to Alan Wolfe, "If the debate over the inclusion of religion in the university teaches us anything, it is that faith is vital, religion ubiquitous, and belief admirable." But, he adds, religion in the university does not attain such virtues. That is why "we have families, churches, circles of friends, and private religious institutions" where the genuine needs and interests of religion can be served. "The inclusive university should be for something else."[48]

Some still might wonder whether the secular character of the university puts too heavy a burden on the religious. The nature of modern intellectual life as the university has come to define it does, indeed, require believing scholars to make choices that are difficult. They may have to live in an apparently schizophrenic manner, separating what they do in the classroom or publish from what they do at home or as part of a community of faith. But here the teaching of many faiths should give comfort to religion's advocates. If this world and prestige in it should not be the primary aim of believers, and if in the world to come the faithful will inherit riches that exceed any perk or privilege the university confers, then the burden believing scholars bear in the university is not too great. This was certainly the implication of Jesus' question to his disciples, "What does it profit a man if he gain the whole world and lose his soul?" (Mark 8:36). If believers really hope they will receive enduring rewards in the world to come, then they should have faith that eternal bliss will more than make up for whatever suffering and ignominy the university exhibits toward them here and now. In effect, Christ's question was a variation on the theme that you can't have it both ways. It may be time for faithful academics to stop trying to secure a religion-friendly university while paying deference to the academic standards of the modern university. If the old religions are right, in the new heavens and new earth there should be plenty of enduring rewards that will make promotion, tenure, and endowed chairs look like so much hay and stubble.

Notes

Abbreviations

AAC   Association of American Colleges
AAR   American Academy of Religion
ACLS   American Council of Learned Societies
AHR   *American Historical Review*
BCSR   *Bulletin of the Council on the Study on Religion*
CCBE   Council of Church Boards of Education
CS   *Christian Scholar*
FCF   Faculty Christian Fellowship
JAAR   *Journal of the American Academy of Religion*
JBR   *Journal of Bible and Religion*
JNABI   *Journal of the National Association of Biblical Instructors*
NABI   National Association of Biblical Instructors
NCRHE   National Council on Religion in Higher Education
REA   Religious Education Assocation

Introduction

1. See David van Biema, "The Gospel Truth?" *Time* 147 (April 8, 1996): 52–59; "In Search of Jesus," *U.S. News and World Report* 120 (April 8, 1996): 47–53; Luke Timothy Johnson, "The Jesus Seminar's Misguided Quest for the Historical Jesus," *Christian Century* 116 (Jan. 3–10, 1996): 16–22; Charlotte Allen, "The Search for a No-Frills Jesus," *Atlantic Monthly* 278 (Dec. 1996): 51–68; and James R. Edwards, "Who Do Scholars Say That I Am?" *Christianity Today* 40 (Mar. 4, 1996): 14–20.

2. Robert W. Funk, Roy W. Hoover, and the Jesus Seminar, *The Five Gospels* (New York: Macmillan, 1993), v, 2.

3. Luis Leon, contributor to "Taking the Bull by the Tail: Responses to the *Lingua Franca* Article," *Bulletin of the CSSR* 26 (Nov. 1997): 83.

4. J. Samuel Preus, *Explaining Religion: Criticism and Theory from Bodin to Freud* (New Haven: Yale University Press, 1987), ix, x, 210.

5. Walter H. Capps, *Religious Studies: The Making of a Discipline* (Minneapolis: Fortress Press, 1995), xiv.

6. Ibid., xviii, xxii, 52, 337–38. For other recent treatments of the academic study of religion which trace the field's roots to Enlightenment rather than Protestant sources, see Daniel L. Pals, *Seven Theories of Religion* (New York: Oxford University Press, 1996); Rodney Stark, *A Theory of Religion* (New Brunswick, N.J.: Rutgers University Press, 1997); and Mark C. Taylor, ed., *Critical Terms for Religious Studies* (Chicago: University of Chicago Press, 1998).

7. Claude Welch, "Reflections on the Academic Study of Religion: Patterns, Problems and Prospects," *ACLS Newsletter* 19 (Oct. 1968): 1–18, quotation on 4.

8. John Frederick Wilson, *Research Guide to Religious Studies* (Washington, D.C.: American Library Association, 1982), 14, 4.

9. "American Academy of Religion," in The American Council of Learned Societies, *A Report to the Congress of the United States on the State of the Humanities and the Reauthorization of the National Endowment for the Humanities* (Washington, D.C.: ACLS, 1985), 4, 3, 8.

10. Harold E. Remus et al., "Religion as an Academic Discipline," in *Encyclopedia of the American Religious Experience: Studies of Traditions and Movements*, vol. 3, ed. Charles H. Lippy and Peter W. Williams (New York: Scribner's, 1987), 1664.

11. Paul V. Mankowski, "Academic Religion: Playground of the Vandals," *First Things* 23 (May 1992): 32, 33.

12. Quoted in Paul V. Mankowski, "What I Was at the American Academy of Religion," *First Things* 21 (March 1992): 39.

13. Mankowski, "Academic Religion," 35.

14. "The Latest Jewish Ghetto," *Chronicles* 19 (Sept. 1995): 6, 5.

15. For just a few of the conservative attacks on the academic literary establishment, see Allan Bloom, *The Closing of the American Mind: How Higher Education Has Failed Democracy and Impoverished the Souls of Today's Students* (New York: Simon and Schuster, 1987); Roger Kimball, *Tenured Radicals: How Politics Has Corrupted Our Higher Education* (New York: Harper and Row, 1990); and Dinesh D'Souza, *Illiberal Education: The Politics of Race and Sex on Campus* (New York: Free Press, 1991).

16. Jonathan Z. Smith, "'Religion' and 'Religious Studies': No Difference at All," *Soundings* 71 (1988): 235, 233.

17. Gerald James Larson, "An Introduction to the Santa Barbara Colloquy: Some Unresolved Questions," *Soundings* 71 (1988): 194.

18. Ray L. Hart, "Religious and Theological Studies in American Higher Education: A Pilot Study," *JAAR* 59 (1991): 726, 744, 748.

19. Sam Gill, "The Academic Study of Religion," *JAAR* 62 (1994): 996.

20. Mark C. Taylor, "Unsettling Issues," *JAAR* 62 (1994): 952–53.

21. Russell T. McCutcheon, *Manufacturing Religion: The Discourse on Sui*

Generis Religion and the Politics of Nostalgia (New York: Oxford University Press, 1997), 21–24, quotation from 22. It should be noted in passing that in Mc-Cutcheon's desire to race to what he believes are these obviously damaging political and economic conclusions about religious studies, he may have over-estimated the dominance of the *sui generis* approach to religion which, no doubt, is large in introductory courses and textbook surveys. But Mc-Cutcheon's conclusion about the state of the field hardly comports with the observations cited above whose major complaint is that no single paradigm guides the academic teaching and study of religion.

22. The classic expression of this view is, of course, Laurence R. Veysey, *The Emergence of the American University* (Chicago: University of Chicago Press, 1965). See also Richard Hofstadter, "The Revolution in Higher Education," in *Paths of American Thought,* ed. Arthur M. Schlesinger Jr. and Morton White (Boston: Houghton Mifflin, 1970), 269–90; and Walter P. Metzger, *Academic Freedom in the Age of the University* (New York: Columbia University Press, 1955), chaps. 1–3. For additional perspective on secularization, see David A. Hollinger, "Jewish Intellectuals and the De-Christianization of American Public Culture in the Twentieth Century," in *New Directions in American Religious History,* ed. Harry S. Stout and D. G. Hart (New York: Oxford University Press, 1997), 462–84.

23. See the essays in *The Secularization of the Academy,* ed. George M. Marsden and Bradley J. Longfield (New York: Oxford University Press, 1992); and George M. Marsden, *The Soul of the American University: From Protestant Estab-lishment to Established Nonbelief* (New York: Oxford University Press, 1994).

24. Louis Menand, "The Limits of Academic Freedom," in *The Future of Academic Freedom,* ed. Menand (Chicago: University of Chicago Press, 1996), 8, 11.

25. On the history of literary studies, see Kermit Vanderbilt, *American Lit-erature and the Academy: The Roots, Growth, and Maturity of a Profession* (Philadel-phia: University of Pennsylvania Press, 1986), and Gerald Graff, *Professing Liter-ature: An Institutional History* (Chicago: University of Chicago Press, 1987).

26. On intellectual life before the rise of professional knowledge, see Thomas Bender, *New York Intellect: A History of Intellectual Life in New York City, from 1750 to the Beginnings of Our Time* (New York: Knopf, 1987), chaps. 1–6.

27. Hart, "Religious and Theological Studies," 730, 732, 764–66.

28. This happens, it should be noted, in as simple a matter as offering courses in the Bible—which consists of sixty-six books written between 3,500 and 2,000 years ago which the Christian church has pulled together and deemed authoritative.

29. This point is made forcefully in Jon D. Levenson, *The Hebrew Bible, the Old Testament, and Historical Criticism: Jews and Christians in Biblical Studies* (Louisville, Ky.: Westminster/John Knox, 1993); and Alasdair MacIntyre, *Three Rival Versions of Moral Enquiry: Encyclopaedia, Genealogy, and Tradition* (Notre Dame, Ind.: University of Notre Dame Press, 1990).

30. On the history of twentieth-century theology, see, for instance, William R. Hutchison, *The Modernist Impulse in American Protestantism* (Cambridge: Har-vard University Press, 1976); Sydney E. Ahlstrom, ed., *Theology in America: The Major Protestant Voices from Puritanism to Neo-Orthodoxy* (Indianapolis: Bobbs-Merrill, 1967); and Kenneth Cauthen, *The Impact of American Religious Liberalism*

(New York: Harper and Row, 1962). For biblical studies, see, e.g., Ernest W. Saunders, *Searching the Scriptures: A History of the Society of Biblical Literature, 1880–1980* (Chico, Calif.: Scholars Press, 1982); Mark A. Noll, *Between Faith and Criticism: Evangelicals, Scholarship, and the Bible in America* (San Francisco: Harper and Row, 1986); and Gerald P. Fogarty, *American Catholic Biblical Scholarship: A History from the Early Republic to Vatican II* (San Francisco: Harper and Row, 1989). And for church history, see, e.g., Henry Warner Bowden, *Church History in an Age of Uncertainty: Historiographical Patterns in the United States, 1906–1990* (Carbondale: Southern Illinois University Press, 1991); Harry S. Stout and Robert M. Taylor Jr., "Studies of Religion in American Society: The State of the Art," in *New Directions in American Religious History*, ed. Stout and Hart, 15–47; and David W. Lotz, "A Changing Historiography: From Church History to Religious History," in *Altered Landscapes: Christianity in America, 1935–1985*, ed. David W. Lotz (Grand Rapids, Mich.: Eerdmans, 1989), 312–39.

1 • Enlightened Christianity and the Founding of the University

1. Andrew Dickson White, *A History of the Warfare of Science with Theology in Christendom*, 2 vols. (New York: D. Appleton, 1896), 1:17–18, 123, 130–31. On Cornell's place in the university movement of the late nineteenth century, see Laurence R. Veysey, *The Emergence of the American University* (Chicago: University of Chicago Press, 1965), chap. 2, passim; George M. Marsden, *The Soul of the American University: From Protestant Establishment to Established Nonbelief* (New York: Oxford University Press, 1994), chap. 6; and Morris Bishop, *A History of Cornell* (Ithaca, N.Y.: Cornell University Press, 1962).

For background on White's understanding of the warfare between religion and science, see Glenn C. Altschuler, *Andrew D. White—Educator, Historian, Diplomat* (Ithaca, N.Y.: Cornell University Press, 1979); Altschuler, "From Religion to Ethics: Andrew D. White and the Dilemma of a Christian Rationalist," *Church History* 47 (1978): 308–24; and David C. Lindberg and Ronald L. Numbers, "Beyond War and Peace: A Reappraisal of the Encounter between Christianity and Science," *Church History* 55 (1986): 338–54.

2. White, *History of the Warfare of Science*, 1:239.

3. White, "Inaugural Address," in *Account of the Proceedings of the Inauguration, October 7, 1868* (Ithaca, N.Y.: Cornell University Press, 1868), quoted in Bishop, *History of Cornell*, 190–91.

4. On White's policies at Cornell regarding religion on campus, see Altschuler, *Andrew D. White*, 94–96.

5. White, *Cornell Era*, May 4, 1877, quoted in ibid., 98.

6. Adler, letter of April 22, 1885, quoted in ibid., 99.

7. "Religion in Colleges," *New York Times*, Feb. 4, 1886, quoted in Paul Charles Kemeny, "The Changing Nature and Role of Religious Worship at Princeton University, 1868–1928: An Institutional, Educational, and Social Examination," Ph.D. diss., Princeton Theological Seminary, Princeton, N.J., 1995, 1.

8. On Eliot, see Hugh Hawkins, *Between Harvard and America: The Educational Leadership of Charles W. Eliot* (New York: Oxford University Press, 1972);

Hawkins, "Charles W. Eliot, University Reform, and Religious Faith in America, 1869–1909," *Journal of American History* 51 (1964): 191–213; and Marsden, *Soul of the University,* chap. 11.

9. See Kemeny, "Changing Nature," 113.

10. James McCosh, *The New Departure in College Education* (New York: Scribner's, 1885), 5, 8–10, 13, 16, 20–21, 22.

11. Charles W. Eliot, "Liberty in Education," in Eliot, *Educational Reform: Essays and Addresses* (1898; repr., New York: Arno Press, 1969), 126–42.

12. James McCosh, *Religion in a College: What Place It Should Have* (New York: A. C. Armstrong and Son, 1886), 10, 11, 12.

13. For instance, Veysey, *Emergence of the American University,* while conceding McCosh's educational progressivism, largely depicts the Princeton president as a defender of the old ways, who insisted on upholding the old liberal arts ideals of mental discipline and Christian orthodoxy. See 22–28, 41–51.

14. J. David Hoeveler Jr., *James McCosh and the Scottish Intellectual Tradition* (Princeton, N.J.: Princeton University Press, 1981), 250.

15. McCosh, *New Departure,* 6.

16. Eliot, "Address at the Inauguration of Daniel C. Gilman," in *Educational Reform,* 43.

17. Eliot, "The Aims of Higher Education," in *Educational Reform,* 234–35, 241–49. See also Hawkins, *Between Harvard and America,* chap. 4.

18. McCosh, *Religion in a College,* 14.

19. On the prevailing understanding of Christianity undergirding university reforms, see D. G. Hart, "Faith and Learning in the Age of the University: The Academic Ministry of Daniel Coit Gilman," in *The Secularization of the Academy,* ed. George M. Marsden and Bradley J. Longfield (New York: Oxford University Press, 1992), chap. 4.

20. See Mark A. Noll, *Princeton and the Republic, 1768–1822: The Search for a Christian Enlightenment in the Era of Samuel Stanhope Smith* (Princeton, N.J.: Princeton University Press, 1989), esp. chaps. 3 and 4; and Noll, "The Rise and Long Life of the Protestant Enlightenment in America," in *Knowledge and Belief in America: Enlightenment Traditions and Modern Religious Thought,* ed. William M. Shea and Peter A. Huff (New York: Cambridge University Press, 1995), chap. 3 (hereafter Noll, "Protestant Enlightenment").

21. See Noll, *Princeton and the Republic,* 36–47; and Norman Fiering, "The Rationalist Foundations of Jonathan Edwards's Metaphysics," in *Jonathan Edwards and the American Experience,* ed. Nathan O. Hatch and Harry S. Stout (New York: Oxford University Press, 1988), chap. 5.

22. Noll, *Princeton and the Republic,* 43.

23. Ibid., 191; Noll, "Protestant Enlightenment," 107.

24. Noll, *Princeton and the Republic,* 191ff.

25. For a sampling of some of the literature on appeal of the Scottish Enlightenment in the United States, see Sydney E. Ahlstrom, "The Scottish Philosophy and American Theology," *Church History* 24 (1955): 257–72; Henry F. May, *The Enlightenment in America* (New York: Oxford University Press, 1976), sec. 4; Theodore Dwight Bozeman, *Protestants in an Age of Science: The Baconian Ideal and Antebellum American Religious Thought* (Chapel Hill: University of North Carolina Press, 1977); Bruce Kuklick, *Churchmen and Philosophers: From*

Jonathan Edwards to John Dewey (New Haven: Yale University Press, 1985); and Mark A. Noll, "Common Sense Traditions and American Evangelical Thought," *American Quarterly* 37 (1985): 216–38.

26. Mark A. Noll, "The Irony of the Enlightenment for Presbyterians in the Early Republic," *Journal of the Early Republic* 5 (1985): 149–75. On the effects of the Protestant Enlightenment on later academic developments, particularly the tradition of moral philosophy, see Allen C. Guelzo, "'The Science of Duty': Moral Philosophy and the Epistemology of Science in Nineteenth-Century America," in *Evangelicals and Science in Historical Perspective,* ed. David N. Livingstone, D. G. Hart, and Mark A. Noll (New York: Oxford University Press, 1999).

27. Marsden, *Soul of the American University,* 84–90.

28. Samuel Stanhope Smith, *Lectures . . . on the Subjects of Moral and Political Philosophy* (Trenton, N.J., 1812), 2:225–26, quoted in Noll, *Princeton and the Republic,* 203.

29. On the influence of the Protestant Enlightenment on the development of America's public schools, see Charles Leslie Glenn Jr., *The Myth of the Common School* (Amherst: University of Massachusetts Press, 1988).

30. Daniel Coit Gilman, *An Address Before the Phi Beta Kappa Society of Harvard University, July 1, 1886* (Baltimore: Johns Hopkins Press, 1886), 3.

31. Quoted in Marsden, *Soul of the American University,* 116.

32. See Hawkins, "Charles W. Eliot."

33. See D. G. Hart, "The Protestant Enlightenment Revisited: Daniel Coit Gilman and the Academic Reforms of the Modern University," *Journal of Ecclesiastical History* 47 (1996): 683–703.

34. See Richard Hofstadter, "The Revolution in Higher Education," in *Paths of American Thought,* ed. Arthur M. Schlesinger Jr. and Morton White (Boston: Houghton Mifflin, 1970), 269–90; Walter P. Metzger, *Academic Freedom in the Age of the University* (New York: Columbia University Press, 1955), chaps. 1–3; Frederick Rudolph, *Curriculum: A History of the American Undergraduate Course of Study since 1636* (San Francisco: Jossey Bass, 1977), 107–9, 203; Rudolph, *The American College and University: A History* (New York: Knopf, 1962), chaps. 13, 16; Lewis Perry, *Intellectual Life in America: A History* (New York: Franklin Watts, 1984), 289–94; Veysey, *Emergence of the American University;* and Mark A. Noll, "Christian Thinking and the Rise of the American University," *Christian Scholar's Review* 9 (1979): 3–16.

On the authority of science and universities in American culture, see David A. Hollinger, "The Knower and the Artificer," *American Quarterly* 39 (1987): 38–55; Jon H. Roberts, *Darwinism and the Divine in America: Protestant Intellectuals and Organic Evolution, 1859–1900* (Madison: University of Wisconsin Press, 1988), xiv–xvi, 235–42; Thomas L. Haskell, *The Emergence of Professional Social Science: The American Social Science Association and the Nineteenth-Century Crisis of Authority* (Urbana: University of Illinois Press, 1977); Haskell, ed., *The Authority of Experts: Studies in History and Theory* (Bloomington: Indiana University Press, 1984); Bruce Kuklick, *The Rise of American Philosophy, Cambridge, Massachusetts, 1860–1930* (New Haven: Yale University Press, 1977); Kuklick, *Churchmen and Philosopher,* chap. 13.

35. Accounts of the antipathy directed at universities by clergymen and denominational college officials are numerous. But the few citations of ecclesiastical opposition are disproportional to the "warfare between religion and

science" thesis. These should be compared to the instances where the wrong politics proved to be far more objectionable to academic administrators. Compare the citations in n. 34 above to Carol S. Gruber, *Mars and Minerva: World War I and the Uses of Higher Learning in America* (Baton Rouge: Louisiana State University Press, 1975); and Ellen W. Schrecker, *No Ivory Tower: McCarthyism and the Universities* (New York: Oxford University Press, 1986).

36. The quotation from the cleric comes from Gilman, "Reminiscences of Thirty Years in Baltimore," in *The Launching of the University and Other Papers: A Sheaf of Remembrances* (New York: Dodd, Mead, 1906), 22–23. On the opening of the university and the appearance of the controversial Huxley, see *The Annual Report of the President of the Johns Hopkins University* (hereafter *AR*) 1 (1876): 3; Gilman, "Reminiscences of Thirty Years," 20–23; and Hugh Hawkins, *Pioneer: A History of the Johns Hopkins University, 1874–1889* (Baltimore: Johns Hopkins Press, 1960), 68–73.

37. McCosh, *Religion in a College,* 9–10, 14–15.

38. By David A. Hollinger's assessment in "Justification by Verification: The Scientific Challenge to the Moral Authority of Christianity in Modern America," in *Religion and Twentieth-Century American Intellectual Life,* ed. Michael J. Lacey (New York: Cambridge University Press, 1989), 116–17, I am guilty here of a neo-harmonist reading of the encounter between Christianity and science in the context of the American university. But in Hollinger's effort to express "'neo-conflictist' caveats" I believe that he fails to acknowledge that Protestant harmonist strategies endured well beyond the apparent triumph of secularism in the late nineteenth century. Though he is correct to observe a real antagonism between the new science and Christian presuppositions, the religious motives of Gilman and White, however tepid they may have been, did not go away, as Hollinger himself observes in another essay where the presence of liberal Protestants in the 1930s at New York University, a self-consciously public and seemingly secular school, apparently takes him by surprise. See Hollinger, "Two NYUs and 'The Obligation of Universities to the Social Order' in the Great Depression," in *Science, Jews, and Secular Culture: Studies in Mid-Twentieth-Century American Intellectual History* (Princeton, N.J.: Princeton University Press, 1996), chap. 4. If the intellectual gospel, as I read it, was more harmonist than conflictist, then it explains the sort of phenomenon Hollinger examines in this essay on NYU.

39. See McCosh, *New Departure in College Education;* McCosh, *What an American University Should Be* (New York: J. K. Lees, 1885); Noah Porter, *The American Colleges and the American Public* (New Haven: Charles C. Chatfield and Co., 1870), chap. 15; John Chamberlain, "The End of the Old Education," *Modern Age* 2 (1960): 343–54; and Burton J. Bledstein, "Noah Porter versus William Graham Sumner," *Church History* 43 (1974): 340–49.

40. The next several paragraphs follow the argument in Hart, "Faith and Learning in the Age of the University."

41. Gilman, "Modern Education," *Cosmopolitan* 23 (1897): 36.

42. Gilman, "Present Aspects of College Training," *North American Review* 136 (1883): 537.

43. Gilman, "Is It Worthwhile to Uphold Any Longer the Idea of Liberal Education," *Educational Review* 2 (1892): 115.

44. Ibid., 118–19.

45. Gilman, "Our National Schools of Science," offprint in the Gilman Papers, Milton S. Eisenhower Library, Johns Hopkins University, 28; "The Inauguration of President Wheeler at Berkeley, October 25, 1899," in Gilman, *Launching of the University*, 230.

46. Gilman, "The Influence of Universities," in his *University Problems in the United States* (New York: Century Co., 1898), 56. For the reception of Darwinism by Protestant clergy, see Roberts, *Darwinism and the Divine in America*.

47. Gilman, "Research—A Speech Delivered at the Convocation of the University of Chicago, June, 1903," in *Launching of the University*, 251.

48. Gilman, "The Characteristics of a University," in *University Problems*, 97.

49. Gilman, "Remembrances—Looking Backwards Over Fifty Years," in *Launching of a University*, 150. Hollinger, "Justification by Verification," provides ample comment on such liberal Protestant understandings of science. For the antecedents of such views, see Bozeman's account of doxological science in *Protestants in an Age of Science*.

50. Gilman, "Johns Hopkins University in Its Beginning," in *University Problems*, 12–13.

51. On the transformation of learning that research universities nurtured, see the essays in Alexandra Oleson and John Voss, ed., *The Organization of Knowledge in Modern America, 1860–1920* (Baltimore: Johns Hopkins University Press, 1979).

52. James Dwight Dana, "Science and Scientific Schools," *American Journal of Education* 2 (1856): 156.

53. James McLachlan, "The American College in the Nineteenth Century: Toward A Reappraisal," *Teachers College Review* 80 (1978): 304.

54. In addition to Marsden's *Soul of the American University*, other works on the influence of religion on university founders include Julie A. Reuben, *The Making of the Modern University: Intellectual Transformation and the Marginalization of Morality* (Chicago: University of Chicago Press, 1996); Conrad Cherry, *Hurrying Toward Zion: Universities, Divinity Schools, and American Protestantism* (Bloomington: Indiana University Press, 1995); and W. Clark Gilpin, *A Preface to Theology* (Chicago: University of Chicago Press, 1996), chaps. 2–3.

55. Eliot, "Inauguration of Daniel C. Gilman," 43.

56. Porter, *American Colleges and the American Public*, 223.

57. See, for instance, Eliot, "Aims of Higher Education," and "The Unity of Educational Reform," in *Educational Reform*, 239–49, 315–39; and Gilman, "Higher Education in the United States," in *University Problems*, 301–3; "Research," 244–48; and "Characteristics of a University," 102–6.

58. "Characteristics of a University," 96.

59. *Autobiography of Andrew Dickson White*, 2 vols. (New York: Century Co., 1905), 2:562, 532, 568.

60. Porter, *American Colleges*, 217.

61. McCosh, *Religion in a College*, 7, 8, 9, 10, 11, 14, 16, 22.

62. See Henry F. May, *The End of American Innocence: The First Years of Our Own Time, 1912–1917* (New York: Oxford University Press, 1959); Daniel Joseph Singal, *The War Within: From Victorian to Modernist Thought in the South, 1919–1945* (Chapel Hill: University of North Carolina Press, 1982); Singal, "Towards a Definition of American Modernism," *American Quarterly* 39 (1987):

8–26; Daniel Walker Howe, "American Victorianism as a Culture," *American Quarterly* 27 (1975): 507–32. The relationship of modernism to modernization presents a problem in this depiction of Victorianism. Singal, for instance, tries to keep modernism and modernization separate while granting that Victorian values were shaped by the social transformations wrought by modernization. But by maintaining such a sharp distinction Singal, along with other historians who interpret modernism as a revolt against Victorianism, overlooks the doubts and ambiguities that began to surface among Victorian intellectuals and ignores how much modernism was a reaction against the highly structured confines of modern society. On the Victorian doubts, see D. H. Meyer, "American Intellectuals and the Victorian Crisis of Faith," *American Quarterly* 27 (1975): 584–603. On Victorians and modernization, see Richard D. Brown, "Modernization: A Victorian Climax," *American Quarterly* 27 (1975): 533–48; and Robert H. Wiebe, *The Search for Order, 1877–1920* (New York: Hill and Wang, 1967), chaps. 5–7. On the relationship between modernism and modernization, see Marshall Berman, *All That Is Solid Melts Into Air: The Experience of Modernity* (New York: Simon and Schuster, 1981); and T. J. Jackson Lears, *No Place of Grace: Antimodernism and Transformation of American Culture, 1880–1920* (New York: Pantheon Books, 1981).

63. David A. Hollinger, "Ethnic Diversity, Cosmopolitanism, and the Emergence of the American Liberal Intelligentsia," in Hollinger, *In the American Province: Studies in the History and Historiography of Ideas* (Bloomington: Indiana University Press, 1985), 59.

64. Hollinger acknowledges the Enlightenment origins of cosmopolitanism in "How Wide the Circle of 'We'? American Intellectuals and the Problem of the Ethnos since World War II," *AHR* 98 (1993): 317–37.

65. This willingness to see the value of the study of nature contrasts with Porter's argument that science would nurture materialism, naturalism, and the like, that is, research and investigation that denied or undermined the spiritual side of nature. For his expression of Victorian dichotomies, see *American Colleges and the American Public,* chap. 11.

66. See, for instance, Andrew Dickson White, who wrote of how his exposure to the "great religions of the world" had caused him to distrust "theological dogmatism." "More and more clear it became that ecclesiastical dogmas are but steps in the evolution of various religions, and that, in view of the fact that the main underlying ideas are common to all, a beneficent evolution is to continue." *Autobiography,* 2:559.

67. For this strand of Victorian culture, see May, *End of American Innocence,* chap. 3.

68. For the links between the Enlightenment and Protestant principles of biblical interpretation, see George M. Marsden, "Every One's Own Interpreter? The Bible, Science and Authority in Mid-Nineteenth-Century America," in *The Bible in America: Essays in Cultural History,* ed. Nathan O. Hatch and Mark A. Noll (New York: Oxford University Press, 1982), chap. 4.

69. Samuel McCrea Cavert, *The American Churches in the Ecumenical Movement, 1900–1968* (New York: Association Press, 1968), 25.

70. For the larger connections between evangelicalism and democracy, see Nathan O. Hatch, *The Democraticization of American Christianity* (New Haven: Yale University Press, 1989).

71. See Philip D. Jordan, "The Evangelical Alliance and American Presbyterians, 1867–1873," *Journal of Presbyterian History* 51 (1973): 309–26; Jordan, *The Evangelical Alliance for the United States of America, 1847–1900: Ecumenism, Identity and the Religion of the Republic* (New York: Edwin Mellen Press, 1982), chap. 4; Cavert, *American Churches,* chap. 1.

72. McCosh, "The Religious and Social Conditions of the United States . . .," *Proceeding of the Evangelical Alliance* (1866): 23, 17, quoted in J. David Hoeveler Jr., "Evangelical Ecumenism: James McCosh and the Intellectual Origins of the World Alliance of Reformed Churches," *Journal of Presbyterian History* 55 (1977): 45, 47.

73. Gilman, "The Christian Resources of Our Country," in Evangelical Alliance, *U.S. Conference, Washington, D.C., 1887: National Perils and Opportunities* (New York: Evangelical Alliance, 1887), 281.

74. Ibid., 283–84.

75. Mann, quoted in Glenn, *Myth of the Common School,* 172, 173.

76. Charles Brooks, *Elementary Instruction* (Quincy, Mass.: John A. Green, 1837), 10–11, quoted in ibid., 149.

77. William James, "The Teaching of Philosophy in Our Colleges," in *Essays in Philosophy* (Cambridge: Harvard University Press, 1978), 3, quoted in Reuben, *Making of the Modern University,* 89.

78. Though many of the authors cited above make this point, especially Mark A. Noll, few have made it as well as James Ward Smith did four decades ago. See his essay, "Religion and Science in American Philosophy," in *Religion in American Life,* vol. 1, *The Shaping of American Religion,* ed. James Ward Smith and A. Leland Jamison (Princeton, N.J.: Princeton University Press, 1961), 402–42.

79. MacIntyre, *Three Rival Versions of Moral Enquiry: Encyclopaedia, Genealogy, and Tradition* (Notre Dame: University of Notre Dame Press, 1990), 179, 185, 222, 225.

2 • Protestant Divinity in the Shadow of the University

1. Archibald Alexander Hodge, *The Life of Charles Hodge* (New York: Scribner's, 1880), 521.

2. On Princeton Seminary's position in American higher education, see Howard Miller, *The Revolutionary College: American Presbyterian Higher Education, 1707–1837* (New York: New York University Press, 1976), esp. chap. 9; and Mark A. Noll, *Princeton and the Republic, 1768–1822: The Search for a Christian Enlightenment in the Era of Samuel Stanhope Smith* (Princeton, N.J.: Princeton University Press, 1989). For Hodge's links to the academic establishment in the natural sciences, see the introduction to Charles Hodge, *What Is Darwinism? And Other Writings on Science and Religion,* ed. Mark A. Noll and David N. Livingstone (Grand Rapids, Mich.: Baker Book House, 1994), 11–28.

3. For some of the debate on Princeton's unoriginality, see Mark A. Noll, ed., *The Princeton Theology, 1812–1921: Scripture, Science and Theological Method from Archibald Alexander to Benjamin Warfield* (Grand Rapids, Mich.: Baker Book House, 1983), 41–45.

4. Gilman, "The Advanced Course at Andover," *Congregationalist* (Sept. 12, 1880).

5. Organizations such as the YMCA, YWCA, and the Student Volunteer Movement, along with chapel provide one index to the extracurricular nature of religious life. For some of the literature on these institutions, see Clarence Prouty Shedd, *The Church Follows Its Students* (New Haven: Yale University Press, 1938); Shedd, *Two Centuries of Student Christian Movements* (New York: Association Press, 1934); Howard Hopkins, *History of the YMCA in North America* (New York: Association Press, 1951); Committee on the War and the Religious Outlook, *The Teaching Work of the Church* (New York: Association Press, 1923), chaps. 10 and 11; Richard Henry Edwards, *Cooperative Religion at Cornell University: The Story of United Religious Work at Cornell University, 1919–1939* (Ithaca, N.Y.: Cornell Cooperative Society, 1939); Seymour A. Smith, *The American College Chaplaincy* (New York: Association Press, 1954); Merrimon Cunningim, *The College Seeks Religion* (New Haven: Yale University Press, 1947), chap. 9; Edward W. Blakeman, *The Administration of Religion in Universities and Colleges: Personnel* (Ann Arbor: University of Michigan Press, 1942); Nathan D. Showalter, *The End of a Crusade: The Student Volunteer Movement for Foreign Missions and the Great War* (Lanham, Md.: Scarecrow Press, 1998); George M. Marsden, *The Soul of the American University: From Protestant Establishment to Established Nonbelief* (New York: Oxford University Press, 1994), chap. 18; Douglas Sloan, *Faith and Knowledge: Mainline Protestantism and American Higher Education* (Louisville, Ky.: Westminster/John Knox, 1994), 74–84, chap. 5; Julie A. Reuben, *The Making of the Modern University: Intellectual Transformation and the Marginalization of Morality* (Chicago: University of Chicago Press, 1996), 113–32; Dorothy C. Bass, "Ministry on the Margins: Protestants and Education," in *Between the Times: The Travail of the Protestant Establishment in America, 1900–1960*, ed. William R. Hutchison (New York: Cambridge University Press, 1989), chap. 3; and Heather A. Warren, *Theologians of a New World Order: Reinhold Niebuhr and the Christian Realists, 1920–1948* (New York: Oxford University Press, 1997), chaps. 1–3.

6. See Charles W. Eliot, "Address at the Inauguration of Daniel C. Gilman," in Charles William Eliot, *Educational Reform: Essays and Addresses* (1898; repr., New York: Arno Press, 1969), 41–46, especially 42–43.

7. On Harvard Divinity School, see George Hunston Williams, ed., *The Harvard Divinity School: Its Place in Harvard University and in American Culture* (Boston: Beacon Press, 1954).

8. For a helpful overview of Eliot's plans for religion at Harvard, see Hugh Hawkins, *Between Harvard and America: The Educational Leadership of Charles W. Eliot* (New York: Oxford University Press, 1972), chap. 4.

9. Eliot, "On the Education of Ministers," *Princeton Review* 13 (1883): 340.

10. Patton, "On the Education of Ministers: A Reply to President Eliot," *Princeton Review* 14 (1883): 52, 53.

11. Ibid., 58.

12. See William R. Hutchison, "Disapproval of Chicago: The Symbolic Trial of David Swing," *Journal of American History* 59 (1972): 30–47.

13. Patton, "On the Education of Ministers," 59–60.

14. White, *A History of the Warfare of Science with Theology in Christendom*, 2 vols. (New York: D. Appleton, 1896), 2:370.

15. Ibid., 2:395.

16. On Harper's career, see James P. Wind, *The Bible and the University: The*

Messianic Vision of William Rainey Harper (Atlanta: Scholars Press, 1987); Marsden, *Soul of the American University,* chap. 14; and Laurence R. Veysey, *The Emergence of the American University* (Chicago: University of Chicago Press, 1965), 367–80. The study of religion at the University of Chicago was different from the departmental structure that would emerge in the mid-twentieth century. Harper placed religion under the auspices of a theological faculty in the Divinity School. Still, despite a different administrative apparatus, religion at Chicago proved to be a harbinger of later developments in religious studies.

17. See Harper, "Shall the Theological Curriculum Be Modified, and How?" in his *The Trend in Higher Education in America* (Chicago: University of Chicago Press, 1905), 245ff. On the curricular changes within the humanities produced by the academic reforms associated with research universities, see Laurence Veysey, "Plural Organized Worlds of the Humanities," in *The Organization of Knowledge in Modern America, 1860–1920,* ed. Alexandra Oleson and John Voss (Baltimore: Johns Hopkins University Press, 1979), 55–57; Veysey, *Emergence of the American University,* chap. 4; Veysey, "Stability and Experiment in the American Undergraduate Curriculum," in *Content and Context: Essays on College Education,* ed. Carl Kaysen (New York: McGraw-Hill, 1973), 1–9; Bruce Kuklick, "The Emergence of the Humanities," *South Atlantic Quarterly* 89 (1990): 195–206; Douglas Sloan, "The Teaching of Ethics in the American Undergraduate Curriculum, 1876–1976," in *Education and Values,* ed. Sloan (New York: Teachers College Press, 1980), 191–254; and Bruce A. Kimball, *Orators and Philosophers: A History of the Idea of Liberal Education* (New York: Teachers College Press, 1986), 191–204.

18. Harper, "Shall the Theological Curriculum Be Modified," 252–55.

19. Ibid., 262–65. For background on Harper's reforms, see Wind, *The Bible and the University,* chap. 5; and W. Clark Gilpin, *A Preface to Theology* (Chicago: University of Chicago Press, 1996), chap. 3.

20. Harper, "Shall the Theological Curriculum Be Modified," 239, 241, 243.

21. Harper, "The University and Democracy," in *Trend in Higher Education,* 3–5.

22. On the utilitarian character of university leaders, see Veysey, *Emergence of the American University,* chap. 2.

23. Eliot, "The Aims of Higher Education," in *Educational Reform,* 251. See also 241–49, and "The Function of Education in a Democratic Society," 401–18.

24. Gilman, "The Utility of Universities," in *University Problems in the United States* (1898; repr., New York: Arno Press, 1969), 55.

25. On the professionalization of knowledge in late nineteenth-century American learning, see the essays in Oleson and Voss, eds., *Organization of Knowledge in Modern America;* Laurence Veysey, "Higher Education as a Profession: Changes and Continuities," in *The Professions in American History,* ed. Nathan O. Hatch (Notre Dame: University of Notre Dame Press, 1988), 15–32; Bruce Kuklick, "The Professionalization of the Humanities," in *Applying the Humanities,* ed. Daniel Callahan et al. (New York: Plenum Press, 1985), 41–54; Robert A. McGaughey, "Transformation of American Academic Life: Harvard University, 1821–1892," *Perspectives in American History* 8 (1974): 237–332; Burton J. Bledstein, *The Culture of Professionalism: The Middle Class and the Development of Higher Education in America* (New York: Norton, 1976).

26. On the tensions between denominational particularism and the kind of

religious cosmopolitanism nurtured by Enlightened Christianity, see D. G. Hart, "The Tie That Divides: Presbyterian Ecumenism, Fundamentalism, and the History of Twentieth-Century American Protestantism," *Westminster Theological Journal* 60 (1998): 85–107.

27. Harper, "The University and Religious Education," in *Trend in Higher Education*, 76.

28. On the main themes of Progressive orthodoxy, see Editors of the *Andover Review, Progressive Orthodoxy: A Contribution to the Christian Interpretation of Christian Doctrines* (1892; repr., Hicksville, N.Y.: Regina Press, 1975).

29. On mid-nineteenth-century American theological developments, see Bruce Kuklick, *Churchmen and Philosophers: From Jonathan Edwards to John Dewey* (New Haven: Yale University Press, 1985), chaps. 11, 13–14; and D. G. Hart, "Divided Between Heart and Mind: The Critical Period for Protestant Thought in America," *Journal of Ecclesiastical History* 38 (1987): 254–70.

30. On the changes at Andover, see Henry K. Rowe, *History of Andover Theological Seminary* (Newton, Mass.: Andover Seminary, 1933), especially chap. 8; Daniel Day Williams, *The Andover Liberals: A Study in American Theology* (New York: Kings Crown Press, 1941; repr., New York: Octagon Books, 1970); and Kuklick, *Churchmen and Philosophers,* chap. 15.

31. Here I follow Kuklick's discussion of the New Theology in *Churchmen and Philosophers,* chap. 15.

32. William J. Tucker, "The Work of the Holy Spirit," in *Progressive Orthodoxy,* 130.

33. William J. Tucker, "The Christian," in *Progressive Orthodoxy,* 133, 136, 138.

34. Ibid., 148.

35. Egbert C. Symth, "Christianity and Missions," in *Progressive Orthodoxy,* 186.

36. Williams, *Andover Liberals,* 121.

37. On Briggs and liberalizing developments in northern Presbyterian theological education, see Mark S. Massa, *Charles Augustus Briggs and the Crisis of Historical Criticism* (Minneapolis: Fortress Press, 1990); Robert T. Handy, *A History of Union Theological Seminary in New York* (New York: Columbia University Press, 1987), chaps. 4–6; and Gary Scott Smith, "Presbyterian and Methodist Education," in *Theological Education in the Evangelical Tradition,* ed. D. G. Hart and R. Albert Mohler Jr. (Grand Rapids, Mich.: Baker Books, 1996), chap. 4.

38. Briggs, "The Scope of Theology and Its Place in the University," *American Journal of Theology* 1 (1897): 51–52, 53, 55.

39. On the Briggs trial, see Massa, *Charles Augustus Briggs,* 104–9.

40. Briggs, "A Plea for the Higher Study of Theology," *American Journal of Theology* 8 (1904): 435, 448.

41. Briggs, "Scope of Theology," 60–61.

42. Briggs, "Higher Study of Theology," 436, 450.

43. Briggs, "Scope of Theology," 39, 48, 49.

44. Ibid., 60.

45. One guide to liberal Protestant efforts to reconcile Christian particularism with other religions was the World's Parliament of Religions of 1893. On that gathering, see Richard Hughes Seager, *The World's Parliament of Religions: The East/West Encounter* (Bloomington: Indiana University Press, 1995); and

Martin E. Marty, *Modern American Religion,* vol. 1, *The Irony of It All* (Chicago: University of Chicago Press, 1986), chap. 2.

46. See, for instance, Arthur M. Schlesinger Sr., "A Critical Period in American Protestantism, 1875–1900," *Massachusetts Historical Society Proceedings* 64 (1932): 523–48; William G. Mcloughlin, *The Meaning of Henry Ward Beecher* (New York: Knopf, 1970); Paul A. Carter, *The Spiritual Crisis of the Gilded Age* (Dekalb, Ill.: Northern Illinois University Press, 1971); and Donald H. Meyer, "American Intellectuals and the Victorian Crisis of Faith," in *Victorian America,* ed. Daniel Walker Howe (Philadelphia: University of Pennsylvania Press, 1976), 59–77.

47. For some of the literature on late nineteenth-century American Protestant intellectual life, see Kuklick, *Churchmen and Philosophers;* Jon A. Roberts, *Darwinism and the Divine in America: Protestant Intellectuals and Organic Evolution, 1859–1900* (Madison: University of Wisconsin Press, 1988); Charles D. Cashdollar, *The Transformation of Theology, 1830–1890: Positivism and Protestant Thought in Britain and America* (Princeton, N.J.: Princeton University Press, 1989); William R. Hutchison, *The Modernist Impulse in American Protestantism* (Cambridge: Harvard University Press, 1976); James Turner, *Without God, Without Creed: The Origins of Unbelief in America* (Baltimore: Johns Hopkins University Press, 1985); Thomas E. Jenkins, *The Character of God: Recovering the Lost Literary Power of American Protestantism* (New York: Oxford University Press, 1997); and Walter H. Conser, *God and the Natural World: Religion and Science in Antebellum America* (Columbia: University of South Carolina Press, 1993).

48. On the professional dimension of late nineteenth-century debates about religion and science, see David A. Hollinger, "Inquiry and Uplift: Late-Nineteenth Century American Academics and the Moral Efficacy of Scientific Practice," in *Authority of Experts: Studies in History and Theory,* ed. Thomas L. Haskell (Bloomington: Indiana University Press, 1984), chap. 5; Thomas Bender, "The Erosion of Public Culture: Cities, Discourses, and Professional Disciplines," in *Authority of Experts,* chap. 3; James R. Moore, "Crisis Without Revolution: The Ideological Watershed in Victorian England," *Revue de Synthése* 4 (1986): 54–78; Frank M. Turner, "The Victorian Conflict between Science and Religion: A Professional Dimension," *Isis* 69 (1978): 356–76; and Roy MacLeod, "The 'Bankruptcy of Science' Debate: The Creed of Science and Its Critics, 1885–1900," *Science, Technology, and Human Values* 41 (1982): 2–15.

49. Hutchison's definition of Protestant modernism as partly the conscious adaptation of Christianity to modern culture, I argue, abetted the American Protestant project of harmonizing religion and science. See *Modernist Impulse,* 1–11.

50. My argument here follows that of Kuklick, *Churchmen and Philosophers,* chaps. 13 and 15, esp. 195–98 and 225–29.

51. Ibid., 198.

52. Ibid., 197–98. On the rise and development of sociology in the new universities, see Dorothy Ross, *The Origins of American Social Science* (New York: Cambridge University Press, 1991); Mary Furner, *Advocacy and Objectivity: A Crisis in the Professionalization of American Social Science, 1865–1905* (Lexington: University of Kentucky Press, 1975); Thomas L. Haskell, *The Emergence of Professional Social Science: The American Social Science Association and the Nineteenth-Century Crisis of Authority* (Urbana: University of Illinois Press, 1977); and Arthur

J. Vidich and Stanford M. Lyman, *American Sociology: Worldly Rejections of Religion and Their Directions* (New Haven: Yale University Press, 1985).

53. These fields were not clearly defined and overlapped with others. For instance, a Semiticist, like the University of Pennsylvania's Morris Jastrow, is sometimes counted for the field of Semitics, and sometimes for the history of religions. The same difficulty plagues the classification of the Old Testament scholar Crawford Howell Toy, and the New Testament scholar George S. Goodspeed, both of whom used history of religions methods to study the Bible. For the way the study of religion blurred the university's academic specialties, see Robert S. Shepard, *God's People in the Ivory Tower: Religion in the Early University* (New York: Carlson, 1991). Religious studies thus at an early stage showed signs of lacking an academic niche that gave it coherence, a problem that has plagued the teaching and study of religion throughout its history.

54. On Haupt's work at Hopkins, see Hugh Hawkins, *Pioneer: A History of the Johns Hopkins University, 1874–1889* (Baltimore: Johns Hopkins Press, 1960), 155–59, 206–7; and Cyrus Adler, "The Beginnings of Semitic Studies in America," in Cyrus Adler and Aaron Ember, *Oriental Studies* (Baltimore: Johns Hopkins Press, 1926), 317–28. On Jastrow at the University of Pennsylvania, see Harold S. Wechsler, "Pulpit or Professoriate: The Case of Morris Jastrow," *American Jewish History* 74 (1985): 338–55; and Shepard, *God's People in the Ivory Tower,* 33–39. On the field of Semitics and its origins as an academic discipline, see Paul Ritterband and Harold S. Wechsler, *Jewish Learning in American Universities: The First Century* (Bloomington: Indiana University Press, 1994); and Bruce Kuklick, *Puritans in Babylon: The Ancient Near East and American Intellectual Life, 1880–1930* (Princeton, N.J.: Princeton University Press, 1996).

55. See H. P. Sullivan, "The History of Religions: Some Problems and Prospects," in *The Study of Religion in Colleges and Universities,* ed. Paul Ramsey and John F. Wilson (Princeton, N.J.: Princeton University Press, 1970), 246–80.

56. On Protestant campus activities for students, see the works cited in n. 5 above.

57. For analogous changes at the University of Chicago, see Wind, *Bible and the University,* 133–46.

3 • The Emergence of a Pattern

1. "Official Document #2: Program for the Convention," *The Biblical World* (Feb. 1903): 10, quoted in Stephen A. Schmidt, *The History of the Religious Education Association* (Birmingham, Ala.: Religious Education Press, 1983), 35.

2. Officers of the REA were listed in *Religious Education* 1 (1906): 37–40.

3. Bacon, "Courses Bearing on the Bible in Practical and Intellectual Life," in Religious Education Association, *Proceedings of the Second Annual Convention* (Chicago: Office of the Association, 1904), 131, 133, 134, 135. On Bacon's career and scholarship, see Roy A. Harrisville, *Benjamin Wisner Bacon: Pioneer in American Biblical Criticism* (Missoula, Mont.: Scholars Press, 1976).

4. For background on the educational efforts of mainline Protestants in the early twentieth century, see Schmidt, *History of the Religious Education Association;* James P. Wind, *The Bible and the University: The Messianic Vision of William Rainey Harper* (Atlanta: Scholars Press, 1987); Dorothy C. Bass, "Ministry on the

Margins: Protestants and Education," in *Between the Times: The Travail of the Protestant Establishment in America, 1900–1960,* ed. William R. Hutchison (New York: Cambridge University Press, 1989), chap. 3; Ronald C. White Jr., "Presbyterian Campus Ministries: Competing Loyalties and Changing Visions," in *The Pluralistic Vision: Presbyterians and Mainstream Protestant Education and Leadership,* ed. Milton J. Coalter, John M. Mulder, and Louis B. Weeks (Louisville, Ky.: Westminster/John Knox, 1992), chap. 4; and Robert W. Lynn, *Protestant Strategies in Education* (New York: Association Press, 1964).

5. Frank Knight Sanders, "The Bible in Religious Experience: The President's Annual Address," in *Proceedings of the Second Annual Convention,* 5.

6. Wallace N. Stearns, "The Report of the Committee of Six: Religious and Moral Education in the Universities and Colleges in the United States," *Religious Education* 1 (1907): 201–25.

7. Ibid., 209–10.

8. Ibid.

9. The accuracy of this report is questionable considering that the University of Chicago, an institution where the faculty of theology was prominent, and Yale University, an institution where the divinity school had strong ties to undergraduate and graduate studies, did not register any faculty in religion.

10. "Report of the Committee of Six," 208.

11. Ibid., 212, 217–18.

12. Richard H. Jesse, "The Supervision of the Religious Life in Educational Institutions," in *Proceedings of the Second Annual Convention,* 125.

13. Ibid., 128, 129.

14. Ibid.

15. On American Protestant appropriations of the Enlightenment, see chap. 1 above.

16. The subhead title comes from Clarence Prouty Shedd, *The Church Follows Its Students* (New Haven: Yale University Press, 1938), a study of church-related religion programs at state and public institutions.

17. This is the verdict of Shedd in ibid., chaps. 1 and 2. On the involvement of the denominations in colleges and universities, see also David R. Porter, *The Church in the Universities* (New York: Association Press, 1925), chaps. 2 and 3.

18. *Minutes of the General Assembly of the Presbyterian Church in the U.S.A.* (1903): 89, quoted in Shedd, *Church Follows Its Students,* 14.

19. *Minutes of the General Assembly of the Presbyterian Church in the U.S.A.* (1904): 161.

20. Ibid.

21. Shedd, *Church Follows Its Students,* 16. One problem faced by these church activities was securing academic credit for courses offered. On this problem, see White, "Presbyterian Campus Ministries."

22. Shedd, *Church Follows Its Students,* 16, 29, 30, 31, 32. Pastors could also receive financial assistance from synods and presbyteries, the regional mechanisms of church government in American Presbyterianism.

23. Atwater, "Sixth Annual Meeting Council of Church Workers," *Religious Education* 8 (1914): 171.

24. Shedd, *Church Follows Its Students,* 104.

25. *Report of Conference of Church Workers in State Universities* (1910): 50, quoted in Shedd, *Church Follows Its Students,* 26.

26. On the religious ethos of American universities, see George M. Marsden, *The Soul of the American University: From Protestant Establishment to Established Nonbelief* (New York: Oxford University Press, 1994); and D. G. Hart, "Faith and Learning in the Age of the University: The Academic Ministry of Daniel Coit Gilman," in *The Secularization of the Academy,* ed. George M. Marsden and Bradley J. Longfield (New York: Oxford University Press, 1992), chap. 4.

27. The CCBE included the Protestant denomination's educational efforts, from Sunday School to seminary. On the CCBE, see Hugh Hawkins, *Banding Together: The Rise of National Associations in American Higher Education* (Baltimore: Johns Hopkins University Press, 1992), 16–20, 58–64.

28. On the AAC during these years, see ibid., 41–44, 58–62, 97–103.

29. On Kelly's early career, see ibid., 17–20.

30. Ibid., 18.

31. Kelly, "The Relation of Biblical Departments to the Curricula of Liberal Colleges," *Christian Education* 5 (1922): 205.

32. Kelly, "The Liberal College and Human Values," *Association of American Colleges Bulletin* 16 (1930): 341.

33. Kelly, "Relation of Biblical Departments," 208, 209. Kelly's views were similar to those of instructors at other Protestant liberal arts colleges. See, e.g., Henry Churchill King (Oberlin), "The Christian Ideal in Education: Methods of Its Attainment," *Association of American Colleges Bulletin* 1 (1915): 28–39.

It should be noted that Kelly made similar arguments about theological education in his *Theological Education in America: A Study of One Hundred Sixty-One Theological Schools in the United States and Canada* (New York: George H. Doran, 1924), a study that eventually resulted in the formation of an accrediting body for seminaries and divinity schools. Here religion was similarly ubiquitous and geared, in Kelly's mind, toward the social problems of modern American life. Institutions that were more otherworldly in orientation did not receive as high marks for their contribution. See especially chap. 7. The most mature and fullest expression of Kelly's educational philosophy and the place of religion in it, an outlook that I would argue was fairly widespread among mainline Protestants and American higher education, can be found in his *The American Colleges and the Social Order* (New York: Macmillan, 1940).

34. On Kent, see *DAB,* 10:343; Seymour A. Smith, *Religious Cooperation in State Universities: An Historical Sketch* (Ann Arbor: University of Michigan, 1957), 25; and Marcus Bach, *Of Faith and Learning: The Story of the School of Religion at the State University of Iowa* (Iowa City: School of Religion, 1952), 42–49.

35. Conrad Cherry, *Hurrying Toward Zion: Universities, Divinity Schools, and American Protestantism* (Bloomington: Indiana University Press, 1995), 46–47.

36. Kent, "Order and Content of Biblical Courses in College Curriculum," *Religious Education* 7 (Apr. 1912): 42, 44, 49.

37. On the council, see Cherry, *Hurrying Toward Zion,* 46–50; Patrick Murphy Malin, "The National Council on Religion in Higher Education," in *Liberal Learning and Religion,* ed. Amos N. Wilder (New York: Harper and Bros., 1951), 324–34; and Smith, *Religious Cooperation in State Universities,* chap. 3.

38. For a contemporary assessment of the schools-of-religion approach to religious education, see Porter, *Church in the Universities,* chap. 5.

39. Burton, quoted in C. Grey Austin, *A Century of Religion at the University of Michigan: A Case Study in Religion and the State University* (Ann Arbor: University

of Michigan, 1957), 37. For background on religious studies at the University of Michigan, Austin should be consulted along with Robert Michaelsen, *The Study of Religion in American Universities: Ten Case Studies with Special Reference to State Universities* (New Haven: Society for Religion in Higher Education, 1965), chap. 1. Especially helpful is the unpublished paper by Peter Laipson, "And the Walls Came Crumbling Down: The Rise and Decline of the Michigan School of Religion, 1920–1930," presented to the History Department, University of Michigan, December 1990.

40. Kent, quoted in Austin, *Century of Religion,* 37–38.

41. Robert L. Kelly wrote, in fact, that nothing could so quickly diminish the influence of religious studies "as the suggestion or even the impression on the part of any section of the University that either the materials to be presented or the persons who are to present them are inferior or unimportant judged from the most exacting scholastic or cultural point of view." "Schools of Religion," *Religious Education* 22 (1927): 606.

42. *Michigan Alumnus* (August 2, 1923): 1120, quoted in Laipson, "Walls Came Crumbling Down," 6.

43. See chapter 1 above for the university builders' understanding of Christianity.

44. See Austin, *Century of Religion,* 37; and Laipson, "Walls Came Crumbling Down," 23ff.

45. On the impulses within evangelical Protestantism that led to the foundation of Bible schools, see Virginia Lieson Brereton, *Training God's Army: The American Bible School, 1880–1940* (Bloomington: Indiana University Press, 1990).

46. *The Michigan School of Religion: A Response to the Appeal of Youth,* 5, 9, quoted in Laipson, "The Walls Came Crumbling Down," 19, 20.

47. Laipson, "The Walls Came Crumbling Down," 13–14.

48. Smith, *Religious Cooperation,* 20–21.

49. On Foster, see Bach, *Of Faith and Learning,* 58–70.

50. "Canadian Theological Colleges and American Schools of Religion," *Christian Education* 12 (1929): 282.

51. Foster, "Schools of Religion at State Universities," *Christian Education* 6 (1923): 188.

52. On Protestant ecumenism in the late nineteenth and early twentieth centuries, see Heather A. Warren, *Theologians of a New World Order: Reinhold Niebuhr and the Christian Realists, 1920–1948* (New York: Oxford University Press, 1997), chaps. 1–3; and D. G. Hart, "The Tie That Divides: Presbyterian Ecumenism, Fundamentalism, and the History of Twentieth-Century American Protestantism," *Westminster Theological Journal* 60 (1998): 85–107.

53. O. D. Foster, "Denominational Cooperation in Religious Education at State Universities," *Christian Education* 4 (1921): 16.

54. See John F. Wilson, "Mr. Holbrook and the Humanities, or Mr. Schlatter's Dilemma: A Review Article," *JBR* 32 (1964): 261.

55. For a brief history, see M. Willard Lampe, *The Story of an Idea: The History of the School of Religion at the University of Iowa* (Iowa City: University of Iowa, 1963). For a longer and more hagiographic account, see Bach, *Of Faith and Learning,* especially chaps. 2 and 3.

56. Foster, "Denominational Cooperation," 15.

57. For a critique of the "melting pot" that bears on relationship between Protestantism and other faiths in the United States, see Stephen Steinberg, *The Ethnic Myth: Race, Ethnicity, and Class in America* (New York: Atheneum, 1981), especially chap. 2.

58. See Benny Kraut, "A Wary Collaboration: Jews, Catholics, and the Protestant Goodwill Movement," in *Between the Times,* ed. Hutchinson, 193–230.

59. Of the vast amount of literature on fundamentalism, George M. Marsden, *Fundamentalism and American Culture: The Shaping of Twentieth-Century Evangelicalism, 1870–1925* (New York: Oxford University Press, 1980); Edward J. Larson, *Trial and Error: The American Controversy over Creation and Evolution* (New York: Oxford University Press, 1985); and Larson, *Summer for the Gods: The Scopes Trial and America's Continuing Debate over Religion and Science* (New York: Basic Books, 1998), provide good overviews of the salient aspects of the Protestant controversies.

60. Kent, *The Fundamentals of Christianity* (Philadelphia: University of Pennsylvania Press, 1925), 10.

61. Ibid., 21, 22, 27.

4 • Religious Studies and the Humanities

1. Strong, *Our Country: Its Possible Future and Its Present Crisis* (1886; repr., 1891), excerpted in William G. McLoughlin, *The American Evangelicals, 1800–1900: An Anthology* (Gloucester, Mass.: Peter Smith, 1976), 210–11.

2. Henry Thatcher Fowler, "The Influence of the Bible on American Democracy," *Christian Education* 3 (1919): 24.

3. "The Use of the Bible in Teaching National Ideals," *Christian Education* 3 (1919): 29.

4. On the rise and development of courses in western civilization, see Gilbert Allardyce, "The Rise and Fall of the Western Civilization Course," *AHR* 87 (1982): 695–725; Douglas Sloan, "The Teaching of Ethics in the American Undergraduate Curriculum, 1876–1976," in *Education and Values,* ed. Sloan (New York: Teachers College Press, 1980), 191–254; and Bruce A. Kimball, *Orators and Philosophers: A History of the Idea of Liberal Education* (New York: Teachers College Press, 1986).

5. Gilkey, "Religion for the Modern Mind: A Summary Statement on Behalf of the Conference," in *Religion in Higher Education,* ed. Milton Carsley Towner (Chicago: University of Chicago Press, 1931), 89, 90.

6. Introduction, in ibid., xiv, xvi.

7. "The Teaching of Religion," in ibid., 168.

8. *Religion in Higher Education,* ed. Towner, ix–xxi.

9. William P. Lemon, "Spiritual Reality and College Life," M. Willard Lampe, "A United Approach," and Charles A. Hawley et al., "A Symposium on Co-operative Projects," in ibid., chaps. 4, 12, and 23 respectively.

10. "The Religious Self-Expression of a University," in ibid., vii.

11. For instance, both Charles Foster Kent and O. D. Foster designed a curriculum of study in religion. For Kent's ideas, see his "The Bible and the College

Curriculum," *Religious Education* 8 (1913): 453–58, and his "Order and Content of Biblical Courses in College Curriculum," *Religious Education* 7 (1912): 42–49. For Foster's approach, see his "Canadian Theological Colleges and American Schools of Religion," *Christian Education* 12 (1929): 281–303.

12. "Teaching of Religion," 173, 167–70.

13. Willard E. Uphaus and M. Teague Hipps, "Undergraduate Courses in Religion at Denominational and Independent Colleges and Universities of America," *Bulletin of the National Council on Religion and Higher Education* 6 (1924): 7; Gould Wickey and Ruth A. Eckhart, "A National Survey of Courses in Bible and Religion," *Christian Education* 20 (1936–37): 9–45; and Hugh Hartshorne et al., *Standards and Trends in Religious Education* (New Haven: Yale University Press, 1933), chaps. 15 and 16.

14. Uphaus and Hipps, "Undergraduate Courses in Religion," 56–57; Hartshorne et al., *Standards and Trends*, 174. The predominance of the Bible and ethics in religious studies continued into the 1940s. In a survey of 62 public and private institutions in six Northeastern states (Connecticut, Maine, Massachusetts, New York, Ohio, Pennsylvania, and Rhode Island), Bible and ethics continued to top the list in the number of courses (Bible, 35%; ethics, 14%), the number of semester hours (Bible, 33%; ethics, 14%), and the number of institutions offering religious subjects (Bible, 94%; ethics, 98%). See Paul E. Johnson, "College Courses in Religion," *JBR* 10 (1942): 147–48.

15. Hartshorne et al., *Standards and Trends*, 174–75. For other indications of the centrality of the Bible in classroom instruction, see G. D. Edwards, "Credit Courses in Religion," *Christian Education* 11 (1928): 740–48; Edward S. Boyer, "Religious Education in Colleges, Universities and Schools of Religion," *Christian Education* 11 (1927): 2–97; Lura Beam, "Classroom Instruction in Religion in Two Hundred Fifty Colleges," *Christian Education* 8 (1925): 211–64; and Theron Charlton McGee, "Religious Education in Certain Evangelical Colleges—A Study in Status and Tendencies," Ph.D. diss., University of Pennsylvania, Philadelphia, 1928.

16. Wickey and Eckhart, "National Survey of Courses in Bible and Religion," 32, 33, 35, 34.

17. Hartshorne et al., *Standards and Trends*, 219.

18. The precise date of NABI's founding is somewhat obscure. For an early account of the organization, see "The Association of Biblical Instructors in American Colleges and Secondary Schools," *Christian Education* 3 (1919): 2.

19. "The Chief Objectives of Our Work," *Christian Education* 3 (1919): 6.

20. "The Proceedings of the National Association: The President's Address," *Christian Education* 8 (1924): 64.

21. Chester Warren Quimby, "The Word of God," *JNABI* 1 (1933): 1, 2, 4, 6.

22. Joseph Haroutunian, *Piety Versus Moralism: The Passing of New England Theology* (New York: Henry Holt, 1932). For background on the book, see Sydney E. Ahlstrom's introduction to the 1970 reprint (New York: Harper Torchbook, 1970), vii–xv.

23. Joseph Haroutunian, "The Bible and Modern Education," *JNABI* 1 (1933): 12, 14, 15.

24. On the shift toward neo-orthodoxy's connection to the defeat of fundamentalists in the mainline Protestant churches, see D. G. Hart, "Evangelicals, Biblical Scholarship, and the Politics of the Modern American Academy," in

Evangelicals and Science in Historical Perspective, ed. David N. Livingstone, D. G. Hart, and Mark A. Noll (New York: Oxford University Press, 1999), 306–26.

25. "The Future of the Bible in the American College," *JNABI* 1 (1933): 8.

26. "A College Program for the Teaching of Religion," *Christian Education* 21 (1937–38): 87, 88.

27. For a classic expression of liberal Protestant views on experience, see Shailer Mathews, *The Faith of Modernism* (New York: Macmillan, 1924).

28. "Riddle, "Why Study The Bible Today?" *JBR* 8 (1940): 68, 71.

29. Beiler, "Some Implications of Our Teaching Aims," *Christian Education* 14 (1930–31): 641.

30. On Victorianism, see Henry F. May, *The End of American Innocence: The First Years of Our Own Time, 1912–1917* (New York: Oxford University Press, 1959); Daniel Joseph Singal, *The War Within: From Victorian to Modernist Thought in the South, 1919–1945* (Chapel Hill: University of North Carolina Press, 1982); Singal, "Towards a Definition of American Modernism," *American Quarterly* 39 (1987): 8–26; and Daniel Walker Howe, "American Victorianism as a Culture," *American Quarterly* 27 (1975): 507–32.

31. Clippinger, "The Liberal Arts College—Whence? Where? Whither?," *Christian Education* 18 (1934–35): 278, 281, 287.

32. Robert Maynard Hutchins, *The Higher Learning in America* (New Haven: Yale University Press, 1936).

33. For a thoughtful assessment of Hutchins, see George M. Marsden, *The Soul of the American University: From Protestant Establishment to Established Non-belief* (New York: Oxford University Press, 1994), 375–80. On reforms of liberal education between the world wars, see Kimball, *Orators and Philosophers,* 177–204; Laurence Veysey, "Stability and Experiment in the American Under-graduate Curriculum," in *Content and Context: Essays on College Education,* ed. Carl Kaysen (New York: McGraw-Hill, 1973), 9–14, 28–31; and Veysey, "The Plural Organized Worlds of the Humanities," in *The Organization of Knowledge in Modern America, 1860–1920,* ed. Alexandra Oleson and John Voss (Baltimore: Johns Hopkins University Press, 1979), 51–106.

34. Beatrice Allard Brooks, "The Place of the Study of Religion in the Liberal Arts Curriculum in the Light of Recent Theories of Higher Learning," *JBR* 6 (1938): 190, 193, 194.

35. Nesbitt, "The Bible in the Curriculum," *Christian Education* 21 (1937–38): 70.

36. In 1936 the *Journal of the National Association of Biblical Instructors* changed to the *Journal of Bible and Religion.* The reason for the new name was to "advocate the right of the Bible and religion to a place in curricular courses as essential to a well-rounded education. . . . We define with due discrimination the rightful place of the Bible, *the great English classic,* as literature, history, and religion in the science of life." Ismar J. Peritz, "The Journal's Future," *JBR* 4 (1936): 100 (emphasis added).

37. See, for instance, H. L. Newman, "The N.A.B.I. and the National Emergency," *JBR* 10 (1942): 222–23; Edna M. Baxter, "The Importance of the Bible in the Present Crisis as Variously Viewed by Religious Educators," *JBR* 11 (1943): 31–35; Henry Nelson Wieman, "Teaching Religion in a War Time," *JBR* 11 (1943): 75–80; Arthur C. Wickenden, "Teaching Religion in War Time," *JBR* 11 (1943): 213–14; M. Willard Lampe, "The War and Religious Learning," *JBR* 12

(1944): 155–59; and Charles W. Gilkey, "Religion in the Post-War World," *JBR* 13 (1945): 3–7.

38. Lampe, "The War and Religious Learning," 158, 159.

39. Wickenden, "Teaching Religion in War Time," 214.

40. Gilkey, "Religion in the Post-War World," 5, 6.

41. Irwin, "The Message of the Exilic Prophets," *JBR* 11 (1943): 103. For other articles in these series, see Muriel Streibert Curtis, "The Relevance of the Old Testament," Ovid R. Sellers, "The Message of the Eighth-Century Prophets for Today," J. Philip Hyatt, "The Message of the Seventh-Century Prophets for Today," and Otto J. Baab, "The Message of the Post-Exilic Prophets for Today," *JBR* 11 (1943): 81–87, 88–92, 93–97, and 104–6, respectively; and Elmer W. K. Mould, "Teaching the Life of Jesus," William Scott, "Gospels in a Developing Church," Laura H. Wild, "The Basic Teachings of Jesus," S. Ralph Harlow, "Teaching the Pauline Epistles," and Mary Ely Lyman, "Teaching the Fourth Gospel," *JBR* 12 (1944): 17–18, 19–25, 26–32, 33–35, and 36–41, respectively. Of the articles on the New Testament only Lyman's made an argument about relevance.

42. Bixler, *The Resources of Religion and the Aims of Higher Education* (Haddam, Conn.: Edward W. Hazen Foundation, 1942), 25, 26.

43. Gabriel, *Spiritual Origins of American Culture* (Haddam, Conn.: Edward W. Hazen Foundation, 1945), 14, 16, 17.

44. *Conversations on Higher Education and Religion* (Haddam, Conn.: Edward W. Hazen Foundation, 1942), 15.

45. Clarence P. Shedd and Granville T. Walker, "War-Time Adjustments in Teaching Religion," *JBR* 12 (1944): 76, 81, 82.

46. "Higher Education for American Democracy," in *Education for Democracy: The Debate over the Report of the President's Commission on Higher Education,* ed. Gail Kennedy (Boston: Heath, 1952), 24; Paul H. Buch et al., *General Education in a Free Society: Report of the Harvard Committee* (Cambridge: Harvard University Press, 1945), 44, 45.

47. Veysey, "Plural Organized Worlds of the Humanities," 57; Theodore M. Greene et al., *Liberal Education Re-examined* (New York: Harper and Bros., 1943), xiv. See also Bruce Kuklick, "The Emergence of the Humanities," *South Atlantic Quarterly* 89 (1990): 195–206; and John Higham, "The Schism in American Scholarship," in his *Writing American History: Essays in Modern Scholarship* (Bloomington: Indiana University Press, 1970), 3–24.

48. See Brooks, "Place of the Study of Religion in the Liberal Arts Curriculum," 187–94; Chester Warren Quimby, "A Symposium on the Teaching of the Bible in American Colleges: Teaching the Bible as Religion," *JBR* 6 (1938): 70–74; Robert Lowry Calhoun, "The Place of Religion in Higher Education," in Jacques Maritain et al., *Religion and the Modern World* (Philadelphia: University of Pennsylvania Press, 1941), 63–71; and John W. Nason, "Religion in Higher Education: The Program of Faculty Consultations," *Educational Record* 27 (1946): 422–32.

49. This follows the argument in D. G. Hart, "American Learning and the Problem of Religious Studies," in *The Secularization of the Academy,* ed. George M. Marsden and Bradley J. Longfield (New York: Oxford University Press, 1992), chap. 7. For religious studies' alliance with the humanities, see also Con-

rad Cherry, *Hurrying Toward Zion: Universities, Divinity Schools, and American Protestantism* (Bloominton: Indiana University Press, 1995), 107–12.

50. Figures come from *Graduate Education in Religion: A Critical Appraisal,* ed. Claude Welch (Missoula: University of Montana Press, 1971), 230–35. For details on some significant programs founded during this period, such as Stanford, Princeton, Indiana University, the University of California, Santa Barbara, and the University of North Carolina, see Robert Michaelsen, *The Study of Religion in American Universities* (New Haven: Society for Religion in Higher Education, 1965).

51. For examples of religion programs, see Merrimon Cunningim, *The College Seeks Religion* (New Haven: Yale University Press, 1947), chap. 13; Michaelsen, *The Study of Religion;* and *Religious Studies in Public Universities,* ed. Milton D. McLean (Carbondale: Southern Illinois University Press, 1967).

5 • Finding a Place for Theology

1. "Faith for a Lenten Age," *Time* 51 (March 9, 1948): 78, 70.

2. Shedd, *Proposals for Religion in Higher Education* (Haddam, Conn.: Edward W. Hazen Foundation, 1945), 6, 9–10 (italics his), 19.

3. For evidence of theology's incoherence in the classroom, see Prentiss L. Pemberton, "Theology for the Undergraduate," *JBR* 10 (1942): 202–7; Lloyd V. Ballard, "A Layman's Theology," *JBR* 14 (1946): 209–13; L. Harold DeWolf, "Changing Emphases in Recent Theology," *JBR* 23 (1955): 103–9; and Clarice M. Bowman, "Can Theologies Communicate?" *JBR* 25 (1957): 293–300.

4. For helpful overviews of academic Protestant theology in the twentieth century, see Walter M. Horton, "Systematic Theology," in *Protestant Thought in the Twentieth Century,* ed. Arnold S. Nash (New York: Macmillan, 1951), 105–21; Claude Welch, "Theology," in *Religion,* ed. Paul Ramsey (Englewood Cliffs, N.J.: Prentice-Hall, 1965), 221–84; Arthur C. McGill, "The Ambiguous Position of Christian Theology," in *The Study of Religion in Colleges and Universities,* ed. Paul Ramsey and John F. Wilson (Princeton, N.J.: Princeton University Press, 1970), 105–38; and W. Clark Gilpin, *A Preface to Theology* (Chicago: University of Chicago Press, 1996), chaps. 3–5.

5. In addition to the works treated below, see Willard L. Sperry, ed., *Religion and Education* (Cambridge: Harvard University Press, 1945); A. J. Coleman, *The Task of the Christian in the University* (New York: Association Press, 1947); George H. Williams, *The Theological Idea of the University* (New York: Commission on Higher Education of the National Council of Churches, 1958).

6. W. A. Visser't Hooft, *None Other Gods* (New York: Harper and Bros., 1937), 125, 126. The Niebuhr quotation comes from the introduction, vii.

7. Ibid., 127, 130.

8. Ibid., 134, 135, 138.

9. Arnold S. Nash, *The University and the Modern World: An Essay in the Philosophy of University Education* (New York: Macmillan, 1943), 40, 25, 12, xvi, 258.

10. Sir Walter Moberly, *The Crisis in the University* (London: SCM Press, 1949), 15, 300–302, and chap. 3.

11. The full title of Van Dusen's book was *God in Education: A Tract for the Times* (New York: Scribner's, 1951).

12. On the fundamentalist controversy in the Presbyterian Church, see Bradley J. Longfield, *The Presbyterian Controversy: Fundamentalists, Modernists and Moderates* (New York: Oxford University Press, 1991), esp. 100–103, 125–27; and D. G. Hart, *Defending the Faith: J. Gresham Machen and the Crisis of Conservative Protestantism in Modern America* (Baltimore: Johns Hopkins University Press, 1994), 115–16.

13. Van Dusen, *God in Education*, 18, 19, 60, 81, 82–83.

14. Ibid., 116.

15. In a statement that showed the political necessity of uniting Protestants, Catholics, and Jews in promoting religion in higher education but that also reflected genuine ignorance of the differences between Christians and Jews, Van Dusen wrote, "In their conception of the religious orientation of all knowledge, of the place of God in education as a whole, the three major faiths of the Western world—Judaism, Roman Catholicism and Protestantism— hold closely analogous if not identical views, for the good and sufficient reason that their conceptions of God and of his relation to Truth stem from the same source" (*God in Education*, 69). That Jews and Christians did not agree about Jesus Christ did not seem to matter to Van Dusen.

16. William Adams Brown, *The Case for Theology in the University* (Chicago: University of Chicago Press, 1938).

17. In the preface Hutchins wrote, "On the main points I not only agree with Mr. Brown; I also applaud his presentation. . . . He sees . . . how profoundly important the Christian sense of the dignity of man is to the political order. His words on this point should be taken to heart by all those who naively identify science with progress and liberty and philosophy with reaction and authority." Brown, *Case for Theology*, vii–viii. (Subsequent page references appear in parentheses in the text.)

18. For contemporary liberal Protestant assessments of world religions, see William Ernest Hocking et al., *Re-Thinking Missions: A Laymen's Inquiry After One Hundred Years* (New York: Harper and Bros., 1932). For background on this book, see William R. Hutchison, *Errand to the World: American Protestant Thought and Foreign Missions* (Chicago: University of Chicago Press, 1987), chap. 6.

19. Brown, *Case for Theology*, 63.

20. Horton, "Systematic Theology," 116.

21. See, for instance, DeWolf, "Changing Emphases in Recent Theology," 103–9; Clarice M. Bowman, "Can Theologies Communicate?," 293–300; Carl Michalson, "Fifty Years of Theology in Retrospect: An Evaluation," *JBR* 28 (1960): 215–21; William Hordern, "Theology in Prospect," *JBR* 28 (1960): 222–28; and Jack Boozer, "Religion and Culture: An Essay on Essays in Appreciation of Paul Tillich," *JBR* 28 (1960): 229–34.

22. Michalson, "Fifty Years of Theology," 219.

23. Boozer, "Religion and Culture," 229, 232.

24. Hordern, "Theology in Prospect," 228. The problem, as Hordern also observed, was that no one was bringing the insights of contemporary theology "to the millions who are more acquainted with Gunsmoke, Maverick, Perry Mason, and Jack Paar than they are with T. S. Eliot."

25. George F. Thomas, ed., *The Vitality of the Christian Tradition* (New York: Harper and Bros., 1944).

26. Amos N. Wilder, ed., *Liberal Learning and Religion* (New York: Harper and Bros., 1951).

27. Hoxie N. Fairchild, ed., *Religious Perspectives in College Teaching* (New York: Ronald Press, 1952).

28. Related efforts along these lines can be found in *College Teaching and Christian Values,* ed. Paul M. Limbert (New York: Association Press, 1951); and the Edward W. Hazen Foundation and the Committee on Religion and Education of the American Council on Education, *College Reading and Religion* (New Haven: Yale University Press, 1948).

29. "The Faith of Ancient Israel," in *Vitality of the Christian Tradition,* ed. Thomas, 2.

30. "The Significance of Medieval Christianity," in ibid., 115.

31. "The Nineteenth Century and Today," in ibid., 184.

32. "Christian Ethics and Western Thought," in ibid., 302–8.

33. "The Christian Tradition in Modern Culture," in ibid., 226, 232.

34. "The Christian Tradition and Physical Science," in ibid., 271, 285.

35. "Religious Implications in the Humanities," in *Liberal Learning and Tradition,* ed. Wilder, 96–97. See also Victor L. Butterfield, "Liberal Learning and Religion in the American College," in *Liberal Learning and Tradition,* ed. Wilder, chap. 6; and the following, all in *Religious Perspectives,* ed. Fairchild: Hoxie N. Fairchild, "English Literature," chap. 2; Theodore M. Greene, "Philosophy," chap. 4; and Alfred R. Bellinger, "Classics," chap. 5.

36. "Biology," in *Religious Perspectives,* ed. Fairchild, 249, 251, 257.

37. "Sociology and Social Psychology," in *Religious Perspectives,* ed. Fairchild, 335.

38. Thomas, "Religious Perspectives in College Teaching: Problems and Principles," in *Religious Perspectives,* ed. Fairchild, 3, 9, 20, 38.

39. On Harvard Divinity School during the early years of the Pusey administration, see Levering Reynolds Jr., "The Later Years (1880–1953)," in *The Harvard Divinity School: Its Place in American Culture,* ed. George Huntston Williams (Boston: Beacon Press, 1954), 228–29.

40. "A Faith for These Times," reprinted in Nathan M. Pusey, *The Age of the Scholar: Observations on Education in a Troubled Decade* (Cambridge: Harvard University Press, 1963), 7.

41. Pusey's quotation of Eliot's 1909 address, "The Religion of the Future," "Faith for These Times," 3, 4, 5.

42. Editorial introduction, *Christianity and Crisis* 35, no. 8 (May 12, 1975): 106.

43. "Whatever Happened to Theology," in ibid., 108–9, quotation from 109. For a longer version of Harvey's argument, see his "On the Intellectual Marginality of American Theology," in *Religion and Twentieth-Century American Intellectual Life,* ed. Michael J. Lacey (Cambridge: Cambridge University Press, 1989), chap. 8. For another critical assessment of academic theology's marginal status, see William J. Abraham, "Oh God, Poor God: The State of Contemporary Theology," *American Scholar* 58 (1989): 557–63.

44. Sydney E. Ahlstrom, introduction to *Theology in America: The Major Protestant Voices from Puritanism to Neo-Orthodoxy,* ed. Alhstrom (Indianapolis: Bobbs-Merrill, 1967), 79.

45. Proving this conclusion depends greatly on the perspective of the one

doing the concluding. But the overall impression created by mid-twentieth-century Protestant theology is that Americans took their primary frame of reference from public and political concerns rather than parochial matters. For evidence of the political character of the American Protestant theological renaissance, see Heather A. Warren, *Theologians of a New World Order: Reinhold Niebuhr and the Christian Realists, 1920–1948* (New York: Oxford University Press, 1997), who shows in a celebrative way the social agenda of Protestant theology. As much as Reinhold Niebuhr asserted the fallenness of men and women, most of his works address the nation's ethical dilemmas rather than the church. What is more neither he nor his brother, H. Richard, produced anything on the order of Barth's *Dogmatics* whose approach started with the categories of Reformation theology rather than contemporary philosophy or public life. The closest Reinhold Niebuhr came to theology proper was *The Nature and Destiny of Man*, 2 vols. (New York: Scribner's, 1943), but it was far removed from the dogmatic tradition of Protestant theology. Paul Tillich's *Systematic Theology*, 3 vols. (Chicago: University of Chicago Press, 1951–63), came closer than Niebuhr but his theology drew so heavily upon existentialism that the loci of Protestant theology appeared to be marginal to Tillich's concerns. One further point of comparison comes from the twentieth-century revival of scholasticism among American Catholicism, where again, unlike mainline Protestant theology whose theology stemmed from denominations' public prominence, the Catholic church's traditional synthesis of philosophical and theological reflection provided the norm for systematic thought. On the neoscholastic revival among American Catholics, see Philip Gleason, *Contending with Modernity: Catholic Higher Education in the Twentieth Century* (New York: Oxford University Press, 1995), chaps. 5–8.

46. Ahlstrom, introduction, 82–83. For the influence of neo-orthodoxy on biblical scholarship and church history see chaps. 6 and 7 below.

47. "Religious Perspectives in College Teaching," in *Religious Perspectives*, ed. Fairchild, 10–11, 28.

48. On the public character of mainline Protestantism during the middle decades of the twentieth century, see William R. Hutchison, ed., *Between the Times: The Travail of the Protestant Establishment in America, 1920–1960* (New York: Cambridge University Press, 1989).

6 • The Good Book for Tough Times

1. Harry Emerson Fosdick, *The Modern Use of the Bible* (New York: Macmillan, 1925), 11, 35, 57, 58–59.

2. Edwin E. Aubrey, *Humanistic Teaching and the Place of Ethical and Religious Values in Higher Education* (Philadelphia: University of Pennsylvania Press, 1959), 80, 92, 27.

3. Filson, "The Study of the New Testament," in *Protestant Thought in the Twentieth Century*, ed. Arnold S. Nash (New York: Macmillan, 1951), 63, 64.

4. Of the secondary works on twentieth-century biblical scholarship in the United States I have relied upon the following: Ernest W. Saunders, *Searching the Scriptures: A History of the Society of Biblical Literature, 1880–1980* (Chico, Calif.: Scholars Press, 1982); Mark A. Noll, *Between Faith and Criticism: Evangelicals,*

Scholarship, and the Bible in America (San Francisco: Harper and Row, 1986); Harold R. Willoughby, ed., *The Study of the Bible Today and Tomorrow* (Chicago: University of Chicago Press, 1947); G. Ernest Wright, "The Study of the Old Testament," and Floyd F. Filson, "The Study of the New Testament," in *Protestant Thought in the Twentieth Century,* ed. Arnold S. Nash (New York: Macmillan, 1951), 17–44, and 47–69, respectively; Krister Stendahl, "Biblical Studies in the University," in *The Study of Religion in Colleges and Universities,* ed. Paul Ramsey and John F. Wilson (Princeton, N.J.: Princeton University Press, 1970), 23–39; Harry M. Orlinsky, "Old Testament Studies," and Robert M. Grant, "The Study of Early Christianity," in *Religion,* ed. Paul Ramsey, The Princeton Studies: Humanistic Scholarship in America (Englewood Cliffs, N.J.: Prentice-Hall, 1965), 51–109, 113–54, respectively; and David L. Barr and Nicholas Piediscalzi, eds., *The Bible in American Education: From Source Book to Textbook* (Philadelphia: Fortress Press, 1982).

5. "Our Aims," *Theology Today* 1 (1944): 4, 5, 7–8.

6. "Whose Word? An Editorial," *Interpretation* 1 (1947): 361.

7. "The House of the Interpreter: An Editorial," *Interpretation* 1 (1947): 50.

8. "Whose Word?," 361.

9. For background on these journals and their relationship to forerunners, see W. Eugene March, "'Biblical Theology,' Authority and the Presbyterians," *Journal of Presbyterian History* 59 (1981): 113–30; and Mark A. Noll, "The *Princeton Review,*" *Westminster Theological Journal* 50 (1988): 283–304.

10. Emile Cailliet, professor of French literature at the University of Pennsylvania, Wilbur Dwight Dunkel, professor of English at the University of Rochester, Kenneth J. Foreman, professor of philosophy at Davidson College, Theodore M. Greene, professor of philosophy at Princeton University, and E. Harris Harbison, professor of history at Princeton University served on the editorial board of *Theology Today.*

11. In the first year of publication, *Theology Today* ran fifteen articles by seminary faculty, seven by college or university faculty, and seven by pastors. By contrast, *Interpretation* published twenty-two by seminary faculty, five by college or university faculty, and nine by pastors.

12. William Adams Brown, *The Case for Theology in the University* (Chicago: University of Chicago Press, 1938), 92.

13. Joseph Haroutunian, "The Bible and the Word of God," *Interpretation* 1 (1947): 302, 303.

14. G. Ernest Wright, "Neo-Orthodoxy and the Bible," *JBR* 14 (1946): 91–93, quotation from 91.

15. Frank V. Filson, "A New Testament Student's Approach to Biblical Theology," *JBR* 14 (1946): 22, 23, 24–26 (quotation on 26).

16. Between 1945 and the early 1960s the *Journal of Bible and Religion* featured numerous articles on biblical theology and by neo-orthodox students of the Bible, a fairly indicative guide to the biblical theology's large share in religious studies. What contributed to this interest in biblical theology was the translation of Rudolf Bultmann's works throughout the 1950s and 1960s. For samples of biblical theology during these years, see Mary Ely Lyman, "The Unity of the Bible," *JBR* 14 (1946): 5–12; Millar Burrows, "The Task of Biblical Theology," *JBR* 14 (1946): 13–15; Robert C. Dentan, "The Nature and Function

of Old Testament Theology," *JBR* 14 (1946): 16–21; William A. Irwin, "Trends and Moods in Old Testament Theology," *JBR* 19 (1951): 183–90; Floyd V. Filson, "New Testament Theology in the Last Decade," *JBR* 19 (1951): 191–96; Winston L. King, "The Freshman and the Eschaton," *JBR* 23 (1955): 75–80; Bernhard W. Anderson, "Changing Emphases in Biblical Scholarship," *JBR* 23 (1955): 81–88; Lawrence E. Toombs, "O.T. Theology and the Wisdom Literature," *JBR* 23 (1955): 193–96; Robert M. Grant, "What We Look for in the New Testament," *JBR* 29 (1961): 20–24; Eric C. Rust, "Interpreting the Resurrection," *JBR* 29 (1961): 25–34; Paul L. Hammer, "Myth, Faith, and History in the New Testament," *JBR* 29 (1961): 113–18; and Lionel A. Whiston Jr., "The Unity of Scripture and the Post-Exilic Literature," *JBR* 29 (1961): 290–98.

17. A. Roy Eckardt, "The Strangeness of Religion in the University Curriculum," *JBR* 25 (1957): 3–12, quotations from 10, 11, and 12.

18. For an example of the variety if not disunity of more technical biblical scholarship, see the essays in Willoughby, ed., *Study of the Bible Today and Tomorrow*.

19. For some of the muted criticisms of biblical theology and neo-orthodoxy, see, for instance, W. Norman Pittinger, "Biblical Religion and Biblical Theology," *JBR* 13 (1945): 179–83; Edgar Sheffield Brightman, "The Neo-Orthodox Trend," *JBR* 14 (1946): 129–30; Robert M. Montgomery, "Liberalism and the Challenge of Neo-Orthodoxy," *JBR* 15 (1947): 139–42; Rolland Emerson Wolfe, "The Terminology of Biblical Theology," *JBR* 15 (1947): 143–47; E. L. Allen, "The Limits of Biblical Theology," *JBR* 25 (1957): 13–18; and Noah Eduard Fehl, "History of Religions and Biblical Studies," *JBR* 27 (1959): 109–13, 182.

20. Eckardt, "Strangeness of Religion," 11.

21. G. Ernest Wright, "Wherein Lies the Unity of the Bible?," *JBR* 20 (1952): 198.

22. George M. Gibson, "Present-Day Fundamentalism," *JBR* 13 (1945): 69.

23. Filson, "New Testament Theology in the Last Decade," 24.

24. See William Foxwell Albright, *History, Archaeology, and Christian Humanism* (New York: McGraw-Hill, 1966), 13–14, 320–22.

25. Ibid., 319. Albright also had some interesting things to say in 1941 about Japan and its religious and cultural inferiority, once again showing the relevance of ancient cultures for modern politics. See his *Archaeology and the Religion of Israel* (Baltimore: Johns Hopkins Press, 1942), 34–35.

26. Bruce Kuklick, *Puritans in Babylon: The Ancient Near East and American Intellectual Life, 1880–1930* (Princeton, N.J.: Princeton University Press, 1996), 187.

27. Brightman, "Neo-Orthodox Trend," 129.

28. Virginia Corwin, "The Teaching Situation and the Bible," *JBR* 19 (1951): 62.

29. Amos N. Wilder, "An Editorial Note," *JBR* 14 (1946): 4.

30. Thomas S. Kepler, "The Liberal Viewpoint," *JBR* 14 (1946): 77, 78–79, 80, 81.

31. Thomas S. Kepler, "The Problem of Modernizing Jesus," *JBR* 17 (1949): 163, 166, 167.

32. Lucetta Mowry, "Jesus and the Ethical Problem of Man," *JBR* 18 (1950): 161.

33. Ralph W. Odom, "An Analytical Approach to the Study of Jesus," *JBR* 25 (1957): 199, 202.

34. On the religious revival of the 1950s, see James David Hudnut-Beumler, *Looking for God in the Suburbs: The Religion of the American Dream and Its Critics, 1945–1965* (New Brunswick, N.J.: Rutgers University Press, 1994); and Martin E. Marty, *Modern American Religion*, vol. 3, *Under God, Indivisible, 1941–1960* (Chicago: University of Chicago Press, 1996), chap. 19.

35. Robert T. Anderson, "The Role of the Desert in Israelite Thought," *JBR* 27 (1959): 42, 43.

36. Lawrence E. Toombs, "Myth Patterns in the Old Testament," *JBR* 29 (1961): 109, 110.

37. Eric C. Titus, "Did Paul Write I Corinthians 13?" *JBR* 27 (1959): 299.

38. Alvin A. Ahern, "The Perfection Concept in the Epistle to the Hebrews," *JBR* 14 (1946): 164–67.

39. John L. Cheek, "The Historicity of the Markan Resurrection Narrative," *JBR* 27 (1959): 192, 197–98.

40. Titus, "Did Paul Write I Corinthians 13?," 302.

41. Ahern, "Perfection Concept," 167.

42. Joseph L. Mihelic, "The Influence of Form Criticism on the Study of the Old Testament," *JBR* 19 (1951): 128. Harold H. Huston wrote in the same issue on "Form Criticism of the New Testament" that this method of study yielded "a frank approach which sees the gospel materials as a resource for today's problems in religious living" (133).

43. Robert W. Funk, "The Watershed of the American Biblical Tradition: The Chicago School, First Phase, 1892–1920," *Journal of Biblical Literature* 95 (1976): 21.

44. A. Roy Eckardt, "Theological Presuppositions for an Introductory Course in Religion," *JBR* 18 (1950): 174.

45. Ibid., 175, 176.

46. J. Allen Easley, "Appreciation of Bible as Literature and Religion," *JBR* 18 (1950): 96, 97.

47. Mary Frances Thelen, "The Biblical Instructor and Comparative Religion," *JBR* 20 (1952): 71.

48. King, "Freshman and the Eschaton," 76, 79.

49. Corwin, "Teaching Situation and the Bible," 57, 62.

50. O. R. Sellers, "New Problems for the Biblical Instructor," *JBR* 19 (1951): 118, 119.

51. William F. Buckley, *God and Man at Yale* (Chicago: Henry Regnery, 1951), 6, 7.

52. Jon D. Levenson, *The Hebrew Bible, the Old Testament, and Historical Criticism* (Louisville, Ky.: Westminster/John Knox, 1993), esp. chaps. 4 and 5, develops well the irony of modern academic biblical scholarship reliance upon communities of faith for supplying the boundaries (i.e., the canon of scripture) for its field of investigation.

53. Bundy and Coffin, quoted in George M. Marsden, *The Soul of the American University: From Protestant Establishment to Established Nonbelief* (New York: Oxford University Press, 1994), 10, 17.

54. On the status of the Bible in American culture, see Martin E. Marty, "America's Iconic Book," in *Humanizing America's Iconic Book: Society of Biblical Literature Centennial Addresses 1980,* ed. Gene M. Tucker and Douglas A. Knight (Chico, Calif.: Scholars Press, 1982), 1–23; and the essays in Nathan O. Hatch

and Mark A. Noll, eds., *The Bible in America: Essays in Cultural History* (New York: Oxford University Press, 1982).

55. Quoted in Patrick Henry, "'And I Don't Care What It Is': The Tradition-History of a Civil Religion Proof-Text," *JAAR* 49 (1981): 41. On the cultural expressions of America's postwar search for consensus that have important implications for the study of religion in the nation's colleges and universities, see Mark Silk, "Notes on the Judeo-Christian Tradition in America," *American Quarterly* 36 (1984): 65–86; and Philip Gleason, "World War II and the Development of American Studies," *American Quarterly* 36 (1984): 343–58.

56. For a development of this point, see D. G. Hart, "Evangelicals, Biblical Scholarship, and the Politics of the Modern American Academy," in *Evangelicals and Science in Historical Perspective,* ed. David N. Livingstone, D. G. Hart, and Mark A. Noll (New York: Oxford University Press, 1999), 306–26.

7 • Church History for the Nation

1. Henry F. May, "The Recovery of American Religious History," *AHR* 70 (Oct. 1964): 79–92, is reprinted in Henry F. May, *Ideas, Faiths and Feelings: Essays on American Intellectual and Religious History* (New York: Oxford University Press, 1982), from which citations below are taken.

2. For the efforts of some historians to chart those waters, see Harry S. Stout and D. G. Hart, eds., *New Directions in American Religious History* (New York: Oxford University Press, 1997); Martin E. Marty, "American Religious History in the Eighties: A Decade of Achievement," *Church History* 62 (1993): 335–77; Marty, "The Editor's Bookshelf: American Religious History," *Journal of Religion* 62 (1982): 99–109; Henry Warner Bowden, *Church History in an Age of Uncertainty: Historiographical Patterns in the United States,* 1906–1990 (Carbondale: Southern Illinois University Press, 1991); John M. Mulder and John F. Wilson, eds., *Religion in America: Interpretive Essays* (Englewood Cliffs, N.J.: Prentice-Hall, 1978); and Leonard I. Sweet, "The Evangelical Tradition in America," in *The Evangelical Tradition in America,* ed. Sweet (Macon, Ga.: Mercer University Press, 1984), 1–86.

3. May, "Recovery of American Religious History," 80, 68. (Subsequent page references appear in parentheses in the text.)

4. For a work in church history that explored the formation of the Bible, see J.N.D. Kelly, *Early Christian Doctrines* (1960; rev. ed., New York: Harper and Row, 1978).

5. Because the chief journals in religious studies did not publish a substantial amount of church history, this chapter depends on primary sources somewhat different from the materials in the previous two. What is more, the wide-ranging fields of theology and biblical studies failed to produce the same kind of survey textbook literature that the relatively limited topic of American religious (read Protestant) history did.

6. Winthrop S. Hudson, "Research Abstracts: Church History (1948)," *JBR* 17 (1949): 187–89, quotation on 187.

7. Leonard J. Trinterud, "The Origins of Puritanism," *Church History* 20 (1951); quoted in Winthrop S. Hudson, "Research Abstracts: Church History (1950–1951)," *JBR* 20 (1952): 101.

8. James Hasting Nichols, "The Art of Church History," *Church History* 20 (1951): 3–9, quoted in Hudson, "Research Abstracts: Church History (1950–1951)," 100–102.; quotation on 101.

9. Hudson, "Shifting Trends in Church History," *JBR* 28 (1960): 236, 237, 238. The Mead quotation on 237 came from *The Chronicle* (July 1949): 139–40.

10. Roland H. Bainton, *Here I Stand: A Life of Martin Luther* (New York: Abingdon Press, 1950).

11. Roland H. Bainton, "Teaching Church History," *JBR* 10 (1942): 103, 104.

12. Hudson, "Research Abstracts: Church History (1950–1951)," 100–102.

13. Claude Roebuck, "Adoniram Judson: A Study in Church History," *JBR* 20 (1952): 239, 243, 244.

14. For background on Sweet and on his influence, see Bowden, *Church History*, 50–57; and David W. Lotz, "A Changing Historiography: From Church History to Religious History," in *Altered Landscapes: Christianity in America, 1935–1985*, ed. Lotz (Grand Rapids, Mich.: Eerdmans, 1989), 320–22.

15. William Warren Sweet, "Religion and Culture in the Middle West," *JBR* 14 (1946): 191. (Subsequent page references appear in parentheses in the text.)

16. May, "Recovery of American Religious History," 73, 74. See Arthur Schlesinger Jr., "The Causes of the Civil War: A Note on Historical Sentimentalism," *Partisan Review* 16 (1949): 969–81, who called upon historians to recognize the importance of moral responsibility and interpret "the great conflicts" of history in that context (979); C. Vann Woodward, "The Irony of Southern History," *Journal of Southern History* 19 (1953): 3–19, who cited Niebuhr explicitly in fashioning a history that dispelled "the illusion of pretended virtue without denying the genuine virtues"; and George F. Kennan, *Russia and the West Under Lenin and Stalin* (Boston: Little, Brown, 1960), who cautioned against attributing evil and righteousness too quickly in understanding the complicated history of the Soviet Union.

17. My assessment here follows Lotz, "Changing Historiography."

18. Ephraim Emerton, "The Study of Church History," *Unitarian Review and Religious Magazine* 19 (1883): 3, 7, quoted in Lotz, "Changing Historiography," 318.

19. Lotz, "Changing Historiography," 320–21. Ironically, despite appeals to the neutrality and objectivity of church historians, Lotz also notes that church historians in the "scientistic" age believed the church was the "one true key to the meaning of humanity's total story," and was "of material importance for the work of theological construction" (320, 321). This is ironic since the norm of science would appear to put the church on a par with all other human institutions. This preferential treatment of the church mirrored the same sort of favoritism Christianity received from Protestant proponents of Enlightened Christianity. See chaps. 1 and 2 above.

20. See chap. 4 above.

21. Lotz, "Changing Historiography," 324.

22. Timothy L. Smith, *Revivalism and Social Reform: American Protestantism on the Eve of the Civil War*, rev. cd. (Baltimore: Johns Hopkins University Press, 1980), 149. The last five chapters (out of fourteen) ran under the following titles: "The Evangelical Origins of Social Christianity"; "The Churches Help

the Poor"; "Christian Liberty and Human Bondage: The Paradox of Slavery"; "The Spiritual Warfare Against Slavery"; and "The Gospel of the Kingdom."

23. See Smith's afterword, where he explains the context in which he wrote the book. Ibid., 249–61.

24. Winthrop S. Hudson, *The Great Tradition of the American Churches* (New York: Harper and Bros., 1953), 50–52.

25. See ibid., 28–32 on Bryce, 37–38 on Tocqueville. (Subsequent page references appear in parentheses in the text.)

26. Ibid., 11. Curiously, Hudson slammed fundamentalists for doing just this. At a time when neo-orthodox theologians were faulting liberal Protestants for committing some of the sins that fundamentalists had observed, such as accommodating science and secularism uncritically, Hudson praised those Protestants who "struggled valiantly at the turn of the century to save the churches from the utter irrationality of identifying the Christian faith with antiquated knowledge *which was demonstrably false*" (12, italics added). Despite Hudson's defense of liberalism, he was clearly on the side of neo-orthodoxy, thus suggesting that the difference between liberal and neo-orthodox Protestantism had more to do with the mainline church's relative confidence in their position within American culture.

27. Ibid., 13, 258.

28. Sidney Mead, *The Lively Experiment: The Shaping of Christianity in America* (New York: Harper and Row, 1963). The Walgreen lectures can be found in chaps. 2, 7, 8, and 9.

29. Ibid., 103, 104.

30. On the rise and fall of religious history as church history, see Lotz, "Changing Historiography," and Harry S. Stout and Robert M. Taylor Jr., "Studies of Religion in American Society: The State of the Art," in *New Directions in American Religious History*, ed. Stout and Hart, chap. 1.

31. Mead, *Lively Experiment*, 187.

32. H. Richard Niebuhr, *The Kingdom of God in America* (Chicago: Willett, Clark, 1937), xiv.

33. May, "Recovery of American Religious History," 74.

34. Bowden, *Church History in an Age of Uncertainty*, chap. 3, quotation on 66. See also Lotz, "Changing Historiography," 322–30.

35. May, "Recovery of American Religious History," 66, 78.

36. Nichols, "Art of Church History," 3–9, quotations on 9 and 8. For other theologically informed reflections on the nature and purpose of church history, see James Hastings Nichols, "Church History and Secular History," *Church History* 13 (1944): 87–99; Sydney E. Mead, "Church History Explained," *Church History* 32 (1963): 17–31; Albert C. Outler, "Theodosius' Horse: Reflections on the Predicament of the Church Historian," *Church History* 34 (1965): 251–61; Arthur S. Link, "The Historian's Vocation," *Theology Today* 19 (1962): 75–89; E. Harris Harbison, "The Meaning of History and the Writing of History," *Church History* 21 (1952): 97–107.

37. See Bowden, *Church History in an Age of Uncertainty*, chap. 3; and Lotz, "Changing Historiography," 322–30. On the resurgence of denominational history, see Henry Warner Bowden, "The Death and Rebirth of Denominational History," in *Re-Imagining Denominationalism: Interpretive Essays*, ed. Robert

Bruce Mullin and Russell E. Richey (New York: Oxford University Press, 1994), chap. 1.

38. Edwin Scott Gaustad, *A Religious History of America* (New York: Harper and Row, 1966), quotation from preface.

39. Ibid., 388, 393. At roughly the same time as the publication of this book, Gaustad wrote for the American Historical Association a short pamphlet with his own perspective on the recovery of American religious history. See Edwin S. Gaustad, *American Religious History* (Washington, D.C.: American Historical Association, 1966).

40. Winthrop S. Hudson, *Religion in America* (New York: Scribner's, 1965), viii, 425.

41. For comparable interpretations from this period, see Clifton E. Olmstead, *History of Religion in the United States* (Englewood Cliffs, N.J.: Prentice-Hall, 1969); H. Shelton Smith et al., *American Christianity: An Historical Interpretation With Representative Documents,* 2 vols. (New York: Scribner's, 1960–63); Martin E. Marty, *Righteous Empire: The Protestant Experience in America* (New York: Dial, 1970); and Sydney E. Ahlstrom, *A Religious History of the American People* (New Haven: Yale University Press, 1972).

On the public aspirations of mainline Protestantism, see William R. Hutchison, "Protestantism as Establishment," in *Between the Times: The Travail of the Protestant Establishment in America, 1900–1960,* ed. Hutchison (New York: Cambridge University Press, 1989), chap. 1.

42. Lotz, "Changing Historiography," 321.

43. Lewis G. Vander Velde, *The Presbyterian Churches and the Federal Union, 1861–1869* (Cambridge: Harvard University Press, 1932), vii.

44. William Warren Sweet, *The Story of Religions in America* (New York: Harper and Bros., 1930), 9, 10.

45. The point here is not that Sweet's account was untrue. The churches did affect the nation and national life had a direct bearing on the churches. Rather, the concern is whether national politics are the best lens through which to understand and explain the life of the churches, for instance, their teachings, forms of government, and liturgical expressions. If Sweet or other seminary church historians had been more interested in the churchly character of the churches, I believe, the narrative would look significantly different. This would not necessarily interest scholars in the American Historical Association. But it might be of interest to the believing students studying in colleges and universities, seminarians, and the congregations to which seminary graduates would eventually minister.

46. See, for instance, John Tracy Ellis, *American Catholicism* (Chicago: University of Chicago Press, 1955); Ellis, ed., *Documents of American Catholic History* (Milwaukee: Bruce Publishing, 1955); John Kromminga, *The Christian Reformed Church: A Study in Orthodoxy* (Grand Rapids, Mich.: Baker Book House, 1949); and D. H. Kromminga, *The Christian Reformed Tradition from the Reformation to the Present* (Grand Rapids, Mich.: Eerdmans, 1943).

47. Paul A. Carter, "Recent Historiography of the Protestant Churches in America," *Church History* 37 (1968): 97–98.

48. See the works cited in n. 2 above.

49. Sydney E. Ahlstrom, "The Radical Turn in Theology and Ethics: Why

It Occurred in the 1960s," *Annals of the American Academy of Political and Social Science* (January 1970), reprinted in *New Theology*, no. 8, ed. Martin E. Marty and Dean G. Peerman (New York: Macmillan, 1971), 38.

8 • Religious Studies and the Failure of the Christian Academy

1. Ruth Wick, "The Commission on the University," *CS* 36 (1953): 155, gives direct credit to Visser't Hooft's *None Other Gods,* and the writings of other Christian academics who lamented the poor showing of religion in the university. On this literature see chap. 4 above.

2. Werner Bohnstedt, "Reports and Notices: The Faculty Christian Fellowship: Its Meaning and Task," *CS* 36 (1953): 154.

3. Douglas Sloan, *Faith and Knowledge: Mainline Protestantism and American Higher Education* (Louisville, Ky.: Westminster/John Knox, 1994), 84–86, 179–85, quotation on 184.

4. E. Harris Harbison, *The Christian Scholar in the Age of the Reformation* (New York: Scribner's, 1956).

5. Ibid., 169, 172.

6. See, for instance, John Dillenberger's review in the *Christian Century* 74 (March 6, 1957): 297–98.

7. Review of Harbison, *Christian Scholar in the Age of the Reformation, JBR* 25 (1957): 254.

8. Roland Mushat Frye, review of *Christian Scholar in the Age of the Reformation, CS* 40 (1957): 61–64, quotation on 64.

9. Jaroslav Pelikan, *The Christian Intellectual* (New York: Harper and Row, 1965), 34. The companion volume to which Pelikan referred was his *Obedient Rebels: Catholic Substance and Protestant Principle in Luther's Reformation* (New York: Harper and Row, 1964). For an earlier treatment of some of the themes in *The Christian Intellectual,* see Pelikan, "The Christian as an Intellectual," *CS* 45 (1962): 6–11.

10. Pelikan, *Christian Intellectual,* 39. (Subsequent page references appear in parentheses in the text.)

11. David O. Woodyard, review of *The Christian Intellectual, Christian Century* 83 (March 16, 1966): 336.

12. "About the Journal: The Editor's Preface," *CS* 36 (1953): 4. The divide between religious studies and other academic subjects was not as airtight as suggested here. Over time the *Christian Scholar* published a substantial amount of theology and philosophical theology. Still, its orientation initially was toward fields outside Protestant divinity.

13. J. Robert Nelson, "A Transforming Influence upon Student Christian Movements," *CS* 36 (1953): 64, 65.

14. Elizabeth G. Wright, "The National Council on Religion in Higher Education," *CS* 37 (1954): 169–70, quotation on 169.

15. On those initial mainline Protestant extracurricular forays into American higher education, see chap. 3 above. Other groups mentioned in the "Reports and Notices" section of the *Christian Scholar* were such mainstream Protestant standbys as the YMCA, the YWCA, and the Hazen Foundation.

16. "Reports and Notices: The Faculty Christian Fellowship—Its Development and Future Plans," *CS* 36 (1953): 55–57.

17. On the FCF, see Sloan, *Faith and Knowledge,* 84–86, and chap. 6; and Phillips P. Moulton, "The Emerging Faculty Christian Movement," *Religious Education* 50 (1955): 64–67.

18. "Reports and Notices: The First National Conference of the Faculty Christian Fellowship, June 18–23, 1953—Park College, Missouri," *CS* 36 (1953): 240, 241, 242–43.

19. "Faculty Christian Fellowship Consultation," *CS* 37 (1954): 555–56.

20. See "Reports and Notices," *CS* 39 (1956): 243–47, 313–23.

21. See *CS* 37 (1954), suppl., 175–349.

22. Dirks's statement appeared in "Reports and Notices: What Is the Commission on Christian Higher Education?" *CS* 39 (1956): 314–15.

23. Sloan, *Faith and Knowledge,* 184, observes that the FCF's newsletter continued into the 1970s but dates the death of the organization in 1967 when the *Christian Scholar* changed its name to *Soundings.* My hunch, however, is that the Protestant denominations' interest in Christian colleges killed the FCF long before the editorial changes at the *Christian Scholar.*

24. All in *CS* 36 (1953): Kenneth I. Brown, "The Terrible Responsibility of the Teacher," 23–28; Philip N. Joranson et al., "The Recognition of Christian Perspective in Liberal Arts Teaching at Beloit College," 29–33; Lester Hale and Wayne E. Weeks, "Witness on Campus," 38–42; Oswald Elbert, "The Christian Ministry to the Campus," 43–46; and John O. Gross, "The College and the Church: A Partnership," 47–52.

25. On the origins of Protestant campus ministry, see Dorothy C. Bass, "Ministry on the Margin: Protestants and Education," in *Between the Times: The Travail of the Protestant Establishment in America, 1900–1960,* ed. William R. Hutchison (New York: Cambridge University Press, 1989), chap. 3.

26. "Editor's Preface," *CS* 39 (1956): 3, 4.

27. George Ernest Wright, "Progressive Revelation," Joseph Haroutunian, "God's People Israel, the Church and the World," and "An Annotated Bibliography on Biblical Theology," *CS* 39 (1956): 61–65, 56–60, and 77–82, respectively.

28. "Editor's Preface," 4–5.

29. Walter Harrelson, "Creation," Howard Clark Kee, "The Biblical Understanding of Miracle," and Krister Stendahl, "Christology—As a Problem of Translation," *CS* 39 (1956): 45–49, 50–55, and 72–76 respectively. Of all the contributors to this issue, only two of the ten authors, Will Herberg and E. LaB. Cherbonnier (religion professor at Trinity College), were not members of Protestant seminary or divinity school faculty.

30. "Editor's Preface," *CS* 39 (1956): 167.

31. Roland Mushat Frye, "To Synthesis Through Community," *CS* 39 (1956): 174.

32. L. O. Kattsoff, "The Priesthood of the Scholar," *CS* 39 (1954): 170, 172.

33. Frye, "To Synthesis Through Community," 179.

34. Clyde A. Holbrook, "The Commitments and Tensions of Academic Men," *CS* 39 (1956): 191.

35. Rene de Visme Williamson, "The Christian Professor's Responsibility to His Colleagues," *CS* 39 (1956): 201–2.

36. Joseph H. Summers, "Christian Literary Scholars," *CS* 47 (1964): 94, 98.

37. Newby Toms, "Eliot's *The Cocktail Party:* Salvation and the Common Routine," and Josephine Jacobsen, "A Catholic Quartet," *CS* 47 (1964): 125–38 and 139–54 respectively.

38. Michael Novak, "Philosophy and Fiction," and Robert Detweiler, "Christ and the Christ Figure in American Fiction," *CS* 47 (1964): 100–110 and 111–24, respectively.

39. Ronald W. McNeur, "Theology and the Medical Sciences: The Possibility of a Meeting," *CS* 46 (1963): 189–99.

40. Otto E. Guttentag, "On Defining Medicine," *CS* 46 (1963): 200–211. See also F. J. J. Buytendijk, "Renewal in the Life Sciences," *CS* 46 (1963): 213–18.

41. Rollo May, "The Problem of the Will, Decision and Responsibility in Psychological Health," *CS* 46 (1963): 235–44.

42. Eugene T. Gendlin, "Experiencing and the Nature of Concepts," and Ludwig B. Lefebre, "Inclusion of the Negative," *CS* 46 (1963): 245–55 and 219–34 respectively.

43. "Christian Theology and Contemporary Medical Trends: The Editor's Preface," *CS* 46 (1963): 186.

44. See Joseph Francis Fletcher, *Situation Ethics: The New Morality* (Philadelphia: Westminster Press, 1966).

45. William R. Mueller, "A Tribute to J. Edward Dirks," *CS* 50 (1967): 3–5.

46. J. A. Martin Jr., "Christians and the University: Retrospect and Prospect," *CS* 50 (1967): 51, 52.

47. Mueller, "Tribute to J. Edward Dirks," 3.

48. "Editorial: *Soundings,*" *Soundings* 51 (1968): 2–3, 4.

49. Richard Schlatter, foreword to *Religion,* ed. Paul Ramsey (Englewood Cliffs, N.J.: Prentice-Hall, 1965), vii.

50. The other volumes in the Princeton series, all published by Prentice-Hall (Englewood Cliffs, N.J.), were: Eric R. Wolf, *Anthropology* (1964); James S. Ackerman and Rhys Carpenter, *Art and Archaeology* (1963); Wen Fong, *Chinese Painting* (1964); Eric A. Havelock, *Classics* (1963); Felix Gilbert, John Higham, and Leonard Krieger, *History* (1965); William Haas and Karl D. Uitti, *Linguistics* (1964); David Daiches and Howard E. Hugo, *Literature* (1964); Walter Sutton, *Modern American Criticism* (1963); Frank L. Harrison, Mantle Hood, and Claude V. Palisca, *Musicology* (1964); Robert H. Knapp, *The Origins of American Humanistic Scholars* (1964); and Roderick M. Chisholm, Herbert Feigl, William K. Frankena, John Passmore, and Manley Thompson, *Philosophy* (1964).

51. See chap. 4 above on the emergence of this common perspective.

52. *Religion,* ed. Ramsey, chap. 3. (Subsequent page references appear in parentheses in the text.)

53. Ibid., chap. 10. In this chapter Holbrook describes graduate education in religion and, without flinching, locates all of the good graduate programs in schools dominated by Protestant theological education.

54. Richard Schlatter, in his foreword, did observe that "a considerable body of American scholars are of the opinion that religious studies are no part of the humanities, no part of the liberal arts, not an objective scholarly discipline." Ibid., ix. But the Princeton Council's series can be read as a sign that that perception was changing.

55. John F. Wilson, "Mr. Holbrook and the Humanities, or Mr. Schlatter's Dilemma: A Review Article," *JBR* 32 (1964): 253–55.

56. Ibid., 255–56, 259, 261. Quotation on 256.

57. Morton White, "Religious Commitment and Higher Education," in his *Religion, Politics and the Higher Learning: A Collection of Essays* (Cambridge: Harvard University Press, 1959), 105.

58. White, "Religion, Politics, and the Higher Learning," in *Religion, Politics and the Higher Learning*, 95.

59. White, "Religious Commitment and Higher Education," 103, 105–8.

60. "Religion, Politics, and the Higher Learning," 95.

61. White, "Religious Commitment and Higher Education," 106–7.

62. For one Protestant response to White's argument along with his reply, see John A Hutchison, "Religion, Prejudice and Education [a review of *Religion, Politics and the Higher Learning*]," *Union Seminary Quarterly* 16 (1960–61): 397–403; and White, "Advocacy and Objectivity in Religious Education: A Reply," *Union Seminary Quarterly* 16 (1960–61): 403–7.

9 • Religious Studies in Post-Protestant America

1. *Abington Township School District v. Schempp*, reprinted in Robert T. Miller and Ronald B. Flowers, *Toward Benevolent Neutrality: Church, State, and the Supreme Court*, rev. ed. (Waco, Tex.: Markham Press Fund, 1982), 361, 352.

2. Sydney E. Ahlstrom, "The Radical Turn in Theology and Ethics: Why It Occurred in the 1960s," reprinted in *New Theology No. 8*, ed. Martin E. Marty and Dean B. Peerman (New York: Macmillan, 1971), 20. This essay should be compared with Ahlstrom's assessment of the religious and theological revival of the post–World War II era in "Theology and the Present-Day Revival," reprinted in *The Sociology of Religion: An Anthology*, ed. Richard D. Knudten (New York: Appleton-Century-Crofts, 1967), 5–16. Leo Pfeffer, "The Schempp-Murray Decision on School Prayers and Bible Reading," *Journal of Church and State* 5 (1963): 165, called it "an historic decision," but the National Council of Churches, "The Churches and the Public Schools: A Policy Statement of the National Council of Churches," *Journal of Church and State* 5 (1963): 176–80, received the verdict with studied aplomb.

3. *Abington Township School District . . .*," 347.

4. Ibid., 370, italics his.

5. Dwight Beck et al., "Report of the NABI Self-Study Committee," *JBR* 32 (1964): 200, 201.

6. William Adams Brown, *The Case for Theology in the University* (Chicago: University of Chicago Press, 1938), 23–24, 88, 89.

7. Henry P. Van Dusen, *God in Education* (New York: Scribner's, 1951), 102, 103, 105–6, 109, 115.

8. Milton D. McLean and Harry H. Kimber, eds., *The Teaching of Religion in State Universities: Descriptions of Programs in Twenty-Five Institutions* (Ann Arbor: Office of Religious Affairs, University of Michigan, 1960), 7, 8, 9, 10.

9. Geddes MacGregor, "Graduate Study in Religion and the University of Southern California," *JBR* 30 (1962): 109, 110, 111.

10. See chap. 1 above.

11. Paul Ramsey, "Princeton University's Graduate Program in Religion," *JBR* 30 (1962): 294.

12. Waldo Beach, "Graduate Study in Religion at Duke University," *JBR* 31 (1963): 38, 39.

13. Robert Michaelsen, "Reflections on the Graduate Program in Religion," *JBR* 30 (1962): 226–27.

14. John F. Wilson, "Mr. Holbrook and the Humanities, or Mr. Schlatter's Dilemma," *JBR* 32 (1964): 259, 255, 254.

15. J. Calvin Keene, "Ramanuja, the Hindu Augustine," *JBR* 21 (1953): 3–8.

16. Floyd H. Ross, "A Re-Examination of Christian Attitudes Toward Other Faiths," *JBR* 21 (1953): 79–83.

17. Will Herberg, "Judaism and Christianity: Their Unity and Difference, The Double Covenant in the Divine Economy of Salvation," *JBR* 21 (1953): 67–78, quotation on 68.

18. On this approach to the study of religion see Philip H. Ashby, "The History of Religions," in *Religion,* ed. Paul Ramsey (Englewood Cliffs, N.J.: Prentice-Hall, 1965), 3–49; and H. P. Sullivan, "The History of Religions: Some Problems and Prospects," in *The Study of Religion in Colleges and Universities,* ed. Paul Ramsey and John F. Wilson (Princeton, N.J.: Princeton University Press, 1970), 246–80.

19. Noah Eduard Fehl, "History of Religions and Biblical Studies," *JBR* 27 (1959): 111.

20. See, e.g., Charles S. Braden, "Research Abstracts: Research in the History of Religions, 1947–1948," *JBR* 17 (1949): 120–23, who includes Chinese religions, religions of India, Islam, and "Primitive" religions; John B. Noss, "Research Abstracts: History of Religions (1955–1956)," *JBR* 25 (1957): 216–21, who includes "Religions in General," ancient religions, religions of India, Buddhism, religions of China, religions of Japan, and Islam; and Noss, "Research Abstracts: History of Religions (1957–1958)," *JBR* 27 (1959): 146–52, who includes religions in general, religions of India, Buddhism, religions of China, Zoroastrianism, and Islam.

21. Fehl, "History of Religions and Biblical Studies," 111, 112.

22. Harry M. Buck Jr., "From History to Myth: A Comparative Study," *JBR* 29 (1961): 225.

23. On the liberal Protestant theological assumptions that informed the history of religions, see Joseph M. Kitagawa, "Humanistic and Theological History of Religions with Special Reference to the North American Scene," *Numen* 27 (1980): 198–221; Kitagawa, "The History of Religions in America," in *The History of Religions: Essays in Methodology,* ed. Mircea Eliade and Joseph M. Kitagawa (Chicago: University of Chicago Press, 1959), 1–30; Kitagawa, "The History of Religions (*Religionswissenschaft*) Then and Now," in his *The History of Religions: Retrospect and Prospect* (New York: Macmillan, 1985), 121–44; William R. Darrow, "The Harvard Way in the Study of Religion," *Harvard Theological Review* 81 (1988): 215–34; John F. Wilson, *Research Guide to Religious Studies* (Washington, D.C.: American Library Association, 1982), 17–19, 101–3; Grant Wacker, "Liberal Protestants and the Challenge of World Religions, 1890–1960," mss. in author's possession, 1986, 20–28; Eric J. Sharpe, *Comparative Religion: A History* (London: Duckworth, 1975); Harold E. Remus, E. Stanley Lusby,

and Linda M. Tober, "Religion as an Academic Discipline," in *Encyclopedia of American Religious Experience: Studies of Traditions and Movements,* vol. 3, ed. Charles H. Lippy and Peter W. Williams (New York: Scribner's, 1988), 1664–69; Kathryn O. Alexander, "Religious Studies in American Higher Education since Schempp: A Bibliographical Essay," *Soundings* 71 (1988): 389–412; Frank Whaling, ed., *Contemporary Approaches to the Study of Religion in Two Volumes* (Berlin: Mouton, 1983, 1985); and Robert D. Baird, ed., *Methodological Issues in Religious Studies* (Chico, Calif.: Scholars Press, 1975).

24. For more neutral and scientific renderings of the history of religions, see Ashby, "History of Religions," 1–50; and Sullivan, "History of Religions: Some Problems and Prospects," 246–80. For a critique of the theology informing this approach, see Russell T. McCutcheon, *Manufacturing Religion: The Discourse of Sui Generis Religion and the Politics of Nostalgia* (New York: Oxford University Press, 1997).

25. On the substance of the AATS report, see J. Allen Easley, "The 'Statement on Pre-Theological Studies,'" *JBR* 27 (1959): 211–15; and J. Arthur Baird, "Pre-Theological Training: An Empirical Study," *JBR* 27 (1959): 303–10. For dissent regarding the AATS's advice to prospective ministers, see J. Paul Williams, "But Don't Major in Religion," *Christian Century* 71 (June 16, 1954): 731–32.

26. H. Richard Niebuhr, Daniel Day Williams, and James M. Gustafson, *The Advancement of Theological Education* (New York: Harper and Bros., 1957), 91.

27. Easley, "'Statement on Pre-Theological Studies,'" 211, 213.

28. Baird, "Pre-Theological Training," 309, 310. For a further response to the AATS report, see Ernest Cadman Colwell, "Closing the Gap between College and Seminary," *JBR* 26 (1958): 107–14.

29. Members of the committee were Easley, Baird, John L. Cheek, Earl Cranston, Edward C. Hobbs, Walter G. Williams, and A. Roy Eckardt, chair.

30. Pre-Theological Studies Committee, "Pre-Seminary Preparation and Study in Religion," *JBR* 27 (1959): 139–42, quotations from 140, 141.

31. Keith R. Bridston and Dwight W. Culver, eds., *The Making of Ministers* (Minneapolis: Augsburg, 1964), xiii. Why Lutherans took such a large part in the production of these studies, both editorially and in its publication, is a consideration that no one seemed to ponder.

32. Keith R. Bridston and Dwight W. Culver, *Pre-Seminary Education* (Minneapolis: Augsburg, 1965), 58. (Subsequent page references appear in parentheses in the text.)

33. Robert S. Michaelsen, "Religion in the Undergraduate Curriculum," in *The Making of Ministers,* ed. Bridston and Culver, 65, 66–67.

34. Paul Ramsey, "Theological Studies in College and Seminary," in ibid., 95.

35. Ibid., 96.

36. James I. McCord, "The Lilly Study and the Theological Seminary," *JBR* 34 (1966): 139–45.

37. J. Arthur Baird, "Maturity in Theological Education and the College Teaching of Religion," *JBR* 34 (1966): 122–29, quotation on 129.

38. Jack Boozer, "Three Revolutions or One?," *JBR* 34 (1966): 130–38, quotations on 136 and 138.

39. Harry B. Adams, "Major Issues in the Lilly Study," *JBR* 34 (1966): 152–56, quotation on 155.

40. Clyde A. Holbrook, "The Lilly Study: Challenge to College and Seminary," *JBR* 23 (1966): 157–65, quotations on 158, 161, and 165.

41. Edmund Perry, "The Lilly Study: An Unfulfilled Promise," *JBR* 34 (1966): 106–14, quotations on 113 and 114.

42. See Bridston and Culver, *Pre-Seminary Education,* chap. 4 on "Professional Training."

43. "The Lilly Study," *JBR* 34 (1966): 96.

44. Claude Welch, ed., *Graduate Education in Religion: A Critical Appraisal* (Missoula: University of Montana Press, 1971). The same year that this study was published, Welch left Penn to become the dean of the Graduate Theological Union in Berkeley, California. (Subsequent page references appear in parentheses in the text.)

45. Ibid., chap. 3, quotations on 37.

46. See, for instance, the collections of essays in *Soundings* 71 (1988); *JAAR* 62 (1994); and Ray L. Hart, "Religious and Theological Studies in American Higher Education: A Pilot Study," *JAAR* 59 (1991): 715–827. The papers in *Soundings* come from the University of California–Santa Barbara Colloquy on religious studies, the articles in the 1994 issue of *JAAR* were devoted to the topic, "Settled Issues and Neglected Questions in the Study of Religion."

47. Charlotte Allen, "Is Nothing Sacred?" *Lingua Franca* (Nov. 1996): 40.

10 • Religious Studies, the Would-Be Discipline

1. Jonathan Z. Smith, "'Religion' and 'Religious Studies': No Difference at All," *Soundings* 71 (1988): 235, 236, 238.

2. From the description of the program at the University of California, Santa Barbara, quoted in ibid., 232.

3. Paul Ramsey and John F. Wilson, eds., *The Study of Religion in Colleges and Universities* (Princeton, N.J.: Princeton University Press, 1970).

4. Paul Ramsey, ed., *Religion* (Englewood Cliffs, N.J.: Prentice-Hall, 1965).

5. See, for instance, Krister Stendahl (Harvard Divinity School), "Biblical Studies in the University"; Arthur C. McGill (Harvard Divinity School), "The Ambiguous Position of Christian Theology"; and William A. Clebsch (Stanford University), "History and Salvation: An Essay in Distinctions," in *Study of Religion in Colleges and Universities,* ed. Ramsey and Wilson, 23–39, 105–38, and 40–72 respectively.

6. Jacob Neusner, "Modes of Jewish Studies in the University," in *Study of Religion in Colleges and Universities,* ed. Ramsey and Wilson, 159–89.

7. McGill, "Ambiguous Position of Christian Theology," 117–18, 119, 120, 133, 137. For arguments since 1970 in support of theology in the university, see George A. Lindbeck, *University Divinity Schools: A Report on Ecclesiastically Independent Theological Education* (New York: Rockefeller Foundation, 1976); "Religious Studies/Theological Studies: The St. Louis Project," *JAAR* 52 (1984): 727–57; and Charles E. Winquist, "Theology: Unsettled and Unsettling," *JAAR* 62 (1994): 1023–36.

8. Stendahl, "Biblical Studies in the University," 31, 33, 36–37, 38–39

9. James M. Gustafson, "The Study of Religion in Colleges and Universities:

A Practical Commentary," in *Study of Religion in Colleges and Universities,* ed. Ramsey and Wilson, 330, 331–32, 335, 336, 338.

10. Tom F. Driver, "The Study of Religion and Literature: Siblings in the Academic House," in ibid., 304, 305.

11. A. Richard Turner, "The Religious as It Appears in Art," in ibid., 299.

12. H. P. Sullivan, "The History of Religions: Some Problems and Prospects," in ibid., 276, 277.

13. See John F. Wilson, "Mr. Holbrook and the Humanities, or Mr. Schlatter's Dilemma: A Review Article," *JBR* 32 (1964): 252–61.

14. For an argument on behalf of diversity and humanistic methods, see John F. Wilson, "Developing the Study of Religion in America," *Journal of General Education* 20 (1968): 190–208.

15. John F. Wilson, "Introduction: The Background and Present Context of the Study of Religion in Colleges and Universities," in *Study of Religion in Colleges and Universities,* ed. Ramsey and Wilson, 20–21.

16. On the history-of-religions approach to religious studies, see Joseph M. Kitagawa, "Humanistic and Theological History of Religions with Special Reference to the North American Scene," *Numen* 27 (1980): 198–221; Kitagawa, "The History of Religions in America," in *The History of Religions: Essays in Methodology,* ed. Mircea Eliade and Joseph M. Kitagawa (Chicago: University of Chicago Press, 1959), 1–30; Kitagawa, "The History of Religions (*Religionswissenschaft*) Then and Now," in *The History of Religions: Retrospect and Prospect* (New York: Macmillan, 1985), 121–44; John F. Wilson, *Research Guide to Religious Studies* (Chicago: American Library Association, 1982), 17–19, 101–3; Grant Wacker, "Liberal Protestants and the Challenge of World Religions, 1890–1960," mss., 1986, 20–28; Eric J. Sharpe, *Comparative Religion: A History* (London: Duckworth, 1975); William R. Darrow, "The Harvard Way in the Study of Religion," *Harvard Theological Review* 81 (1988): 215–34; Harold E. Remus, E. Stanley Lusby, and Linda M. Tober, "Religion as an Academic Discipline," in *Encyclopedia of American Religious Experience: Studies of Traditions and Movements,* vol. 3, ed. Charles H. Lippy and Peter W. Williams (New York: Scribner's, 1988), 1653–69; Philip H. Ashby, "The History of Religions," in Ramsey, ed., *Religion,* 1–50; and Sullivan, "History of Religions," 246–80.

17. Donald Wiebe correctly notes the continuing Protestant themes of presidential addresses before the AAR. See his "Religious Agenda Continued: A Review of the Presidential Addresses of the AAR," in *The Politics of Religious Studies: The Conflict with Theology in the Academy* (New York: St. Martin's Press, 1999), chap. 15.

18. J. Wesley Robb, "The Hidden Philosophical Agenda: A Commentary on Humanistic Psychology," *JAAR* 37 (1969): 3–14; John C. Meagher, "Pictures at an Exhibition: Reflections on Exegesis and Theology," *JAAR* 47 (1979): 3–20; Charles H. Long, "Cargo Cults as Cultural Historical Phenomenon," *JAAR* 42 (1974): 403–14; and William F. May, "Institutions as Symbols of Death," *JAAR* 44 (1976): 211–23. For figures on the publishing trends of the AAR during the 1970s, see Ray L. Hart, "*JAAR* in the Seventies: Unconcluding Unscientific Postface," *JAAR* 47 (1979): 513–16.

19. McCutcheon, *Manufacturing Religion: The Discourse on Sui Generis Religion and the Politics of Nostalgia* (New York: Oxford University Press, 1997), 27.

20. Ibid., chap. 4, quotation from 126.

21. See *Soundings* 71 (Summer/Fall 1988) for the papers presented at Santa Barbara; and "Special Issue: Settled Issues and Neglected Questions in the Study of Religion," *JAAR* 62 (Winter 1994).

22. On the development of comparative religion and the International Association for the History of Religions, see Sharpe, *Comparative Religion,* esp. chap. 12.

23. See, e.g., the proposal on graduate studies produced by the Santa Barbara Colloquy, Gerald James Larson, "Revising Graduate Education," *Soundings* 71 (1988): 415–20, esp. 418 where the author repudiates *sui generis* religion.

24. On the history of anthropological, sociological, and psychological studies of religion, see Murray G. Murphy, "On the Scientific Study of Religion in the United States, 1870–1980," in *Religion and Twentieth-Century Intellectual Life,* ed. Michael J. Lacey (New York: Cambridge University Press, 1989), 136–71.

25. For background on these developments, see John H. Schultz, "Editorial," *BCSR* 1, no. 3 (1970): 2; Robert N. Bellah, "Confessions of a Former Establishment Fundamentalist," *BCSR* 1, no. 3 (1970): 3–6; James E. Dittes, "Confessing Away the Soul with the Sins, or: The Risks of Uncle Tomism among the Humanists. A Reply to Robert Bellah," *BCSR* 1, no. 3 (1970): 22–25; and James Gilbert, *Redeeming Culture: American Religion in an Age of Science* (Chicago: University of Chicago Press, 1997), chap. 11. For a balanced perspective on the contribution of the social sciences to the study of religion, see Mark A. Noll, "'And the Lion Shall Lie Down with the Lamb': The Social Sciences and Religious History," *Fides et Historia* 20, no. 3 (1988): 5–30.

26. Paul M. Harrison, "The Character and Contribution of the Sociology of Religion," in *Study of Religion in Colleges and Universities,* ed. Ramsey and Wilson, 215.

27. Though made in an overly politicized way, this is the worthwhile point made in McCutcheon's *Manufacturing Religion.*

28. The American Academy of Religion Task Force for the American Association of Colleges, *The Religion Major: A Report* (Syracuse, N.Y.: AAR, 1990), 3, 4, 5, 11.

29. Larson, "Revising Graduate Education," 417, 419.

30. See, for instance, Grant Wacker, "A Plural World: The Protestant Awakening to World Religions," in *Between the Times: The Travail of the Protestant Establishment in America, 1900–1960,* ed. William R. Hutchison (New York: Cambridge University Press, 1989), 268–75. Alisdair MacIntyre, *Three Rival Versions of Moral Enquiry: Encyclopaedia, Genealogy and Tradition* (Notre Dame: University of Notre Dame Press, 1990); Jon D. Levenson, *The Hebrew Bible, The Old Testament, and Historical Criticism: Jews and Christians in Biblical Studies* (Louisville, Ky.: Westminster/John Knox, 1993); and Stanley Hauerwas, "A Non-Violent Proposal for Christian Participation in the Culture Wars," *Soundings* 65 (1992): 477–92, offer formidable critiques of the Enlightenment's approach to the study of religion.

31. *Religion Major,* 8–12, quotation on 8.

32. On the habit of American intellectuals at mid-twentieth century making their particular outlook stand for a universal understanding of human nature and society, see David A. Hollinger, "How Wide the Circle of 'We'?

American Intellectuals and the Problem of the Ethnos since World War II," *AHR* 98 (1993): 317–37. Though Hollinger pays little attention to mainstream Protestantism, the example of Protestant educators in the field of religious studies underscores his point.

33. Mark C. Taylor, "Unsettling Issues," *JAAR* 62 (1994): 954. It should be noted that Taylor does not recommend the abolition of religious studies.

34. This and the next several paragraphs reflect the argument made in D. G. Hart, "American Learning and the Problem of Religious Studies," in *The Secularization of the Academy,* ed. George M. Marsden and Bradley J. Longfield (New York: Oxford University Press, 1992), 214–20.

35. For some of the literature on academic professionalization, see Laurence Veysey, "Higher Education as a Profession: Changes and Continuities," in *The Professions in American History,* ed. Nathan O. Hatch (Notre Dame, Ind.: University of Notre Dame Press, 1988), 15–32; Bruce Kuklick, "The Professionalization of the Humanities," in *Applying the Humanities,* ed. Daniel Callahan, Arthur L. Caplan, and Bruce Jennings (New York: Plenum Press, 1985), 41–54; Robert A. McGaughey, "Transformation of American Academic Life: Harvard University, 1821–1892," *Perspectives in American History* 8 (1974): 237–332; Burton J. Bledstein, *The Culture of Professionalism: The Middle Class and the Development of Higher Education in America* (New York: Norton, 1976); Dorothy Ross, *The Origins of American Social Science* (New York: Cambridge University Press, 1991); Mary Furner, *Advocacy and Objectivity: A Crisis in the Professionalization of American Social Science, 1865–1905* (Lexington: University of Kentucky Press, 1975); Thomas L. Haskell, *The Emergence of Professional Social Science: The American Social Science Association and the Nineteenth-Century Crisis of Authority* (Urbana: University of Illinois Press, 1977); and the essays in Alexandra Oleson and John Voss, ed., *The Organization of Knowledge in Modern America, 1860–1920* (Baltimore: Johns Hopkins University Press, 1979)

36. On the effects of federal funding for American universities, especially to assist the development of the natural sciences, see Roger L. Geiger, *Research and Relevant Knowledge: American Research Universities since World War II* (New York: Oxford University Press, 1992); and Richard M. Freeland, *Academia's Golden Age: Universities in Massachusetts, 1945–1970* (New York: Oxford University Press, 1992). On the impact of these developments on the humanities, see Douglas Sloan, "The Teaching of Ethics in the American Undergraduate Curriculum, 1876–1976," in *Education and Values,* ed. Sloan (New York: Teachers College Press, 1980), 244–48.

37. Wacker, "Liberal Protestants," 21ff; Kitagawa, "Humanistic and Theological History of Religions," 209–12; Lyman H. Legters, "The Place of Religion in Foreign Area Studies," *JAAR* 35 (1967): 159–64; Lewis Perry, *Intellectual Life in America: A History* (New York: Franklin Watts, 1984), chap. 8; Sydney E. Ahlstrom, "The Radical Turn in Theology and Ethics: Why It Occurred in the 1960s," *Annals of the American Academy of Political and Social Science* 387 (1970): 1–13.

38. Gerald James Larson, "An Introduction to the Santa Barbara Colloquy: Some Unresolved Questions," *Soundings* 71 (1988): 201.

39. Eric J. Sharpe, "Religious Studies, the Humanities and the History of Ideas," *Soundings* 71 (1988): 256.

Conclusion

1. Claude Welch, ed., *Graduate Education in Religion: A Critical Appraisal* (Missoula: University of Montana Press, 1971). The same year that this study was published, Welch left Penn to become the dean of the Graduate Theological Union in Berkeley, California.

2. Facts about the episode at the University of Pennsylvania come from E. Ann Matter, "The Academic Culture of Disbelief: Religious Studies at the University of Pennsylvania," *Method and Theory in the Study of Religion* 7 (1995): 383–92.

3. Ibid., 386, 387. Of course, Matter borrowed her title from Carter, *The Culture of Disbelief: How American Law and Politics Trivialize Religious Devotion* (New York: Basic Books, 1993).

4. Matter, "Academic Culture of Disbelief," 389.

5. Carter, *Culture of Disbelief,* 209.

6. Ibid., chap. 10.

7. Actually, Richard John Neuhaus made this point almost a decade earlier in *The Naked Public Square: Religion and Democracy in America* (Grand Rapids, Mich.: Eerdmans, 1984).

8. Carter, *Culture of Disbelief,* 8, 189–90, 201–2, 207.

9. George M. Marsden, *The Soul of the American University: From Protestant Establishment to Established Nonbelief* (New York: Oxford University Press, 1994), 6, 429–44, quotation on 431.

10. Warren A. Nord, *Religion and American Education: Rethinking a National Dilemma* (Chapel Hill: University of North Carolina Press, 1995), 2, 5, 378–79.

11. Alan Wolfe, "Higher Learning," *Lingua Franca* 6 (April 1996): 70. Joel A. Carpenter, "Review Essay: Religion in American Academic Life," *Religion and American Culture* 8 (1998): 265–81, concurs with Wolf's suspicion.

12. William Scott Green, "Religion within the University," *Academe* 82 (November–December 1996): 28. In the same issue were the following articles: Martin E. Marty, "You *Get* to Teach and Study Religion," 14–17; Isaac Kramnick and R. Laurence Moore, "The Godless University," 18–23; Joshua Mitchell, "Of Answers Ruled Out: Religion in Academic Life," 29–32; and David A. Hoekema, "Politics, Religion, and Other Crimes Against Civility," 33–37.

13. Marsden, *Soul of the American University,* 429–32, quotation on 431.

14. See George M. Marsden, *The Outrageous Idea of Christian Scholarship* (New York: Oxford University Press, 1997).

15. Marsden, *Soul of the American University,* 436–39.

16. Nord, *Religion and American Education,* 387.

17. Marsden, *Soul of the American University,* 414.

18. Nord, *Religion and American Education,* 306, quotation from Ray S. Hart, "Religious and Theological Studies in American Higher Education," *JAAR* 59 (1991): 716, italics Nord's.

19. Marsden, *Soul of the American University,* 316.

20. W. Clark Gilpin, *A Preface to Theology* (Chicago: University of Chicago Press, 1996), 183.

21. Conrad Cherry, *Hurrying Toward Zion: Universities, Divinity Schools, and American Protestantism* (Bloomington: Indiana University Press, 1995), 295–300.

22. See the discussion of Holbrook above in chap. 8, and the recent criticisms of the field above in the introduction and chap. 10.

23. Douglas Sloan, *Faith and Knowledge: Mainline Protestants and American Higher Education* (Louisville, Ky.: Westminster/John Knox, 1994), 213.

24. Russell T. McCutcheon, *Manufacturing Religion: The Discourse on Sui Generis Religion and the Politics of Nostalgia* (New York: Oxford University Press, 1997), 22.

25. For just a portion of the other contributions to debate over religion in American higher education, see Mark R. Schwenn, *Exiles from Eden: Religion and the Academic Vocation in America* (New York: Oxford University Press, 1993); Philip Gleason, *Contending with Modernity: Catholic Higher Education in the Twentieth Century* (New York: Oxford University Press, 1995); David W. Gill, ed., *Should God Get Tenure? Essays on Religion and American Higher Education* (Grand Rapids, Mich.: Eerdmans, 1997); Bruce Kuklick and D. G. Hart, eds., *Religious Advocacy and American History* (Grand Rapids, Mich.: Eerdmans, 1996); Jonathan Z. Smith, "Afterword: Religious Studies: Whither (Wither) and Why?," *Method and Theory in the Study of Religion* 7 (1995): 393–406; Alan Wolfe, "A Welcome Revival of Religion in the Academy," *Chronicle of Higher Education*, Sept. 19, 1997, B4-B5; George M. Marsden, Jacob Neusner, Stephen Macedo, Glenn C. Altschuler, James Nuechterline, and David G. Roskies, "SYMPOSIUM: God in the Academy," *Academic Questions* 9 (Spring 1996): 10–36; Beverly A. Asbury, "Campus Live in a Time of Culture War," *Soundings* 65 (1992): 465–75; Stanley Hauerwas, "A Non-Violent Proposal for Christian Participation in the Culture Wars," *Soundings* 65 (1992): 479–92; and William J. Abraham, "Oh God, Poor God: The State of Contemporary Theology," *American Scholar* 58 (Autumn 1989): 557–63. One particularly good exchange that deserves special mention because of what it says about the beleaguered status of religious studies came in Charlotte Allen's journalistic account of the field and the defensive response of a variety of religion faculty to her assessment. See Allen, "Is Nothing Sacred? Casting Out the Gods from Religious Studies," *Lingua Franca* 6 (November 1996): 30–40; and Tim Murphy et al., "Taking the Bull by the Tail: Responses to the *Lingua Franca* Article," *Bulletin of the CSSR* 26, no. 4 (November 1997): 78–85.

26. This is the overwhelming conclusion of the contributions to a recent issue of the *CSSR Bulletin* 26, no. 3 (September 1997) on the relationship between religious and theological studies. See Arvind Sharma, "On the Distinction between Religious Studies and Theological Studies," 50–51; Eric J. Sharpe, "The Compatibility of Theological and Religious Studies: Historical, Theoretical, and Contemporary Perspectives," 52–60; Jonathan Z. Smith, "Are Theological and Religious Studies Compatible?" 60–61; Robert A. Segal, "From Theology to Social Science: The Case of William Robertson Smith," 61–64; Delwin Brown, "Academic Theology and Religious Studies," 64–66; Ninian Smart, "Religious Studies and Theology," 66–68.

27. Jon D. Levenson makes this point well in the essays collected in *The Hebrew Bible, the Old Testament, and Historical Criticism* (Louisville, Ky.: Westminster/John Knox, 1993).

28. For an argument that assigns an earlier date to mainstream Protestantism's demise in American intellectual life see David Hollinger, "Jewish

Intellectuals and the De-Christianization of American Public Culture in the Twentieth Century," in *New Directions in American Religious History,* ed. Harry S. Stout and D. G. Hart (New York: Oxford University Press, 1997), 462–84.

29. This is not to say that scientific method, by the wave of its magical wand, yields unqualified coherence. But it does help give some order to the otherwise chaotic enterprise of higher education and makes for fairly good copy in catalogs and other forms of publicity.

30. Kramnick and Moore, "Godless University," 22.

31. Wolfe, "Higher Learning," 72.

32. For a lengthy and critical account of what has happened to Christian institutions of higher learning, see James Tunstead Burtchaell, *The Dying of the Light: The Disengagement of Colleges and Universities from Their Christian Churches* (Grand Rapids, Mich.: Eerdmans, 1998). For a more detailed investigation of what happened to religion at a school that went from a Protestant college to a research university, see P. C. Kemeny, *Princeton in the Nation's Service: Religious Ideals and Educational Practice, 1868–1928* (New York: Oxford University Press, 1998).

33. Welch, ed., *Graduate Education in Religion,* 55.

34. Of course, such studies exist under the rubrics of nutrition and human sexuality. Still, these programs have not received departmental status because university administrators suddenly realized food and sex were important to society. Instead, these fields are offshoots of other well-established branches of learning such as medicine, biology, anthropology, geography, or psychology.

35. Talal Asad, "The Construction of Religion as an Anthropological Category," in Asad, *Genealogies of Religion: Discipline and the Reasons of Power in Christianity and Islam* (Baltimore: Johns Hopkins University Press, 1993), 49.

36. Marsden, *Soul of the American University,* 435.

37. Louis Menand, "The Limits of Academic Freedom," in *The Future of Academic Freedom,* ed. Menand (Chicago: University of Chicago Press, 1996), 6–9, quotation on 9.

38. For a different perspective on the relationship between religion and academic freedom, see George M. Marsden, "The Ambiguities of Academic Freedom," *Church History* 62 (1993): 221–36.

39. Bruce Kuklick faults Marsden for employing contemporary academic fashions to argue for religion's inclusion in the university. See his review of *The Soul of the American University* in *Method and Theory in the Study of Religion* 8 (1996): 79–84. See also Hollinger, "Jewish Intellectuals," 475–76.

For judicious assessments of the debates over the liberal arts curriculum prompted by multiculturalism, see John Guillory, *Cultural Capital: The Problem of Literary Canon Formation* (Chicago: University of Chicago Press, 1993), who makes astute points about the liberal democratic and representative assumptions informing the expansion of the canon; and David Bromwich, *Politics by Other Means: Higher Education and Group Thinking* (New Haven: Yale University Press, 1992), who is especially critical of the idea that higher education must produce graduates whose views conform to the social group from which they descended. For a small sampling of the vast and various recent writings about the purpose and politics of the humanities, see Paul Berman, ed., *Debating P.C.: The Controversy over Political Correctness on College Campuses* (New York: Laurel Trade, 1992), "A Special Issue: The Politics of Political Correctness," *Partisan*

Review 60 (Fall 1993); and David H. Richter, ed., *Falling into Theory: Conflicting Views on Reading Literature* (Boston: Bedford Books, 1994).

40. Nord, *Religion and American Education,* 8. See also Marsden's appeal to multiculturalism, *Soul of the American University,* 432–33.

41. "Higher Learning," 77.

42. Menand, "What Are Universities For? The Real Crisis on Campus Is One of Identity," *Harper's* (Dec. 1991): reprinted in Richter, *Falling into Theory,* 96, 97.

43. H. L. Mencken, "Doctor Fundamentalis," *Baltimore Evening Sun,* January 18, 1937.

44. Paul J. Griffiths, "Why We Need Interreligious Polemics," *First Things* 44 (June/July 1994), 32.

45. R. Laurence Moore, "Learning to Love American Religious Pluralism: A Review Essay," *American Jewish History* 77 (1987): 321.

46. See Gerald Graff, *Beyond the Culture Wars: How Teaching the Conflicts Can Revitalize American Education* (New York: Norton, 1992).

47. This is not to say that religion should be excluded altogether. It naturally arises in any number of disciplines and should continue to emerge in that fashion. The argument here only concerns giving religion special attention as in the case of granting it departmental status.

48. Wolfe, "Higher Learning," 77.

Bibliographical Essay

VERY LITTLE HAS BEEN written on the history of religious studies. As such, it is a subject that offers great freedom since a body of scholarship has yet to establish the best lines of inquiry or interpretive issues in the development of the academic study of religion. The history of academic disciplines or of individual departments or institutions provides one way of understanding religious studies, an approach that falls more or less neatly within the historiography of American higher education. Another is the history of scientific and philosophical reflection on the phenomena of religion, the Kant-to-Freud approach. But because of the predominance of mainstream Protestantism in the teaching and study of religion in American higher education, this book has stressed the influence of organized religion on American colleges and universities in the field of religion. For that reason, the study of academic religion needs to be grounded in the intellectual traditions of American Protestantism.

Protestants and the Enlightenment

Pivotal to American Protestant theological development was the reception and adoption of Enlightenment. Henry F. May's *The Enlightenment in America* (New York: Oxford University Press, 1976) remains the best survey of the various aspects of Enlightenment thought in eighteenth- and early nineteenth-century America with thoughtful discussion of Protestant reactions and reception. Narrower in scope, but equally judicious is Mark A. Noll, *Princeton and the Republic, 1768–1822: The Search for a Christian Enlightenment in the Era of Samuel Stanhope Smith* (Princeton, N.J.: Princeton University Press, 1989), whose interpretation of Presbyterian appropriations of the Scottish Enlightenment is particularly helpful for understanding Anglo-American Protestant assumptions about religion and higher education. Other books covering specific aspects of Enlightenment influence that have influenced this study are: Theodore Dwight Bozeman, *Protestants in an Age of Science: The Baconian Ideal and Antebellum American Religious Thought* (Chapel Hill: University of North Carolina Press, 1977); Herbert Hovenkamp, *Science and Religion in America, 1800–1860* (Philadelphia: University of Pennsylvania Press, 1978); Walter H. Conser, *God and the Natural World: Religion and Science in Antebellum America* (Columbia: University of South Carolina Press, 1993); Donald Harvey Meyer, *The Instructed Conscience: The Shaping of the American National Ethic* (Philadelphia: University of Pennsylvania Press, 1972); as well as several essays in William M. Shea and Peter A. Huff, eds., *Knowledge and Belief in America: Enlightenment Traditions and Modern Religious Thought* (New York: Cambridge University Press, 1995); and David N. Livingstone, D. G. Hart, and Mark A. Noll, eds., *Evangelicals and Science in Historical Perspective* (New York: Oxford University Press, 1999).

Though systematic theology as a specific site of intellectual and Christian discourse has been understudied by both church and intellectual historians, several works demonstrate the influence that Enlightenment philosophy and methods had on American Protestant divinity. Three anthologies are especially useful in making this point by letting theologians speak for themselves: Sydney E. Ahlstrom, ed., *Theology in America: The Major Protestant Voices from Puritanism to Neo-Orthodoxy* (Indianapolis: Bobbs-Merrill, 1967); Mark A. Noll, ed., *The Princeton Theology, 1812–1921: Scripture, Science, and Theological Method from Archibald Alexander to Benjamin Warfield* (Grand Rapids, Mich.: Baker Book House, 1983); and Editors of the *Andover Review, Progressive Orthodoxy: A Contribution to the Christian Interpretation of Christian Doctrines* (1892; repr., Hicksville, N.Y.: Regina Press, 1975). Very important for interpreting the development of nineteenth-century Protestant divinity and its legacy for the twentieth century are: Bruce Kuklick, *Churchmen and Philosophers: From Jonathan Edwards to John Dewey* (New Haven: Yale University Press, 1985); E. Brooks Holifield, *The*

Gentlemen Theologians: American Theology in Southern Culture, 1795–1860 (Durham, N.C.: Duke University Press, 1978); James R. Moore, *The Post-Darwinian Controversies: A Study of the Protestant Struggle to Come to Terms with Darwin in Great Britain and America* (New York: Cambridge University Press, 1979); Jon H. Roberts, *Darwinism and the Divine in America: Protestant Intellectuals and Organic Evolution, 1859–1900* (Madison: University of Wisconsin Press, 1988); J. David Hoeveler Jr., *James McCosh and the Scottish Intellectual Tradition* (Princeton, N.J.: Princeton University Press, 1981); Charles D. Cashdollar, *The Transformation of Theology, 1830–1890: Positivism and Protestant Thought in Britain and America* (Princeton, N.J.: Princeton University Press, 1989); James Turner, *Without God, Without Creed: The Origins of Unbelief in America* (Baltimore: Johns Hopkins University Press, 1985); Daniel Day Williams, *The Andover Liberals: A Study in American Theology* (New York: Kings Crown Press, 1941; repr., New York: Octagon Books, 1970); Kenneth Cauthen, *The Impact of American Religious Liberalism* (New York: Harper and Row, 1962); William R. Hutchison, *The Modernist Impulse in American Protestantism* (Cambridge: Harvard University Press, 1976); Thomas E. Jenkins, *The Character of God: Recovering the Lost Literary Power of American Protestantism* (New York: Oxford University Press, 1997); and George M. Marsden, *Fundamentalism and American Culture: The Shaping of Twentieth-Century Evangelicalism, 1870–1925* (New York: Oxford University Press, 1980).

The place of Protestants in twentieth-century American intellectual life has been decidedly less robust than in previous eras. Nevertheless, several works describe the limits of Protestant influence as well as the factors that have contributed to this situation. One of the best places to begin is with the collection of essays edited by Michael J. Lacey, *Religion and Twentieth-Century American Intellectual Life* (New York: Cambridge University Press, 1989); along with James Gilbert, *Redeeming Culture: American Religion in an Age of Science* (Chicago: University of Chicago Press, 1997). For an assessment of Protestant theologians' efforts over the last century, W. Clark Gilpin's *A Preface to Theology* (Chicago: University of Chicago Press, 1996) is useful. Even though Protestantism is not his primary concern, David A. Hollinger's two collections of essays, *In the American Province: Studies in the History and Historiography of Ideas* (Bloomington: Indiana University Press, 1985), and *Science, Jews, and Secular Culture: Studies in Mid-Twentieth-Century American Intellectual History* (Princeton, N.J.: Princeton University Press, 1996), yield considerable insight into the development of American thought in the twentieth century, the context for Protestantism's decline. A comparative perspective is also useful for situating the place of Protestantism in twentieth-century intellectual life. Here studies of Catholicism and Judaism, such as Patrick Allitt, *Catholic Intellectuals and Conservative Politics in America, 1950–1985* (Ithaca, N.Y.: Cornell University Press, 1993), and Susanne Klingenstein, *Jews in the American Academy, 1900–1940: The Dynamics of Intellectual Assimilation* (New Haven: Yale University Press, 1991), reveal that in some ways the difficulties that mainstream Protestants faced were not unique to them. A study of evangelical Protestants and modern intellectual life has yet to be written, but Rudolph Nelson, *The Making and Unmaking of an Evangelical Mind: The Case of Edward Carnell* (New York: Cambridge University Press, 1987); and George M. Marsden, *Reforming Fundamentalism: Fuller Seminary and the New Evangelicalism* (Grand Rapids, Mich.: Eerdmans, 1987) are instructive for examining the academic ambitions of post–World War II evangelicalism.

General studies of twentieth-century mainstream American Protestantism also cover in summary fashion the main themes of recent Protestant intellectual life. The most reliable guides here are the essays in William R. Hutchison, ed., *Between the Times: The Travail of the Protestant Establishment in America, 1900–1960* (New York: Cambridge University Press, 1989); and the first three volumes of Martin E. Marty's series on twentieth-century American religious history, all published by the University of Chicago Press: *Modern American Religion:* vol. 1, *The Irony of It All, 1893–1919* (1986); vol. 2, *The Noise of Conflict, 1919–1941* (1991); and vol. 3, *Under God, Indivisible, 1941–1960* (1996). On the texture of twentieth-century American Protestantism as well as the efforts of one of the leading denominations in academic religion, the series on Presbyterians edited by Milton J Coalter, John M. Mulder, and Louis B. Weeks, published by Westminster/John Knox in Louisville, Ky., also contains many useful essays and helpful material: *The Presbyterian Predicament: Six Perspectives* (1990); *The Mainstream Protestant Decline: The Presbyterian Pattern* (1990); *The Confessional Mosaic: Presbyterians and Twentieth-Century Theology* (1990); *The Diversity of Discipleship: The Presbyterians and Twentieth-Century Christian Witness* (1991); *The Pluralistic Vision: Presbyterians and Mainstream Protestant Education and Leadership* (1992); *The Organizational Revolution: Presbyterians and American Denominationalism* (1992); and Milton J Coalter, John M. Mulder, and Louis B. Weeks, *The Re-Forming Tradition: Presbyterians and Mainstream Protestantism* (1992).

Religion and American Higher Education

Some model of secularization, whether articulated formally or not, dominates the history of American colleges and universities. The dividing line typically has been the Civil War, with denominational and liberal arts colleges before 1865 providing a form of Christian higher education, and research universities after 1865 abandoning older religious ideals and setting the norms for all institutions. The literature on the so-called revolution in American higher education is large and much of it bears on the theme of religion and higher education because of assumptions about the character of antebellum colleges and the demands that specialized research put on religion in the new universities. The best places to go for the revolution thesis are: Richard Hofstadter and Walter P. Metzger, *The Development of Academic Freedom in the United States* (New York: Columbia University Press, 1955); Laurence Veysey, *The Emergence of the American University* (Chicago: University of Chicago Press, 1965); Hugh Hawkins, *Pioneer: A History of the Johns Hopkins University, 1874–1889* (Baltimore: Johns Hopkins Press, 1960); Winton U. Solberg, *The University of Illinois, 1867–1894: An Intellectual and Cultural History* (Urbana: University of Illinois Press, 1968); J. Richard Storr, *Harper's University: The Beginnings: A History of the University of Chicago* (Chicago: University of Chicago Press, 1966); Hugh Hawkins, *Between Harvard and America: The Educational Leadership of Charles W. Eliot* (New York: Oxford University Press, 1972); Louise Stevenson, *Scholarly Means to Evangelical Ends: The New Haven Scholars and the Transformation of Higher Learning in America, 1830–1890* (Baltimore: Johns Hopkins University Press, 1986); and William C. Ringenberg, *The Christian College: A History of Protestant Higher Education in America* (Grand Rapids, Mich.: Eerdmans, 1984).

Recent writing on religion and higher education does not so much overturn the secularization model as it does nuance it. Instead of making scientists or secular academics the reason for religion's demise in American colleges and universities, historians of late have examined the role of liberal Protestants in giving freer reign to the less overtly religious aspects of specialized study while also striving to maintain a religious presence through voluntary and extracurricular activities. The best place to begin in the literature reevaluating the place of religion in modern American universities is George M. Marsden, *The Soul of the American University: From Protestant Establishment from Established Nonbelief* (New York: Oxford University Press, 1994), together with an earlier collection of essays that Marsden had a hand in assembling,

George M. Marsden and Bradley M. Longfield, eds., *The Secularization of the Academy* (New York: Oxford University Press, 1992). Several other books provide similar perspectives on the influence of liberalizing Protestantism on the newer models of higher learning inaugurated by the research university; they include: Julie A. Reuben, *The Making of the Modern University: Intellectual Transformation and the Marginalization of Morality* (Chicago: University of Chicago Press, 1996); James P. Wind, *The Bible and the University: The Messianic Vision of William Rainey Harper* (Atlanta: Scholars Press, 1987); James Tunstead Burtchaell, *The Dying of the Light: The Disengagement of Colleges and Universities from Their Christian Churches* (Grand Rapids, Mich.: Eerdmans, 1998); and P. C. Kemeny, *Princeton in the Nation's Service: Religious Ideals and Educational Practice, 1868–1928* (New York: Oxford University Press, 1998). Once the research university was in place, Christians came to terms with it in a variety of ways. Douglas Sloan, *Faith and Knowledge: Mainline Protestants and American Higher Education* (Louisville, Ky.: Westminster/John Knox, 1994), looks at the adjustments made by mainstream Protestant theology. For Roman Catholic patterns of negotiation, Philip Gleason, *Contending with Modernity: Catholic Higher Education in the Twentieth Century* (New York: Oxford University Press, 1995), renders astute analysis.

In addition to studies of the residual affects of religion within an academic environment rapidly losing its connections to the church are numerous books that discuss the proper place of religion in American higher education. The literature here is large and still growing. But a sample of the various views can be gleaned from the following: Mark R. Schwenn, *Exiles from Eden: Religion and the Academic Vocation in America* (New York: Oxford University Press, 1993); Warren A. Nord, *Religion and American Education: Rethinking a National Dilemma* (Chapel Hill: University of North Carolina Press, 1995); George M. Marsden, *The Outrageous Idea of Christian Scholarship* (New York: Oxford University Press, 1997); David W. Gill, *Should God Get Tenure? Essays on Religion and American Higher Education* (Grand Rapids, Mich.: Eerdmans, 1997); Richard T. Hughes and William B. Adrian, eds., *Models for Christian Higher Education: Strategies for Survival and Success in the Twenty-First Century* (Grand Rapids, Mich.: Eerdmans, 1997); and Bruce Kuklick and D. G. Hart, eds., *Religious Advocacy and American History* (Grand Rapids, Mich.: Eerdmans, 1996).

The Academic Study of Religion

Gaining an understanding of the origins and development of religion as an academic discipline requires some familiarity with the literature that already exists on the professionalization of knowledge more generally, especially as this process gained momentum under the aegis of the research university. A good overview of disciplinary differentiation and specialization comes from a collection of essays that remains a benchmark in the history of academic life: Alexandra Oleson and John Voss, eds., *The Organization of Knowledge in Modern America, 1860–1920* (Baltimore: Johns Hopkins University Press, 1979). The rise and development of the social sciences has received a great deal of scrutiny, not only to trace the history of academic disciplines, but also as a window to debates about the place of Christianity in the new universities. Important works on the social sciences include Mary O. Furner, *Advocacy and Objectivity: A Crisis in the Professionalization of American Social Science, 1865–1905* (Lexington: University of Kentucky Press, 1975); Thomas L. Haskell, *The Emergence of Professional Social Science: The American Social Science Association and the Nineteenth-Century Crisis of Authority* (Urbana: University of Illinois Press, 1977); Arthur J. Vidich and Stanford M. Lyman, *American Sociology: Worldly Rejections of Religion and Their Directions* (New Haven: Yale University Press, 1985); and Dorothy Ross, *The Origins of American Social Science* (New York: Cambridge University Press, 1991). On comparable developments in the humanities, the following histories are worthwhile: Bruce Kuklick, *The Rise of American Philosophy, Cambridge, Massachusetts, 1860–1930* (New Haven: Yale University Press, 1977); Daniel J. Wilson, *Science, Community, and the Transformation of American Philosophy, 1860–1930* (Chicago: University of Chicago Press, 1990); Kermit Vanderbilt, *American Literature and the Academy: The Roots, Growth, and Maturity of a Profession* (Philadelphia: University of Pennsylvania Press, 1986); Gerald Graff, *Professing Literature: An Institutional History* (Chicago: University of Chicago Press, 1984); Peter Novick, *That Noble Dream: The Objectivity Question and the American Historical Profession* (New York: Cambridge University Press, 1988). Two other important books that examine the culture of expertise that academic specialization has encouraged are Burton J. Bledstein, *The Culture of Professionalism: The Middle Class and the Development of Higher Education in America* (New York: Norton, 1978); and Thomas L. Haskell, ed., *The Authority of Experts: Studies in History and Theory* (Bloomington: Indiana University Press, 1984). Finally, a book that explores the strain that recent academic developments have put upon the boundaries between disciplines is Thomas Bender and Carl E. Schorske, eds., *American Academic Culture in Transition: Fifty Years, Four Disciplines* (Princeton, N.J.: Princeton University Press, 1998).

Because religious studies benefited from the mid-twentieth-century renaissance of liberal education, the literature on general education and western civilization is valuable for understanding the appeal of religion as an academic discipline at its origins. The following are useful guides to these developments: Bruce A. Kimball, *Orators and Philosophers: A History of the Idea of Liberal Education* (New York: Teachers College Press, 1986); Russell Thomas, *The Search for a Common Learning: General Education, 1800–1960* (New York: McGraw-Hill, 1962); Daniel Bell, *The Reforming of General Education: The Columbia College Experience in Its National Setting* (New York: Columbia University Press, 1966); Earl J. McGrath, *General Education and the Plight of Modern Man* (Indianapolis: The Lilly Endowment, 1975); and Daniel Catlin Jr., *Liberal Education at Yale: The Yale College Course of Study, 1945–1978* (Washington, D.C.: University Press of America, 1982).

The alliance between religious studies and the humanities resulted in various problems, one of which concerned the Eurocentrism of western civilization curricula. For some of the more thoughtful contributions to recent debates about the literary canon and liberal education, the following should be consulted: John Guillory, *Cultural Capital: The Problem of Literary Canon Formation* (Chicago: University of Chicago Press, 1993); David Bromwich, *Politics by Other Means: Higher Education and Group Thinking* (New Haven: Yale University Press, 1992); David A. Hollinger, *Post-Ethnic America: Beyond Multi-Culturalism* (New York: Basic Books, 1995); and Gerald Graff, *Beyond the Culture Wars: How Teaching the Conflicts Can Revitalize American Education* (New York: Norton, 1992). For a small sampling of various views about the politics of the humanities, Paul Berman, ed., *Debating P.C.: The Controversy over Political Correctness on College Campuses* (New York: Laurel Trade, 1992); David H. Richter, ed., *Falling into Theory: Conflicting Views on Reading Literature* (Boston: Bedford Books, 1994); and Darryl J. Gless and Barbara Herrnstein Smith, eds., *The Politics of Liberal Education* (Durham, N.C.: Duke University Press, 1992), provide good coverage. Surprisingly, little of this literature comments on religion. But it is still important for seeing the ways in which older Protestant arguments for religion look out of place in the contemporary academy.

Histories of cognate disciplines and Protestant divinity schools and seminaries are also important for understanding both the academic and religious context for the academic study of religion. Bruce Kuklick's

Puritans in Babylon: The Ancient Near East and American Intellectual Life,
1880–1930 (Princeton, N.J.: Princeton University Press, 1996) examines
Protestant contributions to the origins of archeology in the ancient
Near East. On early developments in comparative religion, Robert S.
Shepard, *God's People in the Ivory Tower: Religion in the Early American University* (Brooklyn, N.Y.: Carlson, 1991), covers important individuals and
institutions. Another closely related area of study is Jewish studies,
which receives judicious treatment in Paul Ritterband and Harold S.
Wechsler, *Jewish Learning in American Universities: The First Century*
(Bloomington: Indiana University Press, 1994). Since most divinity
schools and seminaries have been primarily servants of the churches,
their histories do not bear directly on religious studies. But some institutional histories, along with more general studies, are beneficial for
examining the overlap and differences between Protestant divinity and
academic religion. Two works of note include Robert T. Handy, *A History of Union Theological Seminary in New York* (New York: Columbia
University Press, 1987); and Conrad T. Cherry, *Hurrying Toward Zion:*
Universities, Divinity Schools, and American Protestantism (Bloomington:
Indiana University Press, 1995).

Turning more narrowly to the study of religion, because of the
close relationship between Protestant divinity and academic religion,
historians need to keep one eye on traditional theological disciplines
and the other on more scientific (i.e., less confessional) approaches to
the phenomena of religion. The place to start is with secondary literature on biblical scholarship because of the Bible's central place in the
development of religious studies. Reliable guides to twentieth-century
biblical studies in the United States include the following: Ernest W.
Saunders, *Searching the Scriptures: A History of the Society of Biblical Literature, 1880–1980* (Chico, Calif.: Scholars Press, 1982); Mark A. Noll,
Between Faith and Criticism: Evangelicals, Scholarship, and the Bible in
America (San Francisco: Harper and Row, 1986); Harold R. Willoughby,
ed., *The Study of the Bible Today and Tomorrow* (Chicago: University of
Chicago Press, 1947); Gerald P. Fogarty, *American Catholic Biblical Scholarship: A History from the Early Republic to Vatican II* (San Francisco:
Harper and Row, 1989); Burke O. Long, *Planting and Reaping Albright:*
Politics, Ideology, and Interpreting the Bible (University Park, Pa.: Penn
State University Press, 1997); and David L. Barr and Nicholas Piediscalzi, eds., *The Bible in American Education: From Source Book to Textbook*
(Philadelphia: Fortress Press, 1982).

As much as Bible was the original subject matter of religion professors, theology supplied some of the glamour to religious studies, especially the variety associated with the theological renaissance of neo-orthodoxy. Yet, as popular as neo-orthodoxy was, it has yet to receive adequate scholarly treatment by intellectual and religious historians. The works mentioned above by Cauthen and Hutchison should be consulted on twentieth-century American Protestant theology. In addition, for a snapshot of Protestant theological endeavors circa 1950, Arnold S. Nash, ed., *Protestant Thought in the Twentieth Century* (New York: Macmillan, 1951), is valuable. On the theology of Reinhold and H. Richard Niebuhr, Richard Fox, *Reinhold Niebuhr: A Biography* (New York: Pantheon Books, 1985); and Heather A. Warren, *Theologians of a New World Order: Reinhold Niebuhr and the Christian Realists, 1920–1948* (New York: Oxford University Press, 1997), make important contributions.

The literature on church history is much larger even though its influence and popularity may not have been as great for academic religion as was that of theology. Be that as it may, studies of historical writing on American religion are valuable for exploring the opportunities and problems attending the study of religion in the recent and contemporary university setting. The following works are especially important: Henry Warner Bowden, *Church History in an Age of Uncertainty: Historiographical Patterns in the United States, 1906–1990* (Carbondale: Southern Illinois University Press, 1991); John M. Mulder and John F. Wilson, eds., *Religion in America: Interpretive Essays* (Englewood Cliffs, N.J.: Prentice-Hall, 1978); Harry S. Stout and D. G. Hart, eds., *New Directions in American Religious History* (New York: Oxford University Press, 1997); and John Higham and Paul K. Conkin, eds., *New Directions in American Intellectual History* (Baltimore: Johns Hopkins University Press, 1979).

Finally, because of the relatively recent emergence of religion as a field of study, the literature describing religious studies is also young and may be read both as primary sources concerned with definitions prescribing the study of religion and as secondary sources that interpret those norms. Good starting points are volumes that come from the period when religion began to achieve greater academic respectability, especially the two books produced for the survey of humanistic scholarship, sponsored by Princeton University's Council of the Humanities and the Ford Foundation: Paul Ramsey, ed., *Religion* (Englewood Cliffs, N.J.: Prentice-Hall, 1965); and Clyde A. Holbrook, *Religion: A Humanistic Field* (Englewood Cliffs, N.J.: Prentice-Hall, 1963). Another book reflecting the Protestant and humanistic orientation of the field is the festschrift compiled for George F. Thomas, long-time

Princeton University religion professor, Paul Ramsey and John F. Wilson, eds., *Study of Religion in Colleges and Universities* (Princeton, N.J.: Princeton University Press, 1970).

Also important for defining the field were reports sponsored by some of the professional bodies most directly responsible for or involved in the teaching and study of religion. Keith R. Bridston and Dwight W. Culver, *Pre-Seminary Education* (Minneapolis: Augsburg, 1965), led the way in assessing religious studies for the Association of Theological Schools and the American Academy of Religion. Next came Claude Welch, ed., *Graduate Education in Religion: A Critical Appraisal* (Missoula: University of Montana Press, 1971); and Welch, *Religion in the Undergraduate Curriculum: An Analysis and Interpretation* (Washington, D.C.: Association of American Colleges, 1972), cosponsored respectively by the American Academy of Religion and the American Council of Learned Societies, and by the Association of American Colleges. Finally, within the last decade conferences or reports assessing religious studies by members of the guild have been produced which merit serious consideration: they are the "Santa Barbara Colloquy: Religion within the Limits of Reason Alone," in *Soundings* 71 (Summer/Fall 1988); Ray L. Hart, "Religious and Theological Studies in American Higher Education: A Pilot Study," *Journal of the American Academy of Religion* 59 (1991): 715–827; and "Special Issue: Settled Issues and Neglected Questions in the Study of Religion," *Journal of the American Academy of Religion* 62 (Winter 1994).

Since the 1970s textbooks and monographs have increasingly defined religion as an abstract entity that transcends particular religious traditions, thus conceiving the academic study of religion as more objective and less religiously partisan. Among the most recent of this genre are J. Samuel Preus, *Explaining Religion: Criticism and Theory from Bodin to Freud* (New Haven: Yale University Press, 1987); Walter H. Capps, *Religious Studies: The Making of a Discipline* (Minneapolis: Fortress Press, 1995); Frank Whaling, ed., *Theory and Method in Religious Studies: Contemporary Approaches to the Study of Religion* (New York: Mouton de Gruyter, 1995); Daniel L. Pals, *Seven Theories of Religion* (New York: Oxford University Press, 1996); Rodney Stark, *A Theory of Religion* (New Brunswick, N.J.: Rutgers University Press, 1997); and Mark C. Taylor, ed., *Critical Terms for Religious Studies*, (Chicago: University of Chicago Press, 1998).

Index

civilization, 34; and Darwinism, 23; definitions of, 57; and Jews, 87; other-worldliness of, 64; and science, 38
Christianity and Crisis, 131
church and state: conflict between, 95; relationship between, 119; separation of, 120, 161, 164, 171, 203–5
church history, 12, 14–16, 155–57, 161, 164, 167–68; goals of, 163; and history of United States, 168–70; recovery of, 170, 172; and scientific method, 162. *See also* American religious history
Claremont School of Theology, 146
Clark, Tom C., 201
Clarke University, 52
classics, 122
clergy, Protestant, 15–16, 42, 48, 55; authority of, 62; newer understanding of, 59; Protestant conception of, 50; status of, 49; training of, 32, 48–49, 52, 56, 64–65, 211, 213, 220
Cochran, Joseph W., 75
Coffin, Henry Sloan, 151
Colby College, 107, 108
Colgate University, 98, 127
Colgate-Rochester Divinity School, 156
college and university chaplains, 95–96, 184, 202, 243
College of New Jersey, 23–24, 27–28, 47, 49, 50. *See also* Princeton University
Columbia University, 94, 124, 158, 182
Commission on Christian Higher Education, 182, 185
common schools, 43–44
comparative religion. *See* religious studies
Conference of Church Workers in Universities and Colleges of the United States, 95
Cornell University, 11, 21–22, 31–32, 47, 51–52, 70, 96, 98
Corwin, Virginia, 142, 150
cosmopolitanism, 39, 41. *See also* Enlightened Christianity; Enlightenment
Council for the Study of Religion, 4
Council of Church Boards of Education (CCBE), 77, 84, 97–99

Council on Graduate Studies in Religion, 218
Culver, Dwight W., 213–14, 218

Dana, James Dwight, 35
Danforth Foundation, 192
Dartmouth College, 68, 83
Darwin, Charles, 1, 2, 11, 181
Darwinism, 40, 62
democracy, 41, 53–54, 58, 94, 103, 107, 110, 120–21, 127, 156, 164, 169, 244; and religion, 53, 108; and universities, 54
Denison University, 52, 108
denominational colleges, 36, 44, 65, 74, 77, 83, 89, 115, 182, 215, 246. *See also* Christian higher education
Dirks, Edward, 185, 191–92
Disciples of Christ, 28, 74, 76; Christian Women's Board of Missions, 76
divinity schools. *See* theological education
dogma. *See* theology
dogmatism, 59, 73, 81, 123. *See also* sectarianism
Douglas, William O., 200–201
Driver, Tom F., 227
Duke University, 96, 205–6
Dulles, John Foster, 118
Durkheim, Emile, 2–3, 229

Earlham College, 78
Easley, J. Allen, 149, 211
Eckardt, A. Roy, 140, 148–49
Edward W. Hazen Foundation, 81, 96, 107, 126, 192
Edwards, Jonathan, 27–28, 101, 113, 132, 161
Eisenhower, Dwight D., 152
Eliade, Mircea, 229
Eliot, Charles W., 36, 39, 50, 54, 56, 83, 112, 120, 130, 245; and debate with James McCosh, 31–33; and theological education, 48–49, 51–53; and university reforms, 23–26
Emerton, Ephraim, 162
Emory University, 187, 216
Enlightened Christianity, 23, 37, 39, 43, 48, 59, 65, 69, 77, 83, 85, 87, 94, 197,

29–31, 35, 42, 44, 72. *See also* Enlightened Christianity

Protestantism, 11, 12, 15, 29, 40–41, 148–49, 195; and science, 30; and Whig ideology, 29, 41. *See also* fundamentalism; liberal Protestantism; mainstream Protestantism in the United States

psychology, 47, 221; of religion, 103

public schools, 43, 69, 237, 238, 239

Puritanism, 27, 48, 108, 126, 132, 164, 169; study of, 156

Pusey, Nathan M., 130

Ramsey, Paul, 193, 194, 206, 214, 215, 216, 224

Reformation, Protestant, 29, 116, 179–80, 219

Religionswissenschaft. See history of religions

Religious Education Association, 67, 69, 70, 78, 80, 90, 95, 99; and religious instruction, 71–74

religious history. *See* American religious history

religious studies: and academic standards, 211; antagonism to theology, 15, 221, 244; and citizenship, 90; and comparative religion, 62, 64, 65, 103; and departmental status, 52, 96, 111, 118, 221, 198, 247; and dependence on religious communions and traditions, 84, 86, 89, 95, 147–48, 151, 244; and faculty, 70; and graduate education, 111, 218–24; and history of religions, 64, 209, 210, 227, 228; as humanistic subject, 96, 108, 111, 150, 195, 211; and identity politics, 7, 9, 248; and indoctrination, 87, 208; inspirational motives for, 96; involvement of Jews in, 65, 72, 85, 86–87; and literary studies, 13, 14, 221, 250; as major, 96–97, 211, 212, 213; methodology of, 60, 229; and piety of studies, 71, 87; professionalization of, 202–3, 218, 232, 240, 247; and Protestant curriculum of, 62–63, 66, 111, 149, 193, 197, 230; and Protestant

dominance in, 83, 188, 196, 198, 210, 212, 220, 227; rationales for, 54–55, 96; and religious diversity, 26, 207, 208; scientific ideals in, 197, 225, 229; social-scientific approaches in, 229, 230; at state universities, 203–4; stature as academic discipline, 48, 74, 109, 222, 223, 226, 230; and student enrollment, 70, 111; and world religions, 207, 209, 210. *See also* biblical scholarship; church history; ethics; theology

Renaissance, 179–80

republicanism, 41

research universities, 11, 14, 17, 30, 31–33, 34, 37, 43, 47, 52, 62, 66, 130, 131, 162, 232, 243, 246, 248; mission of, 51; and research ideal, 54. *See also* universities

revelation, 28, 30, 40, 121, 140; and general revelation, 27; and special revelation, 6, 27, 75, 240, 248. *See also* Bible

Riddle, Donald W., 104

Rockefeller, John D., 52, 81

Roebuck, Claude, 158–59

Roman Catholicism, 15, 40, 41, 43, 72, 151, 155, 173, 189, 196; and schools of religion, 85, 86–87

Ross, Floyd H., 209

Sanders, Frank Knight, 69

Savage, William, 182

Schlatter, Richard, 193

Schlesinger, Arthur, Jr., 162

Schlesinger, Arthur, Sr., 162

schools of religion, 81, 83, 96–97, 243

science, 17, 22–23, 27–29, 31, 33, 37, 38, 40–41, 44, 49–51, 53, 113, 117–18, 120, 128, 148, 152, 177, 178, 187, 208, 225, 228, 246, 248; civilizing influence of, 40; as ideal, 233; and mental discipline, 34; methods of, 14, 28, 29, 34, 36, 52, 59, 68, 72, 100, 112, 191; and research, 47, 186. *See also* higher education; research universities; warfare between science and theology

Scopes Trial, 31

Scottish Common Sense Realism, 28, 29

Library of Congress Cataloging-in-Publication Data

Hart, D. G. (Darryl G.)
The university gets religion : religious studies in American higher
education / D. G. Hart.
        p.   cm.
Includes bibliographical references and index.
ISBN 0-8018-6210-8 (hardcover : alk. paper)
1. Religion—Study and teaching (Higher)—United States—History.
2. Universities and colleges—United States—Religion.   I. Title.
BL41.H38   1999
200'.71'173—dc21   99-15332